# Affective Equality

D1330392

# Affective Equality

## Love, Care and Injustice

Kathleen Lynch

John Baker

Maureen Lyons

With

Sara Cantillon, Judy Walsh, Maggie Feeley, Niall Hanlon, Maeve O'Brien

*University College Dublin, Ireland*

palgrave
macmillan

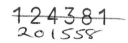

First published 2009 by
PALGRAVE MACMILLAN

Palgrave Macmillan in the UK is an imprint of Macmillan Publishers Limited,
registered in England, company number 785998, of Houndmills, Basingstoke,
Hampshire RG21 6XS.

Palgrave Macmillan in the US is a division of St Martin's Press LLC,
175 Fifth Avenue, New York, NY 10010.

Palgrave Macmillan is the global academic imprint of the above companies
and has companies and representatives throughout the world.

Palgrave® and Macmillan® are registered trademarks in the United States,
the United Kingdom, Europe and other countries

ISBN-13: 978-0-230-21249-7    hardback
ISBN-13: 978–0-230-22719-4    paperback

This book is printed on paper suitable for recycling and made from fully
managed and sustained forest sources. Logging, pulping and manufacturing
processes are expected to conform to the environmental regulations of the
country of origin.

A catalogue record for this book is available from the British Library.

A catalogue record for this book is available from the Library of Congress.

10   9   8   7   6   5   4   3   2   1
18   17   16   15   14   13   12   11   10   09

Printed and bound in Great Britain by
CPI Antony Rowe, Chippenham and Eastbourne

# Contents

# Acknowledgements

We acknowledge the financial support that made this book possible, in particular the support given under the *EU Programme for Peace and Reconciliation, Peace II* which provided the core funding for the project. The completion of this book was also greatly assisted by a Senior Research Fellowship from the *Irish Council for the Humanities and Social Sciences* (IRCHSS) for Kathleen Lynch and by a PhD fellowship for Niall Hanlon. Maeve O'Brien's research was supported by a fellowship from *The Department of Education and Science, Gender Equality Unit*. We would also like to thank the Centre for the Study of Social Justice, University of Oxford and the Faculty of Education, University of Cambridge for hosting visits by John Baker and Kathleen Lynch respectively, while working on the book.

The undertaking of the Care Conversations fieldwork was facilitated by the help of a number of organisations particularly by *The Carers' Association, Caring for Carers Ireland* and the *National Women's Council of Ireland*. We are deeply grateful to all of them for helping us in identifying care households, and for the time, advice and feedback that they gave us in relation to the fieldwork and analysis. We are also very grateful to the members of our Advisory Board who assisted in designing, planning and operationalising the project. Thanks are also due to the various organisations and individuals who assisted Maggie Feeley, Maeve O'Brien and Niall Hanlon in undertaking their fieldwork, most of whom wished to remain anonymous.

We would also like to acknowledge the support of our partners in the EU project on *Equality and Social Inclusion (ESI)* at Queen's University Belfast of which *Affective Equality* was a part. We acknowledge their advice and support and deeply regret that Eithne McLaughlin, who was the lead partner in QUB for the project, is no longer with us to celebrate its completion.

Rarely is a book completed without the support of family, friends and colleagues. We acknowledge the help of all of those who assisted us in so many different ways in the UCD Equality Studies Centre, including Pauline Faughnan, Elizabeth Hassell, Marie Moran, Carlos Bruen and Bernie Grummell. Special words of thanks are due to Theresa O'Keefe and Margaret Crean who gave us so much help in preparing the final manuscript. We are also very grateful to our Masters and PhD students for helping develop our thinking on affective equality, and to the library, computing and support staff of UCD for creating an environment that makes research possible.

While all books are a collective effort, some are more collective than others, and this book is definitely a team achievement. We are deeply appreciative of the love and care given to us all by friends and family while completing this book, those all-too-invisible care workers who granted us the freedom from necessity to write when we needed it.

Finally, we would like to express our deepest appreciation to all the carers and care recipients who took part in the various studies and gave so generously and enthusiastically of their time and understanding. Their experiential knowledge has greatly enriched our academic knowledge and we sincerely hope that the book will lead to more egalitarian policies in relation to love, care and solidary work.

# Preface

## The relations of research production: on writing *Affective Equality: Love, Care and Injustice*

We wrote this book to try to explain to ourselves and others what we meant by Affective Equality. While we had introduced the concept of affective equality in our book, *Equality: From Theory to Action* (Baker *et al.*, 2004), we were aware at that time that we had only touched the surface of this highly important subject. We wanted to develop the concept, to distinguish between it and other, more familiar contexts of equality, and to explore how inequalities arising in the doing of care work can be distinguished both from each other and from inequalities in the receipt of care.

We were encouraged to pursue the subject by very positive responses we received when we presented papers on the theme at conferences and meetings, nationally and internationally. Our Masters and PhD students also encouraged us to work on it further, as did the community, statutory and civil society organisations with whom we try to maintain a continuing dialogue. We knew however that if we were to develop our conceptualisation of affective equality, we needed to do further theoretical work informed by empirical research. And we knew that the research would have to be interdisciplinary and to be open to new ways of examining relations in the caring domain.

While advances in feminist scholarship on care motivated us to write the book (as did, conversely, the lack of attention given to the subject in more mainstream egalitarian thinking), we felt that the complex ways in which inequalities operate in the affective domains of life had yet to be fully explored in the context of our somewhat intuitive distinction between love, care and solidarity. We also wanted to examine the interlinkages between the economic, political and cultural inequalities we identified in *Equality*, and inequalities in the care field, knowing that none of the public institutions of society could function effectively without an infrastructure of care. We were challenged too by our interest in primary care and love labour, because the latter was so often conflated with more generalised forms of care labour in other research. Furthermore, we regarded the analysis of the distinction between what is and is not commodifiable in the care field as of both academic and policy importance, given the growing emphasis in neoliberal societies like Ireland of commercialising state services, including care. We were motivated also to explore relatively neglected issues in the care field, including men's perspectives on caring and how definitions of masculinity interfaced with definitions of femininity to reinforce particular gendered care orders. We wanted to examine the perspective of care recipients in more detail (something that disability scholars had been highlighting for some time), but also the views of children, people who had been in State care, and older people. Given the previous research of a number of the authors on education, we wanted to explore the interface between care, learning and equality in education. We were aware that care and love are also highly idiosyncratic in their operation, and that the context in which care occurs impacts heavily how each is experienced. This motivated us to explore the views of sole carers, same sex and heterosexual couples, older carers, carers of adult children with intellectual and/or physical impairments (and the views of those with these impairments on their care). We knew, however, that trying to understand these cross-sectional studies of care with a multidisciplinary team was not simple. We designed the main Care Conversations study to encompass as many of the care issues as possible, working in partnership with the Carers Association and Caring for Carers Ireland (see Introduction and Appendix).

The work on *Affective Equality* began in 2004 as we finished *Equality*. An Equality Studies team applied for and got funding to do a series of Care Conversation studies under the EU Peace II Programme (2004–2006) in conjunction with Professor Eithne McLaughlin (Queen's University Belfast). Although we had hoped to integrate research from both Northern Ireland and the Republic, this turned out not to be possible, largely because of Eithne's illness and untimely death. We were thereby denied the benefit of her many inspiring insights on the subject of care. *Ar deis Dé go raibh an anam.*

When designing the Care Conversations case studies we recognised that we had to choose between breadth of experience in the care field or depth in a given area; we chose the former given our interests in mapping a wide range of inequalities. We knew consequently that we lacked detailed knowledge of particular aspects of care. While we had had illuminating conversations with men about care, we did not have time to focus in detail on how masculine identities were constructed in relation to care; equally, the care conversations were focused on private family care although some people in society live in State care; and although our research on carers included mothers, it did not explore their experiences in depth. Maggie Feeley, Niall Hanlon and Maeve O'Brien began their doctoral studies with us around the time the Care Conversations study commenced. None of them had come to Equality Studies to focus particularly on care; however as they began to know of the Care Conversations study and to become part of the dialogues about the study, their interests in affective equality developed and each one undertook their own specialised study on the subject: Maggie on the impact of care-less-ness in State care on well-being and on learning; Niall on men's identities as caregivers; and Maeve on mothers' care work with school-going children.

All of the authors of this book were involved in this project in a range of different roles at different times. Kathleen Lynch, John Baker, Maureen Lyons, Sara Cantillon and Judy Walsh worked together as a team in designing, conceptualising and planning the research programme, guided by Pauline Faughnan, our research development colleague. Kathleen did much of the drafting of the research proposal, guided by especially by John in drawing up a conceptual framework, and by Judy and Sara arising from their own cognate work. Maureen played the lead role in working out the details of the empirical research design and undertook most of the Care Conversations, with some assistance from Maggie. Maureen also worked with Kathleen, who was the principal supervisor for the studies undertaken by Maggie, Niall and Maeve. As the Centre's practice is to work through research ideas in dialogues with students and staff, we also benefited from contributions from staff working on other projects at the time and from our other graduate students, especially through dialogues at the fortnightly PhD Roundtable meetings.

The final drafting of the manuscript was primarily Kathleen's responsibility as she was on research leave to do this work in 2006–7, although John played a key role in developing the conceptual framework and editing the final manuscript, while Maureen had responsibility for analysing data and overseeing the analysis of findings. Sara and Judy contributed to different chapters as appropriate, while Maggie, Niall, and Maeve each wrote their own chapters with input and feedback from Kathleen, Maureen and John. We got valuable assistance from Theresa O'Keefe in preparing the final manuscript for publication, while Pauline Faughnan was always at hand to assist in guiding the publication of the work. The administrative skills of Elizabeth Hassell were also enormously helpful in keeping the show on the road at all times. The completion of the book was greatly facilitated by the Irish Research Council for the Humanities and Social Sciences (IRCHSS), which awarded an Irish government Senior Research Fellowship to Kathleen in 2006–7. We are also all of us grateful to our own primary care connections – spouses, partners, children, parents, siblings and others – for their generous support and encouragement throughout this project.

The book is a truly collaborative project therefore, not only between the lead authors, but between those who co-authored chapters, those who wrote individual chapters, those who assisted us through their guidance and comments on the manuscripts at different stages, and the wider communities with whom we engage. It was researched and written in a co-operative manner over a four year period. What made this co-operation possible? One factor was undoubtedly the fact that the core members of the team, although drawn from different disciplines, had worked together not only for the publication of *Equality* in 2004 but on a variety of other projects over the years. There was a great deal of trust and a common purpose and interest in the subject.

Because the UCD Equality Studies Centre has been a project driven by a mission of change-oriented research and teaching, through promoting participatory and emancipatory methods in both teaching and research, it has developed a strong sense of internal solidarity and commitment, and external relations built on similar principles. This has also bolstered trust and collegiality, even in new managerial times!

The book is a hybrid: it has core authors but also assisting authors, as each of us commented and reviewed each others' chapters at different times. It is a product of mutual respect and good will, as well as being a shared intellectual endeavour.

# Introduction

*Kathleen Lynch, John Baker and Maureen Lyons*

Human beings typically have both a need and a capacity for intimacy, attachment and caring relationships. The ability to recognise and feel some sense of affiliation and concern for others is a typical human trait, and everyone needs, at least sometimes, to be cared for. People generally value the various forms of social engagement that emanate from such relations and define themselves in terms of them. Solidary bonds of friendship or kinship are frequently what brings meaning, warmth and joy to life.

Being cared for is also a fundamental prerequisite for human development. All of us have urgent needs for care at various stages in our lives, as a consequence of infancy, illness, impairment or other vulnerabilities. In addition, relations of love, care and solidarity help to establish a basic sense of importance, value and belonging, a sense of being appreciated, wanted and cared about. They are both a vital component of what enables people to lead successful lives and an expression of our fundamental interdependence. Love, care and solidarity therefore constitute a family of distinct but similar relationships that are important for their own sake and for achieving a wide range of other goals. Being deprived of the capacity to develop supportive affective relations of love, care and solidarity, or of the experience of engaging in them when one has the capacity, is therefore a serious human deprivation for most people: it is a core dimension of affective inequality.

Tronto (1993), Bubeck (1995), Kittay (1999) and others have pointed out that caring is both an activity and an attitude. In caring for others, we act to meet their needs in a way that involves an attitude of concern or even love. This duality is characteristic of the wider field of relationships of love, care and solidarity. Love involves acting for those we love and care for, not just feeling for them. Solidarity involves active support for others, not just passive empathy. Because love, care and solidarity involve work, affective inequality also occurs when the burdens and benefits of these forms of work are unequally distributed, and when this unequal distribution deprives those who do the love, care and solidary work of important human goods, including an adequate livelihood and care itself.

1

As we noted in *Equality: From Theory to Action* (Baker *et al.*, 2004) creating equality of condition in affective relations involves developing a society in which people are confident of having ample prospects for loving, caring and solidary relationships. To achieve this goal, it is necessary to change structures and institutions that systematically impede people's opportunities to develop such relationships, including the organisation of paid work, processes of gender-stereotyping and the gendered division of labour, attitudes and institutional arrangements concerning disability, and of course the burdens of poverty and economic inequality. Societies cannot *make* anyone love anyone else, and to this extent the right to have loving, caring and solidary relations is not directly enforceable. (Parents can be legally required to care *for* their children, but they cannot be forced to care *about* them.) But societies can work to establish the conditions in which these relationships can thrive. A key element in this task is to make sure that the work involved in providing love, care and solidarity is properly recognised and supported and that its burdens and benefits are shared equally, especially between women and men. The quality of people's relations of love, care and solidarity is also affected by the other dimensions of equality: equal respect, equal access to resources and equal power. Equality in these other dimensions is important in protecting people involved in relations of love and care from domination and exploitation.

Despite the importance people attribute to love, care and solidarity, and to the institutions that either enable or undermine these affective relations, love and care have for the most part been treated within both liberal and radical egalitarian traditions as private matters and personal affairs. Love and care have not been regarded as subjects of sufficient political importance to be mainstreamed in theory or empirical investigations, while the subject of solidarity is given limited research attention. Sociological, economic, legal and political thought has focused on the public sphere, the outer spaces of life, indifferent to the fact that none of these can function without the care institutions of society (see Chapter 2 for further discussion on the marginalisation of affective relations in academic research).

One of the central concerns of contemporary feminism has been to emphasise the degree to which all societies rely on the love and care typically provided by women to children and other dependants. Feminist-inspired work has played the key role in taking issues of care, love and solidarity out of the privatised world of the family to which they had been consigned by liberal and indeed most radical egalitarians (Benhabib, 1992; Gilligan, 1982, 1995; Held, 1995a; Kittay, 1999). They have drawn attention to the salience of care and love as goods of public significance, and have identified the importance of caring as a human capability meeting a basic human need (Nussbaum, 1995, 2000). They have also exposed the limitations of conceptualisations of citizenship devoid of a concept of care, and highlighted the importance of caring as work, work that needs to be rewarded and distributed equally between women and men in particular (Finch and Groves, 1983; Glucksmann, 1995; Hobson, 2000; Hochschild, 1989; O'Brien, 2005; Sevenhuijsen, 1998).

The complex way in which power relations and exploitation are embedded in all manner of care relations is the subject of a large body of feminist research (Bubeck, 1995; Folbre, 1994; Fraser and Gordon, 1997; Kittay, 1999; Nussbaum, 1995, 2000; Sevenhuijsen, 1998; Tronto, 2002). Feminist-inspired scholars have also contributed to understanding the potential for abuse of dependants in relations of care (Qureshi and Nicholas, 2001). Overall, what feminist scholars have managed to do is to shift intellectual thought from its intellectual fixation with the Weberian and Marxist structuralist trilogy of social class, status and power as the primary categories for investigating the generation of inequalities and exploitations. They have drawn attention to the way the affective domains of life are discrete spheres of social action, albeit deeply interwoven with the economic, political and cultural spheres. Their work has highlighted the ways in which the concerns of ordinary people are ahead of those of many mainstream egalitarian theorists.

In *Equality: From Theory to Action* (Baker *et al.*, 2004: 57–72) we tried to address the affective equality deficit. We identified four major social systems within and through which equality and inequality can be produced, namely, the economic, the political, the socio-cultural and the affective. We argued that the four sets of social relations are deeply interdependent and are central to the organisation of any society. Consequently they exercise an extremely powerful role in determining the levels of inequality within them. Of these four systems, the affective system, which is concerned with providing and sustaining relationships of love, care and solidarity, has received the least analysis and is the central focus of this book. The book is primarily concerned with the empirical analysis of equality within one aspect of the affective system; it focuses on other-centred (primary care) relations, that sphere of social life that is primarily oriented to the care of intimate others (see Chapters 2 and 3). It examines inequalities in the distribution of love and care labouring and, to a lesser degree, in the receipt of love and care. It also examines the inter-relationships between inequality in the affective system and the economic, political and cultural systems, and how this generates and reinforces inequalities in the affective system itself.

## The studies

This book is based on a series of studies of primary care relations focusing on the subjective experiences of intimate care, from the perspective of both those who are caring as well as those being cared for. The main study, on which Chapters 3–7 are based, was a series of Care Conversations undertaken in private households with a wide range of different carers and care recipients. The study was carried out under the direction of Kathleen Lynch and most of the conversations were held with Maureen Lyons. Maggie Feeley, the author of Chapter 10, conducted four of the conversations and assisted in the focus groups. The analysis and write up of the material was undertaken with the support of John Baker, Sara Cantillon and Judy Walsh.

### Care Conversations study

The aim of the main Care Conversations study was to engage in an in-depth exploration and analysis of equality and care in private households, focusing on the subjective experiences of intimate care, from the perspective of both those who are caring as well as those being cared for. The particular focus of the study was on love labouring in *primary care relations:* this is the 'world of primary, intimate relations where there is strong attachment, interdependence, depth of engagement and intensity', where the 'prototypical primary care relationship is that between parents and children' (Lynch, 2007: 555).

In this study, as shown in Table I.1, a total of 21 case studies of care in private households were undertaken (ten involving care of children and 11 involving care of adults with high care needs). Overall, this involved 30 in-depth Care Conversations, held with carers and care recipients (although some persons held both roles. As Table I.1 shows, the 21 households were selected to represent participants from different social classes; they included disabled people, lone carers, couples (heterosexual and same sex), single people, older and younger carers, people from different ethnic backgrounds, and women and men. Both primary and secondary carers were interviewed where appropriate. This methodological approach was adopted in order to achieve an understanding of a diverse range of private household care settings. The focus in the case studies was on having extensive in-depth care conversations. In addition to the 21 household case studies, two focus groups (one middle class and one working class) were conducted involving 14 teenagers; in these focus groups we explored their views on their experience of care as children and teenagers. Given that the household case studies are more representative of the views of carers than care recipients, the interactive conversational material provided by the 14 participants in the two focus groups, primarily concerning their experiences of receiving care, allows for a greater insight into this aspect of the care relationship (see Appendix for a detailed account of the methodology of the main study, including a discussion note on the issue of access to carers and care recipients).

### Three complementary studies on care by O'Brien, Hanlon and Feeley

Chapters 8, 9 and 10 are based on three complementary studies on care that augment the main study. The design of each study and the methodology employed is outlined briefly below.

*Table I.1* Care Conversations with Carers and Care Recipients in Private Households by Background Characteristics (Number Households=21)

| | Care Recipient Characteristics | | | Carer Characteristics | | | | |
|---|---|---|---|---|---|---|---|---|
| Social Class (other group) Composition of Private Care Households | Type of Care Recipients | School/Age Range | Relationship Status | Family Status (in relation to Care Recipient) | Economic Activity Status of Household Carer(s) | Gender | Age Category |
| | A. Dep. Children only, | A. Pre-school only | A. Married, | A. Married/ Cohabiting parents, | **Dual Carer Households (DCH) (n = 9):** | **Dual Carer Household:** | **Dual Carer Household:** |
| | B. Adult Children only, | B. Primary School only | B. Divorced/ Separated, | B. Lone Parent, | A. Both Full-time Employed | A. F/M | A. 31–40 |
| | C. Both, | C. Pre- & Primary School | C. Widowed, | C. Single Daughter/ Son, | B. One Full-time and one Part-time Employed | B. F/F | B. 41–50 |
| | D. Other Family Dependants | D. Second-level School only | D. Cohabiting, | D. Married/ Cohabiting Daughter/ Son | C. One Self-employed and one Full-time Carer | **Single Carer Household:** | C. 51–60 |
| | | E. Second-level School & Post-compulsory Education | E. Always Single | | D. One Self-employed and one Full-time Employed | C. F | D. 61–70 |
| | | F. 21–30 only | | | E. One Full-time Employed and one Retired (on contributory pension) | D. M | E. 71–80 |
| | | G. 31–40 only | | | F. One Part-time Carer and one Retired (on Contributory Pension) | | **Single Carer Household:** |
| | | H. 71 plus | | | G. One Full-time Carer and one unable to work due to illness | | F. 31–40 |
| | | | | | | | G. 41–50 |
| | | | | | **Single-Carer Household (SCH) n = 12:** | | H. 51–60 |
| | | | | | H. Employed Full-time | | I. 61–70 |
| | | | | | I. Full-time Carer & in receipt of State Allowance/ Benefit | | J. 71–80 |
| | | | | | J. Full-time Student | | |
| | | | | | K. Full-time Carer & Farmer | | |

*Table I.1*  Care Conversations with Carers and Care Recipients in Private Households by Background Characteristics (Number Households = 21) – *continued*

| | Care Recipient Characteristics | | | Carer Characteristics | | | |
|---|---|---|---|---|---|---|---|
| Social Class (other group) Composition of Private Care Households | Type of Care Recipients | School/Age Range | Relationship Status | Family Status (in relation to Care Recipient) | Economic Activity Status of Household Carer(s) | Gender | Age Category |
| | (A, B, C, D) | (A, B, C, D, E, F, G, H) | (A, B, C, D, E) | (A, B, C, D) | (A, B, C, D, E, F, G) (H, I, J, K) | (A, B) (C, D) | (A, B, C, D, E) (F, G, H, I, J) |
| Middle Class (n=7) | (5', 1, 0, 1) | (1, 4, 0, 0, 0, 0, 1, 1) | (5, 0, 0, 2, 0) | (6, 0, 0, 1) | (2, 1, 1, 1, 1, 1, 0) (0, 0, 0, 0) | (5, 2) (0, 0) | (2, 3, 2, 0, 0) (0, 0, 0, 0, 0) |
| Lower Middle Class (n=6) | (2, 2, 1, 1) | (0, 1, 0, 1, 1, 1, 1, 1) | (1, 2, 1, 0, 2) | (1, 4, 1, 0) | (1, 0, 0, 0, 0, 0, 0) (2, 3, 0, 0) | (1, 0) (5, 0) | (0, 1, 0, 0, 0) (1, 2, 2, 0, 0) |
| Working Class (n=7) | (1, 2, 0, 4) | (0, 0, 1, 0, 0, 1, 1, 4) | (1, 1, 0, 0, 5) | (1, 2, 4, 0) | (0, 0, 0, 0, 0, 0, 1) (3, 1, 0, 2) | (1, 0) (3, 3) | (0, 1, 0, 0, 0) (1, 2, 2, 0, 1) |
| Immigrant (n=1) | (1, 0, 0, 0) | (0, 0, 0, 1, 0, 0, 0, 0) | (0, 1, 0, 0, 0) | (0, 1, 0, 0) | (0, 0, 0, 0, 0, 0, 0) (0, 1, 0, 0) | (0, 0) (1, 0) | (0, 0, 0, 0, 0) (1, 0, 0, 0, 0) |
| Total (n=21) | (9, 5, 1, 6) | (1, 5, 1, 2, 1, 2, 3, 6) | (7, 4, 1, 2, 7) | (8, 7, 5, 1) | (3, 1, 1, 1, 1, 1, 1) n=9 (5, 4, 1, 2) n=12 | (7, 2) n=9 (9, 3) n=12 | (2, 5, 2, 0, 0) n=9 (3, 4, 4, 0, 1) n=12 |

*Note:* * For a guide to reading this table , see column one. A: this means that 5 of the 7 middle class Care Recipients are' dependent children only', 1 is an 'adult child only' and so on.

Maeve O'Brien's study (Chapter 8) is based on an analysis of mothers' emotional work in education; it examined the ways in which inequalities arising from social class, lone parenting, migrant and ethnic status (including Travellers) impact on intimate care work. It was part of a larger research study that explored the extent and nature of mothers' emotional work in supporting their children's transition from primary to second-level schooling, the inequalities associated with that work, and the meanings that mothers attached to these caring efforts relative to their gender identities and their class and status positions in society.

The study comprised 25, in-depth, taped and transcribed interviews with a theoretically selected sample of mothers whose children had just made, or were about to make, the transfer from first- to second-level schooling. A diverse group of mothers were selected (according to social class, marital status, their involvement in paid work, their sexual orientation, ethnicity and relative to their children's educational needs) in order to understand the nature of how mother's care work was produced relative to different circumstances and identities (see Table I.2).

The interviews with the mothers were semi-structured and focused on mothers' daily routines of care and the specific care work that supported school transfer. Importantly, they allowed mothers the space to discuss the meanings that caring held for them (see O'Brien, 2007: 163–165 and 2008: 140–141 for a detailed description of the methodology employed in the larger study).

*Table I.2:* Mothers by social group, marital status, work status and particular educational needs (Chapter 8)

| Group/ class Identity | Relationship status A. Married B. Separated C. Cohabiting D. Always Single | In paid work | A. Full-time B. Part-time C. Community Employment | Child with a Learning impairment |
|---|---|---|---|---|
| | A, B, C, D, | | A, B, C | |
| Middle Class (n=14) | (9, 2, 2, 1) | 10 | (8, 2, 0) | 4 |
| Working Class (n=7) | (3, 2, 1, 1) | 6 | (0, 3, 3) | 1 |
| Traveller (n=2) | (1, 1, 0, 0) | 1 | (0, 0, 1) | 1 |
| Immigrant (n=2) | (2, 0, 0, 0) | 0 | (0, 0, 0 ) | 0 |
| Total (n=25) | (15, 5, 3, 2) | 17 | (8, 5, 4) | 6 |

*Source*: O'Brien (2008).

*Table I.3*   Profile of Men's Groups Interviewed (Chapter 9)

| Group Interest | Participants | Brief Group Description |
| --- | --- | --- |
| 1. Fathering | Paul | Separated Fathers Rights Group |
| 2. Exclusion | Dave & Tom | Community Development Group |
| 3. Racism | Peter | Traveller Advocacy Group |
| 4. Sexuality | Geoff & Alex | Gay Men's Support Group |
| 5. Spirituality | Fran | Catholic Religious Order |
| 6. Elderly | Paddy | Older Men's Group |
| 7. Employment | Declan | Construction Workers Trade Union |
| 8. Social Networking | Denis | Men's Club |

*Source*: Hanlon, N. (2009) Men and Masculinities and Caring Study (ongoing)

Niall Hanlon's study (Chapter 9) analysed men's perception of masculinity and caring drawing on in-depth interview material with ten key members from eight different types of men's groups (see Table I.3). The study is based on a purposeful sample of men's groups chosen to reflect a diversity of men's interests defined by significant inequalities and divisions among men including those based on social class, religion, age, geographical location, ethnicity, sexuality, and family and marital status (see Table I.3). Hanlon's exploratory study is the first phase of a larger research project examining the relationship between masculinities and primary caring. It examines how Irish men define and construct their masculinity in relation to love and primary caring, and explores the hypothesis that dominant definitions of masculinity write out caring from men's lives by constructing masculinities antithetical to caring practices.

Finally, Maggie Feeley's study (Chapter 10) examined the relationship between care and literacy learning among people who had spent their child-hoods in institutional care and who are currently attending a support centre for people who have been in care. The chapter draws upon a wider ethno-graphic study involving 28 men and women in the 40 to 65 age group who had spent much of their lives in State care (see Table I.4). To compare the care biographies of those who learned and those who did not become liter-ate while in care, those selected to participate in the study were equally divided between those whose literacy needs had been met at school and those who had finished school with unmet literacy needs. Respondents spent different lengths of time within the care institutions and this is recorded showing first age of entry and total number of years. The sample was purposively selected in terms of gender and literacy status. In addition, a range of subgroups was randomly selected from within the pool of persons who were now getting aftercare support. Two respondents were of mixed race. One man came from an Irish Traveller family. Two women had mild learning difficulties and one man was dyslexic. Respondents came from a range of belief groups and none, and were also representative in terms of

*Table I.4*    Literacy status of research participants by gender, age category, age at entry into care, total years in care and highest formal educational attainment (Chapter 10)

| Literacy Status Leaving School | Gender A. Female B. Male | Age Category A. 40–49 B. 50–59 C. 60–69 D. 70 plus | Age Going into Care A. Under 1 B. 2–5 C. 6–10 D. Not disclosed | Total years in Care A. ≤5 B. 6–10 C. 11–15 D. 16–20 E. Not disclosed | Education – Highest Level Attained A. None B. Primary Cert C. Junior Cert D. Leaving Cert E. FAS course F. 3$^{rd}$: Cert/Dip. G. 3$^{rd}$: Postgrad. H. Other |
|---|---|---|---|---|---|
| | (A, B) | (A,B,C,D) | (A,B,C,D) | (A,B,C,D, E) | (A,B,C,D,E,F,G,H) |
| Met (n=12) | (8, 4) | (3,7,2,0) | (3,5,3,1) | (1,5,1,4,1) | (1,1,1,2,1,2,2,2,) |
| Partial (n=2) | (2, 1) | (2,1,0,0) | (1,1,1,0) | (0,1,1,1,0) | (2,0,0,0,0,1,0,0) |
| Unmet (n=13) | (5, 8) | (5,6,1,1) | (1,5,7,0) | (3,2,6,2,0) | (3,1,6,1,1,0,0,1) |
| Total (n=28) | (15, 13) | (10,14,3,1) | (5, 11,11,1) | (4,8,8,7,1) | (6,2,7,3,2,3,2,3) |

*Source*: (Feeley, 2007).

sexual orientation with two respondents identifying as homosexual. With one exception, all of the respondents were working class in origin (see Feeley, 2007 for a more detailed description of the methodology).

Although the material in this book is based on four distinct empirical studies, there is clearly a close relationship among them. We intend each of the chapters to be intelligible in its own terms – entailing a certain amount of repetition – but the book as a whole is structured to make an overall case for the importance of affective inequality and to contribute to a better understanding of its contours, causes, effects and remedies. It is for this reason that we begin with a review of the way affective (in)equality has been treated in egalitarian theory (Chapter 1) and a theoretical taxonomy of love, care and solidarity, from which some key normative conclusions emerge (Chapter 2). The final chapter attempts to bring together the main conclusions and theoretical implications of the empirical work that makes up the body of this work.

The findings confirm the prevalence of a gendered order of caring, especially in terms of how primary caring is distributed in and between households (Chapters 5, 7 and 8). As noted in *Equality: From Theory to Action*, none of the primary social systems are autonomous from other systems, so inequalities within the economic, political and cultural systems impact on the affective system. We found the impact of inequalities in economic resources, but also of cultural and social resources (capitals) (Chapter 5 and 8) and time (Chapter 7) to be considerable for all types of carers, and care recipients (Chapter 10). The intersectionality of inequalities that we identified in *Equality: From Theory to Action* was also a major theme to emerge from the studies: social class, marital and family status and age, all strongly influenced the way primary caring and receiving operated, and especially the resources, including time and energy, that one had for loving and caring (Chapters 5, 8 and 10). Although we did not focus in detail on the relationship between disability and caring (this was part of the original research design but we were unable to examine the issue for the reasons outlined in the preface), and were unable to examine the relationship between citizenship status, ethnic identity, sexual orientation and care in depth, both the Care Conversations study and the studies by O'Brien (Chapter 8) and Hanlon (Chapter 9) show how disability, ethnic status (including Traveller status), sexual orientation and citizenship status impact on care in distinct ways. Power inequalities operating outside love labouring relationships also impacted on caring particularly the social recognition given to loving and caring and the material resources allocated to support them. Power inequalities worked internally within care relationships as well, defining who is expected to do the burdensome forms of love and care work, and how care recipients determine the conditions of their own caring (Chapters 3, 6, 7 and 10). It is clear that caring and loving are low status activities and are not given respect and recognition in the public sphere, especially not by men; however, they are valorised and prioritised in the personal sphere even though such personal validation has considerable economic and status costs (Chapters 3, 4 and 9).

A major finding of the studies is that both carers and care recipients recognise the ways in which the nurturing work involved in love labouring cannot be assigned to others without altering the very nature of the relationships involved. The importance of the analytical distinction between what is and is not alienable in care terms, what we can pay others to do on our behalf and what we cannot, cannot be underestimated. It means that there is a form of primary caring that assumes a personal commitment from primary carer(s) that is relatively unbounded. This type of caring generates a very particular type of care rationality, one that is grounded in the immediacy and urgency of primary care needs, and is morally and other-centred driven (especially for women at this point in history) in a way that is different from economic rationalities. Consequently the Care Conversations and other studies show that while paid carers are vital for assisting love labouring, they cannot substitute for it. Feelings and commitments that are an integral part of an ongoing relationship are not available for hire (paid carers often develop such relationships, but contracts of employment cannot require them to do so). While paid care services were regarded as indispensable for supporting love labouring (and grossly under-funded and under-resourced), they were seen as supplementary to love labouring rather than a substitute for it. Parents could and did pay people to care for their children (and adult children did the same for their parents). However, they recognised that although paid carers built their own relationships with their children they could not replace the parents' relationship (Himmelweit, 2005). Given the inalienability of love labouring, it was inevitable that primary care relations were deeply emotionally engaged, not only for carers but also, as shown in Chapter 10, for those who did not have love invested in them.

This book highlights the depth, complexity and multidimensionality, as well as the gendered character, of affective inequality. It demonstrates the centrality of love labouring to personal identities, as well as its vulnerability to the lack of material supports, time and respect it is granted in the public sphere.

# 1
## Which Equalities Matter? The Place of Affective Equality in Egalitarian Thinking

*Kathleen Lynch, John Baker, Sara Cantillon and Judy Walsh*

There is a deep ambivalence in Western society about caring and loving generally (hooks, 2000). This ambivalence has found expression in the academy. In both liberal and radical egalitarian traditions, love and care have for the most part been treated as private matters, personal affairs, not subjects of sufficient political importance to be mainstreamed in theory or empirical investigations, while the subject of solidarity is given limited research attention. Sociological, economic, legal and political thought has focused on the public sphere, the outer spaces of life, indifferent to the fact that none of these can function without the care institutions of society (Fineman, 2004; Sevenhuijsen, 1998; Tronto, 1993). Within classical economics and sociology in particular there has been a core assumption that the prototypical human being is a self-sufficient rational economic man (*sic*) (Folbre, 1994; Folbre and Bittman, 2004). There has been little serious account taken of the reality of dependency for all human beings, both in childhood and at times of illness and infirmity (Badgett and Folbre, 1999). That fact generates two very important forms of inequality: inequality in the degree to which people's needs for love and care are satisfied, and inequality in the work that goes into satisfying them. These are the core of what we call 'affective inequality'.[1]

In *Equality: From Theory to Action* (Baker *et al.*, 2004: 57–72) we tried to address the affective equality deficit. We identified four major social systems within and through which equality and inequality can be produced, namely, the economic, the political, the socio-cultural and the affective. We argued that the four sets of social relations endemic to these systems are central to the organisation of any society, and thereby exercise an extremely powerful role in determining the levels of inequality in a given society. Of these four systems, the affective system, which is concerned with providing and sustaining relationships of love, care and solidarity, has received the least analysis. The aim of this book is to make a contribution to that analysis. The point of this chapter is to provide a sense of how the affective system, and inequality within it, have been treated by the 'social' sciences, particularly sociology and education, and by economics, law and political theory. Obviously each of these fields is too vast to be fully surveyed in one chapter, but what we hope to do here is to illustrate the relative neglect and general biases that have characterised mainstream work in these disciplines as well as to indicate some of the contributions recent scholarship has started to make.

## Affective inequality in sociology, education and related disciplines

The importance social scientists attribute to economic, political and cultural relations in generating inequality is predictable in social scientific terms. Both Marx and Weber agreed that it was within the economy that basic material inequalities in wealth and income are generated (although they clearly differed in how they interpreted the operation of class relations within it, and the role they attributed to the economy in determining other inequalities). In addition, Weber, and scholars in the Weberian tradition, have shown how cultural and political systems operate in many ways relatively independently of the economy, and at times generate discrete forms of inequality.[2]

Talcott Parsons, working within a Durkheimian, structural functionalist perspective, also attributed primacy to the economy, the polity and culture. Neither Marxist, functionalist nor Weberian social scientists identified any major role for the affective system of social relations independent of the economy, polity or status order. The affective domain was defined as being dependent on other social systems; it was regarded as a by-product of economic, political and cultural action, not an autonomous site or field of social behaviour. Moreover, because it was defined as a private, highly feminised and emotionally-driven sphere, it was not seen as a priority subject for social scientific investigation.

The subordination of the affective domain found expression in the hierarchically organised division of labour within the social sciences. Social work, social policy and social care research did address issues of care but this work lacked the status of research focused on the economy, culture or politics.[3] In the policy field, research on care gained most credence when it was focused on the interface between the public and the private sphere, most especially where it focused on the relationship between care and the state. Thus, the relationship between unpaid informal care and the welfare state was a major theme in social policy research on care throughout the 1970s (Williams, 2001: 475–478). Due to the growing influence of feminist scholarship within established disciplines in the 1980s, social science research began to pay attention to gender relations within caring and in particular to the role of women as carers (Finch and Groves, 1983; Waerness, 1987). The work of Graham (1983) and of Gilligan (1982) purported to highlight differences in women's and men's sense of social and moral identities and how each of these interfaced with care, while Finch (1989) focused attention on the normative structures that impacted on care work. The rise of the disability movement generated a critique of the dependency narratives in care discourses in the 1990s. The unequal power relations between the providers and recipients of care was a major subject of research among disability studies scholars including Oliver (1990), Finkelstein (1991), Morris (1993) and Oliver and Barnes (1991).

The role of the state in determining the dynamics of care provision never left the policy frame however. As state investment in public services and welfare supports was challenged with the emergence of neoliberal policies from the early 1990s onwards, there was a renewed focus on the role of the state, including its role in determining relations of care and gender (Daly, 2000, 2002, 2005; Glendinning and Millar, 1992; Leira, 1992; O'Connor *et al.*, 1999; Ungerson, 1993, 1995, 2000). The gendered character of care was increasingly recognised in social policy therefore, albeit often through a state lens.

### Sociology

Mainstream sociology was and is more male-dominated than social policy and social care research. The primary focus of sociology has always been on matters in the public sphere; it is a highly gendered discipline (Smith, 1987), although it is also a discipline that feminists recognise for its contribution to the development of feminist thought (Jackson, 1999). The dominance of the so-called 'founding fathers' (Marx, Durkheim and Weber) in the early phases of sociological thinking was replicated at the end of the twentieth century with the emergence of a new set of male leaders: Bourdieu reinterpreted Marx, Parsons followed in Durkheim's footsteps, while Randall Collins, Goldthorpe and Giddens, among others, were closely aligned with the Weberian tradition.

The 'fathers' of sociological thought in each generation imposed (often unwittingly) a male cultural arbitrary[4] on alternative voices, be these female, disabled, ethnic or from some other marginalised group. The net effect was that certain questions were not asked, or if asked, not taken seriously (Oakley, 1989). The deference to the male voice meant that the worlds that women controlled and inhabited in a way that men do not, the care world in particular, were interpreted through a patriarchal lens. This practice was exemplified in the sociology of the family, where power inequalities within households and the unequal division of care and other forms of domestic labour were largely unproblematised in early work (see Parsons and Bales, 1956 and Hannan and Katsiaouni, 1977 for two different examples). There was a deep symbolic violation of the feminine in this practice although it went largely unnoticed until pro-feminist scholarship began to challenge the received wisdoms of mainstream sociology (Connell, 1987; Delphy and Leonard, 1992; Oakley, 1976).[5]

The emergence of postmodernist thinking with the work of Foucault in particular did break up the coherence of the sociological framework; it focused attention on issues of power and its operation and circulation in cultural spaces. While it did not open up issues of affective relations in particular, it did create a space for challenging the grand narratives of social scientific thought, including the grand narratives that had trivialised affective relations and the emotional work within them.

Influenced by the publication of Foucault's work in English (*The Birth of the Clinic*, 1973; *Discipline and Punish*, 1977; *The History of Sexuality*, 1978), sociological research expressed growing interest in the human body and mind as sites of disciplinary control at the end of the twentieth century. The ways in which the disciplinary technologies of the state and other powerful social institutions were employed to monitor, shape and control human consciousness generated an interest in the sociology of the emotions, which is closely linked to the affective system because so many emotions are embedded in relations of love, care and solidarity or their opposites. Research on the affective domain gained increasing recognition in sociological thinking in the late twentieth century (Barbalet, 2002; Hochschild, 1983, 1989; James and Gabe, 1996; Kemper, 1990; TenHouten, 2006). Scholars such as Reay (2000), Sennett and Cobb (1977) and Skeggs (2004) have documented the ways in which social class inequalities are not only experienced economically but also emotionally, as social judgements on tastes, lifestyle and values. Sayer (2005) has linked the lack of attention given to normative issues in the social sciences to the failure to investigate the emotional impact of injustices, particularly the way social class injustices are experienced as negative moral judgements.

While the opening up of the emotions and emotional work to social scientific investigation has been a significant development in the social sciences, it cannot easily undo the long-standing neglect of affective relations as a fit subject of research. Connell (1995, 2002), Kimmel (2005) and Seidler (2007) have documented how the neglect of the affective domain has contributed to the lack of research on masculine identities and hegemonic conceptions of masculinity in particular. One area of social scientific research where the neglect of affective relations has not only had an impact on scholarship but also on public policy is the field of education.

## Affective relations and education: an exemplary case

The trivialisation of the world of love, care and solidarity, and of feeling and emotion more generally, has had a profound impact on thinking in education. As 'fallible' emotions were not taken seriously in social scientific research, neither were they taken seriously in education. Education was and is defined as being about the development of reason (Callan, 1997, 2004; Dewey, 1916; Rousseau, 1911). Under the influence of Piaget, formal education increasingly focused on the development of abstract reasoning, notably mathematical reasoning. The primacy of abstract reasoning was underwritten by Bloom's (1956) educational taxonomy of educational objectives (cognitive domain) which ranked modes of cognition on a hierarchical scale. Bloom's taxonomy was widely disseminated and set the agenda for evaluation and testing in the post-war era. His equally important taxonomy of educational objectives for the affective domain (Krathwohl *et al.*, 1964) was never developed either by educators or governments.

Contemporary educational thinking continues to draw heavily from Piagetan thinking, emphasising the development of logical mathematical intelligence and abstract reasoning (Gardner, 1983). Even the growing recognition of emotional and personal intelligence within developmental psychology (see Gardner, 1983, 1993, 1999; Goleman, 1995, 1998; Sternberg *et al.*, 1986; Sternberg, 2002) has not unsettled the focus of education on the development of the logical mathematical and linguistic capabilities for servicing employment. There is a strong focus on the relevance of emotional intelligence for measurable achievement; it is generally defined as a capability that enhances and supplements other marketable capabilities including academic attainment (Cherniss *et al.*, 2006; Goleman, 1995; Grewal and Salovey, 2005; Lopes *et al.*, 2006; Vandervoort, 2006).

There is a strange irony in the development of academic interest in defining and measuring emotional intelligence. Despite the obvious ways in which emotional intelligence is crucial to the development of human capabilities to love, care and engage in solidary relations with others, and to moral education (Cohen, 2006), the advance of neoliberal thinking has led to defining it as yet another measurable and testable public sphere skill, to be deployed largely in the development of the public, market-led persona. At the heart of this shift is an assumption that the ideal human being is not only a self-sufficient and rational citizen, but also quintessentially an *economic* citizen (Lynch *et al.*, 2007). The focus of the Lisbon agreement on preparing citizens for the 'knowledge economy' within the EU exemplifies this trend, as knowledge is reduced to the status of an adjective in the service of the economy. At the individual level, the purpose of education is defined in terms of personalised human capital acquisition, making oneself skilled for the economy: 'the individual is expected to develop a productive and entrepreneurial relationship towards oneself' (Masschelein and Simons, 2002: 594).

### Why educators neglect the affective domain

The neglect of education for emotional work, particularly for love, care and solidarity work, arises for a number of reasons. First it arises because the model citizen at the heart of classical liberal education is a 'rational' (in the narrow sense) citizen and a public persona; thus the student is being prepared for economic, political and cultural life in the public sphere but not for a relational life as an interdependent, caring and other-centred human being. Cartesian rationalism, encapsulated in the phrase 'Cogito ergo sum',[6] succeeded in embedding an understanding of 'the person to be educated' as an autonomous, rational and increasingly economised being, one who largely ignores the relational caring self (Noddings, 1984).[7] The dependant citizen is left outside the educational frame in the Rational Economic Actor (REA) model (Lynch *et al.*, 2007).

The close and growing link between formal education and employment also contributes to the neglect of the affective. Because educationalists tended to take the definition of the person-to-be-educated from mainstream social and psychological thinking, they also tended to adopt these disciplines' core assumptions as to what constitutes work. Within the social sciences, only work for pay, or work within the market economy, has been defined as real work (Harrington Meyer, 2000; Pettinger *et al.*, 2005). The equating of work with economic self-preservation and self-actualisation through inter-action with nature (Gürtler, 2005) meant that education is seen as prep-aration primarily for economic productivity.[8] What is seen as 'private' care labour can easily be ignored within this paradigm, while training for paid care labour, because it is assimilated to other forms of employment, emphasises professional detachment rather than emotional involvement.

A further reason why care has been ignored in the academy and in edu-cation is because of the way scholarly work itself is produced; it is a by-product of the domain assumptions of dominant researchers across disciplines (Gouldner, 1970).[9] The social relations of research production and exchange operate on the premise that one has sufficient personally-controlled and care-free time to think, to write and rewrite: one needs freedom from necessity to be an academic (Bourdieu, 1993). Given that not all caring (especially love labour: see Lynch, 1989, and Chapter 2 below) can be delegated without being transformed, those who have non-transferable dependency demands on their time and energy either cannot write, or cannot write much. They are less likely to be *care commanders*, people who are in positions of power and can delegate essential care and love work to others. In contrast, those who are in a position to globalise their point of view are generally people who have time to do the promotional work that international academic scholarship requires, not only writing and research time, but care-free travel time, networking time, conferencing time and general self-promotional time. Those who have named and known the world academically are disproportionately people (mostly men) whose paradigmatic and domain assumptions are formed in relatively care-free contexts. The domain assumptions of research production, distribution and exchange have been care-free assumptions and these have determined priorities both social scientifically and educationally.

## Concluding remarks

While sociologists have examined issues of inequality in depth, the focus of much of this work has been on economically-generated inequalities, especially class inequalities (Grabb, 2004; Romero and Margolis, 2005). Affective inequalities constituted by the unequal division of care labour within and outside households, and by unequal access to love, care and solidarity, have only become the subjects of research under the growing influence of pro-feminist scholarship. Feminist scholars have moved sociology and related disciplines away from their fixation with the Weberian and Marxist trilogy of social class, status and power as the defining terms of inequality and exploitation. They have drawn attention to the way the affective domains of life are discrete spheres of social action, albeit deeply interwoven with the economic, political and cultural spheres.

## Economics and the affective domain

Like sociology and education, economics has not traditionally been concerned with the affective domain and issues of love, care and solidarity. The emphasis in neoclassical economics, the dominant approach within economics, on methodological individualism, rational choice theory and the distinction between the public and private spheres helps to explain not only the neglect of the affective domain but also the marginalisation of women's economic contribution. Notwithstanding this, quite a number of areas of theoretical and empirical work within economics implicitly touch on the affective domain including labour market theory, reinterpretations of work and the division between paid and unpaid labour, efforts to incorporate non-market activity in national accounting systems, the use and critiques of the concept of altruism, particularly as it relates to the household, the emergence of new home economics of the family and the subsequent application of game theory to the economics of the family. It has, however, been with the rise of feminist economics from the 1980s onwards that issues of care labour have been explicitly addressed in a comprehensive manner.

Part of the agenda of feminist economics is to investigate the apparently 'value free, politically neutral, gender blind' assumptions and values embedded in the neoclassical paradigm, particularly in those areas that cross the affective domain and bear directly on women's lives and experiences. For example, in examining the wage gap between men and women, neoclassical economics focuses on women's rational choices as the explanation that justifies the higher earnings of men, whereas gender analysis examines how gender-specific social expectations about women's roles and caring obligations affect their labour market experiences (Barker, 1998). Similarly, Strassman (1993) examines the often implicit assumption that people are responsible for taking care of their own needs and take only their own needs and wishes into account, arguing that while it may fit the profile of a select few, it fails completely to recognise the economic reality for children, older people, those with disabilities or many others who do not have independent, or sufficient access to economic resources.

**Paid and unpaid labour**

Conventional economic analysis defines 'work' as paid employment. This view is increasingly contested as producing a one-sided picture from which distorted and inefficient policy outcomes result. Economic life depends on both paid work and on the unpaid activities undertaken in the 'private'/ domestic sector. In recent years data collection on unremunerated work, currently outside most national accounting systems, has been undertaken in several countries with a view to explicitly recognising and incorporating the economic contribution of unpaid work. But the emphasis on market activity remains, epitomised in Pigou's (1932) view that gross domestic product decreases when a man marries his housekeeper, and the crucial interdependency between paid and unpaid economic activities is underplayed.

The unpaid domestic sector provides caring services directly to household members, as well as to the wider community, that contribute to individual socialisation and to the production and maintenance of human capabilities, thereby developing 'the social fabric, the sense of community, civic responsibility and norms that maintain trust, goodwill, and social order' (Himmelweit, 2002). Caring services are also provided by employees in the public and private sectors of the paid economy. Obviously some of this paid work takes place within households and there is both paid and unpaid work in the voluntary sector, which is a significant provider of care services and a net contributor to the social and economic infrastructure. A key issue however is that while both men and women work in all arenas, there is a marked gendered division of labour and it is predominately women's time that is stretched between work in the unpaid economy and the paid economy. The terms 'double day' and 'second shift' have been used to describe the phenomena of increasing numbers of women who are income earners yet at the same time continue to perform their traditional roles as household managers and care providers.

While the paid and unpaid economies are interdependent there are also fundamental differences. A key difference is the motivation to care for others. Gendered social norms play a significant role in creating a sense of responsibility which may compensate for or even outweigh monetary reward. The motivation of self interest, the extent of which is exaggerated even in the paid labour market, makes little sense when applied to situations in which work is not directly rewarded at all (Folbre and Weisskopf, 1998). Again, unpaid labour is distinctive insofar as a lot of the work cannot be delegated to others. As discussed later in this book, many aspects of caring work are non-commodifiable. Caring labour is relational – it entails not only the performance of physical tasks but also the development of a relationship. Parents can pay someone to care for their children and those entrusted with the task may do it very well, but the relationships they are building with those children are their own: they cannot build the parents' relationship (Himmelweit, 2005). So, insofar as the aim of caring is to develop a particular relationship, it cannot be contracted out to others. Finally, productivity increases in caring labour are difficult to achieve. As personal relationships form the basis of care there is a limit to how far they can be stretched. It is unlikely therefore that society can reduce the total amount of time devoted to caring labour across the whole economy without damaging the quality of care provided. An example of this aspect of quality is the educational sector, where the desire to reduce the ratio of teachers to children is sometimes put forward as an economic efficiency objective.

Despite the differences between paid and unpaid labour at individual and household level, the decisions made about caring and employment are entwined, an issue which labour market theory and labour market policy are increasingly being forced to acknowledge. Care is increasingly being recognised as a significant economic issue (Himmelweit, 2005), not just in terms of its contribution to the economy but in light of the more conventional point that unpaid care labour presents a practical limit to the growth of the economy, by being an obstacle to the expansion of employment and especially to increased female labour market participation. Care responsibilities for children and elderly parents remain the most significant variable affecting women's labour force participation and hours of employment (Gardiner, 1997).

### Economics of the family

A significant interface between economics and the affective domain is in what can be generally classified as the economics of the family, which is concerned with the way decisions are made and resources are allocated within families. This field of study draws together different areas of economic enquiry such as unpaid labour, female labour force participation, population, social policy, game theory and bargaining models. It has also exposed a key weakness in methodological individualism, which for consistency has had to resort to a false dichotomy between selfishness in the market place and altruism in the family (Folbre and Hartmann, 1988).

Economic theories of household behaviour are commonly divided into two types – unitary and collective models (which incorporate co-operative and non-co-operative bargaining models). The former assume that a household behaves as if it were a single individual decision maker maximising the total utility of the household whereas the latter tries to recognise the potentially conflicting preferences of individual members and posits a form of decision making which takes into account the differing positions and choices of individual members. Both of these models conceptualise the family unit as a producer as well as a consumer, so that a household acts like a firm insofar as it produces outputs, invests in real assets and generates non-commodifiable goods such as children, care and happiness for the welfare of the family.

The most well-known and frequently cited example of a unitary model is Becker's New Household Economic Theory (Becker, 1981). Becker's model is problematic for reasons that are well-documented (for example, see Berg-mann, 1995; Lundberg *et al.*, 1997; Nelson, 1994). These include his assumption about women's economic dependency; the necessity of the head having enough control of income for others to depend on him for transfers; the assumption that the head cares about other family members while they themselves are completely selfish; the assumption that household decisions depend on total income and it is irrelevant who receives that income; his analysis of time as a scarce resource; and his theory on the specialisation of labour and classification of non-market work as leisure, which makes invisible and devalues the care work and love labour carried out within the home. Furthermore, the unitary model is not supported by empirical evidence (Browning *et al.*, 1994; Cantillon *et al.*, 2004; Cantillon and Nolan, 1998; Woolley and Marshall, 1994).

The shortcomings of the unitary model have led to a number of alternative approaches that focus on the individuality of household members and explicitly address the questions of whether, and if so how, individual preferences lead to a collective choice. These models, based on game theory, draw attention to the process of co-operation and conflict in families and in particular to how that conflict is bargained over and negotiated. These models attempt to correct the pervasive gender bias of earlier models such as the 'benevolent male dictator' or women's supposed comparative advantage in household work. They provide more plausible explanations of household expenditure patterns and of how inequality in the labour market reinforces inequalities in the home and they identify factors influencing the division of resources such as divorce legislation and social policy. However, while these models may be an improvement on unitary models they still have many shortcomings. In particular the ideology of individualism which underlies these models has been increasingly questioned. Sen (1990) argues that women and other oppressed people may not have an accurate sense of their own interests while Nelson (1996) argues that a parent's care may be better understood as a 'commitment' rather than an action motivated by their own interests. While still a long way from a well-developed, non-individualistic model of the family, the game theoretic approach has begun to shift economists' views of the household so that inequalities in power and wealth among household members cannot be as easily ignored nor can the household be treated as an undifferentiated optimising unit (Folbre, 1994).

## Non-monetary work and national accounting systems

Unpaid household work has not, by and large, been included in national accounts, with the resultant undervaluing of the contribution of women's work. The exception to this has been the Nordic countries, which since the 1930s have included unpaid household work in their national account estimates in a desire to provide a comprehensive picture of all economic activity in society and to explicitly record women's economic contribution. In the Anglo-American tradition only goods and services that were exchanged for money were included in the first international standard of national accounts published in 1953. As the limitations of using Gross Domestic Product or other systems of national accounts as a welfare indicator became clearer in the 1970s, particularly in relation to environmental concerns, the issue of non-market activities and the question of women's unpaid labour in the household came onto the agenda. Waring (1988), Eisner (1989), Iron-monger (1996) and others pioneered approaches to computing the value of unpaid work into satellite accounts that are consistent with the national account framework. In addition to the restrictive definition of economic activity in national accounts, part of the problem is the notion of value itself. In economics, value is defined in terms of market value, making it difficult to assign a value to goods and services that are not marketed. This is solvable for goods and services that could be sold on the market, such as subsistence crops or garden vegetables consumed by the producers, as a market value can be imputed for them. The same approach can be taken for some other non-market activities, including a lot of household work and also some caring work. However, some of this work transcends market value in that it makes a vital contribution to satisfying human needs that cannot be captured by its market value. Some of the work on developing 'quality of life' indicators represents an attempt to measure such values (Nussbaum and Sen, 1993). Other aspects of these contributions to social reproduction and the fabric of society, such as fostering friendships and other relationships, are of such intangible quality that it is impossible to place a market value on them. That is, not all work of value, in a sense that is clearly relevant to the economy, has a market price.

### Concluding remarks

This very brief overview shows that there is interesting work being done in economics on issues of love and care, but also that this whole field is only beginning to be developed. Feminism in particular has put care work and its value on the agenda of economics. Yet economics continues to have dif-ficulties dealing with unpaid labour, with modelling economic relationships within families, and with constructing adequate ways of assessing the value that unpaid care work contributes to the economy.

## Affective inequality and law

Law is deeply implicated in constituting and perpetuating the social insti-tutions that shape affective inequality. Until fairly recently, however, legal scholarship has neglected this fact. As in other fields, feminism has been the key influence in drawing attention to the role of law in sustaining affective inequality, but feminists are divided on its capacity to address this inequality, particularly in terms of legal rights. Although the affective system extends well beyond the family and into many other social institutions, the family plays a key role in this system and is our main focus here.

## Affective inequality in legal theory

As Michael Freeman (1994) observes, legal theorists generally neglected the affective context until the arrival of feminism. Martha Fineman (1995: 23–24) also notes that 'the family has been only marginally evident in legal theory or jurisprudence, including feminist legal theory' and comments on the scholarly tendency for 'those relationships conceptually contained in the private sphere [to receive] little sustained critical attention except as they relate to the public domain'.

Recent work in feminist legal theory has gone some way towards redressing this neglect of the family and of the affective system more generally. Feminist theorists have not just critiqued a host of laws that impact upon the affective, but have probed the role of the legal system in generating and sustaining affective inequalities. Such scholarship has tended to focus on the consequences of unpaid caregiving for (female) care providers (Fineman, 2004), prompted by a concern that such labour is a site of gender inequality that has not been tackled by the major law reform efforts of the past few decades. More generally, a body of legal writing, such as that concerning children and sexual minorities, has begun to engage with the conditions of access to relationships of love, care and solidarity.

An example of this new approach is Fineman's (2004) view that care must be reconstituted as a public good. Responsibility for ensuring that care work does not lead to poverty and social exclusion should be taken out of the private sphere and reframed as a collective responsibility. Under this renegotiated 'social contract' each individual engaging in caring labour would have a range of socio-economic rights met by the state, rather than by family members. Fineman (1995) also argues that the legal category of marriage should be abolished; instead the relationship which should be valued and protected is that of Mother/Child, where 'Mother/Child' is taken as a metaphor for all relationships that involve intimate caring (e.g. son/ elderly parent).

O'Donovan (1989: 146) notes that all of those who go to law find a language imposed upon them, and that this language incorporates certain values. In liberal legal systems, the values contained in that language have been identified as liberty and autonomy. These are values of sharply defined commitment, not of open-ended obligation; of free choice, not of family duty; of contract not of trusting relationship. She maintains that women's concern for others and for continuity and connection is an alternative model of justice. The idea that women have a 'different voice' (Gilligan, 1982) has played an important but controversial role in the debate over the importance of legal rights in promoting equality.

## Law's presence in the affective domain

Because of its regulatory role in society, law is implicated in many social practices. Law both reflects and constitutes social relations (Ewick and Silbey, 1998; Gordon, 1984; Hunt, 1993; McCann, 1994). It promotes certain ideals at the expense of others (for example, by telling us what types of 'families' deserve recognition) and plays a powerful role in shaping and regulating identity. Legal discourse is said to construct gender identity by, for instance, applying notions of the 'good mother' (Biggs, 1997) or 'good father' in custody disputes, the 'deserving housewife' or homemaker in family property disputes and so on (Smart, 1989). As Brophy and Smart (1985: 1) put it:

> Law sets the parameters to what is considered 'normal', for example marriage, sexual relations, the way we care for our children. ... We cannot 'opt out' of these legal parameters by adopting unconventional lifestyles or by avoiding heterosexuality. The law still has something to say about our domestic lives and intimate relations, and we cannot assert its irrelevance by ignoring it.

An example of this process is the distinction between the 'public' and the 'private'. As Yuval-Davis (1997: 80) puts it, the 'construction of the boundary between the public and the private is a political act in itself'. In law, the public/private distinction is used in different ways in different contexts. As Karl Klare (1992: 1361) observes:

> There is no 'public/private distinction'. What does exist is a series of ways of thinking about public and private that are now constantly undergoing revision, reformulation, and refinement. The law contains a set of imageries and metaphors, more or less coherent, more or less prone to conscious manipulation, designed to organise judicial thinking according to recurrent, value-laden patterns.

Feminist scholars have exposed law's contradictory and complex relation to the affective context. The affective is in fact highly regulated. Laws proscribe certain forms of sexual contact, prescribe ideal family forms largely through privileging heterosexual marriage, and regulate abortion and other reproductive technologies. Non-intervention is itself a form of regulation because it protects established practices (Freeman, 1994; O'Donovan, 1989).

## How family law reinforces inequality

The manner in which law constitutes families has implications for both primary forms of affective inequality – the unequal distribution of care work and the care deprivations experienced disproportionately by certain groups. For a start, law has been complicit in conveying the ideological message that certain aspects of the 'private' should remain outside the preserve of state action and regulation. For example, male dominance was shielded by case law and statutes that explicitly excluded women from the public sphere and did not extend individual rights into the domestic sphere to which they were confined (Olsen, 1983; Taub and Schneider, 1998; Vogel, 1988). In this way, law has acted to preserve existing power relationships and social arrangements and to reinforce the *status quo*. Liberal legal doctrines such as the social contract and its attendant liberal rights sheltered certain forms of interpersonal oppression while sanctioning governmental interference in the lives of poor and deviant families. In Ireland, for example, severe forms of affective inequality were experienced by women who gave birth outside marriage and by the (mostly) working class children who were effectively incarcerated in various homes and institutions while theoretically being in the care of the state (Feeley, 2007; O'Sullivan, 1998; Raftery and O'Sullivan, 1999).

Feminist writers have exposed the devaluation of care within the legal field, objecting to the interpretation of work performed in homes as unproductive love and affection rather than as productive labour (Fineman, 2004; Roberts, 1997; Siegel, 1994; Silbaugh, 1996; Williams, 2001). Assessment of what types of activities or work should be 'rewarded' with a share in the family home has been a highly contentious issue before courts in several countries (e.g. Khadiagala, 2002; Siegel, 1994; Wong, 1999; Yeates, 1999). Where provision is made for the redistribution of property between (married) family members, some recognition is afforded to the value of care work at a horizontal level. Such measures, however, ensure that the costs of social reproduction are largely privatised (Boyd, 1999), a pattern that has become concentrated and (re)formed under neoliberalism (Cossman and Fudge, 2002). For example, the World Bank's land reform agenda is, according to Manji (2003, 2005), premised on the continued exploitation of women's unpaid work. It treats the household as an undifferentiated unit, overlooking the fact that the family often functions as an ideological and material site of gender-based oppression.

Much legal practice assumes the inevitability, or at least primacy, of the family centred on heterosexual partners. Stychin (1995: 7) argues that 'legal discourse is an important site for the constitution, consolidation and regulation of sexuality and, in particular, the hetero-homo sexual division.' While the European Court of Human Rights has adopted a more progressive stance, it has done so on terms that cling to a binary model of gender difference (Grigolo, 2003). Gay and lesbian people are posited as individuals with immutable characteristics that mark them out as 'different' and as deserving of toleration. The background norm against which these 'others' are measured – the heterosexual family unit – is not problematised (Gotell, 2002; Stychin, 1995).

Another way the law has reinforced affective inequality is in its rules concerning adoption. Traditionally adoption was predicated on an exclusive model, under which what was effectively ownership of the child passed exclusively from the birth parents to the adoptive parents. The effect of this practice was to completely sever the tie between birth mothers and children and to place the child with a new nuclear family, often with severe emotional costs to all of the parties concerned. Open adoptions that enable ongoing contact between birth parents and children are now routine practice in many jurisdictions.

Of course, it is not just in the affective sphere that family law has served to reinforce inequality. Throughout its history, the effect and to a large extent the purpose of family law has been to ensure that children inherit the socio-economic status of their parents. Family law has also played an important role in perpetuating racism, for example by prohibiting interracial marriages and sexual relations (particularly those between white women and black men) and by racialised laws of descent' (Pateman and Mills, 2007: 141–147).

### The debate over rights

Rights play a central role in the operation of the legal system, but feminists have had very different views about the potential of legal rights for addressing inequality. MacKinnon (1987), for example, believes that a key mechanism for the institutionalisation of male power is the law's claim to gender neutrality and objectivity, epitomised in the appeal to abstract rights. Naffine (1990) shows how the ostensibly autonomous, contracting individual is gendered: men's dependencies and needs are met within the unacknowledged private sphere, thus women's domestic work sustains the 'paradox of the man of law' (p. 149). By equating liberty with state non-interference, the right to privacy including the decisional autonomy of the family cordons off aspects of this important sphere of life from public scrutiny. Separation is valorised above connection leading to the devaluation of care work in judgements pertaining to both interpersonal relationships and the state-individual axis considered in socio-economic rights jurisprudence.

Gilligan and MacKinnon have both argued that an emphasis on rights reflects male values and male power. In Gilligan's (1982) view the ethic of rights comprises the male voice, whereas the female voice is the ethic of care. Her research leads her to the conclusion not that the male voice should be suppressed to make way for the muted female voice, but that properly adult moral conceptions integrate both ethics. Her work has generated much debate and criticism in feminist legal theory. For example Scales (1986: 1381) comments that Gilligan's work 'tempts one to suggest that the different voices of women can somehow be grafted onto our rights and rule-based system'. Scales is opposed to what she sees as the facile idea that incorporation of the female voice into a rights-based system could be anything other than mere incorporation, arguing that the inevitable result is the further repression of the contradiction between the two voices: 'Incorporationism assumes that we can whip the problem of social inequality by adding yet another prong to the already multi-pronged legal tests' (Scales, 1986: 1382).

Another argument regularly advanced against rights is that they promote an adversarial stance instead of the sort of co-operation that makes for good social relations. Mary Ann Glendon (1991), for instance, argues that the proliferation of rights goes hand-in-hand with the impoverishment of political argument, with every person asserting their private entitlements against each other or the state instead of trying to come to a mutual agreement or compromise on matters that affect all parties. A related objection concerns the 'implicit individualism of the liberal legal subject' (Lacey, 2004: 21). Feminists such as West (2003, 2004) and Naffine (1990) problematise the abstract individual rights-bearer at the heart of liberal legalism, maintaining that rights discourse obscures the extent to which we are interdependent and valorises separation instead of connection.

Moreover, as Scheingold (1974: 76) persuasively argues, a problem with articulating rights claims is that they 'cut both ways – serving at some times and under some circumstances to reinforce privilege and at other times to provide the cutting edge of change'. Measures designed to transcend the public/private dichotomy to some extent, such as the recognition of domestic violence as a harm that should be cognisable as a legal wrong, have met with quite a degree of success. Yet the entry of liberal rights into the private sphere did not result in equality of power, resources or other dimensions (Minow, 1990). Many early successes in the arena of reproductive rights were not based on egalitarian arguments but rather derived from rights to marital privacy which were heavily imbued with patriarchal assumptions (Flynn, 1995). Constitutional anti-discrimination guarantees have been deployed to remove the remaining vestiges of formal status hierarchies between married men and women (Doyle, 2004, ch. 7), but have not altered the substantive position of spouses, as becomes apparent in case law on the value of care work.

Robin West (2003: 90) starkly proclaims: 'Rights have never been viewed, within liberalism, as a source of support for caregivers.' While historical justifications of gender roles rested on women's nature, contemporary liberalism seems to base their justification on women's choice. The minimal protections afforded to caregivers derive from a conception of charity as opposed to validating such work as a matter of right. West does suggest, however, that liberalism can be expanded to embrace a right to care.

Despite these criticisms, many feminist legal scholars continue to believe that rights have an important potential for promoting gender equality. Minow (1990: 301) argues that we need not dispense with citizenship, equality, and other human rights because of their limitations, but that we should 'reconceive rights as a notion that upholds the rights in relationships among mutually dependant members of the community'. Rights also retain their appeal as a means of ensuring that the self is not effaced by adherence to communitarian norms, which can lead to erasure of the female as subject within the family (Minow and Shanley, 1996).

In reply to the charge that rights discourse generates conflict between individuals and so threatens co-operative social relations, one response is that rights themselves do not fuel adversarial positions but are in place in the event that relations break down (Waldron, 1993). In addressing marriage Waldron (1993: 374) writes that formal rights and duties do not constitute the relationship but rather operate as a type of safety net. Minow (1987: 1874) further argues that those who invoke rights discourse actually affirm community because in doing so they 'invest themselves in a larger community, even in the act of seeking to change it'.

The case for rights is strengthened by reflecting on the distinction drawn by liberal legal systems between rights and needs (Vogel, 1988: 315). Waldron (2000) argues that the language of rights is preferable to the language of needs because it provides a way that self-respecting individuals can articulate determinate claims as moral equals. White and Tronto (2004) agree to an extent with Waldron but further contend that 'needs' ought to be reconfigured. Explaining that 'needs' tend to be associated exclusively with subordinate groups they comment:

> Needs talk is at odds with 'self-respect' only if we cannot conceive of needy selves as citizens. Recent feminist scholarship has challenged both the concept of autonomy and its common equation with economic self sufficiency, and the connections between autonomy and liberal citizenship. Ultimately all selves are needy. But because the liberal conception of citizenship is tightly linked to a conception of independence and autonomy, this fact is often obscured. (White and Tronto, 2004: 433)

With regard to the objection that rights are incompatible with relationality, a number of feminist theorists have claimed that rights too are relational. Both Young (1990: 25) and Nedelsky (1993) argue that legal rights are not singular objects possessed by individuals but social relationships, which are reduced to a written text in order to be captured by law. As Minow (1987: 1884) argues, because legal rights 'arise in the context of relationships among people who are themselves interdependent and mutually defining' they are best configured as 'simply the articulation of legal consequences for particular patterns of human and institutional relationships'. Nedelsky (1993: 13) makes both a normative and empirical claim in asserting that all rights are relational: 'In brief, what rights in fact do and have always done is construct relationships – of power, of responsibility, of trust, of obligation.' While the surface inquiry conducted by a court may present an understanding of rights as shielding the individual from the tyranny of the majority, a question of rights 'trumping' the common good (Dworkin, 1977), the actual structure of decisions reveals that they are vehicles for achieving various collective goals. Pildes (1998: 731) observes that judicial review 'requires courts to determine the scope of rights with reference to the justifications government offers for limiting them. That is because rights are better understood as means of realising certain collective interests; their content is necessarily defined with reference to those interests.' Thus legal reasoning is already relational but arguably tends to prioritise proprietary-object relations rather than ones framed around egalitarian principles.

The goal, therefore, should be two-fold: to expose the unarticulated premises and invisible mechanisms through which relational principles enter the law and to ensure that those principles foster human connections that advance rather than impede substantive equality. If courts were to adopt such a relational view of rights, property, for example, could be regarded as a system that shapes the contours of human relationships. In doing so courts would be more attentive to the kinds of relationships we want the legal rules to foster or discourage.

If rights are to be taken seriously in the affective sphere, a key question will be whether to assert a 'meta right' to care (West, 2003). Work on the positive rights required to ground such a meta right to care dovetails with critical legal scholarship on socio-economic rights (Pieterse, 2004). Critical legal scholars have pointed out that the civil and political rights that take prominence in most Western constitutions need to be underscored by the social rights required to exercise them (Jackman and Porter, 1999). This point can be extended to include rights relating to love and care.

## Concluding remarks

Law's treatment of love and care is, therefore, somewhat paradoxical. Legal systems have a profound effect on affective relationships, defining what is normal and reinforcing inequality. But legal scholarship has only recently addressed these issues from an egalitarian point of view. This scholarship has opened up new ways of thinking about the role of law and important debates about how it can be used to promote equality. The debate about rights is an example of the many issues that remain to be resolved.

## Affective equality and political theory

As we note in Chapter 2, affective equality ranges across a family of concepts, including love, care and solidarity. The idea of love, however, has received less detailed treatment from political theorists than the discussion of care (which sometimes makes reference to love: see below). Issues of solidarity are related to extensive debates about the concept of community in recent political theory, but these tend to concentrate on issues of shared values and identities rather than on the parallels between love, care and solidarity. In this section, therefore, we restrict our discussion of affective equality in political theory primarily to feminist work on the theme of care.

We focus on a few key moves in the debate about care and equality rather than attempting to survey the entire literature.

## A brief overview

As in the social sciences, political theory has traditionally been concerned with the 'public' sphere, defined primarily in terms of the coercive political relations of the state and the economic relations of market economies, and therefore with inequalities of income and wealth, status and power. Rawls's *A Theory of Justice* (1999), which has been the dominant work in Anglophone political theory since its publication in 1971, is a clear example of the primacy of the public sphere so defined. Regarding the private sphere, Rawls repeatedly refers to 'the family' as playing an important role, but only insofar as it contributes to the formation of citizens (405 ff.) and to inequalities of opportunity (64, 265, 448).

The most powerful early criticism of Rawls's treatment of the family, Susan Moller Okin's *Justice, Gender, and the Family* (Okin, 1989), attacks Rawls and other political theorists for neglecting the distributional, status and power inequalities within families, and their consequences for inequalities in the public sphere. Okin treats the gendered division of labour as a central factor in generating these inequalities. But although she identifies child care as integral to this division of labour, she does not focus on the unequal success families have in satisfying their members' needs for love and care, and she treats domestic abuse and violence as indicators of unjust power relations (128–129, 152) rather than as affective injustices in their own right. Rawls's reply to Okin (Rawls, 2001: 163–168) concedes that women's 'disproportionate share of the task of raising, nurturing, and caring for their children' is a 'long and historic injustice' (166) but his attention remains fixed on how this inequality affects moral development and equality of opportunity.

Part of the academic impact of the women's movement from the 1980s onwards was to put care itself onto the agenda of moral and political philosophy. However, the way that this was generally framed was in terms of an alleged tension between care and justice, and therefore, implicitly, between care and equality. Perhaps the most widely-cited work in this vein was Carol Gilligan's *In a Different Voice* (1982), which maintains that women adopt a contextualised, care-based moral perspective in contrast to the allegedly abstract, deductive, rule-based forms of morality seen as typical of western philosophy in general and epitomised by both of its dominant Kantian and utilitarian traditions.[10]

In the 1990s, however, a number of important works emerged that challenged the idea of a simple choice between justice and care. On the one hand, feminist political theorists offered powerful critiques of the adequacy of the dominant tradition for understanding social justice, precisely because of its neglect of issues of care and dependency. In particular, Eva Feder

Kittay's work, *Love's Labour* (1999), systematically criticises traditional theories of equality, and Rawls's theory in particular, from a point of view that takes human dependency seriously. Kittay argues that the issue is not to choose between equality and care but to develop a 'connection-based' conception of equality that recognises that dependency is a typical condition of human life, that dependants need care, and that dependency workers – those who provide this care – need support in doing so. She maintains that 'the good both to be cared for in a responsive dependency relation if and when one is unable to care for oneself, and to meet the dependency needs of others without incurring undue sacrifices oneself is a primary social good in the Rawlsian sense' (Kittay, 1999: 103). From a somewhat different perspective, Martha Nussbaum's development of the capability approach (Nussbaum and Sen, 1993; Nussbaum, 1995, 2000) identifies care-related factors such as love and affiliation, as well as protection from assault and abuse, as central human capabilities that an adequate theory of justice needs to promote.

Concurrently there was a growing realisation that the 'ethics of care' approach could not be divorced from questions of justice. For example, Diemut Bubeck (1995) shows that an ethics of care perspective leads inevitably into important issues of justice, such as how to avoid the exploitation of women as carers, how to address inequalities in meeting people's need for care, and how to promote an equal distribution of the burden of caring. More generally, she points out that questions of justice inevitably arise from conflicts of interest between those who need care, those who provide care, and third parties who benefit from the care work of others – the latter two categories consisting predominantly of women and men, respectively, and therefore playing a central role in the reproduction of gender inequality.

### Major themes

These theoretical developments contain three major themes, not always integrated. First of all, there is an emphasis on the needs that human beings have for various kinds of care. The literature has tended to focus on particular phases or conditions of life in which people are especially vulnerable and therefore clearly dependent on others, such as infancy, childhood, illness, frail old age and some cases of disability. While these examples bring out very clearly the inevitability of the need for care, they also generate some problems. With respect to disability, the discussion is sometimes insufficiently informed by the social model of disability, which distinguishes between disability and impairment and rejects the assimilation of impairment to incapacity. As a result, it is sometimes assumed that all disabled people need care of a kind or to a degree that non-disabled people do not need. This assumption is strongly contested by many disability activists.[11] However, some of the cases discussed, such as Kittay's powerful discussions of severe mental impairment, show that the opposite assumption is also mistaken, and that certain forms of impairment do require specific forms of care. A more general problem with concentrating on vulnerable conditions is the implication that typical healthy adults are *not* dependent on others and do not need care. Our own view is that interdependency is the standard condition of human beings and that the need for love, care and solidarity is ubiquitous. It is only in very exceptional circumstances that individuals may be said to be fully independent.

The idea that love, care and solidarity are general human needs has not been easily incorporated into mainstream liberal egalitarian theorising, largely because of a reluctance, stemming from Rawls, to build into a theory of justice anything that belongs to a substantive conception of human well-being. Rawls's 'primary goods' are defined precisely as 'things which it is supposed a rational man [sic] wants whatever else he wants' (Rawls, 1999: 79). In response to the claim that love and care are a basic human need, liberally minded political philosophers typically claim that these belong to a specific conception of human well-being and that their inclusion therefore violates the requirement that theories of justice should be neutral among conceptions of the good.[12] Kittay's reply is that the goods of being cared for when one needs it and being able to care for others when one has to do so meet Rawls's own standards for primary goods, because they are goods that everyone needs as a condition for pursuing their own ends. Drawing on Rawls's later work, *Political Liberalism* (1993), Nussbaum argues that there is a general, cross-cultural 'overlapping consensus' on the value of such goods. On either account, they can be included in a theory of justice without privileging any particular conception of well-being. A slightly weaker, third position leading to a similar conclusion is to argue that even if there is a small number of people who genuinely do not need or at least do not want any love or care in their lives, this is no different from any of Rawls's other primary goods, since there are also people who do not want certain basic liberties or more than a minimal amount of income. On this view, it is enough for egalitarian theories of justice to focus on goods that nearly everyone needs. Strict neutrality among all conceptions of well-being is simply too strong a requirement.

The second major theme of the literature is its concern with the work of caring. At least two issues have been raised here. The first, and historically the earliest, is the gendered division of labour and the fact that the largely unpaid work of caring is done primarily by women. Although Okin's (1989) focus is on the effects of this division of labour on gender inequalities in income, power and status, more recent discussions in political theory have also emphasised the unequal work burden imposed on women by this division of labour (for example, Bubeck, 1995; Fraser, 1997: ch. 2). What has made this inequality difficult to incorporate into mainstream theories of equality is a tendency for such theories to ignore inequalities of work burden altogether.

A second question about care work is how to support those who care for others. Okin argues that the ideal solution is to abandon the gendered division of labour; in the meantime, she proposes that there should be a mandatory splitting of household income so that wives in traditional roles are no worse off materially than their husbands (Okin, 1989: ch. 8). This proposal emphasises the material needs of care workers, but of course they also have their own care needs. Drawing on the tradition of caregiving to new mothers, Kittay articulates:

> a principle of *doulia: Just as we have required care to survive and thrive, so we need to provide conditions that allow others – including those who do the work of caring – to receive the care they need to survive and thrive.* (Kittay, 1999: 107, emphasis in the original)

An egalitarian ideal of support for carers should therefore attend to the whole range of their needs.

A third major theme is that the *relationship* between caregiver and care recipient can be more or less egalitarian. Returning to an earlier point, there has been a tendency to focus on situations in which the relationship is taken to be asymmetrical, i.e. where one person provides care and the other receives it. It is easy to imagine that this asymmetrical relationship could not possibly be egalitarian in character, but interestingly enough the character of its presumed inequality has been perceived in very different ways. On the one hand, it looks as though care recipients are in a privileged position, since they are the beneficiaries of the work of caregivers without having to give back anything in return. As Bubeck (1995) notes, the 'ethic of care' places potentially limitless demands on caregivers. By contrast, one can see caregivers as the privileged parties to the relationship, because of their power over vulnerable care recipients. Although Kittay recognises that care recipients also exercise a kind of power over the carer, based on the moral claim that their needs must be met, she nevertheless views the relationship as one of unequal power, since the care recipient may have very little capacity for agency (Kittay, 1999: 33–35). Asymmetrical relations of care may also be marked by unavoidable inequalities of love and affection, if the care recipient is incapable of reciprocating the caregiver's love; and of respect and recognition, if the care recipient is incapable of adopting these stances towards the caregiver.

All of these points indicate that there may be limits to the degree to which the relationship between caregivers and care recipients can be fully equal. But this does not necessarily show that the aspiration for equality is misguided. Even in the asymmetrical cases under discussion, aspects of the relationship can be egalitarian in character. For example, Kittay writes movingly about her intellectually-impaired daughter Sesha's capacity for love: 'That is what she wishes to receive and that is what she reciprocates in spades' (Kittay, 1999: 152). Unless there is some reason in principle why the relationship *should* be one of unequal power, love or respect, the fact that an equal relationship may not always be possible is not a fundamental objection to making it as equal as possible.

Because of the emphasis on asymmetrical relations, there has been less discussion in the theoretical literature of relationships of mutual care. Such relationships do not raise the same difficulties for equality as asymmetrical relationships: it is both possible and, arguably, desirable for mutual carers to treat each other fully as equals, with equal respect, power and care.

### Concluding remarks

Although feminist philosophers have powerfully criticised mainstream political theory for its neglect of the affective domain, it has been an uphill battle. Partly because of the 'care *versus* justice' position, issues of inequality in caring relations have often been neglected. Recent feminist work has revealed a number of key themes for egalitarians – the need for care, the work of care, and the quality of the relationship between caregiver and care-recipient. These themes are explored in depth in the rest of this book.

## Conclusion

In this chapter we have reviewed some of the approaches taken towards affective equality in a number of relevant academic disciplines. The story that is common to all of them is that scant attention was paid to the affective system and its constituent inequalities before these were focused upon by feminist scholars, mostly since the 1980s. Even now, after at least two decades of scholarly attention, issues to do with love, care and solidarity and the work that goes into sustaining them are largely confined to branches of academic disciplines that are labelled as 'feminist' or 'radical' rather than being recognised as central issues. The theme of affective equality has still to become truly integrated into mainstream sociology, education, economics, law and political theory.

In the chapters that follow, we hope to contribute to that aim. Chapter 2 sets out a general taxonomy of love, care and solidarity, and draws out some normative implications. The empirical studies set out in Chapters 3 to 10 reveal the importance and complexity of affective inequality. Chapter 11 attempts to bring together the main conclusions of those chapters and to develop their theoretical implications.

# 2
# Love, Care and Solidarity: What Is and Is Not Commodifiable

*Kathleen Lynch and Judy Walsh*

This chapter provides a three-fold taxonomy for analysing other-centred work, distinguishing between work required to maintain primary care relations (love labour), secondary care relations (general care work) and tertiary care relations (solidary work). A central theme of the chapter is that primary care relations are not sustainable over time without love labour; that the realisation of love, as opposed to the declaration of love, requires work.[13]

Drawing on a wide range of theoretical and empirical sources, including a study of caring undertaken by the authors, the chapter argues that there is mutuality, commitment, trust and responsibility at the heart of love labouring that makes it distinct from general care work and solidary work. It sets out reasons why it is not possible to commodify the feelings, intentions and commitments of love labourers by supplying them on a paid basis. The chapter also explores the scope and limitations of paying for secondary care work, and the ways in which solidarity can be both positively and negatively employed in terms of social justice.

The chapter opens with a brief comment on the status of caring work. It then reviews the research literature in the field and provides an explanation as to why love, care and solidarity (LCS) are vital for human self-preservation and self realisation, both collectively and individually. The main focus of the chapter is on outlining a three-fold taxonomy of care that distinguishes between the kinds of work involved in sustaining love, care and solidary relations.[14] We then present a brief analysis of the implications of neoliberal politics for love labouring, examining the ways in which gender, social class and migration interface with care commanding, and outlining the significance of economic resources for care work. The chapter closes with a discussion as to why love labour in particular is not commodifiable.

## The status of care work

The traditional scholarly understanding of work has equated it with self-preservation and self actualisation through interaction with nature (Gürtler,

2005; Pettinger *et al.*, 2005). It has been blind to the importance of other-centred work arising from our interdependencies and dependencies as affective, relational beings. In particular it has ignored the centrality of caring for the preservation and self actualisation of the human species. Yet, care labour produces social outcomes and takes at least three distinct forms, namely love labour, general care labour and solidary work. Primary care relations, in particular, are not sustainable over time without love labour, and the realisation of love, as opposed to the declaration of love, requires work. Love labouring is affectively-driven and involves at different times and to different degrees, emotional work, mental work, cognitive skills and physical work (the distinction between love labour, general care labour and solidary work is examined in detail below). Without such labouring, feelings of love or care for others can simply involve rhetorical functionings, words and talk that are declaratory in nature but lack substance in practice or action. Verbal utterances of affection, care or solidarity (which may be valuable in and of themselves) become empty forms of rhetoric when they are not complemented by undertakings on behalf of others. The rhetorical problem is not unique to primary care relations; it also arises in relation secondary care relations or solidary relations although these are not the primary focus of this chapter (see Moran, 2006 for a discussion of the use of social inclusion as a rhetorical device in the political sphere).

Caring is low status work generally undertaken by low status people, especially when it is engaged in full-time. In most countries, people who are working full-time as carers at home (mostly women) are not defined as working. Personal service workers, especially carers, are poorly paid and have low status. In the United States (in 2006) child care workers had a mean annual wage of $17,120 which was lower than that of cleaners and janitors at $19,750 or those employed in food preparation and serving related work at $19,690 (U.S. Department of Labor, 2007). In Ireland, as in many other countries, care workers employed in the care sector have the same status as semi-skilled workers such as bar staff, goods porters and mail sorters, which is the second lowest occupational ranking. If care workers are employed in private households as domestic staff they are classified as unskilled workers and are at the bottom of the occupational ranking (Central Statistics Office, 2003).

The low status and wages of full-time carers reflect the deep disrespect there is for caring in society. As we demonstrated in Chapter 1, this lack of respect is reflected in the academy. Sociological, economic, legal and political thought has focused on the public sphere, the outer spaces of life, indifferent to the fact that none of these can function without the care institutions of society (Fineman, 2004). Within classical economics in particular there has been a core assumption that the prototypical human being is a self-sufficient rational economic man (*sic*) (Folbre, 1994). There has been no serious account taken of the reality of dependency for all human beings, both in childhood and at times of illness and infirmity (Badgett and Folbre, 1999).

## Debates about care

As noted in Chapter 1, care research now spans all the social sciences and cognate areas and is being advanced by feminist scholars in a wide range of disciplines including sociology, social policy, philosophy, economics, politics, education and law.[15] The objective of this chapter is to extend the work of feminist scholars by analysing the differences between forms of care, especially between what is and is not commodifiable in the sense that it can be provided on a paid-for basis. A core assumption of this chapter is that the affective domain of life centred on caring constitutes a fourth structural system of social relations focused on providing and sustaining people as emotionally and relationally engaged social beings. The affective relations within which caring is grounded constitute a field of social action within and through which inequalities and exploitations can occur, just as they can occur in the economic, political or cultural sphere (Baker *et al.*, 2004).

## Why love, care and solidarity matter

> While conditioned in fundamentally significant ways by cultural considerations, dependency for humans is as unavoidable as birth and death are for all living organisms. We may even say that the long maturation process of humans, combined with the decidedly human capacity for moral feeling and attaching, make caring for dependants a mark of humanity. (Kittay, 1999: 29)

Being loved and cared for is of central importance for having a minimally decent life; caring, in its multiple manifestations, is a central human capability serving a fundamental human need (Nussbaum, 1995, 2000). Being loved and cared for is not only vital for survival in infancy, early childhood or times of illness or vulnerability, but throughout human life. Even when we are not in a state of strong dependency, we are relational beings, emotional as well as intellectual, social as well as individual (Gilligan, 1995). All people have the capacity for intimacy, attachment and caring relationships. Bonds of friendship or kinship are frequently what bring meaning, warmth and joy to life. Being deprived of the capacity to develop such supportive affective relations, or of the experience of engaging in them when one has the capacity, is therefore a serious human deprivation and injustice.

Whether people subscribe to other-centred norms or not, their own existence is dependent on the successful enactment of such norms (Fineman, 2004; Sevenhuijsen, 1998). No human being, no matter how rich or powerful, can survive from birth without care and attention; many would die at different points in their lives, if seriously ill or in an accident, without care. The inevitability of interdependency does not just apply in personal relationships, but also in work places, in public organisations, in voluntary groups or other social settings. While it is obvious that we cannot flourish personally without support, encouragement and affirmation, even in our paid work lives we can only flourish fully if we work with others who are nurtured, fed and supported so they are willing and able to work.

Being cared for is not only a prerequisite for survival therefore, it is also a prerequisite for human development and well-being (Engster, 2005). Relations of solidarity, care and love help to establish a basic sense of importance, value and belonging, a sense of being appreciated, wanted and cared about. They play a vital part in enabling people to lead successful lives, and are an expression of our fundamental interdependence (Held, 1995a; Nussbaum, 1995). To deprive or deny someone the experience of care and love, or to be indifferent towards or inhibiting of their acts of solidarity, is to deprive them of one of the great goods of human existence.

A further reason why relations of care, love and solidarity matter is because the development of love, care and solidary relations involves effort, time and energy. Maintaining love and care relations involves work that is often pleasurable but also burdensome. Hochschild's (2001) work shows that the demands of caring for young highly dependant children are seen as work, so much so that people do try to escape them, in particular by spending longer hours in paid employment than they have to. As discussed in Chapters 6 and 7 below, the love labouring involved with young children, and with older parents with special needs, is often seen as 'hard work'; it can be pleasurable and burdensome even at the same time. Insofar as love, care and solidary work is burdensome, it needs to be distributed equally between the members of society, between women and men in particular. The pleasurable aspects of this work also need to be distributed equally.

Love, care and solidarity matter also because care work produces outcomes that can be seen and felt if not always easily measured. The outcomes are evident in the presence of emotionally resourced family members, friends, colleagues, neighbours or partners. We recognise the presence or absence of love and care in the lives not only of those familiar to us, but even among strangers, especially where we have to engage with them. The outcomes of solidarity are also visible in collective form, in the political energy and commitment that so many civil society groups and individuals produce when they work together in other-centred ways (Borg and Mayo, 2007). Ironically, the primacy of love, care and solidarity is often most visible in their absence. It becomes visible in social institutions such as prisons where people are not only deprived of basic civil liberties such as freedom of movement or freedom of association, but also of the freedom to engage in love and care relations. It also becomes visible when powerful states enact laws and terms of trade that are seriously disadvantageous to poor people in different parts of the world, or when wealthy states enact immigration laws that exclude vulnerable people from entry (Seglow, 2005).

One of the most important outcomes of care work is the creation of *nurturing capital*,[16] i.e. the capacity to nurture others, that is available to us personally, socially and politically. The amount of nurturing capital available includes a) that inherited from the love, care and solidarity invested in people historically, both individually at an intimate level, and collectively as social and political beings, and b) that which is created anew in each generation. The levels of nurturing capital available are visible in the amount of personal love and care people have received in the intimate sphere of life, and in the degrees of solidarity that exist in public spheres including places of work, public services and the physical, social and cultural environment. Thus, nurturing capitals are both inherited and recreated on an ongoing basis throughout life. These nurturing capitals affect people's ability not only to relate to others at an intimate level, but also to flourish and contribute in other spheres of life.

Because love, care and solidarity matter for the survival and development of humanity and for the effective functioning of economic, political and cultural systems, their importance cannot be denied. Someone has to do this nurturing work on a daily basis, and much of it is unpaid. Knowing the differences between what caring can be put out for hire and what cannot is vital not only for promoting gender equality in the doing of care, but also for knowing what kinds of public policies should be enacted to support different forms of care labour.

## The relational realities of caring

Human beings are ethical, committed and emotional, as well as economic, political and cultural; the sets of values that govern people's actions in everyday life and the emotions that accompany them are central to how people live and define themselves (Sayer, 2005: 5–12). People struggle in their choices between what is good and the not-so-good; their lives are governed by rules of lay normativity in much of their social action (*ibid.*: 35–50). Because human beings live in affective relational realities, they also have emotional ties and bonds that can reinforce their motivation to act as moral agents, to act 'other wise' rather than 'self wise' (Tronto, 1991, 1993) – though of course they can also work the other way. One of the defining struggles in the lay normative world is the struggle over how to balance concerns and commitment to others with personal and career self-interests (Ball *et al.*, 2004), tapping into and managing corresponding emotions. Within the broad field of love, care and solidarity, there are significant differences in how these norms and emotions operate.

## Concentric circles of care relations

Human life is lived in a wide range of care networks. The three major contexts where these operate are visually represented in Figure 2.1 as care circles. Care circles are sets of relational realities connected to each other (and with the material world we share with other species) in complex and often unobservable ways (Gilligan, 1995).

There are three major life-worlds or circles of 'other-centred' relational care work. First, there is the world of primary, intimate relations where there is strong attachment, interdependence, depth of engagement and intensity; the prototypical relationship in this circle is that between parents and children. Even if little love labour is invested in this sphere by the parties to this intimate world, these relationships retain a high level of care significance. Secondary care relations involve outer circles of relatives, friends, neighbours and work colleagues where there are lower order engagements in terms of time, responsibility, commitment and emotional engagement. Tertiary care relations involve largely unknown others for whom we have

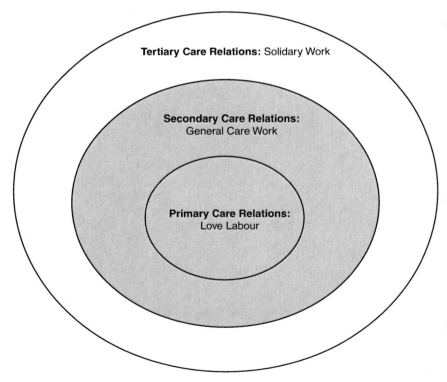

*Figure 2.1*   Concentric Circles of Care Relations (*Source*: Lynch *et al.*, 2007)

care responsibilities through statutory obligations at national or international levels, or for whom we care politically or economically through volunteering or activism. Within each of these circles of care, people live in varying states of dependency and interdependency. And each care reality is intersectionally connected to the other, moving along a fluid continuum from care-full-ness to care-less-ness.

The world of care is not an isolated and autonomous sphere. It is deeply interwoven with economic, political and cultural relations, and inequalities in the latter can undermine the capacities and resources to do love, care and solidary work (Baker *et al.*, 2004). It is no accident of history, for example, that those who are in prison are not only disproportionately from very poor households, but are also very likely to have suffered severe care deprivations and to have lacked equality of access to education and other social goods (O'Mahony, 1997). Structural injustices exacerbate affective deprivations.

In primary care relations, labours of abuse and neglect can replace love labouring, not only denying someone the benefits of love labour but damaging the person through abuse and/or neglect. Equally in the secondary care relations fields, other-centred care labouring may or may not take place. Highly competitive work environments do not generate cultures of care and concern among colleagues (Ball, 2003). Neighbourhoods mired by poverty or violence are not likely to produce the kind of trust that underpins neighbourly care or so-called 'social capital' (Leonard, 2004). In the global or national sphere of social action, opportunities to express solidarity through forms of fair trade, debt cancellation or the curbing of sex trafficking are greatly undermined when governments and multi-lateral agencies conspire against them in their own interests. There is therefore nothing inevitable in the love, care and solidarity (LCS) world; the relational sphere provides contexts where they can be either fostered or destroyed, not least because economic, political and cultural injustices interpellate with affective relations and frame their character.

In characterising LCS relations, it is important to recognise that they are embedded in relations of time and space that are politically and gender constituted (Adam, 1995; McKie *et al.*, 2002). Time is not experienced simply as chronological time, it is socially defined time, known and defined by life cycle and other events (Adam, 2000). And care is a central narrative in the social definition of time especially where there are relations of dependency. Because time is a finite resource in human existence, it limits the range of care relations that any given person can engage in. Moreover, each human being is indivisible in terms of her or his person. She or he is not able to bilocate and most people have a limited capacity to complete more than one task at a time. The way care is organised therefore is deeply bound up with time and space. It is governed by rules of finiteness, and by the limitations of energy and resources.

## Mapping other-centredness

Table 2.1 identifies the features of love labour that distinguish it from both secondary and tertiary care labour. The features identified are not only those that have been observed by a wide range of scholars who have researched the care field (Bubeck, 1995; Finch and Groves, 1983; Harrington Meyer, 2000; Hochschild, 1989, 2001; Kittay, 1999; McKie *et al.*, 2002; O'Brien, 2005; Reay, 2005; Tronto, 1991; Williams, 2004), but also those that have emerged from the findings of the Care Conversations study discussed in Chapters 3–7.

What is clear from the work of care researchers is that care work generally involves not only *emotional work* and *moral commitment*, but also *mental work* (including a considerable amount of planning), *physical work* (doing practical tasks including body work such as lifting, touching and massaging) and *cognitive work* (using the skills of knowing how to care). Caring is a multifaceted set of endeavours especially when it takes love labouring forms; it not only involves all of the senses, it also engages the mind and body in a complex range of interlocking practices and thought processes. In Table 2.1, the differences between love labour, secondary care labour and solidary work are presented in summary form. The right-hand column lists a range of characteristics that are typically present in care work, though to various degrees and with qualitative differences. The remaining columns set out the typical features of good, effective care work. So they represent what the different forms of care work could typically be expected to look like when they are done successfully. In practice, each kind of work will vary significantly, and sometimes succeed despite lacking some of the features listed in the table. The next section of this chapter discusses these features in detail.

### Love labouring

Love relations refer to relations of high interdependency that arise from inherited or chosen dependencies or interdependencies and are our primary care relations. Love labouring is the work required to sustain these relations (Lynch, 1989). It is undertaken through affection, commitment, attentiveness and the material investment of time, energy and resources. It is visible in its purest form in relations of obligation that are inherited or derived from the deep dependencies that are integral to our existence as relational beings (parent-child relations being the most obvious types).

Love labour is *emotionally engaged work* that has as its principal goal the survival, development and/or well-being of the other.[17] There is an intense sense of *belongingness* and *trust* in primary care relations when they are positive, and of distrust and isolation when they are neglectful, exploitative or abusive that does not hold for other care relations. Although it has a material dimension, when the distribution of resources is involved or where practical tasks have to be undertaken, love labour is fundamentally emo-

*Table 2.1*  Mapping other-centredness: love, care and solidarity

| Features of Care Work | Forms of Care Work | | |
| --- | --- | --- | --- |
| | Love Labour | Secondary Care Labour* | Solidary Work** |
| Discovering what needs to be done (**Cognitive work**) | Getting to know someone very well and learning how to meet their deepest needs | Identifying someone's needs for care and knowing how they can be met | Learning about distant others and finding out how to support them in a solidary (as opposed to charitable) way |
| Emotional engagement (**Emotional work**) | Intense and prolonged (may be positive or negative) | Moderate and variable | Politically emotional rather than personally emotional |
| Commitment and Responsibility | Long standing and sustained | Temporary and contingent | Variable – can be long standing or temporary |
| Time frame | Prolonged | Variable | Variable |
| Moral imperative | Strong and compelling especially for women | Limited and bounded | Determined by law, culture and personal values |
| Trust | High | Moderate and variable | Variable but can be reasonably high |
| Sense of belongingness | High | Moderate and variable | Variable but can be reasonably high |
| Attentiveness including advance planning (**Mental work**) | Close attention to the person as a whole | Attention to specific, relevant factors | Attention to strategically important factors |
| Scope (range of relevant considerations) | Extensive | Bounded | May be bounded or extensive |
| Intensity | High | Low and bounded | Variable |
| Mutuality | High interdependency whether voluntary or not | More circumscribed | Not necessarily present |
| Practical tasks including **Physical work** | High | Moderate and variable | Variable but can be reasonably high |

*  Secondary care work varies considerably depending on whether it is set in the context of professional care relationships or voluntary relationships.
** Solidary work also varies in character depending of whether it is determined by state action, custom or culture and whether it is voluntary.

tionally driven work that enhances humans as emotional beings. This is not to suggest that love labour actions are entirely altruistic, as the bonds that develop in the caring dimensions of human relationships have the potential to be mutually beneficial, even if the benefits to the caregiver are sometimes disproportionately small, contingent or temporally distant. However, it is arguable that love labour is essentially other-centred in that it is directed in the first instance by the good of the other rather than the good of the self. It often has little marginal gain for the carer in either the short or longer term and may in fact involve a net loss to them financially, socially or emotionally. To recognise the potential gains from love labour for the labourer is not to deny the power differentials that can occur in such relations, and the potential costs to the caregiver, especially if the love work is undertaken in structurally exploitative care relations (Bubeck, 1995; Delphy and Leonard, 1992). To recognise the role of love labour is also not to deny the abuse and neglect that takes place when the trust that is central to love labouring relations is broken or exploited.

Love labour is generally characterised by relations of strong *mutuality*; there is a sense of mutual dependence no matter how poor the relationship may be. While one party to the relationship may undertake much more love work than the other, the structurally defined care recipient is not necessarily a silent or powerless partner, a passive receptacle for someone else's love labour. While people who are very vulnerable due to illness or infirmity may be in this position, care recipients can and do exercise power and control even in vulnerable situations. They can show appreciation for care or fail to show it; they can call on the moral imperatives to care available in the culture to enforce their care expectations and in that way can exercise care commands on carers (Bubeck, 1995). The mutuality that is at the centre of love labour relations is also a relationship of (variable) power and control exercised through the medium of care.

One of the defining features of love labour that distinguishes it from *secondary care labour* more generally is that it is not only a set of tasks, but a set of perspectives and orientations integrated with tasks. It is a feeling and a way of regarding another while relating to them. While it involves respect for the other like all forms of care, it involves more demanding forms of *attentiveness and responsiveness* than would apply to other forms of care (Engster, 2005). It denotes not just the activity of thinking about people or having them on one's mind, although this may be part of it. It also refers to the very real activities of 'looking out for', and 'looking after' the other, including the management of the tensions and conflict which are an integral part of love labour relations. For the person who has the primary responsibility for the care of vulnerable others in particular, it involves drawing up the care map for the other. It involves carrying the care map in one's mind at all times, and overseeing its implementation in terms of scope and quality throughout the care journey. In the case of children or adults with full-time dependency needs, it is quite literally a 24-hour care map (what is called a 'caringscape' by McKie *et al.* (2002)). In cases where there is a dependency relationship but more autonomy in the care recipient, it is a less detailed map and the care journey does not require the same level of checking, or rerouting where care falls down.

Love labour variously involves *physical and mental work as well as emotional work*. It involves practical physical tasks such as cooking favourite meals for a child or partner (not just feeding them so they are not hungry), listening to cares and worries as required, massaging the body, or giving financial and physical help if needed. At the mental level, it involves holding the persons and their interests in mind, keeping them 'present' in mental planning, and anticipating and prioritising their needs and interests. Emotionally, it involves listening, affirming, supporting and challenging, as well as identifying with someone and supporting her or him emotionally at times of distress. While love labour varies in level of intensity and degree of commitment depending on the care context and depending on cultural and legal norms, it does involve making some kind of *commitment* to continuity over time, although the length of that commitment can vary: the moral and legal imperative to care for dependant children is clearly much stronger than it is to care for a parent long-term; care for friends is more loosely defined in terms of the commitment expected, as indeed is the care for sisters or brothers especially in Western societies.

At times love labouring is experienced as heavy work, especially where it involves prolonged care of persons who are multiply dependent and/or with whom there neither is nor is likely to be any great reciprocity in care terms; at other times it is simple pleasure. Although women are generally more likely than men to be morally impelled to undertake love labouring work, especially where it involves taking leave from paid work, there are differences among women. Sometimes family care is organised in highly individualised agreements between family members and/or between the carer and care recipients (see Chapters 3–7 below).

While primary care relations also require secondary care labour to sustain them, they can be distinguished sociologically from secondary care relations on a number of grounds. Neither the *moral imperative* to care, nor the expectations of trust, mutuality and attentiveness that are part of love labouring relations, are present to the same degree in other care relations. There are also higher levels of *time* invested in love labouring relationships, and more of the self invested within them than applies in other care contexts. And they involve levels of commitment and responsibility that do not necessarily apply in other spheres. The care that is available to others in love labouring is personally defined and non-transferable, as it is given in the contexts of pre-established relationships with a unique history and assumed future involving continuity and attachment (Barnes, 2006: 8–9).

Distinguishing between love labour relations and secondary care labour is important for heuristic purposes although the boundaries between these forms of care labouring are often blurred. Love labouring relations can and do change to secondary care relations when friendships or intimate relationships mutate over time. Sometimes the primary love labourer becomes the care recipient such as when a parent becomes dependant due to illness or infirmity. Equally, secondary care friendships at work or elsewhere may develop into love labouring relationships. Although most people who are engaged with others in intimate primary relationships both engage in and receive the benefits of love labouring simultaneously within that relationship, others may be the love labourer in one person's life and the primary beneficiary of love labour from a different person. A prime example of this is when the love labour that partners can invest in each other is paralleled by the love labour they may individually or collectively engage in for dependent others, be these children or adults.

### Secondary care relations and general care work

Outside of primary care relations, there are *secondary care relations* that operate at one or more removes from the intimate in terms of trust and expectation. These secondary care relations are lower order interdependency relations. They operate according to second-order degrees of other-centredness. While they involve care responsibilities and attachments, they do not carry the same depth of feeling or moral obligation in terms of meeting dependency needs, especially long-term dependency needs, although depending on the context, they can change to primary relationships over time. There is a degree of choice and contingency about secondary care relations that does not apply to primary relations.

Neighbourly friendships or work friendships are likely to belong to this category of care relation as they are context specific and can and do end when the context changes. (One is not expected to continue to live by and befriend neighbours no matter how close one is to them, if work or immediate family obligations require moving house). Relations with relatives outside of the immediate family are also generally of a secondary rather than primary character as they do not carry the same dependency demands in Western cultures.

While it is analytically helpful to distinguish between the nature of the care work done in intimate, primary relations from the care work undertaken in secondary relations, there are borderline cases. For example, what someone does for colleagues at work or for neighbours or close associates, though it may be limited in terms of time, scope and responsibility, may have the emotional intensity and attentiveness characteristic of love labour. The primary/secondary distinction is in reality a continuum rather than a sharp division.

Neither are secondary care relations confined to the familial and the personal. Secondary care work cements relations of solidarity in community, associational and work relations as well as in intimate relations (Glenn, 2000; Kittay, 1999; Tronto, 1991). Within employment contexts, where there is a lack of a care ethic for workers, where people have no time to listen to one another, to take account of personal needs and to modify work practices so that they are supportive of caring, there is an inevitable deterioration in the quality of work relations; the contrary is also the case. Lack of time to engage in voluntary and community associations also impoverishes the quality of life in neighbourhoods, in voluntary organisations, in community bodies from sports clubs to tenants' and residents' associations. The emotional work involved in maintaining bonds of solidarity and care is fundamental to the fabric of social and political life.

An obvious question that arises in relation to care is the status of paid care relations. Paid care work is definitively emotional work, although it can be undertaken with varying degrees of emotional engagement. What distinguishes such professionally-defined care relations from love labouring in particular is their contingent quality; they cease with the contract of employment. There is no contractual or clear moral obligation to care when the contract ceases. This is not to deny that those who undertake paid care work often do establish deep emotional relations, for which they are not paid (Meagher, 2002). People who work as paid carers do not necessarily leave their moral sense about caring and their emotions outside the professional door (Nelson and England, 2002). It is not appropriate to suggest therefore that good emotional work or good care is done in families and poor emotional work in paid care. Families can be and are exploitative at times in the way they care, while paid care relations can be supportive and involve commitment.

## Tertiary care relations and solidary work

There is also a tertiary care sphere that is more collective in form and context, and operates outside of face-to-face relationships. *Tertiary care relations* are essentially relations of solidarity that can be enacted without intimacy or personal engagement with the other. They are public care relations involving solidary work that sustains people as public persons. Care as solidarity manifests itself in two primary forms, either as statutory obligation or as voluntary or community work in civil society. Solidarity is expressed in statutory regulations in states that require members of society to fund public goods and services through taxation and other policy provisions, even though they may be only a minor beneficiary of same. It is also evident in the voluntary and community work that is undertaken without payment, particularly in civil society organisations.

Solidary work refers to a wide range of other-centred public care work and can be both national and international in its scope: it includes work involved in sustaining public goods and services that may be of little or no immediate value to oneself, campaigning for homeless people, prisoners' rights or better welfare services, or working on global solidary campaigns. It can also involve simply providing financial support for campaigns and activities that express solidarity with others, or working politically and/or organisationally within one's own society to create solidarity. Sometimes solidary relations are chosen, such as when individuals or groups work collectively for the well-being of others, but they can also be obligatory when they are constituted legally by the state or local authority of which one is a member. Non-statutory solidary work is typically governed by social norms.[18] These can be strong moral imperatives in some cultural contexts.

Solidarity as represented by us here is about an ideal, a moral principle in its own right. 'By... putting oneself in the place of concerned others, it is possible in principle to respond adequately to the interests of all members of the communication community' (Cook, 2001: 96). However, this idealised view of solidarity is not socially inevitable; it has to be constructed. Bonds of social cohesion can also be inward looking, self-centred rather than other-centred. Strong internal bonds can operate as a force for exclusion rather than inclusion (*ibid*.). This happens frequently when states enact laws and policies that grant rights and privileges only to selectively defined communities (normally their own citizens) regardless of the social need of the excluded (Seglow, 2005; Shachar, 2003). What happens in these cases is better described as social closure than as solidarity; groups aggregate rights and privileges to themselves consolidating internal cohesion at the expense of, and often against, others (Parkin, 1971).

## Implications

### Neoliberalism and care

In the neoliberal political framework, there is a core assumption that all services are best provided via the market (Harvey, 2005). In line with this thinking, both day care and state child care are increasingly being privatised in many countries. Care for older people is also moving steadily towards the market, and is frequently advertised as a commercial opportunity for investors, giving good financial returns. Given the endemic income and wealth inequalities in capitalist societies, what is conveniently ignored in the neoliberal framework is that unequal economic resources will inevitably lead to unequal access to care services. This point is already well-established in the fields of both health (Wilkinson, 2005) and education (Gamoran, 2001; Lynch, 2006).

In any case, the failure to understand the nature of care and to make the analytical distinction between forms of care makes it easy for neoliberals to argue for providing care on the market. Care can be easily represented as a generic and undifferentiated set of practices which is no different substantively from heating, transport or other services. (There are of course a host of reasons why essential services such as transport, health, education, etc.

should not be provided by profit-driven interests, but it is not possible to deal with these here.)

Yet, the sets of social relations within which care work is embedded frame the nature of caring. As discussed below, there are severe problems with the very idea of commodifying primary care, not just because it is impossible to pay someone else to maintain *your own* relationship with someone you care for, but also because the trust, continuity and attachment characteristic of love labour cannot be secured by contract in contemporary labour markets. While paid care is necessary as a support for primary care, it cannot substitute for it. When even a secondary care relationship is set within a system of social relations focused on profit or gain in particular, it is self-evident that the nurturing characteristics of this relationship (such as careful attention to needs, emotional engagement, trust and attentiveness), are likely to be either precluded, subordinated or made highly contingent on the profit-margins expected. This is very evident in human service relationships such as nursing where the move to provide health care on a for-profit basis had tended to undermine the time available for care and personal attention (Toynbee, 2007).

What care, love and solidary relations have in common is that they all involve relations of dependence and interdependence, relations of giving and receiving; they are other-centred to a greater or lesser degree. Because they have an other-centred character, they cannot be entirely marketised without undermining the care or solidarity they embody. One of the distinguishing features of love labour relations in particular (but also of the other-centred dimensions of care and solidary relations) is, therefore, that they are not commodifiable. We pursue this point in detail below.

## Care commanders: gender, class, ethnicity and migration

Caring does not take place in a vacuum; it takes place in a globally nested set of class, gender and racialised relations. The moral imperative to undertake care work in all forms is much stronger for women than for men (Bubeck, 1995; O'Brien, 2005). The division of care labour is gendered, classed and raced locally and globally (Tronto, 2002). Women bear disproportionate responsibility for care work, be it in the informal world of work in the family or in the formal world of the care economy (Daly, 2001; Folbre, 1994; Reay, 2005). As most care labour is unpaid, especially love labouring given its intimate and inalienable quality, those who perform it incur a material net burden due to forgone earnings. Simultaneously they enable others (mostly men) to pursue more materially beneficial activities, notably paid work and leisure. There is a very real case for claiming that women's exploitation as carers is the main form of exploitation that applies specifically to women (Bubeck, 1995: 182–183).

While women undertake more care work than men in all classes, poorer, working class, ethnic minority and migrant women undertake disproportionately high levels of caring (Ehrenreich and Hochschild, 2003). The wealthy and the powerful can generally claim immunity from care responsibilities, especially the more burdensome forms of care. They tend to be care commanders. Care commanders have immunity from all but the more formal caring-for and tending-to responsibilities. While they are expected to be present at significant life transition events – birth celebrations, weddings and funerals – they have no obligations to do everyday care, be it visiting, tending, lifting, feeding, collecting or delivering, especially if there is an eligible woman there to do it. Their status, power and/or wealth enable them to be 'free riders' on somebody's (mostly women's) care work (Fineman, 2004). They are granted immunity from caring by interfacing class, race and gender norms. What is notable about globalised codes of glamourised, high status masculinity is that they are definitely not other-centred (Connell, 2002). Hegemonic masculinity is aggressive, unattached and available to out-compete others (other men in particular) (Connell, 1995). High status for both men and women is inversely related to the doing of love, care and solidary work as the idealised workers are 'zero-load' workers: these are without care, detached from care relations by ignoring them, by paying others to do care work for them, or by commanding others to do it without pay.

## Nurturing capitals and resources for care

Although the focus of this chapter is on the differences between forms of care, it is important to note the interface between the affective domains of life and other social and economic relations. The quality of love, care or solidarity a person can give is influenced by financial resources; not least because of the scope money offers to pay other people to perform the more burdensome parts of care, leaving more time for the more pleasurable and mutually sustaining parts. The quality of the love or care also varies with the wealth of emotional resources available to sustain it. Those who have received much care in life, be it at the personal, community or state level, are 'care-rich'. They have had the time and resources of others invested in them. This may be it in the form of intimate love labour devoted to them in the form of emotional support, listening, attending and/or presence in the mindful care of another; or as beneficiaries of the voluntary and community efforts of others to secure services such as public parks, sports activities etc., for them locally; or by the political efforts of others working in solidarity to protect their rights as workers, older people, children etc. The care invested in them provides them, other things equal, with an increased capacity to care for others. In a sociological sense they can be said to have considerable *nurturing capital* although there is no language in society to name this and to indicate those with considerable care capacities. Those who are care-rich may not just owe a dependency debt, as Fineman (2004) suggests, but may also have a wealth of nurturing capital that they can work to 'redistribute' (Gheaus, forthcoming).

## The non-commodifiable nature of love labour

While certain care tasks are commodifiable, and there is a case for substantially improving the conditions of its commodification to preclude exploitation (Meagher, 2002), love labour cannot be commodified in the same way. The emotional work involved in loving another person is not readily transferred to a paid other by arrangement; neither can it be exchanged. To attempt to pay someone to do a love labour task (having a meal with a partner, visiting a friend in hospital, reading a story to a child or making an ageing parent's favourite meal) is to undermine the premise of care and mutuality that is at the heart of intimacy and friendship (Strazdins and Broom, 2004).

This is not to suggest that paid care is neither desirable nor necessary. Public care often supplements informal care rather than substitutes for it (Waerness, 1990: 122–123). Where intimate care is poor or even abusive, paid care is necessary and often preferable at the very least to supplement weak forms of care; however, it is fundamentally different. The existence of commodified care systems, either in the form of public care institutions or private therapy for those who can pay for it, does not mean the end of intimacy or solidary relationships. It may indeed signify the very opposite, a demand for greater satisfaction in personal lives by having certain basic caring needs provided for on a paid basis (so one has time for the more pleasurable forms of love labouring) or by developing one's emotional life via therapy to enable one to have more fulfilling personal relations.

What makes commodification of care work problematic is the attempt to commodify its non-commodifiable dimensions. Mutuality, commitment and strong feelings for others (and the human effort that goes with expressing these) cannot be provided for hire as they can only be produced over time in relations of intimacy and engagement. The nurturing work that produces a sense of support, solidarity and well-being is generally based on intentions and feelings for others that cannot be commodified as it is not possible to secure the quality of a relationship on a paid basis. Furthermore, one cannot provide love labour on the same rational basis that one can provide other personal services because of its nature, it is not bounded; it cannot be packaged. The rationality of caring is different from, and to some degree contradicts, scientific and bureaucratic rationality (Waerness, 1984). There is no hierarchy or career structure to relations of love labouring; they cannot be supplied to order. There is no clear identifiable project with boundaries illuminating the path to the realisation of the goal. Indeed, as the goal is the relationship itself, there is no identifiable beginning, middle and end. The goal or objective is often diffuse and indefinable. As Chapters 3–7 will illustrate, the differences between the rationalities underpinning love labouring and those governing paid employment was a continuous theme in our Care Conversations. The reality of social life is that one cannot pay someone to love someone else; one cannot pay someone to make love to one's partner and claim that this is a substitute for oneself; one cannot pay someone to visit or talk to a friend in hospital and claim that the visit is from oneself.

Love labour time is not infinitely condensable; you cannot do it in less and less time (Folbre and Bittman, 2004). The illusion of 'quality time' is that one can have it in condensed or reduced time, ignoring the fact that it is the preliminary time in the (positive) presence of the other that allows for the trust and understanding to develop that enables quality time to exist (Tronto, 2003: 123). It is not possible to produce 'fast care' like fast food in standardised packages. If we go the McWorld route in caring what we will get is not care but 'pre-packaged units of supervision', attending without intimacy or personal interest in the welfare of others (Badgett and Folbre, 1999: 318).

Those aspects of relationships that boost confidence, inspire strength and encouragement, give people a sense of belonging, and a sense of being wanted and needed and of being free, cannot be commodified as they can only exist in a context where there is some choice or decision to care and commit oneself for the sake of the relationship and not for payment. This is not to deny the reality of the 'compulsory altruism' which has been a feature of so many women's lives, nor is it to suggest that those who care should not get paid for certain types of caring work. Quite the contrary, payment for certain aspects of caring often has a positive rather than a negative effect on care relationships, as it makes the relationship between the carer and the person being cared for more reciprocal and more equal (Qureshi, 1990); it also creates time for the pleasurable aspects of love labouring. What is being suggested therefore is that the labour involved in love, care and solidarity should be materially supported, as it is a public good, not that it should be bought and sold on the market. The attempt to turn love and care into a commodity can only result in the destruction of love and care itself.

## Conclusion

The aim of this chapter has been to provide a general taxonomy of love, care and solidarity and to draw out its implications. We have argued that care is a crucial kind of work, although it is accorded low social status and material rewards, and we have set out the case for why love, care and solidarity matter: because of their importance to human survival and well-being, because of the work they require, and because of their socially important outcomes. Care is intrinsically relational, but the relations involved can be usefully analysed into three categories, that we have called primary, secondary and tertiary care (Figure 2.1). Using these categories, we went on to suggest that the different forms of care differ significantly in their typical features (Table 2.1). In particular, we argued that primary care or love labour is typically much more intimate, prolonged, intense and demanding than secondary and tertiary care work. The distinctiveness of love labour has important social and political implications. The neoliberal project of allocating all care to the market neglects the tensions between the emotional engagement of care and the logic of profitability. The low status and high demands of care generate a social distinction between care commanders and care providers that is deeply implicated in the oppression of women and also in relations of class, ethnicity and international migration. Good care requires adequate resources of several kinds; we commented on how this connects inequality in the affective realm with inequality in other social systems. The chapter ended with a discussion of the non-commodifiable nature of love labour.

The arguments in this chapter have been based on a wide literature. Although they have inevitably been informed by the research set out in the rest of this book, the aim has been to provide a general orientation rather than detailed research findings. Chapters 3–10 explore issues of care work, and particularly primary care, in much greater depth. In Chapter 11 we return to the broader picture and discuss the wider implications of those studies.

# 3
# Love Labouring: Nurturing Rationalities and Relational Identities

*Kathleen Lynch and Maureen Lyons*

This chapter opens with a brief review of traditional scholarly interpretations of work and the reasons for the marginalisation of care work. It then outlines the reasons why care is a form of work. Drawing on a set of 30 in-depth Care Conversations with carers and care recipients (see Introduction and Appendix), it goes on to map carers' understandings of their primary care relations in terms of the love labouring they do to maintain and develop these. The latter part of the chapter focuses on the issue of commodification, outlining how and why primary carers rejected paid-care alternatives to their own caring. It outlines the ways in which nurturing rationalities override economic rationalities, and how people's relational identities as carers play a central role in determining their life priorities.

## What is work?

What is defined as work in scholarly terms varies across philosophical and sociological traditions (Pettinger *et al.*, 2005). Work is equated with economically productive work in the materialist tradition; it is defined as that which contributes to human-historical 'progress' (as exemplified in the work of Marx). Within the phenomenological tradition, work is equated with individual cultivation and self-perfection, it is less about being economically productive than about being individually productive (exemplified in the thinking of Marcuse and Kirkegaard) (Gürtler, 2005). In neither of these traditions is the work of care, or the reproduction of the human species through care, defined as socially valuable work.

Mainstream sociological and economic analysis is less concerned with the purpose of the work (whether it be for economic return or self-realisation) than with its status in terms of pay. In industrial sociology and in classical economics, work was traditionally conceptualised in terms of whether it was paid or unpaid, which was taken as equivalent to whether it was in the public or the private sphere (Pahl, 1988). This perspective has resulted in work being dichotomised as either 'real' work for paid employment or unpaid domestic labour. This dichotomous view of work not only ignores care work, but also voluntary, community and activist work (Glucksmann, 1995; Taylor, 2004).

Scholarly recognition of care as a form of work grew throughout the 1980s and 1990s as feminist scholars challenged classical views of work across disciplines (Folbre, 1995; Glucksmann, 1995). Feminists not only highlighted the role of emotional work within mainstream employment, thereby bringing the 'private' world of emotions into the public sphere (Hochschild, 1983), but also demonstrated why domestic work and care work are real forms of work, albeit work that is often unpaid (Beechey, 1987; Feldberg *et al.*, 1979; Finch and Groves, 1983; Delphy and Leonard, 1992). They showed that care was like other forms of work in that it serves human needs, has observable, intended outcomes, uses complex skills, requires time and effort and often involves challenges and some stress.

Despite these achievements there is still a historical residue of denial, both in popular discourse ('does your wife work?') and in policy discussions of the conflict between paid work and care work, the unequal gendered division of care labour, and the role of the state in supporting care work (Gürtler, 2005; Harrington Meyer, 2000; Kittay, 1999; Pillinger, 2000; Williams, 2001). There is also little understanding of which aspects of caring can be provided on contract and which cannot (Lewis and Giullari, 2005); the differences between secondary care labouring, which can be commodifed, and love labouring which cannot are only minimally understood. Likewise, the differences between the nurturing rationalities that govern caring and the economic rationalities that are employed in other spheres of life have received little empirical attention. The object of this chapter and those following is to address these deficits.

## Why care work is marginalised

The marginalisation of care work arises in part from the general ambivalence about caring and loving that exists in society. Love has been sentimentalised, sexualised and commercialised to a degree that the word is a synonym for the trivial and the trite in terms of human relations (hooks, 2000). The sexualisation of love in particular has led to the term being associated with pleasure and desire, something fleeting, contingent and ephemeral. While caring is not trivialised the way love is, it is definitively a low status and highly feminised activity which is viewed as a private and personal concern (see Chapter 2).

The reluctance to name care as work arises also from the public allegiance to the traditional feminine (as opposed to feminist) ethic of care which defines care as a moral obligation (for women in particular) governed by rules of selflessness and self-sacrifice (Gilligan, 1995). It is defined in this deeply patriarchal code as a 'duty' not a job (an example of this is the Irish Constitution, Article 41, 2.1, 2.2 which defines women's role in the home as 'duties'). Given the influence of traditional gender understandings in framing our desires (Butler, 1993, 1999), it is not surprising that they also frame public understandings of what is defined as socially useful work.

The assumption that care is a private matter, a personal affair and not a form of work is also related to dominant conceptions of citizenship. The idealised citizen in Western democracies is not a caring one; the public citizen is assumed to be primarily a rational economic actor (REA) who consumes and makes choices in a market-led economy (Duncan and Edwards, 1997; Lewis, 2003; Lister, 2001; Sevenhuijsen, 2000; Tronto, 2001). The allegiance to the REA model of the citizen is not entirely new; it is deeply rooted in Western political thought (Fraser, 1997; Held, 1999; Lynch *et al.*, 2007).

While the contemporary neglect of care as a form of work is explicable in light of the valorisation of economic productivity as a measure of human standing, it also arises from the glorification of never-ending consumption as the primary purpose of leisure in the neoliberal age (Harvey, 2005). Living in a world that is advertised constantly as boundless in terms of consumption possibilities means that there is little social sense of 'having enough' in the collective psyche. There is always more to be had, more products to be bought, more holidays to go on, and a bigger car or house to own. The 'other-centredness' that is endemic to love, care and solidarity work is deeply suppressed in cultural contexts where personal acquisition, power and status are prioritised.

There is no doubt that another, related reason that caring is not recognised as work is because women do most of the unpaid (and paid) care work. This holds across several cultural and political contexts, and over extended periods of history (Bettio and Platenga, 2004; Daly, 2001; Ehrenreich and Hochschild, 2003; Finch and Groves, 1983; Folbre, 1994; Hochschild, 1989, 1997; McKie *et al.*, 2002; Strazdins and Broom, 2004). As the feminine is an inferior category to the masculine, that which is associated with the feminine (care work in this case) is also defined as inferior (Millett, 1969).

Even when it is provided on contract, care work is lowly paid, unregulated, insecure and exploitative (Ehrenreich and Hochschild, 2003; Standing, 2001; Tronto, 2002). Much of care work is also dirty work involving the management of human waste and this further contributes to its lowly standing (Hughes *et al.*, 2005).

The lowly status of care work creates a vicious circle of exploitation as domestic care workers are drawn increasingly from the ranks of poor, migrant women (Bettio *et al.*, 2006; Daly, 2001; Harrington Meyer, 2000). When care work is undertaken by family members for those with long-term high dependency needs, it is often done at high personal cost without adequate support or respite services, something that further reinforces its marginal and invisible status (Brody and Saperstein, 2004; MacDonald *et al.*, 2005).

## Care as work

Caring can be broadly defined as work that involves looking after the physical, social, psychological, emotional and developmental needs of one or more people.[19] Like other work, caring involves language and thought, but unlike many other forms of work, it also involves empathetic understanding of the other to meet their individual needs (Bubeck, 1995: 29).

Care is work without which humanity as a species could not survive. In early infancy, humans experience a prolonged period of dependency; as life expectancy increases, old age also bring degrees of dependency, and for some this involves high levels of dependency on the care of others. People with significant intellectual disabilities are also likely to be highly dependent on the care of others for much of their lives (and often require carers to have care plans in place – including substantial economic provision – if it is likely that they will die before dependants). Moreover, at times of sickness or ill health, all human beings are dependent. Human well-being is not only reliant on care in times of high dependency, it is also reliant on the interdependent forms of care that benefit people mutually in friendships, intimate relations, neighbourly activities, collegial work relations, and working for solidarity with human kind locally and globally.

Care is also work in the sense that it produces a definite, intended output: love and care contribute greatly to general health and well-being; they give a sense of belonging, of being wanted and appreciated; a sense of being needed and desired (see Cohen, 2006 for a review of research on the impact of care in education). Those who are denied the benefits of love, care and solidarity are visibly deprived in their emotional and mental health (see Chapter 10).

Care is work because it requires competence, skill and learning to do it well. It also takes time and effort and levels of attentiveness and responsiveness at the emotional level that are not required in much non-care work. And care also involves stress due to the fear of failing the care recipient (Standing, 2001: 18; Tronto, 1993: 127–134).

What is most invisible about care relations is what is most universal about them, namely that virtually all of humanity are engaged in some form or other of caring for most of their lives. While care work involving high dependency is visible both in its demands and outcomes (with young children or with people who are ill), other forms of care work are less so, but are nonetheless real in their effects. The mutual care given by friends or partners to one another frequently gives meaning and purpose to life (O'Connor, 1998; Roseneil, 2004). Care of colleagues at work, care of neighbours, acts of solidarity with persons unknown to us personally but to whom we wilfully make financial or material commitments through taxation, donations, or voluntary labour, create the wider circles of solidarity (or lack of solidarity) in the national and global order. It is possible, therefore, to locate people structurally in terms of what circles of care they are engaged in, how many circles if any they are engaged in, and how they themselves are part of other peoples' circles of care (see Chapter 2).

Caring can be distinguished from other forms of human service work, such as teaching and nursing, that have a strong care dimension, but caring is not their sole purpose. Care is central to education but primarily as a process that enables learning; likewise in nursing, care is generally a means to restoring health (although palliative care work is an exception as it is more purely a care task). Care work can also be distinguished from human service work that is purely commercial in character, such as flight attending and serving in shops or restaurants. In these cases there is a level of personal attentiveness required but the primary goal is not to care but to sell the product or to provide a service for commercial return (Hochschild, 1983).

It is also possible to map our care relations to the animal, bird and environmental world in terms of levels of care. We have close relations with some animals, notably our personal pets or companion animals, and a type of secondary relationship with others, namely animals we like and care for while they are alive because they are of use to us (domestic animals such as cows, pigs and sheep). Other animals we care for but do not relate to (certain endangered species) while others are not within our care trajectory as they are seen as a threat or as pests (wild rodents, or foxes in sheep farming areas).

## Conversations on care and love as work

The Care Conversations held with a wide variety of carers (see Appendix for details) produced narratives about primary care relationships that were interwoven with different messages about care. Caring was seen as pleasure, fun and joy at times, but also as relentless, hard and sometimes overwhelming work on other occasions. Those who denied that care was work at one moment would say it was work within the same part of the conversation; those who said it was work often said that it was also pleasurable. While some people were fluent in talking about their care worlds, mostly women including two lesbian couples who had made very conscious decisions to be mothers, others had difficulty in finding words to express their feelings. Some men (particularly Séan, a father of three young children, Tony who was caring for his mother and uncle, and Alex a father of two young children) said they had never thought about such issues. They just did things that needed to be done without reflection or analysis.

Our conversations with carers were principally focused on their primary care relations, although we did also ask about their own secondary care responsibilities, and we also interviewed adults who were not always carers. For those who were primary carers for dependant adults or children, it was clear that they regarded their primary caring responsibilities as a central task in their lives. Their care identities defined who they were and involved a variety of different forms of other-centred work. Their narratives were also characterised by a discourse of nurturing: in the case of children it was focused on their happiness in the present and their security in the future; with adults and older people, the focus was on respecting their wishes and desires for comfort or for presence. The work involved not only *emotional work* (listening and engaging) and *moral commitment* (being trustworthy and reliable), but also *mental work* (including a considerable amount of planning), *physical work* (doing practical tasks including body work such as lifting, touching and massaging and other work like cooking and doing laundry) and *cognitive work* (using the skills of knowing how to care) (see Table 2.1, Chapter 2). Primary caring as love labouring was a multifaceted set of endeavours; it not only involved all of the senses, it also engaged the mind and body in a complex range of interlocking practices and thought processes that were morally bounded.

## Love labouring for adults

### Guilt and the moral imperative to care

Those who were caring long-term for older relatives or adult children who had special care needs were most likely to see care as work. However, care work for intimate others was unlike other forms of work in some striking ways. It was deeply emotionally laden work that was bounded by moral imperatives about what was appropriate and good care. There were no certainties and people's own sense of being a moral person was tied up with their identity as carers.

Valerie was a woman who had given up a career with considerable prospects to take care of both her parents who were incapacitated through illness. Although she was devoted to her parents and was caring for them for seven years at the time of interview, she was adamant that caring was hard work and that it involved a lot of planning, expertise and physical work:

> *Oh definitely it is work, and sometimes it is very arduous! I mean to keep two sick people organised is like a military operation, you're talking oxygen, you're talking nappies, you're talking clean underwear, their juice or a drink, their medication, I mean, the plan has to be there, because without one of those things in that plan the whole system will just fall, you know?* (Valerie, single, caring full-time for both parents)

Care work was also relentless when people were unable to tend to their own basic needs:

> *Well it's basically 24 hours a day, seven days a week. I mean you are on call all the time, … you cannot leave them, it's a case of you have to be here,*

*which is very trying so I do look forward to that respite week, and I try to put as much into that week as possible, you know, to get out and about.* (Valerie, single, caring full-time for both parents)

Valerie felt that care for older people like her parents presented a huge moral dilemma for which there was no answer. Although she was overwhelmed by the way her life had been taken over by the care of her parents, and even though her brother and sister (neither of whom lived in Ireland) suggested that she should place her parents in residential care she could not do this (although her family could afford it) as she felt that her parents would be very upset and would suffer. The labouring she did for her parents could be done by others in a technical sense but not in a relational sense as they now had become used to her caring:

*I think just everybody's life should be important to them. I really feel that nobody should have to suffer. There is no solution.... I feel that if they had gone into residential [care] in the initial stages, it would have been somewhat easier, but to do it now! [implies by gestures that it is not an option]* (Valerie, single, caring full-time for both parents)

Although she knew that she would be unable to keep caring for her parents indefinitely due to the physical demands of the work:

*As time goes on ... there will come a time when I can't do it and I would have to accept that.* (Valerie, single, caring full-time for both parents)

Caring was not only physically demanding, it also engaged people emotionally in a way that was morally compelling. Valerie was torn by guilt and anxiety about leaving her parents and returning to her job:

*You know that the onus is on you, if you go away and they possibly go into care, one of them dies, that's on your conscience then, you think if I hadn't left them that wouldn't have happened, so it's like a catch 22 situation ... I would feel that, I think you're damned if you stay, and I think you're damned if you go, so I feel like, or maybe I've just got rose-tinted glasses on that I can't, you know, see the trees from the forest, I just don't know!* (Valerie, single, caring full-time for both parents)

Nora was a separated woman, caring for an adult son with a physical impairment, who also saw care as work:

*Well caring to me, caring is a full-time job. It is actually fuller than a full-time job, than if you were in a job and you were going out at nine in the morning and working until six in the evening. You could come home and that is your day over. When you are a carer, your day is not over at six [o'clock]. You could be going until twelve if things weren't right.* (Nora, separated, caring full-time for adult son)

Tony was caring for his mother who lived with him and an uncle who was unwell who lived nearby. A man of few words, Tony felt that care was work, and like Valerie he regarded it as work about which you had no choice:

*It is work, and if you have to do it, you have to do it.* (Tony, single, caring full-time for his mother and uncle)

Tom, who was caring for his father who was unable to walk, also saw care as work, albeit a form of work that was without boundaries. Because it was boundless, he did not think anyone else would do it:

*How could you put a value on it? You couldn't put a value on it, you couldn't quantify it. And if I were to get somebody in and they were working an eight hour shift you would need three people, they would work eight hour shifts and then they are gone home. They would have to be paid. What carers are only working eight hour shifts a day? There is no break.* (Tom, single, caring full-time for his father)

While Tom and Tony did not have sufficient income to pay someone to care for their respective parents full-time, each of them knew that they had options in relation to placing their relatives in state-aided care. As will be discussed below, they did not consider this an option that their respective parents would like and so it was not considered. Tom, in particular, did not believe that his father could get the quality of care he gave him anywhere else. Like Valerie he experienced a lot of guilt about care:

*With care you are probably aware there is a lot of guilt; guilt goes with it. 'I could do more' or 'I can't go away' or 'if I go away who will look after them?' It is like having a baby in the house, you wouldn't entrust a baby to someone else and if you did you would feel guilty. It is the same with a carer.* (Tom, single, caring full-time for his father)

### Care as pleasure

Not all of those who were caring for adults saw care as work, and those who saw it as work at times also recognised that care had pleasurable moments. Two mothers who were caring for their adult children with intellectual impairments disagreed that care was work. Sara was married and was caring for her adult daughter at the weekends. Sara's husband was no longer employed after suffering a stroke. Consequently he was no longer able to help Sara with the care of their daughter and in fact required a certain amount of care by Sara. Her daughter was in residential care from Monday to Friday:

> ... *it is not a chore for me to look after my daughter. If I was looking after the woman down the road it is a different thing but looking after my daughter is a privilege.* (Sara, married to John, caring part-time for daughter and husband)

Mary was a widow and the full-time carer for her adult son who had both physical and intellectual impairments. She saw caring as demanding but it was not like paid work:

> *That [caring] is not work to be honest with you, that is not a 'caring role' as such, that is a more enjoyable thing... Yes and it is lovely to have him and I wouldn't see that as a chore at all.* (Mary, widow, caring full-time for adult son)

Tom articulated the contradictory emotions that primary caring involves and the sense of mutual love it entails:

> *Sometimes I tear my hair out but then he will come up with a gem or I might be at the end of my tether after a very hard day with him. 'Tom,' 'What dad?' 'I love you.' That defuses the whole thing then. As he says himself those are the three loveliest words in the English language. 'I love you' and he does.* (Tom, single, caring full-time for father)

Our conversations with Tom also show how his whole identity was bound up with being a good carer:

> *'Am I living?' and the answer I made was 'I am living looking after him; that is my aim in life to look after dad.' It is a cliché but it is a privilege and a pleasure to look after him.* (Tom, single, caring full-time for father)

### Love labouring for young children

Those who had care responsibilities for young children were less inclined to see care as work as they noted the many pleasurable moments in caring. However, the conversations were interspersed with almost contradictory statements about caring. Care was not seen as work when it was spontaneous but when people were sick or tired it was more difficult:

> ... *it is work, definitely it is work. It is actually I would say very hard work at times, sometimes it is a pleasure but sometimes it is pressurised and it is work ... Let's say like last year at one stage they [her two children] were both sick at the same time for the same week, now that was work. I felt at the end that*

*that was exhausting because we were on full time demanding care for the week so then it is work, but that is occasional. It is mutual anyway, it is a shared thing, I don't think it is work actually.* (Jane, partner of Jill, primary carer of two young children)

Elizabeth was also parenting two young children; she also felt that care was work at times but not all the time:

*I suppose it can be work. If you had to bring them to school and get them dressed, like there is a lot involved in caring, there is work, yes ... I feel that there are times that it has to be work and sometimes you come home or at the weekends and you just want to watch TV, you really just don't want to ... yes sometimes it is work and you just have to make a decision that they need certain things and you just have to do it. Most times it's not, most times you're delighted to be with them and that whole involvement is wonderful but then sometimes you are sick, you're fed up but you have to do it because they are your babies.* (Elizabeth, partner of Nuala, secondary carer of two primary school children)

Donal, who was co-parenting one pre-school child with his partner Geraldine was also ambivalent about whether care was work or not:

*Em, it is and it isn't, it's work at half six in the morning (laugh), but at six in the evening it is not work, you know, so, it's a big of both really! ... Yes when you are happy to take care of your daughter, but sometimes you'd be happier just to sleep (laugh)!* (Donal, married to Geraldine, co-carer of one pre-school child)

Parents of children with special learning needs and supports were able to compare the work involved in parenting a child who did not have such needs with a child who did, and they saw the latter as demanding in terms of the time and attention it required. As Alex, father of two children, one of whom has an intellectual impairment, explains:

*I think it is work all right. It's hard work, certainly in Noel's case given the type of care that is required over and above say what Cathy would have taken. There are a lot more conscious decisions and concentration needed when you are working with Noel, well not working, but even playing with him and talking to him, bringing him anywhere. Conscious of what he needs, to get the message across to him rather than just have to say it to Cathy, ... It's almost like ... having a child with an intellectual disability ... it's like having your first child again. You know nothing and you are on a continual learning path, ... and if your second child is the same as your first then you just go through the same things, at least, you know. Whereas our second one was not, Noel had different needs and we are continuously learning. That is work, it's hard work.* (Alex, married to Debra, secondary carer of one primary and one pre-school child)

Alex felt however that it was not right for him to call it work:

*Yeah, well hard work is probably the wrong thing to say because it's certainly satisfying [caring for Noel] but it is different to the work we had to put into Cathy when she was four years of age.* (Alex, married to Debra, secondary carer of one primary and one pre-school child)

Paula, lone mother of four children, saw care as work when it demanded more effort and energy than you felt you could give:

*It is work I suppose when it doesn't come naturally.* (Paula, divorced, primary carer of one second-level child and three adult children)

More generally, Paula believed that child care outside of the family environment was hard work. She spoke of the difficulties she had in recruiting people to work in the crèche at her workplace:

*… but people don't want to be working in child care anymore. Because they see it as hard work. The girls would rather have a cleaning job than going in and working in a crèche, that's to be quite honest with you. I wouldn't work in child care myself even though a lot of my work is around children in terms of family support and stuff like that. But it is hard work and it is not recognised as hard work by the powers that are there because it's just taken for granted that it gets done.* (Paula, divorced, primary carer of one second-level child and three adult children)

Overall, the conversations with parents of young children displayed a sense of hope and enthusiasm that was less frequently articulated by carers of adults. Because children were growing and developing, care work was seen a creating something positive for the future. Parents enjoyed seeing children develop:

*Just being able to see her development on a daily basis, there's something new every single day, even, I mean it might be something very simple, and, for example, she might, one day she might do something where she couldn't do that the other day, just little things like that that you really appreciate and savour!* (Donal, married to Geraldine, co-carer of one pre-school child)

Watching their achievements:

*It is more of an achievement having kids and rearing them and seeing all the various stages they go through. Getting them over challenges and little milestones and all the things that you know, like starting school and walking and talking, all that sort of stuff. There are lot of challenges you can't get anywhere else, certainly not in a job. I don't know, certainly not in any job I have ever had, not in my background, it is very difficult to get that sort of challenge anywhere else.* (Alex, married to Debra, secondary carer of one pre-school and one primary school child)

And being with them:

*I suppose you don't look on yourself as being a carer as such ... you love them and it is great to have that feeling of so much love and enjoyment in your children.* (Clodagh, married to Séan, co-carer of three primary school children)

### Love labouring as commitment

Séan was a married father from the West of Ireland who was very engaged in the care of his children and both he and his wife saw him as an equal partner in care. He was a person who insisted that he never thought about looking after the children as work:

*Séan: Minding the kids – work? No, no – that's just a straight 'No'.*
ML: So how would you describe it?
*Séan: Minding the kids, is it? Well, I don't think much about it. You do it – I wouldn't describe it! I have no problem at all with it. You do what you have to do like. I don't even think about it to be quite honest with you.* (Séan, married to Clodagh, co-carer of three primary school children)

Yet he admitted that caring for his three young children did involve a lot of tasks:

*Like by the time you get home in the evening and cook the dinner, there isn't a whole lot of time for much else. When homework is done and you get them ready to go down to bed it is 9 or 10 o'clock. You are not far off going to bed yourself at that stage. You would be away early in the morning and you would be very tired – so you would just do the things you have to, to keep going.* (Séan, married to Clodagh, co-carer of three primary school children)

His wife Clodagh did not see care as work in the sense that it was like work that you got paid for, she saw it in a more complicated sense as commitment and work you do out of love, which could not be equated with work you did for pay:

*It's hard, but it's not work. It's not work like the work that you have to go into every day, it is something that if you didn't have it to do ... I mean it is part of your life! I mean if someone told me in the morning your job is gone I would go, I will get another job, so be it! But if someone told me in the morning I didn't have to care for my kids or I didn't have them or something were to happen to them, I would scream, I would go to pieces, I really would! It's not work. It's your family! ... It's commitment. It's a commitment that is natural, that is there, that is not to say it is easy and it is not that I am not roaring at them and shouting at them and one of them might tell me that they hated me because I am shouting at them but I wouldn't be without them. It's not, ... mm, it is hard work ... but it's something you do out of love, so it's not work if you understand what I mean.* (Clodagh, married to Séan, co-carer of three primary school children)

Many of those with whom we had care conversations about their children were ambivalent about naming care as work. It was seen as work when it was involuntary (when you had to do it and did not feel like doing it), tiring (attending to a child at 6am when you wanted to sleep or being attentive to someone after a long hard day at paid work), when it was incessant (24 hours a day and 365 days a year with no break) or demanding (when it required resources, time and energy that you did not have, when children were sick, etc.). It was not seen as work when it was more spontaneous, when it was appreciated, when care and love were reciprocated and when the work was respected by others.

Although care was seen as both work and non-work at the same time, it was unlike other forms of work in crucial respects. It involved emotional and moral engagements and commitments to persons that were neither clearly time-bounded nor task limited. The pleasures and joys, fears and anxieties that came with love labouring were integral to the relationships between the carer and care recipient. Indeed, the nature of relationships greatly determined the level of pleasure or fear/anxiety/guilt that was experienced by carers (and care recipients). There is a sharp contrast between Maeve, who had always had a difficult relationship with her mother, and Tom or Tony or Pearse who had very good relationships with their respective parents.

## What is and is not commodifiable: the inalienability of nurturing

In much of the research literature, care is defined as a singular entity; it is not disaggregated. It is assumed that some ideal type care regime can be devised where care can be provided on a paid professional basis that will answer the needs of both carers and care recipients equitably. The solution to the care problem is primarily constructed as a problem of service provision, regulation and adequate pay. While it is self-evident that the payment of a good living wage for carers is a prerequisite for promoting the dignity of care workers and care recipients (bearing in mind that many people are in both categories simultaneously), what our data suggests is that care needs to be disaggregated and what can be provided for pay and what cannot need to be identified and separated from each other.

Given the integral role that feelings for others play in primary care relations, not all of the work involved in caring for intimate others is capable of being provided on a hired basis, not least because one cannot contract out one's feelings for others and the character of a relationship. People distinguished in their conversations between the work that could be done by others on a paid or support basis in crèches or through respite services (what we have called secondary care labour) and what could not (what we have called love labour). There was a distinction made between what was alienable in terms of care labour and what was inalienable. While the technical aspects of care could be commodified, what could not be commodified was the quality of care that was contingent on a set of relationships where there was commitment, longstanding intimate knowledge and a strong sense of other-centredness. Even when people paid for care, they were also managing the secondary care relationship by monitoring the quality of care provided. Primary carers believed that the control, planning and responsibility for care, and the undertaking of relational-specific tasks, could not be devolved to paid carers.

What made love labour different from secondary care labour was not only that the work had to be done, but the belief that responsibility for the work could not be reneged on. One of the other defining differences between secondary care labour and love labour was the place of nurturing in the relationship. People who were primary carers saw themselves as having a nurturing role, a developmental role in relation to their children at multiple relationship levels, and a facilitating and empathising role with the adults who were in their care. They also saw themselves as carers over indefinite periods of time while recognising that they might not be physically or mentally capable of fulfilling that role at a future date.

While people wanted to have care support services, including child care and respite services, they regarded these as supplementary to primary care relationships. The resistance to placing adults in institutional care exemplified the strength of feeling about caring most of all.

## Institutional care as care of last resort

While there are certainly huge cultural variations in what people think is appropriate or acceptable care for themselves or others with high dependency needs, there is no doubt that all people are concerned about the quality of care they receive if they are dependant (Barry, 1995). People want the best care possible for themselves and others. Those who are in need of care and are aware of the care options are mindful not only of the quality of care but of 'not being a burden' on others; what is defined as burden-some varies greatly cross-culturally as does the concept of good care itself (*ibid.*).

Ireland does not have a good history of institutional care (Fahy, 1999; McDonnell, 2007), although the issue of quality in institutional care is by no means confined to Ireland (Toynbee, 2007). Historically children were only placed 'in care' if there was no adult willing or able to care for them, while homes for people who were old, ill or severely disabled were developed throughout the nineteenth century as places of containment rather than places of care. It is not surprising therefore that against this cultural backdrop, no matter how demanding care work was seen to be, institutional care was seen as a last resort especially for those with long-term care needs. The vulnerability of highly dependant people, and in particular their inability to exercise control over their own lives in an institutional environment was a fear for both carers of adults and of vulnerable young children.

This fear of institutional care was founded on personal experiences in some cases. Nora was a carer in her 70s of one adult son with a physical impairment and two other adult children who had a physical impairment but also suffered from mental ill-health. She had worked in various care homes and was adamant that none of her family would ever be placed in homes where they would have:

> ... *no power over their own lives; you are just a thing; you are an instrument. You are lifted and sat in a corner and that is it ... they are not someone else's responsibility. They are your own. And why give them to strangers? I don't think it's fair.* (Nora, separated, caring full-time for adult son)

Nora was also aware of her pending old age; she was equally adamant that she did not want institutional care for herself from what she knew of it through working in a home for older people:

> ... *I lived through it. I told my family, I said should I be on my hands and knees, I don't want to be a burden to anybody, just get me a ... spot out the back there, I will do my own thing as long as I can, as long a I live, I do not want to be put in a home ... I don't want to ... Because I saw too much! I saw us going out to thatch houses away out in the middle of nowhere and I saw this old crater [sic] sitting in the corner as happy as Larry and an open fire and smoking her old pipe and she was as happy as Larry. We took her out against her wishes and put her onto an ambulance and we took her into the county home and we put her in a tin bath in the middle of the floor and she was put into that and all her clothes were taken off her and her hair was cut and she was scrubbed and scrubbed and she was put in this white nightdress and she was put in a bed with white sheets and I wished she was dead. The old crater could have been left where she was and somebody went in and took her in a warm meal and cleaned up a bit for her and left her there.* (Nora, separated, caring full-time for adult son)

Debra and Alex had two young children, one of whom had an intellectual impairment. Although their son was only four years of age their biggest fear was that he would be placed in institutional care:

> *I think the biggest, my biggest, the biggest thing that I want or don't want for Noel is I don't want him to be institutionalised ... a residential facility, then I mean for example he would mm ... be in his pyjamas every night at 8 o'clock even if he was 50 years of age ... so you know if he was sick he would still have to go to his day care centre because of the staff, you know, so there are a lot of little personal things ... Also I think institutions are institutions. I mean the word institution, right, is eh I mean it's a lot less of a big word than it used to be but there is still, no matter how pretty they are they are still the same and to some extent the sterility.*(Debra, married to Alex, primary carer of one pre-school child and one primary school child)

Debra and Alex were planning to save for a house they could share with Noel when he got older so he could live relatively independently:

> *Mm, and eh, and financially I think, you know, at the moment in my head is the kind of idea of well when we are older if we could afford to buy a house that has two flats, you know, and it could be integrated for Noel if he isn't independent enough to live at all on his own but if he had a wife or a girl-friend or something potentially they could live. And when we die, potentially we could leave the house to [name of NGO] on the basis, or somebody, on the basis that you know with some trusting arrangement that Noel is allowed to live there as a community home with a few other people. You know that kind of thing.* (Debra, married to Alex, primary carer of one pre-school and one primary school child)

Anita was caring for her daughter with an intellectual impairment, Beth, at home. While Beth attended a day centre five days each week, she lived at home the rest of the time. Anita had tried placing her daughter in residential care twice but as her daughter had not settled in either home she had abandoned the effort after a two-year trial. While Anita was positive about the first home Beth attended, she never understood what led to her daughter having a breakdown there at the beginning of her second year. She was quite sceptical of institutional care because it was not what it appeared to be when it was promoted to her. Speaking of the second home Beth attended, which was in the UK where they lived at the time, she said:

> *Not as good at all as it promised to be. It didn't work out like ... in actual fact it was a disaster. It was a beautiful house but very badly organised and they had six clients there when Beth went in ... We had nothing but*

*problems; she was put on an anti-depressant ... she used to spend her time*
*watching out the window waiting for me to come. She wasn't alright; it was a*
*total wrong place for her to be.* (Anita, separated, caring full-time for adult
daughter)

Although Valerie found caring for her parents to be a very demanding task,
the fact that she had minded both her parents at home and kept them out
of institutional care was regarded as an achievement in itself:

*... the fact that they haven't spent the last seven years in an institution, you*
*can always look back and say you did your best. And I certainly did! Hope-*
*fully! Whereas if they did go to an institution you would have to live with*
*that, rightly or wrongly! So I think it was not in my make up to be able to do*
*that. So that is the top and bottom of it really.* (Valerie, single, caring full-
time for both parents)

Placing someone close to you, especially a child with a physical or intellectual impairment or a vulnerable parent or partner, in care was deemed to
be a choice of last resort. Carers were aware that care recipients would not
want to go into care and this also influenced decisions:

*I have to do it [caring]. I don't see any other way and that's that. Either*
*that or haul them into some, you know, some kind of places that they*
*wouldn't want to go to. Or I wouldn't want them to go to, either, to*
*be honest with you. No, that would not be much of a solution either.*
(Melanie, married to Peter, full-time carer of husband and three adult
children)

Melanie and others believed that to care for a vulnerable person properly,
one had to know them well and want to care for all their needs:

*Like the way I see it is that it is only someone like me, like their mother,*
*or say in relation to Peter his wife, it is only someone like that who will*
*really care enough to want to look after all their needs and that. Sure*
*who else would ever know them the way I do?* (Melanie, married to Peter,
full-time carer for husband and three adult children)

Nora's fear of being in long-term residential care was such that she was
most determined her own children who have a particular physical impairment would not go into care:

*Now I wouldn't want them to ever be institutionalised. That is why I*
*taught Rory to do everything for himself because I was told that there*
*was a home for him in [the area]. I said he would never end up in a home,*

*not over my dead body!* (Nora, separated, caring full-time for adult son)

Most carers claimed that what they needed was better financial support for caring:

> *The Child Benefit is a joke, it's just a disgrace, it is almost nothing, that's a shame. At least for single parents the Child Benefit should be higher even though there is one single child. They should make this ... Child Benefit ... make it bigger. If you don't have to give the parent financial support then give it to the child if he is in a lone parent family, I think, because it's not fair the way it is.* (Regina, divorced, primary carer of second-level child)

Better access to care services, especially respite care, was their other main priority. Anita, who is a separated mother of an adult child with an intellectual impairment, explained how respite services for her daughter were cancelled on a number of occasions. Even organising respite care was very difficult, and it was not always available:

> *So that day when I rang Respite first of all their answer phone was out of order, which it had been for weeks so you couldn't leave a message. I continued ringing but nobody answered, eventually I got the social worker which was lucky to get her because she would be in and out so often and I told her the situation ... And she said 'Anita I don't hold out much hope' and I said 'Sheila I am not able to look after the child.' What I was looking for was [for the Respite services] to take her, give her her dinner, give her her bath and bring her home at bedtime. So then I actually got [Mr X] who is the head of disabilities in the Health Centre and the reason I got [X] was because I had his mobile because ... I am also involved in the [mentioning specific impairment] group for the region and [X] came to a couple of meetings. So I had his mobile and I rang him in desperation and told him the situation, he didn't know what to do. So he said 'Anita I will ring you back.' So he rang me back and said 'the two women that work for you, can you not get either of those to help?' and I said 'they have already done their hours for this week'... So Respite wasn't even open that night, we only discovered that afterwards.* (Anita, separated, primary carer of adult daughter)

People felt they had to fight for services they were entitled to. This was both demeaning and exhausting and added to the stress of caring:

> *... you would have to fight, oh yes, you have to be always constantly looking for things because otherwise you don't get it. ... It is you, you have to fight for them, you have to be always fighting their corner from day one.* (Mary, widow, caring full-time for adult son)

## What is inalienable?

While no one doubted that other people could physically care for their children with physical or intellectual impairments or for their adult relatives who were very dependent, those interviewed believed that this would be a very different kind of care from what they could be given by those who were committed to them. What was inalienable was the quality of the relationship:

> *You know you don't have the same relationships with people who are only there eight hours of the day five days a week or whatever. So I just don't think quality of life is the same.* (Debra, married to Alex, primary carer of one pre-school and one primary school child)

> *Nobody is ever going to take the same thought or care that a mother or a member of the family does. I think that is generally the way it is anyway. Maybe you get the odd carer from outside who is exceptional but I would say that is more the exception than anything else.* (Melanie, married to Peter, primary carer of husband and three adult children)

While Valerie recognised that she might not be able to mind her parents at home indefinitely, she knew that they would have less freedom and independence if they were in care:

> *But like they've been used to being out and about, and going visiting, although that hasn't happened recently, but it would be very difficult for them to adjust to full-time care.* (Valerie, single, caring full-time for both parents)

## Trust and fear of neglect

One of the issues that most exercised carers, including parents of young children, was trust. Pearse knew a number of other people who were also carers for older relatives. He was very sceptical of the quality of care for older people outside of their home environment. For him the issue was not just quality of care but the fear of neglect of vulnerable people:

> *I have investigated all those places and what I am saying now is the truth because I have investigated [hospitals and nursing homes] ... I know one particular person in hospital at the moment in St. John's and he is bedridden and he is wetting the bed and he is not properly looked after ... and the fellow's [relatives] will take him home again.* (Pearse, single, primary carer of mother)

Trying to find someone or some place one could trust, and people with whom the children would be safe was an overriding concern for parents (Vincent and Ball, 2001). Women articulated this anxiety more than men because they were the people who generally negotiated the child care arrangements:

> *And it was just a question of trying to get a name of somebody, like a child-minder that somebody had used ... as a childminder and, you know, a bit of recommendation. The lady that gave it to me – her children had been minded by a person, I am not talking about for maybe six months or a year but someone whose children had been minded maybe until they were older, and it wasn't a question of taking a chance or a risk, I knew that Alicia would be safe with her.* (Clodagh, married to Séan, co-carer of three primary school children)

Clodagh, who returned reluctantly to work for financial reasons, cited her desire to reproduce 'home' as much as possible in the childminding environment. She wanted her children:

> *... to be in a family background. To be in the middle of, you know, the way it wasn't a crèche. Because I feel they have to, I mean, [pause), they [the children) do little jobs for her and they don't have to do them but she will expect them to do little jobs or even maybe, [pause), tidy away stuff or you know, so it's a bit like replicating home.* (Clodagh, married to Séan, co-carer of three primary school children)

> ML: They could literally go to bed and be sick at the childminder's, can they?
> *Clodagh: Yeah, they can and they are at home and they feel at home.*
> (Clodagh, married to Séan, co-carer of three primary school children)

None of the parents of young children whom we interviewed had a single continuous child care arrangement from infancy. All had a series of arrangements. Cathy's experience was not untypical. Her interview highlighted the anxiety and sense of risk that people had about child care and the dilemmas that arise from having to manage care and paid work for women in particular:

> *... I was quite upset because there was a couple of things that happened in the crèche which were very upsetting for parents, especially a new parent, I mean, unqualified staff, you know you think you've found a really good arrangement for your child and then it starts to kind of unravel and you realise that it's not as good as it was made out to be, ... a very distressed child, em, a child that wasn't feeding very well, and medication that was being given in the wrong dosage, you know, which really caused, caused tension at home. ... but then luckily we decided that we'd kind of stand back a bit, I got a couple of weeks off work to sort things out and try and find something, and I looked really long*

*and hard to make sure I got a childminder, and that next arrangement was grand then, that went on until I had my second child.* (Cathy, married to Michael, co-carer of two pre-school children)

Cathy and Michael decided to pay for a childminder at home and Cathy did all the necessary background work to find the best person:

*... I got references, and ... I think it is actually em, if you get kind of word of mouth recommendations it stands for a lot really.* (Cathy, married to Michael, *co-carer of two pre-school children)*

Eventually Cathy changed jobs and took work nearer to home so that she could use local child care. The new arrangements allowed both her husband and herself to play a greater part in caring for their children.

The anxiety that exists around using paid child care for young children or institutional care for adults arises in part from the lack of trust in these forms of care, and the difficulty of monitoring personal care for vulnerable adults and children even when carers are formally qualified to do the work. Personal care by strangers is seen as risky where vulnerable people are involved (Lewis and Meredith, 1988; Twigg and Atkin, 1994). Cathy's experiences exemplified this. She did not think that having formal care qualifications guaranteed good care:

*... I think all the child care qualifications in the world are not going to be the thing that gives you good care, if the person is not really interested and I think that that to me [is crucial] ..., and there's a lot of, you know, people going into child care just because there are lots of jobs in it and they're getting trained in it, and they haven't got the attitude or the interest in working with children, and that's quite worrying I think.* (Cathy, married to Michael, co-carer of two pre-school children)

The problem is further complicated by the relational knowledge that intimate care requires and which can only be developed over time (Barnes, 2006, Pickard and Glendinning, 2002). The reasons people seek intimate others to care therefore is not because they have some blind allegiance to an outdated ideology about what is good care. They seek it because those who are close to them personally have the depth of knowledge that is derived from intensive interaction on a daily basis over a prolonged period of time. Knowing that the carer will have an extended knowledge of one's needs increases the trust. For this reason primary caring or love labouring is not a service that can be supplied on a simple hire and fire, market basis; primary caring relations involve knowledge and trust that can only develop through long-term involvement (Ball and Vincent, 2005; Duncan *et al.*, 2004).

The fear that the care of a stranger would not equal intimate care was exacerbated by the fear of possible vested interests among care providers, not least the need to keep the care business running:

> *The manageress of the Home (when I look back now I can see it all) didn't want to let her go because don't forget that every room was money. So any time I had to talk about how upset Beth was ... (I used to take her in every weekend and I would go out on a Wednesday and take her into town and we would have tea and a scone and do a little bit of shopping. The weekends were murder trying to get her back so there was obviously something terribly wrong.)... But the manageress would keep blaming me, she kept saying if I left her alone to settle it would have been all right but ... it was a totally wrong place for her to be.* (Anita, separated, caring full-time for adult daughter)

## Conclusion

This chapter began with a general discussion of the nature of work and the reasons that care work has been marginalised. We argued that care has as much of a claim to being work and the activities people undertake for payment. The bulk of the chapter consisted in analysing Care Conversations conducted with a range of carers. These showed that although all of the carers spoke of the work involved in caring, those responsible for adults in need of care were more inclined to describe their care as work, while those caring for young children were more ambiguous. Both sets of carers recognised that care work had specific characteristics that stood in the way of its being commodified, both because they could not pay others to sustain their own loving relationships with those they cared for, and because it was very unlikely that paid care would have the long-term, intimate and caring involvement that is necessary for good care. We conclude below that these facts are related to a deeper fact about the rationality of caring.

### Care as work and the inalienability of love labouring

While caring can be pleasurable and joyful at times, it is also seen as work. It is regarded as hard work where the carer is attending to a person who is highly dependent and who has a need for constant attentiveness over time. In our Care Conversations, caring was seen as work that produced socially valued outcomes, the development of a child and the provision of high quality personal and committed attentiveness to the needs of vulnerable others. The carers distinguished between when care work could be done for pay and when it could not. There were relationally integrated emotional and moral aspects to caring (love labouring) that were grounded in trust and that could neither be simulated nor bought on a simple hire and fire basis. While paid care services were regarded as indispensable for supporting love labouring (and grossly under-funded and under-resourced) they were seen as supplementary to love labouring rather than a substitute for it.

The planning and controlling of intimate care was regarded as a core love labouring task. Neither did carers think it was feasible or realistic to expect people who were paid carers to give the 24-hour care that primary carers had to give at times. While care tasks such as tending or cooking for someone were alienable in the technical sense, they were often seen as inalienable in a relational sense. One could not pay others to have the orientation to care tasks that one felt oneself. Feelings and commitments that were an integral part of an ongoing relationship were not available for hire.

One of the defining differences between secondary care labour and love labour was the matter of nurturing. People who were primary carers saw themselves as having a nurturing role, a developmental role in relation to their children at multiple relationship levels, and a facilitating and empathising role with the adults who were in their care. They also saw themselves as carers over indefinite periods of time while recognising that they might not be physically or mentally capable of fulfilling that role at a future date. Although they recognised that high quality paid care could potentially be nurturing and could sometimes initiate long-term relationships, they had found from experience that this was very unlikely to happen.

## Relational identities and nurturing rationalities

One of the striking messages from the Care Conversations was that care rationalities are different to economic rationalities. Almost all of the people we conversed with made some, and in some cases significant, economic and personal sacrifices in order to prioritise the care of those they loved. As most of those who were primary carers were women, most of the sacrifices were made by women (for further discussion on the gendered nature of caring, see Chapter 5). Debra took a job share arrangement to spend more time with her two children and in particular to care for her son with an intellectual impairment; Geraldine worked an early shift (being at work at 7am) in order to have more time with her baby daughter in the evening; Maeve gave up taking in a student to supplement her income in order to care for her mother; Cathy moved job to a lower paid position so that her husband and herself could have more time with their children; Jane took 6 weeks' unpaid leave in summer in order to have time with her partner Jill and their two children; Tom and Tony devoted huge amounts of time to the care of their parents and a sick uncle (in Tony's case) at a cost to their livelihoods and their social life; and Valerie gave up her prestigious career to be a full-time carer.

People struggled to find words to name their care labours, variously describing it as demanding, joyful, stressful, time consuming, fun, natural, exhausting and fulfilling; the lack of a language to name the different forms of care could be a study in itself (see Uttal, 2002). The named reasons for caring varied, although for any one person there were multiple motives; at times it was a sense of duty and obligation that was the primary care narrative; other times the language of desire, longing and aspiration was more pronounced; the languages of guilt, hope, affection, responsibility and lack of choice were also dispersed throughout the interviews. What was clear was that care was embedded in a set of relationships which had a history and an assumed future and so was integral to the sense of purposes, values and identities people held in life. To renege on *responsibility* for caring (even if some of the tasks had to be assigned to others) was to assign the person for whom one was caring an 'unwanted' caring status and to identity oneself as a person 'who was not caring'. People saw their primary care relations as integral to who they were, both as carers and as care recipients. Maeve who was caring for her mother exemplified this. She spoke about finding it difficult to care for her mother, who could be quite demanding, but whom she felt obligated to care for because of her sense of herself as a caring person, and because her mother would be deeply hurt if she was placed in residential care (see Chapter 5 for further discussion of this).

Caring was not seen therefore as a set of discrete tasks that could be separated completely from the relationship in which they were embedded, and the identities of those involved. Because of this, only certain aspects of care could be handed over to others or paid for at times without undermining the relational identity of both carer and care recipient. Care is not just a practical dilemma about a set of tasks to be undertaken, it is also an emotional and moral dilemma about who one is relationally and what is best care.

Clearly the range of reasons for care, and the range of reasons for resisting institutional care, have a very different character from those typically ascribed to economic actors. Yet they are easy to understand: they are clearly rational. Being embedded in the relationships that these carers had with the people they cared for, and intelligible in terms of those relationships, they could be said to express a nurturing rationality that is quite distinct from the rationality of economic actors.

# 4
## Care-less Citizenship? Public Devaluation and Private Validation

*Kathleen Lynch and Maureen Lyons*

Given the influence of liberal thinking on Western political thinking, it is not surprising that issues of love, care and solidarity are also conspicuous by their absence from major debates about public policy (Baker *et al.*, 2004: 28–29). Caring is defined as a private matter, an inadmissible subject within serious politics. Yet, the state plays a major role in determining the conditions for caring in most Western societies: it regulates paid working hours and thereby the amount of time one has available for care; it regulates housing, transportation and education in a way that either inhibits or enables caring; and it determines the levels of public solidarity that exist through systems for redistributing wealth, and through the levels of social expenditures devoted to care and solidarity services. Regulatory mechanisms within welfare and legislative codes also affect the power and subordination of both carers and care recipients, with respect to each other and to third parties such as social workers and the police.

Drawing on a set of 30 in-depth Care Conversations with carers and care recipients (see Introduction and Appendix), this chapter shows how all types of carers feel invisible and undervalued in their various forms of care work, although there are important gender differences in this regard. The chapter also demonstrates how the life world of caring is a space where carers claim the value of care for themselves; carers are not passive recipients of negative labelling. They articulate a strong resistance to the lowly evaluation attached to caring; they contest the values of the public spheres that assume the presence of love and care work while ignoring its existence. People are willing and able to contest economic rationalities and articulate the primacy of nurturing rationalities.

Having outlined the sense of frustration that carers feel about the lack of respect for their work in the earlier parts of the chapter, we devote the last section to making sense of these contradictory discourses about caring: the validation for caring in the private world and the lack of respect for caring in public policy. We argue that while it is true that the gendered identity of carers plays a major role in determining the lack of respect for care work (Bubeck, 1995), as does the fact that carers and care recipients are seen as unproductive, vulnerable and even 'wasteful' in a strong capitalist society (Hughes *et al*., 2005), a further reason why caring and care recipients are not valued is because the concept of the ideal citizen is not a 'careful' one (Lister, 1997). The prevailing concept of the citizen lacks a concept of dependency and interdependency as it is premised on the ideal of the political participant, the publicly engaged, self-determining person. Care recipients are clearly not citizens in the politically engaged sense, especially where they have severe intellectual disabilities or where they are highly dependent due to age or illness (Lanoix, 2007). Carers are also invisible in this politically engaged definition of the citizen as their care work controls their time, forcing them to disengage from political action, and indeed from employment when they lack care support services. Revaluing care thus requires a reconceptualisation of citizens as interdependent.

## Lack of respect for care and love work

What exercised carers most in the course of our Care Conversations was not the fact that caring was demanding or tiring at times, since that was seen as endemic to love and care relations, but rather the absence of care support services and the attitude that this absence seemed to express. The conversations all focused at some stage on the lack of value placed on care in politics and public policies. Most people saw care as work that was 'taken for granted' or given 'token support'. Although most carers received vital support and affirmation from their own informal social networks, the minimal degrees of public respect and formal assistance available were a different matter. The lack of political respect for caring was felt equally strongly by all carers, be these women or men, couples or single parents, older carers or children caring for parents.

### Women and the lack of respect for care

Regardless of the relational conditions women and men cared within, they all felt a lack of respect for their work. For some the problem was lack of appreciation and financial support for what was very onerous care work, work which if done in a home or hospital would be funded in full.

Melanie, who had multiple care responsibilities, exemplified the anger, frustration and exhaustion that comes with being expected to do too much care with too few resources. She was well aware that many people who had adult children with intellectual disabilities had placed them in long-term care although she could not bear to do this as she had been in institutional care herself and felt it would not be an appropriate care environment. When asked if she thought society appreciated what she did, Melanie said:

> *No, I don't think so ... well the government certainly doesn't ... after all I am doing, and all the money I am saving the government they still don't see that they should make it a bit easier for me. Not having to worry about money and paying the bills would at least help ... If they were somewhere, it would cost a lot. There seems to be no appreciation of that.* (Melanie, married to Peter, caring full-time for three adult children and husband)

Mary was a widow in her 50s caring for her adult son who had a physical and intellectual impairment. While she thought services were better in some ways in Ireland than in Canada (where she had lived with her son) she did not believe that politicians cared except *'maybe at election time, they pretend they care'*. Nora, who was a pensioner, held similar views. She was the primary carer for her son who had a physical impairment, and two daughters who lived close by who had a less severe form of the same physical impairment, one of whom also had ongoing mental health problems. In her view, the Ministers and politicians made empty promises in nice words and in so doing showed a lack of respect for caring:

> *Yeah, when [X] was minister for social welfare, they brought her [to the local town] and [we] said the money we were getting wasn't enough for the work the carers were doing, like you know. But all [X] said was 'Look at all this stuff [I] have to do'. She was to try to get more and all this but you get the same thing all the time ... Nothing at the end of the day, nothing ... Sympathised, and very polished and very nice, you know, all that to talk to, understands your situation and they sympathise with you but that is not much good like you know.* (Nora, separated, caring full-time for adult son)

For Paula, a divorced mother of four, the lack of appreciation of care was more general and applied to mothers in particular:

> *I think that being a mother is the most thankless task in the world anyway ... because it's taken for granted particularly in Ireland in terms of the whole culture and the whole thing, that's just the way it is, it's taken for granted. Nobody really cares at the end of the day ... I think that it's society that doesn't appreciate it, the government doesn't appreciate it either.* (Paula, divorced, primary carer of one second-level child and three adult children)

Paula believed however that it was because women were assumed to be 'naturally' carers that care was not valued:

> *... and it's a thing that is just not valued because it is expected you are a woman and these things are expected that you will do them. And we do.*

(Paula, divorced, primary carer of one second-level child and three adult children)

Unlike Paula, Jane saw the care problem, especially child care, as a parental issue rather than a women's issue *per se*. She believed that there was a need for some kind of financial contribution towards the cost of care for children:

> *I think if a parent or parents want to go out to work and have their children in child care I think that needs to be facilitated and I think they should have either tax credits or get tax back to allow them or a child care payment per month. Some financial contribution towards the cost of child care, a significant contribution. Or if a parent chooses to stay at home I think they should get money for it because they are contributing to society in that way. They are giving up the possibility of working outside the home. So I think it needs to be a package really to suit whatever circumstance the child care is being done in, either at home or more formal care or whatever.* (Jane, partner of Jill, primary carer of two primary children)

While Jane believed that care was of great importance, she thought it was largely taken for granted:

> *There should be a lot more acknowledgement and the value of that role should be valued in loads of different ways. Through cultural interpretations as well, it is not all monetary but monetary [reward] always goes a long way in relation to most things. So there are loads of ways of acknowledging caring as being valuable but it isn't [valued] ... it is just given, it is just done.* (Jane, partner of Jill, primary carer of two primary children)

Cathy was married with two children and she also believed that care was not taken seriously, especially for women who wanted to enter paid employment:

> *I mean they're always talking about women getting back into the work force, but there's absolutely no support to help them get back into it, so I mean, to me now, if there was job sharing available and child care available and flexible working time and family friendly work practice, an awful lot of people would go back to the work force, but it's not there, it is not encouraged really.* (Cathy, married to Michael co-carer of two pre-school children)

Like many of the people we interviewed, Cathy had a memory and history of care in her own family that led her to think that carers were lowly valued, particularly people who care for adults who were ill or in need of intensive caring:

> *I mean you only have to look in you know, my own family situation, in terms of my mum now, caring for my dad, ... she was treated appallingly because she was caring for him at home and the amount of times people said well do you want to put him in a home, and she was like no, no, I want to get support to care for him at home. But she really got minimal support, and she was saving the state a fortune, and she was caring for him better than the state could have done, but they weren't prepared to accept their responsibility, in that. ... Carers are just totally not recognised by the state for the value of the work that they do, ... having seen now my own family and the way my mother was treated you know. She was a 70 year old woman, caring full-time for an 87 year old man who was terminally ill, and she got hardly any support, really bad, really bad.* (Cathy, married to Michael, co-carer of two pre-school children)

### Men and the lack of respect for care

Men who were primary carers were as adamant as women that care was not valued. Tom was caring for his father (who had needed full-time care) for almost ten years and he felt that care was simply not recognised. Carers were invisible people:

> *We don't exist, we get the usual pat on the head at election time ... patronised. We don't exist. As long as you are prepared to do it they will wring their hands and say you have done a great job and leave it to that.* (Tom, single, caring full-time for father)

He was also scathing about politicians, their 'hypocrisy' and their failure to promote an more equal distribution of wealth, a distribution that would fund state services for those in need of care:

> *... most people [carers] have been through it so they understand but politicians, especially the government are like something out of the Twilight Zone. ... the cake could be spread out more evenly. You have a lot of wealthy people in this country who are not paying tax and it is the poor working man who is caught for PRSI, he is caught for VAT, he is caught for every bit of tax going and you have the billionaires that can pay accountants to get out of paying tax. So there is no equality in this country. ... I am saving the state thousands.* (Tom, single, aged 50 to 60, caring full-time for his father)

Tom was actively resisting the state's devaluation of carers. He outlined the contents of a letter he had written to a government minister after hearing him on television saying he *'had taken care of carers in the budget'*. Given that he himself had a physical impairment and was a carer, Tom was especially annoyed as he read out his letter:

> *'I am a ful-time carer since '87 with a disability so perhaps you could explain to me how I was looked after in the budget. ... Maybe I was asleep when all these benefits were coming around but I certainly didn't benefit. ... I would appreciate a waffle free reply.'* But I have as much chance of getting a waffle free reply from you as I have of getting an invitation to the Pope's wedding. [This last comment was not in the letter] (Tom, single, caring full-time for father)

Donal, who was married with one young child, also felt that care was not valued, especially child care:

> *There is, well ... I just feel there's absolutely no focus on care, or child care within the government, I mean, from just what you hear they don't want to, or haven't really thought it through or whatever, but there doesn't seem to be any, there's no incentive at all to raise children and there's no reward for raising children, it is just something that a parent is expected to do and there's no compensation for that, in terms of, of finance or lifestyle or time off, or whatever, so, certainly it is not a focus.* (Donal, married to Geraldine, co-carer of one pre-school child)

Carers were not overly optimistic about change although they did resist the care-less model of the citizen imposed on them. Alex, who was married to Debra (who was also employed), and who had two young children, reflected this sense of frustration with the state:

> *It's particularly bad, but that is the way it has been for a long time and I don't see it changing in the future. My mother looked after her father at home for 11 years before he died and there was never any recognition from the state for that. We obviously have kids and Noel has special needs and there is very little recognition for all that work that we do. Anything you need you have to go looking for it yourself. There is no organised state help for any of the special needs that Noel has. But even on the standard child there is very little in the way of organised help or care, I just think they could do an awful lot more.* (Alex, married to Debra, secondary carer of one pre-school child and one primary school child)

Although men agreed with women about the low public status given to care, there was an important gender difference in the way they were viewed in more informal social circles. As we discuss more thoroughly in Chapter 5, women were seen as the default carers: it was taken for granted that women would care. By contrast, men who took on caring roles were seen as exceptional and worthy of praise. As Geraldine put it:

> *Donal, anything he does he's the hero, you know, I mean in other people's eyes for doing anything for Trisha. ... And then circle of friends and everything like that, you know the comparatives aren't the same, you know his peers or people that he would get the opportunity to compare himself to, he can always come off best.* (Geraldine, married to Donal, co-carer of one pre-school child)

### Lack of respect for care – lone carers

Lone carers felt isolated and vulnerable due to the lack of support services for caring. Lone parents of young children lived in a world of contractions; they could not afford to pay for child care, yet they needed to be employed to have a reasonable standard of living. Taking part-time employment was not always an option owing to the need for flexibility to care for children in particular, a flexibility that was not always granted by employers. Even if children were in school, they had to picked up (often at different times). Those who had children with disabilities had to attend clinics and appointments where there were queues and waiting lists, all of which assumed the parent had total time flexibility. Low-income lone parents felt they were 'blamed' for being welfare dependent but their care responsibilities meant that they could not enter employment without becoming neglectful parents. The lone parent problem was especially acute for women who comprise the great majority of lone parents (CSO, 2007b).

Regina's position typifies the dilemmas faced by a lone parent with young children. She came to work in Ireland from Eastern Europe when her son was young. Although she had a university degree when she arrived, she experienced a lot of economic hardship, problems that were greatly exacerbated by the lack of affordable child care services. She spoke about how child care services were free in her country of origin, as they were state-supported, and this made it easy to work. However, in Ireland she could only work part-time, basically when her son was in school:

> *I started to work part-time because I couldn't work while my son wasn't in school ... And I had no child care for him and I couldn't afford to pay child care because [with] the part-time work as a single parent I couldn't manage. And in six years living in Ireland I moved six times from one private rented accommodation to another ... being a single parent with a child it is very hard to get accommodation and it was the idea of being a foreigner* [implying here that she experienced considerable difficulty in getting

housing because she was not Irish]. (Regina, divorced, primary carer of second-level child)

She did not think the challenges faced by migrant workers like herself or lone parents generally (most of whom are women) were taken seriously by politicians:

> *They talk from their ivory tower, I don't know who elected them and they just show that they are populist and they are flashy in their expensive cars and they talk with rough language in rough English just showing that they are kind of part of the people and it's just double faced – it makes you sick.* (Regina, divorced, primary carer of second-level child

The lack of financial support for one parent families on low incomes was a major concern for some of those interviewed. Sasha had three young children two of whom had sensory impairments. She could not undertake paid work without fully funded care supports, and the latter was not available to her. Her reliance of welfare payments made it extremely difficult for her to survive economically and she felt there was little understanding of her position:

> *Like I think it is very unfair how I am on my own with three children and how low my payment is like, like I think that I should be entitled to more money to rear them. Like but [pause] like when I went to the clinic to ask for more money to help pay for the playschool she said I was better off finding Séan's father and asking him for maintenance. They don't seem to get it that that does not work and that I am on me own rearing three children, on me own and living on €70 a week! You know, so!* (Sasha, single, caring for one pre-school and two primary school children)

Nora, who was a pensioner, was also living on welfare payments. She felt that politicians had little understanding of how difficult it was to live on social welfare:

> *I would love as I said to [the Minister] I would love you to take my salary for a month and give me your salary for a month and see which me or you are the wellest off at the end of the month. And [the Minister] just laughed.* (Nora, separated, caring full-time for adult son)

The lack of respect for carers meant that the vital and onerous work that benefits everyone was being carried out with inadequate resources and minimal respect and recognition from political institutions. Most full-time carers we spoke with felt isolated, exploited and let down by public representatives in terms of care support services. This was especially true of people who had children with intellectual disabilities or differences or degenerative health conditions.

Anita was politically active in working for services for children and adults with intellectual impairments. She exemplified those carers who resisted their lowly status. In her view, young adults with an intellectual impairment, like her daughter Beth, were a low priority in terms of government spending. Speaking of getting further education and care for daughter, she compared the educational options that her sons had when leaving school with those of her daughter. When they were leaving school, they eagerly waited for examination results to see what their options were:

> *It is the opposite [for Beth] ... you have to see if you can find a place that will have her, not where she would like to go. They are bottom of the list ...* (Anita, separated, caring full-time for adult daughter)

She explained how she had fought for services for her daughter and other young people with this type of intellectual impairment:

> *So I went in to the Minister's office with that as well and said 'take a look at this, so this is a money issue, I'm not a genius but I'm not stupid, so I know we need two or three more houses. If you can't afford to buy them, rent them. What sort of service is there for the young people like Beth?* (Anita, separated, caring full-time for adult daughter)

### Employers and the lack of recognition for care

It was not only state agencies that were seen to undervalue care, those who were employed also stated that their employers did not want to recognise that people had to attend to their care responsibilities. Donal was an auctioneer and had recently established his own business. While he had strong personal commitments to caring for his baby daughter and managing his work around her needs, he claimed that family friendly policies were simply 'never discussed' in his own company nor in the various companies in which he worked previously:

> *Donal: Even in my previous incarceration [sic] I'd say, it was never discussed.*
> ML: And this has always been in the context of private sector work?
> *Donal: Yeah, always ... Now you mention it, I see what you are saying but I've never thought about it before to be honest.* (Donal, married to Geraldine, co-carer of one pre-school child)

When Donal was asked how he thought caring for children fits in with paid work, his reply was blunt:

> *Donal: It doesn't! It really doesn't when you think about it, you're expected to do your job, particularly in the private sector!*

ML: Yes.

*Donal: Absolutely, sink or swim! ... there is absolutely no thought put into it at all, regarding child care.* (Donal, married to Geraldine, co-carer of one pre-school child)

Cathy had lived in another EU country before returning to Ireland and believed that attitudes to care in Ireland were especially unsupportive:

> *Employers would always expect you almost to compromise the children, and your family life really, I think you know, that ... the general feeling is that you should be this super person that fits it all in but you should never compromise your work for your family. And I suppose that's probably a bit of a sweeping statement now, but I feel that it is all about the employer and much less about the welfare of the family and the employee and ... I really think that that balance is very bad, and I suppose again, having not always worked in Ireland, I think it's acutely bad in Ireland compared to other place.* (Cathy, married to Michael, co-carer of two pre-school children)

Clodagh worked for a large bank where she claimed there was little consideration of the care needs of children, especially given that so many of the employees were people with young children:

> *I suppose when you have a history of 20 odd years with a company you expect, you know, more. ... but I wouldn't say as a company they are very family friendly.* (Clodagh, married to Séan, co-carer of three primary school children)

Clodagh noted how the banks advertised themselves as being family friendly but that was not her experience as a parent with three young children:

> *When you see it and read about it and being family orientated, hello! It's not family orientated or anything like it! There are plenty of places and ways where I definitely don't see it. And it is very much at the behest of maybe your own local manager and if he [sic] isn't you know, ... if he is not inclined to be supportive you can be just left waiting and hanging and wondering.* (Clodagh, married to Séan, co-carer of three primary school children)

Like most of those we spoke with, she viewed caring as a woman's responsibility. She assumed she would be the person to seek a reduction in her hours of work to have more time to care for the children although her job was more secure and as well paid as her husband's. In her view, 'family friendly' policies operated on an *ad hoc* basis with concessions being granted at the whim of the branch manager:

> *I know I am going to find it difficult getting reduced hours and I know people have found it very difficult to get hours to work their family life around it. But against that then I know people who have found it easy to get hours, and for what reason, who knows? There should be a level playing field that you are not wondering – 'will I get it, won't I get it', that it's not … you know, dependent on a whim of somebody up the line whether you get it or not. There should be kind of a statutory entitlement there that if you have children … there isn't structure and I find it very annoying that there isn't. It's so ridiculous, especially in a place like the bank who have so many women working for them.* (Clodagh, married to Séan, co-carer of three primary school children)

Clodagh had entered the bank with basic secretarial training and had no specialised skills that she could use to transfer easily outside the banking sector. This reduced her employment options and increased her dependency on the bank. While Alex had also entered the financial services sector with Leaving Certificate (second-level school) qualifications he had been able to move company as he had acquired considerable further skills in his previous job. The knowledge that his skills were in demand enabled him to be more flexible in his approach to doing care work as he had other employment options outside of his current employer:

> *And, you know, I know I can do my job and still have a fairly good flexible arrangement to be able to care for the kids the way I want to. So once I have done the sort of thing I want to do in my new role I am going to revert back to working as flexibly as I can, regardless of the way the bank wants me to work. If that doesn't work out, it doesn't work out, I will certainly be looking at options at that stage. I suppose I am at the stage in my career now that I know I can do certain things and I don't need the bank to restrict me in the way I want to do it. So if I can't be satisfied in the job and the work life balance if you like, if I can't have that flexibility and satisfaction I will be more inclined to compromise on the job rather than the life aspect of it.* (Alex, married to Debra, secondary carer of one pre-school child and one primary school child)

The ability to manage care relations on one's own terms was limited to those who had flexibility in their jobs, that is, having flexibility on their terms rather than on the employer's terms. Some had flexibility because the employer had good job share arrangements in place (in Debra's case) or because of their skills (Alex), while others were only able to have flexibility by being self-employed (Jill in consultancy; Tony in farming; Donal as a self-employed businessman). For those who were unskilled or trying to get skills but who were caring alone without family supports (such as Sasha and Regina respectively) there were no real options in terms of employment; they could not afford the child care costs that would enable them to enter employment.

## Making sense of the validations and devaluation

There are two very different worlds of evaluation operating in relation to caring, one public and one private. There is a public sphere of policymaking, employment and formal politics where carers and care recipients are not highly valued except at a rhetorical level. And there is a private world where love, care and solidarity work is highly valued and protected often at a high personal cost to the carer.

The carers to whom we spoke were keenly aware of these two contrasting sets of evaluations. Women and men, lone parents and couples, carers of older people, sick people or children, were all of one mind about the low public status of care work. Yet, all of those interviewed valued their own care labouring and that of others highly, especially the love labouring they regarded as vital for their well-being.

How do we make sense of these contradictory sets of discourses and policies? In *The Human Condition* (1958) Arendt suggests that the low status of certain forms of work is related to classical understandings as to what constituted valued work for human beings. The work of 'homo faber' (humans as makers of things), of 'animal laborans' (the work humans must do of necessity to maintain life itself) and of 'animal rationale' (intellectual labourers) were, she notes, distinguished hierarchically from each other. The work of animal rationale was accorded highest status and that of animal laborans, lowest status. Women were assigned to the *laborious* work necessary for maintaining life, work that was not a defining feature of humanity: 'Women and slaves belonged to the same category and were hidden away, not only because they were somebody else's property but because their life was "laborious", devoted to bodily functions' (*ibid*: 72). That the low status of caring may arise from its association with managing bodily functions, especially vulnerable bodies – 'leaky bodies' – has been identified by a range of contemporary feminists as a framework for understanding the low status of women generally, and by implication for understanding the low status of care work (Irigaray, 1991, 1977; Shildrick, 1997).

Hughes *et al.* (2005) have drawn on the work of Irigaray and Shildrick to promote the metaphor of 'waste' as a means for understanding the trivialisation of both those defined as carers *and* care recipients. Doing care work is seen as engaging in a low-level life because it involves managing the most basic of human waste, be it babies' nappies, bedpans or other bodily excretions (*ibid.*: 266–268). They claim, however, that it is not just caring that is not valued but care recipients. Because *care recipients* are often seen as 'wasted' people,[20] people who are unable to produce goods and services according to the breadwinner and citizen worker models, Hughes *et al.* maintain that this contributes to the view that the care world is a useless world.

While there is no doubt that the low status of carers generally is related to their association, both personally and performatively, with managing wasteful and wasted bodies, this is not an entirely satisfactory explanation. Not all work with vulnerable or 'leaky' bodies is defined as low status. Doctors' work, especially surgical work, is intense and sometimes bloody body work; it is focused on managing and ameliorating sick and wasted bodies. Yet, it is not low status. However, unlike care work, surgery is public work; it takes place in highly visible and increasingly specialised technologised environments. Thus, the context within which the 'body' work takes place and the perceived skills it entails each have a role in determining its value, not just the work itself.

The gender of the typical worker in the field also impacts on its status. By comparison with the 'body managing' world of surgery, the care world is a largely feminine one. And what is feminine is defined as inferior regardless of the work women do (de Beauvoir, 1948). Even when women enter into the work of *animal rationale* or *homo faber,* they still find that their work is not granted equal standing (Boland, 1995; Smith, 1987). To understand the lowly status of caring and care recipients, therefore, we need to recognise the importance of the gender of the worker. There is no profession or job that women dominate that is comparable in status and power to that of men, even when that job of work is in the public sphere (Witz, 1992).

Caring is also devalued because of the way dominant conceptualisations of citizenship equate full citizenship with activity (increasingly under neoliberalism, with 'productivity') in the public spheres of life, be it in the economy, politics or culture. Cartesian rationalism, encapsulated in the phrase 'Cogito ergo sum',[21] prevails, promulgating a care-less view of the ideal citizen. The dominant understanding of citizenship is one that valorises autonomy and independence, and devalues vulnerability, dependence and interdependence, all of which are endemic to caring (Kittay, 1999).

The ways in which the 'care-less' view of the citizen sets the agenda for different fields of social action is made visible in education where future adult citizens are being prepared. The focus is on educating the citizen to achieve her or his potential in the public sphere of life, while ignoring the relational caring self (Lynch *et al.*, 2007). Within the neoliberal framework, in particular, the purpose of education is defined in terms of personalised human capital acquisition, making oneself skilled for the economy: 'the individual is expected to develop a productive and entrepreneurial relationship towards oneself' (Masschelein and Simons, 2002: 594). No serious account is taken of the reality of dependency for all human beings, both in childhood and at times of illness and infirmity (Badgett and Folbre, 1999).

The dependant citizen is left outside the frame in the Rational Economic Actor (REA) model. The way the REA world operates relationally is illustrated in Figure 4.1 below: a Hobbesian view of the world is assumed. The only recognised interdependencies are those that operate through competition for resources (marked by the Xs between individuals).

What neoliberalism is now doing, which classical liberalism did not do, is glorifying 'economic man' above the cultural or politically engaged citizen. The ideal type citizen is the cosmopolitan worker built around a calculating entrepreneurial self. It is a worker unencumbered by care responsibilities, freely available to play the capitalist game in a global context, be it as migrant labourer or market capitalist (Connell, 2002). Connell suggests that this concept of the idealised care-less worker-citizen is closely aligned with hegemonic conceptions of masculinity that equate masculinity with dominance and control. It is deeply disrespectful of the relationally engaged, caring citizen which it defines as weak and vulnerable. Instead it validates consumption and possessive individualism as defining features of human identity. Competitive individualism is no longer seen as an amoral necessity but rather as a desirable and necessary attribute for a constantly

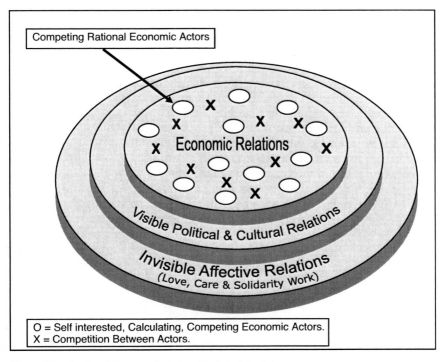

*Figure 4.1* Rational Economic Actor Model of Society

reinventing entrepreneur (Apple, 2001; Ball, 2003). Such a model of citizenship is not only care-less, it is anti-care.

The rise of neoliberalism internationally from the early 1990s onwards has strongly endorsed the individualised and entrepreneurial view of the citizen (Beck, 2000; Harvey, 2005). Like many other countries, Ireland has embraced the neoliberal framework with a vengeance (Allen, 2007; Kirby, 2002); and the idealised entrepreneurial citizen is only intermittently contested (Coulter and Coleman, 2003).

## Conclusion

This chapter has shown that carers are acutely aware of the low public status of caring, despite the value that is placed on it in personal relations. The lack of recognition is felt by both men and women, and especially by lone parents, and it is a feature of both the state and the economy. Yet there is nothing intrinsic to caring or loving that makes these activities wasteful or meaningless except the fact that they have been privatised while being publicly devalued and silenced. The idealised rational economic actor (REA) model of the citizen, that valorises the entrepreneurial self, has taken hold and with it a new macho-masculinised public sphere has emerged. This sphere disallows the use of the language of care and love in the public domain and in so doing silences carers and care recipients. If issues of love and care cannot enter public *discourse* as matters of serious political concern they cannot enter the world of *policy*, and if they are not on the policy agenda they are not on the *political* agenda. They are confined to the sub-altern world of 'weak publics' and excluded from the dominant world of 'strong publics' (Fraser, 1997).

Rather than accepting the patriarchal metaphor of wastefulness to define and understand the low status of caring, or focusing on its connection with the femaleness of caregivers, it might be helpful to contest the binaries that exist between the personal and the public spheres, and to challenge the care-less model of the citizen that the public so strongly endorses in a neoliberal, strong capitalist age. Care is a relational matter; the relationship between carers and care recipients is paralleled by one between the personal sphere and the public sphere. Recognising the interdependence of spheres and of persons is central to understanding the dynamics of care, to contesting the care-less and anti-care definitions of citizenship, and to rejecting the consignment of carers and care recipients to wasted spaces.

# 5
# Gender, Social Class and Lone Caring: The Intersectionality of Inequalities

*Kathleen Lynch and Maureen Lyons*

As carers are not singular in their identity, caring is done under very different conditions depending on the resources, abilities, power and status of both the carers and care recipients. There are deep inequalities among carers themselves that reflect and exacerbate inequalities in other social systems. While the gender inequalities in the doing of care work are well recognised in the research literature (Lewis, 1998), there is a need to explore how other differences in social class and family status intersect with gender and determine the conditions of caring.

In this chapter we examine both women's and men's accounts of their caring in our set of 30 in-depth Care Conversations with carers and care recipients (see Introduction and Appendix), confirming the importance of gender as a factor that shapes care work. We also examine differences among both women and men in terms of how social class and family status (caring alone or with others) impact on caring.

## Women as 'natural carers'

In her analysis of the way mothers managed their care work with children moving between primary and second-level school, O'Brien (2005, 2007; see also Chapter 8) found that women felt morally impelled to do most of the 'transition' work. They were the people who took responsibility for the child's well-being as they moved from one form of education to another; it was a task they felt obliged to do by virtue of being mothers. The gendered essentialism identified by O'Brien is consistent with other research that has examined gender inequality in the family, including the ways in which the family unit disguises and sanctions inequality in the doing of care and love work. The notion of 'moral imperative' or 'self sacrifice' in particular comes through in research that has examined differences in food consumption within families (Cantillon *et al.*, 2004; Goode *et al.*, 1998). These studies found that not only were women more likely to "go without", but that this was implicitly sanctioned within a hegemonic family discourse that saw the welfare of the children as the primary responsibility of the woman. Family discourses of gendered caring normalised the idea that the woman should make sacrifices for the welfare of their children. Cantillon *et al.* (2004) also found that within about 5% of all couples (in a national sample of 1,124 heterosexual couples) the woman was skimping on her meal, though the man was not, to try to ensure the rest of the family had enough. In over half these cases the woman skimped on her own meal due to lack of money. Not surprisingly therefore, women from low-income families were even more likely to experience personal deprivation in order to make ends meet (*ibid.*). The tendency for the woman to make personal sacrifices has been found to be substantially stronger in households characterised by financial systems where women are in charge of stretching household finances but do not have total, or even shared, financial control (Vogler, 1994).

### Gendered order of caring

Our study confirms O'Brien's, Cantillon's and Goode *et al.* findings about the perceived role of women. The majority of those with whom we spoke held very strongly gendered views about who was the most appropriate carer. However, there was some resistance to the moral imperative on women to care, even if it was only articulated by a minority of women and men. Interestingly, the gendered narratives on caring were also reflected in our focus groups with young people who were primary care recipients. Mary, a widow caring for an adult son with a physical and intellectual impairment gave a typical response:

> *I don't think anyone could do it as well as I can do it. Not meaning that I am better than anybody else but just that because I am his mother ... nobody loves a child more than his mother you know.* (Mary, widow, caring full-time for adult son)

The gendered moral imperative was so deeply internalised that many people regarded it as an innate disposition. There were no class, age or gender differences in the belief in the gendered care order, although there was evidence of resistance from several of the women and some men. Susan, who was caring for her son alone on a low income, typified the essentialist perspective:

> ML: Do you think there's a difference there between men and women, in terms of caring, in the sense of the caring work that is done?
> *Susan: I think there is a difference, we've different understanding and a different kind of like, I think women are a lot more geared for caring, like I mean I think it comes more **natural** to women than it does to men.* (Susan, single, primary carer of one second-level child) [Bolded text emphasis added]

Melanie, who was caring for her husband and three adult children, also held strongly gendered views on the division of care labour. She believed women were more naturally caring:

> *Well emotionally you know yourself, women and men are different, I think that **women are more caring**, you know, of all that.* (Melanie, married to Peter, caring for husband and three adult children) [Bolded text emphasis added]

The fact that women were doing the work was proof to Melanie that it must come more naturally to women:

> *I don't think men do much caring to be honest with you. If you look around you will see that it is mostly women who are doing it.* (Melanie, married to Peter, caring for husband and three adult children)

Debra, a middle class professional woman, held similar views. She believed that children needed their mother and the mother wanted to be with her children:

> *I believe that children need their mother. And too, the mother needs the children. So I mean, I would hate to think that in 20 years time I would let them go, and I really do think Alex will think that. You know, I am on at him a lot about that, I really think that Alex will look at his children when they are grown up and say they grew up so fast.* (Debra, married to Alex, primary carer of one pre-school and one primary child)

Alex believed that the arrangement whereby his wife Debra took greater responsibility for caring was a 'natural' and a 'want' on her part. She was the person who 'wanted' to take part-time work:

> *The opportunity was there for her to do it and, I don't know, from what we discussed at the time, it was more of a **natural** thing for her to do it. She just seemed **to want to do it**; it wouldn't have been as much of a 'want' from my perspective. It would have been for her so it was a relatively easy decision to make, both the environment was there in her job and **she wanted to do it**. So it was really just a matter of me supporting that decision, it was relatively easy really when I think about it.* (Alex married to Debra, secondary carer of one pre-school and one primary school child) [Bolded text emphasis added]

Some of the fathers interviewed (Alex and Donal in particular) claimed, however, that women themselves contributed to the gendered division of labour and the assumption that it was more natural for women than men to care for children. Donal spoke about how the crèche (run by women) would phone his wife Geraldine rather than him about the baby, even though he was the person who brought the baby in most days. Alex noted that because he did not collect and deliver the children to school or to their minders as often as Debra, it was assumed he was not as knowledgeable about the children. He spoke about how when his own family were asking about the children they would ask to speak to Debra:

> *Like if my mother is asking anything about the kids, she will always ask for Debra first and my sisters would be ringing up and they want to know something about Noel ... they will ask for Debra first.* (Alex, married to Debra, secondary carer of one pre-school and one primary school child)

Even though Cathy did not believe that men were unable to do care work, and she had encouraged her husband to do more care work as the children had got older, she also observed how she operated within gendered care codes at times. The assumption that women would be the carers was the default position:

> *I'd have to say my husband now has definitely kicked up a gear since they got bigger, he really wasn't that great when they were babies, and that was probably me as well, me sort of, thinking only a mother can do these things ... I think in* **retrospect I probably pushed him out, inadvertently** *when they were a lot younger, when they were babies.* (Cathy, married to Michael, co-carer of two pre-school children) [Bolded text emphasis added]

As she believed she should be caring for her children all the time, Cathy also spoke about the guilt she felt because she was not with her children during the day:

> *I'd think 'some other woman is minding my children during the day and I want to be the centre of it all in the evening'.* (Cathy, married to Michael, co-carer of two pre-school children)

The belief that women were naturally more caring was articulated by both young and old. In the focus groups with teenagers, some spoke about mothers being more expressive in care terms. However, they saw this as a problem for men as well as women; men had not learned how to do caring in an expressive way:

> *I think a lot of the time, mothers are* **naturally** *more caring in that affectionate way, and fathers do care as well but they find it harder to express it because they are not used to that. They probably did not see their own Dad*

*doing it when they were growing up.* (Roger, member of second-level middle class Focus Group) [Bolded text emphasis added]

## Doing the care work

The gendered assumptions that operated about primary caring had very practical implications in terms of the amount of care work women did compared with men. Being a primary carer did not just mean being present and doing the everyday work of caring, the hands on work, it also meant being the planner of care, the person who took responsibility for the quality of care. Women were definitively the care planners:

*So it's more, I think of it more as, mm, making sure your children's needs are met, whether they are emotional needs or whatever or just in terms of reaching their potential. And almost without ... I would feel that I am really the person that does that. ... Like Alex doesn't seem to take, ... he takes all the responsibility that I ask him to take for doing specific jobs but **he doesn't do any decision-making, you know,** unless I go to him and say 'look we need to make a decision about something'. He is not in that space at all.* (Debra, married to Alex, primary carer of one pre-school child and one primary school child) [Bolded text emphasis added]

The young people we interviewed in both focus groups also noted that their mothers did more of the hands on work of caring, even when they mothers were employed:

*My Dad doesn't do cooking, cleaning, washing or anything like that ... but she [Mum] is not the traditional housewife who stays at home; she works and she has her own life.* (Roger, member of second-level middle class Focus Group)

Clodagh and Séan were among the few interviewees to challenge gendered assumptions about care:

*I would do whatever has to be done – like I would do it alongside Clodagh except ironing, I cannot iron.* (Séan, married to Clodagh, co-carer of three primary school children)

Clodagh agreed with Séan's assessment:

*There is no such thing as that's your job and that's my job. Now maybe ironing, that's a different story! He doesn't do it, and I hate the ironing, but he doesn't do the ironing. But I mean anything else is just, you know, we both muck in!* (Clodagh, married to Séan, co-carer of three primary school children)

Despite their professed desire to share care work equally, Clodagh did do more care work than Séan. She was operating under the default position of primary carer. It was she who generally collected and delivered children from school and the child minder. She was also the person who took the children to the doctor if they were sick, and who took time off if the children were very sick. Clodagh was also the person who had the primary role in liaising with the child minder.

### Resistance to the gender care order

Although women felt morally impelled to care, and they generally did more care work than men, they did not subscribe wholeheartedly to the gendered care ideology. They often resisted being the primary carers, and many saw the injustices involved for women in doing disproportionate amounts of care work.[22]

Cathy typified the position of these women. While she was very interested in caring for her children, she claimed that her husband had a very gendered view of the division of domestic labour and care labour. Early in their marriage there was a lot of negotiation, and some tension over the issue:

> ... you know, without putting too fine a point on it, I mean I was knocking the rough edges off him in terms of domestic bliss for a number of years, in terms of, you know, cooking, cleaning, sharing responsibilities ... so certainly if I'd had a baby on top of that, em, I think oh I think it could be hugely difficult to be honest. (Cathy, married to Michael, co-carer of two pre-school children)

Despite her intense interest in her children, Debra also expressed some resistance to the unequal division of care labour between Alex and herself:

> I think I more feel the burden of ... **I am doing more than my fair share of the work**, you know, in that 'you can go to football and I can't' because you know 'if you are at football I have to be here'. You know, we can't get babysitters all the time but I wouldn't think that would be fair. So I began to feel sometimes you know when you get your little ... and I think 'I am not getting my space here' and you get a bit frustrated or you get, you know, that time of the month or whatever, and that is where it comes out in me. **You know, I am doing three-quarters or four-fifths of the work.** (Debra, married to Alex, primary carer of one pre-school child and one primary school child)[Bolded text emphasis added]

While Melanie believed that the division of care labour was somewhat more gender balanced now than in the past, she believed that 'in the caring side of things, women end up doing more than men.' (See also findings on social (leisure) time and care responsibilities in Chapter 7). She documented in some detail how her husband pursued his interest in music in the evenings after work when their children were young. He was out most nights of the week; she had to care for four young children on her own from morning until bedtime which she found 'tough going'. She also lost out in maintaining friendships through being tied to caring:

> *Of course **I wasn't happy about it**. When I looked at how much time Peter would have to himself. Like I would have had friends but a lot of my friends, I had kind of dropped away from them because you didn't want to go to them with four children during the day or even on a Sunday. They were too hard to manage because of their disabilities and all and so you couldn't really go anywhere in comfort with them and I didn't even have a night [out] in the week.* (Melanie, married to Peter, caring full-time for husband and three adult children) [Bolded text emphasis added]

Melanie outlined three scenarios as to how people became carers, either they chose it in some way, volunteered for it, or had to do it as there was no one else available. In her view, men only became carers when they had little choice in the matter, that is, when there was no suitable woman available to do it:

> *Maybe sometimes a man around here would end up caring for their wife or something. They very rarely do caring otherwise... well according to the way it is, **it's women, unless the men have to do it** I think it's women who opt for it or volunteer to do it.* (Melanie, married to Peter, caring full-time for husband and three adult children) [Bolded text emphasis added]

Maeve, who was caring for her mother with the support of her two sisters, but not her brother, held similar views:

> *I think women would be more inclined to care for her parents or his parents whereas men would be more inclined to care for their wives.* (Maeve, married to Frank, part-time carer of mother)

Paula was one of the people who did not hold gender stereotyped views about the division of care labour. However, she did not believe men and women were equal in terms of the amount of care work they undertook. And she herself had primary care responsibility for her four children:

> *I see even down in my own area that the men would be going golfing at the weekend where the women would be there doing the windows ... That's the roles that people fall into ... In the main **I feel men have a better deal than women when it comes to the caring element ... It's hard not to***

*feel **hard done by**, it's just hard.* (Paula, divorced, caring for one second-level child and three adult children) [Bolded text emphasis added]

It is clear from our interviews that there are gender power struggles going on over caring and related work. Cathy believed that there was an emerging challenge to traditional gender norms. She claimed that some *'men were struggling'* with the fact that they were not always the main or sole breadwinner in the home. She believed men who were not in high status jobs or who were unemployed found it especially difficult as roles changed. And there was little guidance on how to manage this change:

*I find ... it more difficult, you know, with men that are not working or are lower skilled. That's even more difficult, they're quite displaced sometimes, 'cos you know, if they're not working, they don't have a function in the economy and often they don't have a function in the home either ... It is trying to find new, a new place yeah, so I think that that's quite difficult really and a lot of families are working through some of that stuff and ... learning that stuff on their feet really.* (Cathy, married to Michael, co-carer of two pre-school children)

### Men, care and retaining the breadwinner status

Men who were primary carers in our conversations were aware that they were quite exceptional in either being a sole carer of an older parent or heavily involved in their children's care. Yet none of the men we interviewed, unlike the women, had had to give up their 'breadwinner' status entirely to be primary carers. When women were available to do caring, there was a default assumption that caring was women's work. This was true for care of both adults and children. When Mary (a widow caring for her intellectually and physically disabled son) was asked who would care for her son if she was not available or was unable to get respite support, she automatically said 'I suppose my daughter would have to take him'. Maeve, who was the primary carer of her 90-year-old mother also noted how it was her two sisters and herself (but not her two brothers) who shared in the caring of her mother – even though all of them were married with families. Clodagh spoke about how she would ask her sisters to care for the children if she needed help.

The men who did do a lot of primary care had a 'hero-like' status sometimes, something that did not hold for women. Speaking of the arrival of a new baby and the impact on their lives, Geraldine stated:

*I suppose I would feel the pinch more than Donal, because Donal, anything he does **he's the hero**, you know, I mean in other people's eyes for doing anything for Trisha ... And then circle of friends and everything like that, you know the comparatives aren't the same, you know his peers or people that he* *would get the opportunity to compare himself to, he can always come off best. But that is because most of them have wives that stay at home and the men would probably never do anything with the kids.* (Geraldine, married to Donal, co-carer of one pre-school child) [Bolded text emphasis added]

Geraldine believed that this assumption that men were exceptional was reinforced in the media where caring fathers were glorified if they changed nappies:

*If there's anything on the TV, you know you'd see somebody being interviewed and it's like 'oh yeah hands on dad' and 'you do nappies?' and 'ah yeah I do nappies', and then 'ah you're brilliant for doing that'! You must be kidding me, you know that's just horrendous like you know that that's validated somebody's role. You don't see women being asked if they do nappies, you know, oh yeah hands on mum you're changing their nappies ... it wouldn't even be questioned!* (Geraldine, married to Donal, co-carer of one pre-school child)

Cathy spoke about how deeply ingrained attitudes were in relation to men doing domestic work; her husband's sisters were amazed he could cook. When he visited them, they would tend to cook for him:

*I can remember the first time my husband and myself cooked together in front of his family, and his sister nearly dropped off her standing, 'cos he'd lived in England for 12 years but she didn't know he could cook. She was shocked, and she would still, she would still treat him like that [cook for him], you know whereas in his own home now, he's changed that role for himself.* (Cathy, married to Michael, co-carer of two pre-school children)

It was not assumed that men would care for children on equal terms, and Geraldine and other mothers, and one man, Donal, noted how the child-minder or crèche would automatically phone the mother rather than the father if there was a problem with the child.

The assumption that men were not carers also impacted on Tony who combined caring for his mother and managing a very small farm. He did not apply for the Carer's Allowance because it was assumed by himself and his sister it was only an entitlement for women:

*But it never crossed my mind, actually it never came into my own mind that Tony would ... maybe be entitled to something. Because I felt again ... he thought there had to be some woman in the house full-time.* (Marion, married, sister of Tony who is the primary carer of mother and uncle)

Although the men we interviewed said they did not view paid work as the overriding priority in their lives, paid work was central to their identities especially among the middle class men who were on career paths in their jobs. They had occupational ambitions, albeit ambitions that were bounded by other considerations including care.

Alex, who was quite successful in his financial services career, spoke about the importance of keeping a balance between paid work and his care life:

> *The commitment I have made is that I won't be compromising on the life piece; it would be the work piece.* (Alex married to Debra, secondary carer of one pre-school child and one primary school child)

Yet Alex did not countenance the idea that he might go part-time in his job, an option taken by his wife Debra after the birth of their son with an intellectual impairment, although at the time Debra went part-time she had a more secure, considerably more senior, and better paid job than Alex. In his view, it would have been *'highly unusual'* for a man to go part-time and *'it wasn't the done thing'*:

> *It may have been possible [to go part-time], it would have been **highly unusual**. I think it would still be unusual, although there are, I have heard of men who have done that kind of thing. I still think it would be highly unusual though, probably possible within the (name of Insurance company) environment; it's a very open and friendly environment for that kind of thing. In the bank I am in now, probably not, and certainly in the first company I joined (after the Insurance Company), **it certainly wasn't the done thing**. So I think it depends on the company you were in, the length of time you are in the environment and what the management are like.* (Alex, married to Debra, secondary carer of one pre-school child and one primary school child) [Bolded text emphasis added]

While women had developed a strong sense of duty in relation to care work, especially in relation to the care of their own children, men did not have the same sense of duty. Alex, who was employed in financial services, was open about having no wish to be the primary carer:

> *Whether or not I would have wanted to do it, at the time, probably not, in fact at the time **I didn't want to do it!** It wasn't the sort of choice I would have made, you know.* (Alex, married to Debra, secondary carer of one pre-school and one primary school child) [Bolded text emphasis added]

Not all men held stereotypical views of men caring. Tom, who was caring for his invalid father, challenged gendered views of carers and disliked the way people assumed all carers were women. He believed that male carers were not that different to women carers. He felt they *'aren't acknowledged'*, apart from politicians saying *'you are doing a great job'* which raised his *'hackles'*. Tom was very clear on the importance of caring for his father and would not consider taking on paid work:

> *If I had to work I would have to leave Dad in bed all day and when I came in the evening maybe change him or else put him into a home.* (Tom, single, caring full-time for father)

For Tom, this was not an option he would consider. As it was, he found it difficult to take time off. He reported how guilty he felt leaving his father, a guilt which is normally associated with women:

> *... there is a lot of guilt; guilt goes with it. 'I could do more' or 'I can't go away' or 'if I go away who will look after them?' It is like having a baby in the house, you wouldn't entrust a baby to someone else and if you did you would feel guilty. It is the same with a carer.* (Tom, single, caring full-time for his father)

Tom did not think he was typical of other men however. He believed that many men 'were spoilt' and did not learn to care for themselves. He believed that the reason most men got married was because they were unable to care for themselves:

> *... that is why most men get married, they don't get married for love, they get married for someone to look after them and do the cooking and the washing.* (Tom, single, caring full-time for his father)

Pearse was a small farmer, and was the primary carer of his mother. He chose to give up a labouring job in the building trade to be at home. However, Pearse was able to farm and care for his mother at the same time. He did not lose his breadwinner status by being a carer:

> *Well the way I looked at it is that she needs a bit of minding anyway and I said I would do it. Once I was in the farm I would be doing farming and that. But as I said the facilities aren't good, the amount of money you get would not be that [great] ... but I would be farming as well and both things come so you would be able to manage the farm and that but you wouldn't be able to manage anything else.* (Pearse, single primary carer for his mother)

Unlike Tom's father, Pearse's mother was not bedridden and because of that he did not find caring difficult. However, he did comment that although his sisters lived in the same county, they rarely visited and any support he received as a carer was from a local care organisation.

When men undertook primary care work, they were accorded recognition for this work that did not apply to women. They were seen to be exceptional, almost heroic by being carers. Almost all of the men we spoke with were also attached to the paid labour market, no matter how tenuously (except Tom who said he was 'unable to work due to long term illness and a physical impairment'). Two of the three single men who were primary carers (in all cases of one of their parents) were able to maintain a male breadwinner role in society while caring. Each one had inherited the family farm and care of the surviving parent was part of the responsibility that came with that inheritance. Thus, while they suffered a loss of income in being carers (especially at a time when there were many opportunities for well-paid building work outside of farming) they did not lose their male status as paid workers (their breadwinner status) – unlike Valerie who gave up a very good career, and Maeve who gave up her income from students, in both cases to care for parents.

While there are gendered rationalities and moralities in relation to care as Duncan *et al.* (2003, 2004) suggest, these are located in cultural and relational-specific contexts. In rural Ireland when land is inherited by a son, he has traditionally inherited the care of his parents who continue to live on the farm. (The same would apply to an inheriting daughter except that they are less likely to inherit land.) Care moralities are not therefore an entirely female preserve; men can also be governed by these rationalities depending on the economic and class context. Although there is evidence that men only care when there are no women there to do the care work (Gerstel and Gallagher, 2001), the economic and marital status of men is also a factor in determining this practice. Low-income farmers like Tony and Pearse, both of whom were single, had become primary carers partially through inheritance but also because of their lack of other care and financial commitments. Gendered norms interfaced with marital and economic status to determine their care roles.

## Social class matters

To have good public services, including caring services, a state must invest in them. However Ireland has one of the lowest rates of social expenditure within the EU. It ranks fourth from the bottom in terms of investment in social protection, education and health within the 27 member states, spending just 27.5% of Gross Domestic Product (GDP) on these services, which is only 2–3% above Lithuania, Latvia and Estonia, three of Europe's poorest countries. In contrast, Sweden spends almost 50% of GDP, Germany spends 45.6% and Austria spends 42.6% on social expenditures. Even Poland, at 33.6%, and the Czech Republic at 31.7% have significantly higher investment in social expenditures than Ireland (CSO, 2007b: Tables 4.1 and 4.2). The lack of social investment in services generally is reflected in the care field. In an EU study of child care in 2004, Ireland was ranked lowest (along with the UK) in terms of child care supports and maternity leave (European Commission, 2004: 8). Ireland was ranked the worst of the original 15 member states in terms of public child care provision and Denmark was the best (*ibid.*, 2004).

As it is poorer people who rely most on State services in a class-divided society like Ireland, and as lack of investment in such services means that they are not widely available and are not fully resourced, it is lower income households who are hurt most by the lack of state investment in care supports such as respite and child care. Not surprisingly therefore, the Care Conversations show that the form of care that people can offer varies with their income and resources and their social class. The cost of caring is spread out to other family members where services are missing.

Tom was a man who left school at the end of compulsory education and had worked at various unskilled jobs. He was on invalidity/disability pension due to ill health and had a medical card as his income was very low.[23] However, he found that there were many hidden costs in caring for an older, highly dependant person like his father, costs that were not covered by the allowance available to carers:

> *And if you apply for anything, you have to pay for most things. Things like nappy wipes for Dad, baby oil, baby lotion, Sudocrem, these have to be bought; he has to get these things. As well as that there is fruit, there are four lots of fruit. You can't get those on a medical card. This is my fourth liquidiser because the other three packed up because I use it every day. And when I give him meat, it has to be pureed for him.* (Tom, single, aged 50 to 60, caring full-time for his father)

Even when his father was in respite care, it was not satisfactory as the public hospital he was in lacked the resources to care for him properly:

> *... they couldn't handle him because if he wanted to use the bathroom they had to put him in the hoist ... The odd time then when they hadn't the hoist (the hoist is up in the main part of the hospital so they must have had only one hoist for the whole thing) they couldn't manage ... There had to be two or three to help him, to take off his trousers and clean him or whatever ... They weren't prepared to do that, they weren't geared for it. He was too disabled, that is what they told me, and this was over three years ago so I have him every day [since then].* (Tom, single, caring full-time for his father)

Professional couples with good incomes, like Jane and Jill and Debra and Alex, were in a very different place to Tom in the world of caring. They could make choices about caring and could generally afford the kind of care they wanted. They exercised control over the care supports they got in a way that poor carers did not.

Jane and Jill were a professional couple with third-level education. Jane explained how both she and her partner Jill could afford the care they needed to supplement their own caring. They could afford private care for their children when they needed it:

> *We pay for Tomás to go to crèche, we pay for him to go to a childminder. If we want to go out for a night we have to pay for that unless we get somebody else to mind them. It is not huge money, it is not a mortgage type of payment that you would have if they were both going to child care.* (Jane, partner of Jill primary carer of two primary school children)

Debra and Alex were also people with third-level education and professional occupations. They were able to afford pre-school care for their young son and had recently bought a holiday home that was very accessible where they could take breaks with their children. They were also greatly supported by Alex's mother with caring. It was the combination of a good income, grandmother support, and not having other adult caring responsibilities, that allowed Debra to do paid work two full days and one half day each week:

> *I don't have a poverty issue; I don't have an elderly parent issue. I also have a huge support particularly from Alex's mother ... the days I work full days Alex's mother looks after them which is just marvellous. So not only ... do I not have an issue of having to care for our parents, our parents are helping us so you know like it makes a huge difference ... She lives quite locally ... So she comes to the house in the mornings, which is brilliant ... Well he [Noel the youngest child] does go to this toddler group but she takes him.* (Debra, married to Alex, primary carer for one pre-school and one primary school child)

Elizabeth was also a middle class mother and had a successful business. She was keenly aware of the importance of having money. As one of her children had dyslexia she was also aware of the high costs involved in accessing services due to lack of publicly funded care supports:

> *We were only talking about it, the money that we are spending on him, especially at the beginning getting analysed and getting different packages. And it is a couple of hundred euro here and a couple of hundred euro there for an hour to see somebody. We didn't really have to think about it ... but if you did you would be in trouble.* (Elizabeth, partner of Nuala, secondary carer of two primary school children)

In contrast to these households, Séan and Clodagh had fewer options about working full-time. Séan's job was in sales and involved a lot of travel each week. His wife Clodagh worked in a bank branch in a middle income paid position. While Clodagh did not wish to work full-time they had little choice in the matter financially:

> ML: What were the main considerations in coming to your decision for both of you to work full-time?
> *Séan: Money – financial! Both of us needed to work to make things work. There wasn't any other consideration really – I mean it wasn't possible to have any other consideration.* (Séan, married to Clodagh, co-carer of three primary children)

Séan was not in a position to negotiate with his employers about care work. Like the other carers of children in particular, he was always worried if his children were sick as he had no flexibility to take time off. Speaking about what would happen if children were sick and who would take time off, Séan said:

> *Well, I'd say it would be Clodagh in general, like. You see, I cannot take time out unless I have someone to cover me. It doesn't come into it like. The shops are yours and if you didn't turn up you would be blamed, not [the company]. Like it is you that is coming in, into the shop I mean, so sickness don't come into it like.* (Séan, married to Clodagh, co-carer of three primary school children)

Caring is endemically unpredictable in its requirements; to do caring and loving well requires flexibility and adaptability. However, for most people in paid employment, there is little flexibility in terms of hours of attendance. The paid work world is assumed to be care-less, in the sense that it does not have to accommodate caring, unless legally required to do so. As noted by Clodagh in relation to non-mandatory family-friendly policies, their operation is at the discretion of the employer, not of the employee. Not surprisingly therefore, jobs such as those involved in sales, banking, administration, etc., do not have the kind of flexibility that caring requires. While those who are self-employed in areas like consultancy, or in certain types of employment where discretion has been negotiated by trade unions (such as 'term' leave given during school holidays to civil servants), are able to be flexible around caring, most people lack this flexibility and this is especially true for those in routine jobs that require little skill. As unskilled workers can easily be replaced they do not seek flexibility for caring for fear of losing their jobs. Social class impacts on care, therefore, in two very distinct ways: on the one hand it makes paid care unaffordable for low-income workers in a privatised care system, and on the other, it limits people's flexibility as primary carers owing to lack of autonomy in low-income jobs.

## Caring alone

While those who were living in partnerships faced challenges in caring, arising from their social class, or their gender, those who were sole carers experienced the greatest challenges. This happened both because of isolation and because of the difficulty of living on a single income.

The rhetoric of 'community care' or 'family care' which is so strong in public care narratives tends to conceal not only the fact that it is women who do most of the caring but also the isolation and lack of resources experienced by lone carers. There is an implicit assumption in the concepts of family or community care that there is a group there to support carers, or at the very least a partner or other supporting person in carers' lives. There is little public commitment to put support services in place for those who do not have them within their own family (or sometimes friendship) circle.

### Lone carers of young children

The Care Conversations tell a story that is in line with similar research internationally with lone parent carers (Oliker, 2000). Not only was the cost of child care premised on the assumption that it is funded from a double-income household budget, lone parents also had to manage the emotional and social isolation that was part of being a lone parent family. Being stigmatised was also part of the experience of those who were single parents.

The one parent families with young children whom we talked with (Susan, Sasha, Paula and Regina) had not availed of paid child care as they could not afford it. Being the sole primary carers of young children made it impossible to combine care work and paid work, not only because child care was too expensive relative to earnings, but also because of the difficulty of managing the time logistics around paid work and caring. Paula, whose children were now older, could not afford paid child care when her children were very young. She lived solely on the lone parent family allowance until the children went to school. Sasha was living exclusively on the lone parent family allowance at the time of our conversation as her youngest child was too young to go to school. She wanted to work part-time but she could not manage to get even a few hours of work due to the tight schedule she had to follow collecting and dropping off the older two children to school, which was a bus ride away.

Even though Susan was in employment and Regina was studying for a postgraduate degree, neither could afford paid care. Susan relied heavily on her own parents who were very supportive, particularly her father who was able to mind her son in the evening after school. This enabled her to take a course she needed to do for work. She felt uncomfortable about having to do this but she had little choice:

*I'm doing a management course at night time and I don't get in ... until about quarter past ten and there's no way I'd leave him [her son] that long, from six 'til a quarter past ten. And it's far away, so if anything happened, if I left him in the house ... So my da, because my ma works nights, my da minds him, he comes in from work at six and Sam is there when he comes in so he gives Sam his dinner on a Monday and Sam goes, like I drop Sam straight there about ten to six, after work before that.* (Susan, single, primary carer of second-level school child)

While having family support enabled Susan to stay in paid employment, it also induced guilt and anxiety. It was not without emotional cost:

*So I always think oh god like I asked my dad ... and I know it's only temporary, it's only for a few months but, they're very good, they're very, very obliging like that but I just don't want them to think, ever think that I'm taking advantage, do you know what I mean.* (Susan, single, primary carer of one second-level school child)

Regina was from Eastern Europe and had no family in Ireland. She was divorced and was completely alone in care terms. She was living in private rented accommodation which was expensive, unstable and difficult to access as someone seen as a 'foreigner'. She also had very little money:

*I mean I never go out, never ever, I can't afford to go out. I don't smoke, I don't drink at all, I just count each penny, lots of my clothes are second hand.* (Regina, divorced, primary carer of one second-level school child)

As noted in Chapter 3, Regina believed that the lack of support for one parent families was crippling on every front as child benefit was too low. She described child benefit as *'a joke'* because it was so low relative to the cost of living especially for lone parents. Her migrant status also made life difficult for her as her qualifications (degree and diplomas) and experience from her home country were not recognised:

*They always say 'You have no experience in business in this state.' You have everything, your diploma is from (name of country) you have experience there. [But they say] 'No you have no experience you didn't get the job.* (Regina, divorced, primary carer of one second-level school child)

The irony for her was that she got no financial support while pursuing a part-time postgraduate course which she needed to obtain employment:

*If you are in part-time studies you lose everything. You lose the grants from the government, from the corporation [local authority].* (Regina, divorced, primary carer of one second-level school child)

Low-income lone parents of children had very constrained lives financially, emotionally, socially and in terms of mobility. Even when lone parents were in employment, being a primary carer was not only costly but was a responsibility that could not be easily devolved to others. Like all parents, it tied them to times and spaces which were not flexible and which could not be negotiated (McKie *et al.*, 2002). While couple-based households could negotiate the interface between time, space and paid work among themselves, lone parents had no such option.

### Lone carers of adults: being overwhelmed

Caring for adult dependants has significant long-term implications for carers in terms of their health, income, pension, sleep, leisure and quality of life generally (see Bittman 2004 for a review). When long-term care for one or more adults is being provided by only one person, especially if the person is co-resident, the demands are even greater (*ibid.*).

While the lone parents to whom we spoke struggled to manage care and paid work, or care and welfare, or paid work, care and education, they saw this as a clearly defined phase of life no matter how arduous. Carers of dependant adults did not hold this view. They could see no immediate end to their caring lives, a life that was often seriously constrained by lack of supports and services.

Melanie was caring for her husband who had a physical impairment and two adult children who had intellectual disabilities. Her experience of care was one of exhaustion and lack of hope for the future:

> *And like when you are minding children, like they grow up and then they will be gone but I know that this is not going to happen with them. You know? That means that it goes on, there is no end to it.... I don't know to be honest if they will ever get to the independent stage that I would like them to get to.* (Melanie, married to Peter, caring for husband and three adult children)

Her sense of exasperation was compounded by the lack of supports available, again reflecting the lack of value placed on this care:

> *You are just on your own so much with it, carrying this heavy burden that you cannot really share with anyone and no matter how hard it is you just have to keep going with it. I think that is the hardest part. Maybe if you had a lot of family or someone you could rely on to help you with things it would be a bit easier.* (Melanie, married to Peter, caring for husband and three adult children)

Caring created a sense of exhaustion and frustration when it had to be given without adequate resources or respite. Valerie was caring for both her mother and father whose health had deteriorated steadily over a seven-year period. She found the work relentless. While she did get reasonably good respite support from her local community hospital (and great support by

Kathleen Lynch and Maureen Lyons 111

comparison with other carers we spoke to as she had a right to one respite week out of every four weeks though this did not always happen because of bed scarcities), she did not find it sufficient. The demands of caring for two sick people were such that she was worn out by the time she got respite:

> *But you just have to keep telling yourself, the week's respite coming, you'll, you know, hang on, hang on, and it is, bearable but only just. When one of them is sick, but see when two of them [are] sick, the adrenalin really is pumping, and your nerves are just through the roof, I don't think any human being should have to do it, I mean I really don't … I do look forward to that respite week, and I try to put as much into that week as possible, you know, to get out and about … You are completely worn down and as I say, the stress would get to you more than anything, I mean there's many a time I find I just can't cope with it, but what choice do you have?* (Valerie, single, caring full-time for parents)

While Valerie was quite resigned about the relative lack of support for carers, Anita was not. She was actively involved in fighting for support and respite services for children and adults with intellectual disabilities. She mentioned problems with lack of respite and support for her daughter 26 times in the course of the conversation. As she saw it, the only way to get care supports was to fight for them:

> *I have a battle on my hands to get what I need for her and anything that I have got so far has been a battle. Nothing was handed to us right from Day Centre to the extra help … Three or three and a half years ago I came home from England and I waited almost a year for services.* (Anita, separated, caring for adult child)

Even when respite services were available they were not always ideal. Those who had low incomes had no choice but to use the service offered no matter how unhappy they were with it. Tom explained how three years previously an arrangement had been made to take his father into a day care centre each Wednesday. He noted how the physiotherapy that was supposed to be available at the time did not materialise and that consequently 'his arm is completely locked, his fingers are bent in'. Care involved physical work such as lifting and dirty work where people were incontinent. In Tom's case the day care arrangement only lasted one month:

> *I got a phone call from [name of hospital] on a Wednesday, [after] he was going for a month: 'we can no longer handle your dad, he is too disabled.' Now they were the professionals but what they wanted down there in the Day Centre is what I would call 'the walking wounded'. That was grand for a*

*month but after the month was up they couldn't handle him.* (Tom, single, caring full-time for father)

## Conclusion

In this chapter we have shown how gender, class and family status structure inequalities in care. The world of caring is highly gendered: unpaid family caring exists as a social space where women are the default carers unless there is no suitable woman available. In Ireland, 99% of those doing full-time unpaid home-related work, much of which is care work, are women (Central Statistics Office, CSO, 2007b: 10), and so are most of those doing paid care work. The patterns are the same in other OECD countries including the US and Canada (Bittman, 2004). The responsibility for caring is not experienced equally by all women however (or men if they are primary carers). Low-income carers are especially vulnerable, being unable to afford many of the care supports they need at the time that they need them. Consequently, they are forced out of employment, often when their children are young, as they cannot afford good quality child care; their unemployment further exacerbates their poverty. Low-income carers of adults often have to wait for extended periods of time to access state care services as they cannot afford to buy readily available private services. When they do get support, such as respite or home help, it is often for short periods and is not adequate for what they need. Moreover, low-income carers who are employed are often working in jobs that lack both the autonomy and flexibility that enables them to manage caring in their own terms.

Lone carers, be it of children or adult dependants, are also heavily burdened in care terms, especially due to the lack of accessible and affordable care-support services. While couple-based households can share care responsibilities, no matter how unequal that division of care may be, no such option exists for sole carers. Those who are sole carers and poor have little independence; they experience social isolation, stress, lack of leisure and general exhaustion. Those who are unpaid carers of adults are especially burdened by caring if they are poor and without supports. The demands of caring are exacerbated by a lack the hope of an independent future, and the challenge of living within an uncertain time frame.

The care-less view of the citizen that informs public policy-making means that those who were already economically vulnerable are made even more vulnerable by their caring due to under resourcing. This was especially true for lower income women and men, and for lone carers of adults and of children.

In mapping affective inequality, then, we need to take not just gender but also class and family status into account. Generally speaking, the effect of gender is to disadvantage women *vis-à-vis* men in the affective system. However, class-based inequality means that on the whole economically advantaged carers are better placed than economically disadvantaged ones. Moreover, those living in families where the care can be shared between two adults are better off than lone carers, primarily because of the lack of emotional and practical support from others. These factors of gender, class and family status intersect to produce complicated patterns of affective inequality.

# 6
## Love Labouring: Power and Mutuality

*Kathleen Lynch, Maureen Lyons and Sara Cantillon*

Most research on care is taken from the perspective of the carer (Hughes *et al.*, 2005). Within this work, the carer is represented as the giver, the care recipient the receiver; the care recipient has needs, the carer is less needy; the carer is strong and able bodied, the care recipient is weak and vulnerable. This understanding of care portrays it as a deeply asymmetrical relationship and leads us to expect marked power inequalities within it, with the caregiver exercising power over care recipients.

This chapter challenges these understandings. We begin by discussing the issues generally, in light of the stance taken by many disability activists on the relationship between care and power. Then, using data from our set of 30 in-depth Care Conversations with carers and care recipients and our two focus groups with teenagers (see Introduction and Appendix), we examine the views of carers and some care recipients about their experience of love and care in the primary care settings. We show the way power and control is exercised over carers and illustrate the mutuality and interdependency that is at the heart of love labouring forms of care in particular. This chapter is particularly concerned with power relations *within* care relations. Chapter 7 takes up some issues of power relations between those who care and third parties who benefit from their care work.

### Disability, care and power

There has been a strong reaction to the representation of care recipients as 'needy' or a 'burden' by activists in the disability movement, with some activists in the UK disowning the concept of care entirely (Wood, 1991). Disabled scholars have highlighted the ways in which the organisation of care for disabled people has traditionally been both disempowering and oppressive. It has provided the rationale for the institutionalised dependency of many disabled people, and thereby compromised both their quality of life and life chances (Oliver, 1993). Morris (1991, 1993) has also critiqued feminist work for being insufficiently attentive to the oppressive ways in which care operates from a disabled person's perspective. The solution to the problem of dependency has been presented as that of Independent Living and direct payments to personal assistants for disabled people in particular. As noted by Shakespeare (2006: 136), however, Independent Living is an option that has been most availed of by those who have static permanent physical impairments and people with chronic or degenerative illnesses and impairments. People who need extra special care and support, ranging from children to very old people who are frail,[24] are often not in a position to organise independent living or direct payments to personal assistants. So while independent living is suited for those who desire it, and have the capacity to organise it and manage it, many severely dependant persons are not able to avail of it even if they do desire it. Moreover, all types of care arrangements have strengths and limitations, in terms of flexibility, reliability, privacy, risk, agency, choice, privacy, responsibility and control (*ibid.*: 149). Autonomy is undoubtedly a priority value for some, and this frequently finds expression in the Independent Living movement. However, autonomy may not be prioritised or desired by others, as it may involve too high a level of responsibility, energy and risk. This is especially true for those with profound intellectual and physical disabilities (Kittay, 1999).

What the Disability Studies perspective also fails to highlight is that even though some people have higher care needs than others throughout life, over the life span, everyone is at some time a net care recipient (Shakespeare, 2006). There is no caregiver who has not at some time been a care recipient no matter how poor that care may have been (Lynch, 2007). Carers and care recipients cannot be treated as distinct categories of people, who only either provide care or receive it. Although severely physically and intellectually disabled people are unlikely to be caregivers, there are a wide range of people who move between caregiving and receiving at different times in life, or at different periods in the one day. A person may spend time caring for an intellectually disabled child all day and spend the evening when the child is in bed getting support and care from a friend or partner. Most parents who are intense carers when children are young become net care recipients if they live to be old and frail and/or to develop severe impairments.

Drawing a neat dichotomy between the carer and care recipient is also not appropriate given the interdependencies, reciprocity and mutuality that is endemic to primary care relations in particular. Caring is embedded in relations of mutuality and reciprocity (Strazdins and Broom, 2004). No matter how limited the reciprocity may be, care relations have a reciprocal dimension, even if it is giving or withholding a nod or a hand to show appreciation on the part of a vulnerable care recipient. Where care is given within families or defined communities, care relations exist over protracted periods of time, and reciprocity may take the form of a generalised reciprocity (Sahlins,

1972) where the person from whom one receives care is not necessarily the person to whom one provides it.

Even though disability researchers have rightly focused on the power that the carer exercises over the care recipient, and the fact that caring is not always done for noble motives, care is not always given on the carer's terms, not least because of the power of the care recipient to refuse certain forms of care and because of the cultural mores that exist in relation to care. While one party to the relationship may undertake much more love and care work than the other, the publicly defined care recipient is not necessarily a silent or powerless partner, a passive recipient of someone else's love labour. People who are very vulnerable due to illness or infirmity can and do show appreciation for care or fail to show it; they can call on culturally available moral imperatives to care to enforce their care expectations. Moreover, the profoundness of their needs calls forth a level of attention that may not be desired by the carer. It is through the impact of culturally defined moral imperatives to care that care recipients exercise control over women carers in particular (Bubeck, 1995; O'Brien, 2007).

With very young children, and adults who are vulnerable and unable to communicate their needs, the imperative to care is not just culturally defined, it also arises from their deep dependency; the command to care arises from having to provide for survival needs. The failure to meet the survival and elementary care needs of vulnerable dependants is highly visible and this visibility exercises its own control on carers. So while vulnerability can and does allow for the carer to exercise power over the care recipient, it also enables the care recipient to exercise some unspoken power over their carers as the neglect or abuse of care recipients can and does become visible, often within a short time. If society fails to monitor the care of the vulnerable either in family or institutional settings, however, then the power of dependency itself to make carers' neglect or abuse visible is limited accordingly.

What is also not sufficiently attended to in the disability discourse on care is the fact that human beings live in affective relational realities especially in their primary care relations; they have emotional ties and bonds that compel them to act as moral agents, to act 'other wise' rather than 'self wise' (Tronto, 1991, 1993). Their lives are governed not only by the demands of economically and politically determined survival, but also by the rules of lay normativity (Sayer, 2005: 35–50). Arising from their affective relational existence, trust and commitment are central to the primary care relations of most human beings. Love labourers are expected to be trustworthy and committed over extended periods of time. They do not do care work on a hire and fire basis like paid care labourers and as such are bound by sets of long-term expectations. While such expectations vary in scope and intensity cross-culturally, and are deeply gendered, trust remains central to the primary care relationship. Care recipients exercise control on carers therefore through the trust fund that underpins the primary care relations; it is this trust fund that generates guilt, guilt on the part of carers that they are not doing enough and on the part of the care recipients that they are expecting too much.

Thus, while the feminist literature on care highlights the extraordinarily high levels of care work that women do relative to men, and while disability researchers highlight the importance of reducing unnecessary care dependencies for disabled people, there is a need to recognise that care relations are also embedded in relationships of interdependency, mutuality and reciprocity, and trust. While the carer does exercise power over the care recipient, it is a power that is tempered by cultural mores and conventions, by the survival needs of dependants, and by an assumption of trustworthiness that is often central to individual identities. There are also relations of mutuality and reciprocity within care relations that are not always visible to the outside observer.

## Power in care relations

For many decades, a model of care has taken root, both within families and in institutions, in which carers are assumed to be virtuous (including secondary paid carers). Little or no attention has been given to care recipients' perspectives, including those of children (Archard, 1993). Even though carers exercised power without much direction or regulation especially when caring for adults, and at times abused their power, the privacy of the family was sacrosanct in the liberal political framework (Hobson, 2000). Those service providers who provided care in the public sphere often exercised a colonial-style relationship towards disabled people and other highly dependant persons, developing careers through prolonging their dependencies. These subjects were not admissible in public discourse however. A paternalistic and charity model of care prevailed, reinforced by ideology and scholarship that viewed those who were vulnerable, for whatever reason, as people who did not need to have agency (McDonnell, 2007). The potential for the abuse of power in care relations was and is considerable therefore, as care relations are assumed to be trustworthy, and the trustworthy tend not to be questioned. The care power of parents is lightly policed, and is only sanctioned if they engage in very serious transgressions through gross neglect and abuse. Everyday abuses, including the slapping or hitting of children, is not an offence in most countries, unless it takes extreme forms. The abuse of power through the neglect and violation of older people within families and care homes is only beginning to be recognised internationally.

However, to focus too much on the potential abuse of power in care relations may hide the reality that the primary care that is provided in love labouring is personally defined and non-transferable, as it is given in the contexts of pre-established relationships with a unique history and assumed future involving continuity and attachment (Barnes, 2006: 8–9). Relations of attachment are no different to other human relations in that there is a power dimension to them, but power can be exercised both ways. In the case of primary relationships, the power the care recipient exercises over the carer is embedded in the trustfulness of that relationship. Even if the trust is broken, primary relations are defined by expectations of trust, and the reneging on this is a deviation from what is expected. Inattentiveness, neglect and abuse by carers is recognised as such and sanctioned if and when it becomes known. One of the clearly defined ways in which care recipients exercise control over their carer therefore, is by bringing the cultural norms of care into the care relationship and relaying that to the carer by naming their love and care desires.

People with intellectual disabilities, older people, people with physical disabilities and teenagers who took part in our Care Conversations and focus groups were all aware of their power in their relationships. Even though carers realised they had power to leave and place the highly dependant person in some form of institutional care, especially if caring for adult relatives, they were also aware that choices were limited at times. Those for whom they cared exercised power over them by communicating expectations of trustfulness and by relaying the cultural codes that prescribed particular forms of care as most desirable. Their vulnerability as care recipients also acted as a break on the power of carers as the latter knew they sometimes had little choice about the level of care they needed to provide.

### Exercising power: moral agents, cultural codes and survival requirements

While Valerie was committed to the care of her parents and claimed she was doing this work voluntarily, it was also evident that her parents' desires played a central role in continuing to care for them at home. She saw herself as a moral person, a person who had made a decision not to place her parents in institutional care even though the cost was very high for her personally:

> *They haven't spent the last seven years in an institution; you can always look back and say you did your best. And I certainly did! Hopefully! Whereas if they did go to an institution you would have to live with that, rightly or wrongly! So I think it was not in my make up to be able to do that. So that is the top and bottom of it really.* (Valerie, single, caring full-time for parents)

It was not entirely a free choice for Valerie however, as her parents exercised power over her in determining the kind of care they received. They were not passive recipients of care. Valerie noted how her parents wanted the security of her presence, being around and available, even if they did not need her at that given moment:

> It's a case of 'I'm ok so, you, as long as I can see you are there in the back-ground' ... they are I suppose more into themselves, they want to be looked after; they want to be cared for regardless of the cost. They don't even think about it and it's the fear aspect as well. Thinking well 'if she goes, I'm going too' (Valerie, single, caring full-time for parents)

Her mother was strongly resistant to the idea of going into a nursing home and Valerie was well aware of this:

> Yes but Mummy would make it very clear, like 'I'm not going in there!' And it makes it worse when they have their mental faculties; you know they're totally there, totally compos mentis! Whereas with somebody that wasn't all there, you can kind of cajole them or some poor people don't know if it's night or day, they don't know what is going on and so it might not matter to them as much. (Valerie, single, caring full-time for parents)

The pressure to care according to prescribed cultural norms took different forms but was articulated by care recipients nonetheless. Maeve was a co-carer of her 90-year-old mother and was well aware of her mother's desires to be cared for in her old age by her own family:

> Mum would be so proud of her family that ... 'they look after me' and I know she has said that she would hate to go into a nursing home and she would hate to be looked after like that. And the aspect of her family not wanting to look after her that would upset her as well. (Maeve, married to Frank, part-time carer of mother)

Her mother's desires exercised a strong control over Maeve even though it caused her inconvenience at times and a loss of income as she had to give up renting a room to a student in her house to care for her mother.

Monica, a widow in her late 70s who was being cared for by her adult daughter, spoke about how the moral imperative (on women especially) to care for their parents was a longstanding cultural expectation. She had cared for her own mother and her mother had cared for her mother:

> It was always the thing ... something you had to do. You had to look after your parents. Well anybody that I knew ... that was what you saw, and my mother was the same with her own [children]. My grandmother lived with us you know. (Monica, widowed, being cared for by co-resident single daughter)

Mary, a widow in her late 50s, was caring for her son Declan who had both intellectual and physical disabilities. She found it difficult at times, especially since her husband died and her two adult children moved away:

> *I suppose there are times that you just feel how come I got landed with this but I mean that would only be the rare occasion.* (Mary, widow, caring full-time for adult child)

Not to care for Declan, while she was able to, was unthinkable:

> *He is mine and he is here and I have to look after him and I will continue to look after him. I just couldn't walk away from him and put him into a Home ... it is a totally different thing looking after your own child because they are part of you.* (Mary, widow, caring full-time for adult child)

The control that care recipients exercised over carers also arose from their extreme physical dependency. Tom's father was unable to move without help and needed constant assistance. He relied almost totally on Tom, and Tom was aware of the implications of this:

> *I don't leave him by himself, he can't be left by himself. I would be afraid God forbid if anything happened when I was out and he was here by himself ... I was down with my brother during the week and they wanted me down to stay for a couple of days but with care you are probably aware there is a lot of guilt; guilt goes with it. 'I could do more' or 'I can't go away' or 'if I go away who will look after them?' It is like having a baby in the house, you wouldn't entrust a baby to someone else and if you did you would feel guilty. It is the same with a carer.* (Tom, single, caring full-time for father)

While Tom was a primary carer, he was also disabled himself. He saw dependency and interdependency as an inevitable feature of human existence:

> *You have to go through it [being cared for] yourself. And at some stage of our lives we will be either one or the other or both, we will either be someone who is cared for or we will care for someone or we will be both.* (Tom, single, caring full-time for father)

Seeing dependency as inevitable was not an uncommon view. Pearse, who was the primary carer of his mother, had a similar perspective. He believed that if you lived your life with someone, caring for them was part of what you contracted to do:

> *If a man is living with a wife he would look after the wife anyway, it's the same thing, it is no different ... We'll say you could have an old person to look*

*after or you could have a wife to look after. You have children to look after anyway and it's the same thing ... and that is the way I feel about it.* (Pearse, primary carer for mother)

The power that care recipients exercise over carers is not always articulated. It is assumed and unspoken especially in the case of children. Their deep and prolonged dependency calls forth a power over carers that is assumed rather than stated. The implicit power that children exercise over parents was evident with parents who had very young children. Debra was the mother of Noel, aged 2, who had an intellectual impairment and health problems. She was keenly aware of the implications of this for care even though Noel could not speak about his physical and intellectual needs. She had taken a job share arrangement at work to accommodate the care work involved in managing his health and disability needs:

*He would be a more than average sickly small child. Not very bad but you know I spend a lot of time at the doctor's, you know. I spent a lot of time trying to look at his hearing and different kinds of things, right.* (Debra, married to Alex, primary carer of one pre-school and one primary school child)

Sara and her husband were also bound by the security of routine that her intellectually impaired daughter Phoebe needed; she held power over them in this regard, albeit not in a conscious way:

*She lives her life by routine so ... my husband and myself are living Phoebe's routine. I cannot go anywhere without first considering Phoebe. She goes to 7:30 Mass on a Saturday night, I couldn't go because I had a meeting, I had to have a taxi take her to Mass and take her home again.* (Sara, married to John, caring part-time for daughter and husband)

Some care recipients were also aware that they had needs and were able to exercise the command for care. Monica was an older person who was now living with her daughter. She had made it clear to them that if she were to get care supports, what she wanted was *'care in the home ... I would hate to go into a Home'.* She felt that she had made demands on her daughter that might have been excessive at one time. However, it was fear that drove her to make those demands:

*I suppose it is fine to say that you will never demand of your children. It is fine in theory, yes. I would say at one stage when I was very sick about four or five years ago (I was sick here for about two or three months before I went into hospital) and I was very demanding of Denise ... Yes, I knew I was doing it but I couldn't help it. I was frightened ... I had this fear that she would go out and*

*I would be left.* (Monica, widow, being cared for by co-resident single daughter)

Monica was keenly aware of the implications of her expectations. Yet the fear of deep dependency, and the neglect that might arise from this, was an overriding concern:

> *You have fears, of course you have fears, you know, that you won't be able to do things for yourself ... That is the biggest thing of all ... That is hard, yes ... I would find it very hard and my friend says to me all the time, sometimes we talk, and she'd say to me 'I wouldn't like to have to go into a Home', but at the same time I wouldn't like to think that you would be dependent and more or less a burden on anybody. What the solution is, I don't know what the answer to it is. But there is an awful fear of nursing homes and they are not making it any better for us now.* (Monica, widow, being cared for by co-resident single daughter)

The care expectations that Monica placed on her family were not unrelated to her lack of choice about care. As she was living on the statutory old age pension, she knew she had few choices about the quality of care she would get if she had to leave her own home. Her social class status impacted on her care choices:

> *If you haven't got the money you don't have many choices do you? ... If you haven't got the money, no! Otherwise you would need to have a lot of family support that you would have the guarantee of someone to look after you either in your own home or living with them. ... I suppose I am lucky to have that at the moment. But you never know what the future brings and sure very few people have the sort of money that it would take to be in a good nursing home ...* (Monica, widow, being cared for by co-resident single daughter)

The power to exercise a preference in terms of care is not the preserve of adults. It can also happen with children. Jane explained how her partner Jill and herself had to change their morning routine to suit their youngest child who wanted to spend an extra half an hour with his parents before play school rather than with his childminder:

> *For a while we dropped him to his childminder for the half hour and she would bring him to the crèche but he really didn't like that so we changed it and now we bring him. He really reacted going to the childminder for the half hour, it was disruptive for him ... so we listened to that and responded and now we do it, or I generally do it.* (Jane, partner of Jill, primary carer of two primary school children)

## The necessities of life: food

In all of the conversations with carers, there was talk of food preparation as a central function of caring. Cooking took time and was a major focus of many carers' days. Some people prepared meals a day in advance to have them partially ready when they came in from work in the evening; this was especially true for those with young children. Susan spoke about how she had a system of food preparation for herself and her young son:

> *I'd make the dinner but I'd leave it kind of like half prepared from the night before and before I go out in the morning I'd leave him probably a sandwich or noodles. He's able to make noodles in the microwave so I'd leave those [for when he came in from school].* (Susan, single, primary carer of one second-level school child)

Séan and Clodagh, who had three children in primary, school had a similar practice:

> *The way we work it is when we come in, in the evening they will have had their dinner and then when we come home in the evening we have our dinner ready from the night before. But Séan is also getting ready the dinner for the next day and that dinner goes with them to the childminder's for the next day.* (Clodagh, married to Séan, co-carer of three primary school children)

For those tending to the needs of older people or people with special food requirements, the preparation of food was a significant task requiring considerable planning and mindfulness. The needs and preferences of the care recipients exercised strong control over the timing of meals and the way food was prepared. The time and attention that Tom devoted to preparing food for his father and maintaining a balanced diet for him exemplified the importance of food in care. Because Tom was conscious of the very hard life his father had had as a young boy he was focused on giving him the best of care:

> *He is not like a normal person in that when I give him his meals I have to do it in courses; when I give him his breakfast in the morning I give him first of all cranberry juice and sometimes I might boil a herb for him, lemon balm and I put a bit of honey in that. Then he will have a cereal and through the cereal then I would put whatever fruit is there, a banana maybe, and Danone multi-vitamin stuff and whatever juice is there. I juice the fruit and I give him fruit juice; then he will have his cup of tea and his bit of bread and maybe some bread and cheese. Then around 12 o'clock maybe a cup of de-caf and maybe a biscuit of two. Then he will have his lunch about 1:30 ... I give him his dinner and then put him down to bed, change him and clean him and put him down. Then I might lie down myself for an hour or two and get up around 5pm and*

*if he wants to use the toilet I will look after him there and then clean him and give him his tea around 5:30. And the tea pot is going until 9 o'clock and then 8:30 or 9:00 I will give him a cup of cocoa or drinking chocolate and a sleeping tablet and his pain killers and then put him to bed and hold his hand until he goes to sleep.* (Tom, single, caring full-time for father)

Maeve's 90-year-old mother Bridgid liked her food and she liked to have company when she was eating. Maeve tried to ensure that there was regularity in the timing of meals and she kept her company when she was eating. She organised lunch at mid-day to suit her mother and prepared a full breakfast each day:

*Well up in the morning about 8 o'clock and prepare breakfast; she likes juice, porridge, tea and toast. She has an enormous appetite, she really has, I think that is what keeps her going. This would be on a Monday, Tuesday and Wednesday ... We would always sit down for breakfast together.* (Maeve, married to Frank, part-time carer of mother)

While Maeve was aware that having company while eating was not immediately essential for her mother's physical well-being, she knew that this was something that was a pleasure for her mother, something that made her life meaningful. Given that her mother might have few other pleasures in her day, she felt morally impelled to enable her to have this enjoyment. This desire to attend to her mother led to extra work for Maeve in terms of managing meals, as some other family members did not want to eat with her mother because she had difficulty managing food, spilling it and missing her mouth at times:

*I know that [my sister's] husband doesn't like mum at the table eating because she just has dreadful table habits and dribbles and things like that, it doesn't bother me and it doesn't bother [my husband] Frank.* (Maeve, married, part-time carer of mother)

Keeping company with people while they were eating was important for those whose social lives were curtailed due to health, a physical impairment or age. Anita explained how her daughter who has an intellectual impairment, Beth, liked to have somebody with her when she was having breakfast so Anita was available to share breakfast with her each morning.

### Safety

Feelings of safety were also important in care and for older people this meant having someone nearby whom one could call on immediately in times of need. Tony's mother was in her 80s and was fearful of being left alone. Her fears were very rational and arose from the fact that she unable to walk independently due to vertigo. She feared falling if she walked, so she did not want to be left alone:

> *She is not happy now if she is left on her own. When I am gone from her now, she is waiting until I come back again.* (Tony, single, caring full-time for mother and uncle)

Valerie spoke about a similar desire on the part of her parents, their wish that she would be 'there in the background' even if they had no particular need for her at the time. Monica, who was being cared for by her daughter, was also very focused on access to care and feeling safe. She spoke a lot about safeguards. When her daughter who lived with her was away she would tell her other children to:

> 'Keep your mobile on' and I would keep the mobile on and have it beside me when I am in bed ... And I'd say, 'If I ring in the middle of the night you do know it is me'; so I always have those safeguards. (Monica, widow, being cared for by co-resident single daughter)

The power that care recipients exercise over carers is not just a culturally determined form of power, it derives from their survival needs, their need to be fed, to be safe, and a basic social need for company. Highly dependant persons such as Tom's father who was unable to walk, or Beth, Anita's daughter who had an intellectual impairment, were not just in need of food, they needed meals at very specific times and/or very particular types of food. Meals were also important social events in the lives of people who are isolated due to infirmity or a physical impairment. Maeve was conscious of her mother's need for company at meal times as was Anita of her daughter Beth's needs; both carers organised the times and format of meals to suit the needs of those they cared for while Tom ensured a highly regular routine of meal times for his father which not only involved feeding him but demonstrating affection and attentiveness in the process.

## Teenage children's views on care: the power of presumption

Care was something that teenagers presumed they would get. It was not a problematic to be negotiated. The love labouring of their parents was an expected food on the table of emotional life. Given that parents are required by law in most countries to care for their children in their dependant years, it is not surprising that the young teenagers with whom we held conversations were mindful of their parents' obligations to care for them. Care was seen as a given; it was something that was inevitable, expected, an assumed provision in their everyday existence:

> *I think it is an unfamiliar association between 'care' and home; it's just that it is a given, do you know what I mean? Like in a way it is taken for granted ... It is not a word that is associated with home in that kind of way. It is like care is there but it is taken for granted, that kind of way.* (Mark, member of teenage middle class Focus Group)

The young people in this youth group saw care as providing the very basics of life, food, shelter and clothing. It was not seen as a problem or something to be negotiated, it was a right, a given:

> *I think it's mostly about food, things like basic needs, food and clothing and just basic shelter. I think care is like somewhere to sleep, pretty much.* (James, member of second-level middle class Focus Group 1)

Care at home meant being fed to some. Michael equated care with food:

> *Food ... Probably because I eat a lot. That is where most people would get most of their food. I think food and being fed it is a very important part of care.* (Michael, member of second-level middle class Focus Group)

While food was an important signifier of care for teenagers, including the quality of food and the care with which food was prepared, food was also a metaphor for care:

> *And it could go deeper, as in like rather than just feeding your stomach, feeding your imagination, not just food for your stomach, but food for our mind, food for growing up and things like that.* (John, member of second-level middle class Focus Group)

In the youth group involving working class students, food was also centrally associated with care, although care was also about attention, affection and financial resourcing:

> *Dinner ... love ... Bedtime stories when you were little ... They'd give you a hug ... They buy you new clothes and things ... They give you money ... Always on your side.* (Declan, Alan, Shane, Chris and Thomas, from second-level working class Focus Group)

Young people were also able to exercise control over carers through articulating their expectations about what they wanted in care terms.

Susan, who was a single parent rearing her teenage son, Sam, remarked on how Sam used to say: *'if only you were waiting at the door when I came in from school with a hot dinner'*. She found this *'pulling on your heart strings'* very difficult but she could not meet his desires as she had to work full-time to maintain a reasonable standard of living.

## Mutuality and interdependency

The love labouring that is involved in primary care relations is set in the context of existing relationships with assumed histories and futures. It is not bounded within a fixed contract of time in most cases. And the love labouring that is invested yields emotional and social returns. With few exceptions, the given-ness and other-centredness that is endemic to love labouring reproduces love labouring capacities in the care recipients. There is a reciprocity at the heart of love labouring relationships that reproduces the capacity to give and to care in the other as it is being exercised. This mutuality serves as an important counterweight to the exercise of power, whether by carers or care recipients.

Rory was in his 30s and had metabolic degenerative disease since birth; his sole income was his disability benefit. He had had an organ transplant and other complications with his illness. His mother Nora was in her 70s, and his recognised carer. Yet, both Nora and Rory recognised that he was an important support in his mother's life in both practical and emotional ways. Rory helped his mother care for his two sisters, both of whom were not well, by driving her to see them and by having meals ready when she returned. He did this work although he was in pain much of the time and was on several different medications, all of which had side effects that had to be carefully managed. When asked if he saw himself as being both a carer and a care recipient, Rory said:

> I never look at it like that, it is just something you have to do and try and do like I mean you see someone in trouble you help them out, you know? … I would see like if mum goes over there I will be here, you know, and I will have dinner or something like that made here you know, like that is my job. You see she can get nothing done, she might be over there four or five hours a day and there say when Caitriona wasn't well she was there for four or five days a week, six days a week. (Rory, single, care recipient with physical disability)

Although Nora worried a lot about Rory's health and was watching always at night to make sure he was breathing:

> … the main thing is that he's just such a worry now in your life. You are watching. I would call him 'Are you alright Rory?' If I don't see any movement I would call 'Are you alright?' You know you will never sleep content because

*you are worried about the angina and that, especially in the middle of the night.* (Nora, separated, caring full-time for adult child)

But she also found him to be a great source of support:

*We are so close, you know, he is like a brother to me, like a sister to me. You know, it's like something I never had, you know. It's so hard, I didn't have a family, no one really belonging to me.* (Nora, separated, caring full-time for adult child)

People with intellectual disabilities were also able and willing to express care and concern that was appreciated by their carers. Anita found caring for her autistic daughter, Beth, difficult on her own, due especially to the lack of support services and respite. Yet she did get some rewards from the relationship:

*Well I love when she is in good form and she has the loveliest face when she is laughing; it is not all doom and gloom. It is hard work but when you see her enjoying herself … she is a character at the back of it all, she really is a character. When you put your worries aside, she really is a character.* (Anita, separated, primary carer of adult daughter)

Beth explained how she told Anita that she cared for her and appreciated what she did:

*Beth: Yes, I love her … I say 'I love you to bits Anita'.*
ML: And what does Anita say to you?
*Beth: 'I love you to bits.'* (Beth, single, care recipient of Anita)

Showing mutual concern was not the preserve of adults. Regina explained how her teenage son listened to her in the evening about her work. They listened to one another:

*Sometimes if I'm home he wants to talk to me, talking about the day and always asking me 'How was your day, how were your students, what did you do?' and I ask him 'What did you do and how were your papers and did you have to submit something?'. And he is so into conferences, present-ations, papers and he knows 'Oh mummy's busy' and I let him know because I think it is important that the child should know.* (Regina, divorced, primary carer of one second-level school child)

But while young people were appreciative of what their parents did for them, they seemed to find it difficult to declare appreciation except in a basic way. The most commonly cited way of showing appreciation was by saying 'Thanks' or 'Thanks for everything'. The students in the city youth project were in their mid-teens and working class. They felt that going beyond saying thanks would be difficult:

> ML: So you would never sort of say 'God I think you are great, thanks so much for doing that for me, I really appreciate...?'
> *Shane: I don't think I could do that to my ma on her deathbed!*
> ML: Why is that?
> *Shane: I don't know.*
> ML: Do you think your mum or dad would like to feel they were appreciated? Would they like to hear that?
> *Chris: Yes.*
> *Diane: I'd say they know.*
> ML: How do they know?
> *Diane : You do things in return and you show it by saying 'thanks' anytime they do anything for you.* (Second-level working class Focus Group 2)

Those teenagers who were older and middle class were more forthcoming about recognising their parents' contribution to their well-being and the costs of what they had received:

> *They have done so much for me and they never ask us for anything. We always buy them stuff and they always say 'Don't get anything for us' and that kind of way. And they have spent huge chunks of money that they don't really have on presents.* (John, second-level middle class Focus Group)

> *It is only recently I have started realising. I look around my room and I find old things and I realise all these things would have cost loads. And I always ... when I was younger, I felt as if we were rich even though we were really poor ... And my Dad gave up alcohol because of me and my sister, that it wouldn't be good for us to see Dad drinking and stuff.* (Mark, second-level middle class Focus Group)

In the case of very young children, reciprocity had a somewhat different character. Elizabeth admitted that caring for two young children was exhausting and pressurising but she also found it hugely enriching. The children's love for her gave her a sense of importance:

> *It is completely wrecking, our lives are completely changed ... and yet you wouldn't change a minute of it ... I suppose the whole sense of love, that whole excitement of being with them, of going home and they are screaming the minute they hear me. They scream and jump and up and down and I think I am the best in the world, so I have rejuvenated myself from having the kids ... So for me it is the sense of love that I get from them makes me feel that I am great.* (Elizabeth,

cohabiting with same sex partner Nuala with whom she has 2 young children, aged 30 to 40, secondary carer, self-employed).

Donal, who was the father of a baby girl also spoke about how even a small baby can give affirmation:

> *It's fantastic, I mean, she smiles and she lights up your day! Yes! Absolutely!*
> (Donal, married to Geraldine with whom he has 1 young child, aged 30 to 40, co-carer, self-employed).

Although primary care relationships are fraught with contradictions and conflicts, the overriding outcome of the relationship is usually one of mutual concern and interdependence. Mary, who was caring for her son with intellectual and physical disabilities, valued his company although they did have their conflicts especially over what to watch on television:

> *We fight a bit over TV and that, he has his own television but he doesn't really want to go to his room, for some reason he wants to be here with me. Sometimes I compromise and say 'all right I will go to the sitting room and watch the News and you can watch the Simpsons.' But he is not too difficult. He is great company, since my husband died at least I have someone to chat with and to sit and watch television with and he is great company that way and I am not on my own.* (Mary, widow, aged 50 to 60, caring full-time for her adult son who has both intellectual and physical disabilities)

The mutuality and interdependency of care relationships is an important value in itself, but it also tempers the power relations between carers and care recipients. On the one hand, it shows that each person is vulnerable to the power of the other to withhold their care. Conversely, each is vulnerable to the power of the other to demand good care. This mutual power, based on mutual vulnerability, helps to prevent the abuse of power, although the degree to which it does so will clearly vary among care relationships.

## Conclusion

Feminist scholars have emphasised the work involved in care for dependants, often (but by no means always)[25] ignoring the care recipients in the analysis. Disability rights scholars have emphasised the limitations of both feminist and traditional social policy models for assuming that disabled people are inevitably dependant and needy. They have argued for replacing a model of care and dependency with one of rights and autonomy.

While we fully accept the criticisms disability rights theorists have made of disabling practices, we have argued that they are mistaken in rejecting the need and importance of relations of care. Our data shows that care and love labouring is a two-way street. Those who are in positions of dependency are not without control or power in the care relationship, although we accept that the capacity to exercise power varies with contexts and cultures about the status of care recipients and carers.

Control is exercised in a range of different ways. The command to care for children when they are minors is legislated for in most jurisdictions. While caring for other family members, for partners or friends is less tightly controlled and regulated (except in the basic case of economic rights and entitlements particularly in marriage), cultural norms and mores play a powerful role in determining what are acceptable forms of care and love labouring. The way people enact these cultural norms is mediated by the everyday moral codes that exist in some form in all societies compelling us to be other-centred to a greater or lesser degree. The well of trust and guilt within which care relations are embedded is highly personalised and idiosyncratic, although highly gendered as well with an especially strong expectation in most cultures that women are the primary carers. The command to care is also exercised through having to meet basic necessities of living for dependants, the need for food, shelter, cleaning, clothing and social interaction. Meeting high dependency needs is only subject to negotiation in limited ways as survival itself depends on it.

Another reason that depicting care recipients as dependants without power is a misrepresentation is that those who are officially defined as care recipients may also be carers as our conversations with Rory and with Pearse's mother showed. Moreover, Tom who was engaged in a very demanding care role with his father, was himself disabled and receiving disability benefit. While we did not focus on teenagers' role as carers, a number of young people in the focus groups noted that they had responsibility for caring for younger children after school until their parents came home. Children may be dependants but they can also be carers (Wihstutz, 2007).

Love labouring is a two way street also in terms of relational gain. Those who are carers not only invest time, energy and attention in the care of others, they also receive affection, attention and appreciation in return, albeit in highly variable ways and to greatly different degrees. To the extent that caring is reciprocal, the power relations involved in caring work in both directions.

Taken together, these characteristics of the care relationship are a challenge to views that emphasise the asymmetry of care and the power that this generates. While it is undeniable that some care relationships, especially those at the secondary and tertiary levels, are highly asymmetrical, our Care Conversations show that primary care relationships in particular are typically far more balanced than is often assumed.

# 7
# Time to Care, Care Commanders and Care Footsoldiers

*Kathleen Lynch, Maureen Lyons and Sara Cantillon*

This chapter uses data from our set of 30 in-depth Care Conversations with carers and care recipients (see Introduction and Appendix) to examine the way unpaid care work interfaces with employment in terms of time demands. It also explores the ways in which time for love labouring is squeezed out increasingly through the use of so-called flexible time schedules, the intensification of work and time spent commuting to and from work.

The gendered nature of care commanding is also examined. The chapter highlights in particular the ways in which inalienable forms of love labouring are assumed to be primarily a woman's responsibility. While some women are care commanders, people who can delegate primary care responsibilities to others, most are not in this position; they remain care's footsoldiers, people who do the unavoidable and essential care and love work.

## Time for care

Time is a limited commodity as human beings have a finite existence. Within that finite life, all tasks have a duration; they take up time, and moving between spaces to do different tasks also takes time, both mobility time and mental readjustment time. The way time is used is not only a function of its finiteness, it is also determined by the fact that each human being is indivisible in terms of their person. She or he is not able to bilocate, and most have a limited capacity to complete more than one task at a time. Thus time is a valuable resource that has to be negotiated between tasks.

Our experience of clock time is not simply quantitative however; it is framed by tasks and mediated through relations of power (Adam, 2000; Melucci, 1996). Love, care and solidary work is embedded within 'timescapes' and spatially bounded 'caringscapes' that are both highly political and strongly gendered (Adam, 1995; McKie *et al.*, 2002). The dominant cultural, economic and political frameworks in a given society determine the meaning of love and care time, the terms of its availability, including who does it, on what terms and at what times.

The salience of care as a time-consuming activity has received greater attention in recent years, not least because more and more women who were traditionally devoting most of their time to care are now in employment (Folbre and Bittman, 2004; CSO, 2007b). The move to the paid labour market has only marginally altered the gendered division of care labour however, with time use studies indicating that women still tend to do more 'housework' regardless of what time they spend working outside the home (Bianchi *et al.*, 2000; Bittman, 2004; McGinnity *et al.*, 2005). Caring tasks, both paid and unpaid, remain a hugely female preserve (Pettinger *et al.*, 2005). Women remain the footsoldiers of care and men are still those who are most likely to command others to care on their behalf. The scope that individual women have to negotiate their way around being primary carers is much more culturally constrained, with wives often becoming carers of parents-in-law rather than sons (Abel, 1991).

Because women spend more time doing care and care-related tasks, this impacts on the leisure time that women enjoy. A national study of the difference in living standards between husbands and wives found that husbands were not only more likely to have a regular pastime or hobby than their wives, they were also more likely to have an evening or afternoon out each week to pursue their own interests (Cantillon *et al.*, 2004). One of the major reasons why wives did not have a regular hobby or spend the same amount of time on evenings and afternoons out, was because of child care and other household responsibilities. Where husbands did not have time out or regular leisure activities, this was more likely to be attributed to lack of money or lack of time for some reason other than caring responsibilities. Similarly with respect to education, where wives wanted to have access to further education and could not avail of it, 25% attributed their difficulties to lack of child care supports; in contrast, just 4% of husbands attributed their inability to engage in further education to lack of child care supports (*ibid.*).

The conflict between care time, leisure time and paid work time is exacerbated by the patriarchal values that are encoded in various forms of employment, particularly in better paid skilled occupations and professional occupations. Many occupations are governed by masculinised norms that pre-date flexibility-driven capitalism, and are designed around men's relative immunity from care work (Halford and Leonard, 2001; Williams, 2001). Work in secure skilled employment in the building trades, for example, or in careers such as accountancy or senior corporate management assume almost complete flexibility around overtime, long hours, freedom to travel, meetings and socialising for work. None of these practices are wholly compatible with the non-transferable and immediate demands of primary caring.

Conflicts between care time and paid work time arises increasingly within contemporary capitalism as the demand for increasing supplies of flexible workers (rather than flexible employers) generates new conflicts over time.

Conflicts arise not only from reconciling the demands of caring with paid work (Hochschild, 1997) but also from longer hours of paid work (Gershuny, 2000), often as a result of employers' flexibilisation strategies (Beck, 2000; Green, 2001). Work is also becoming more intensified in its demands (Green, 2006). Flexibilisation has generated a serious challenge to the notion of 'normal working hours'; there has been a massive increase in shift work, employment at weekends, evenings and nights, and with this a decline in extra pay for working unsocial hours as the definition of what is normal extends later into the night and earlier in the morning (La Valle *et al.*, 2002). The official response of governments and employers has been to initiate so-called 'family-friendly policies' and 'work-life balance' policies although these are typically voluntary codes, the implementation of which is at the discretion of each employer and manager. Even where flexible hours are available, they are generally encoded in a way that only facilitates certain kinds of workers, either those in lower status and less skilled jobs (Hogarth *et al.*, 2000, cited in Coyle, 2005), or those whose skills are in unusually high demand (Coyle, 2005). Flexible working time is also interpreted by employers as increasing the opportunities for part-time work, yet part-time working does not usually generate sufficient income for people to live independently. Because many part-time jobs are low paid, people may have to take a few jobs to survive, and this means organising care in shifts as well. Unpredictable flexible working hours, shift work and work at unsocial hours are especially difficult to reconcile with care responsibilities. While the flexibilisation of working hours is more regulated in some European countries than others, and is clearly more advanced in the UK and Ireland than in Germany, France or the Netherlands, the outcome is the same wherever it is enacted:

> Despite official discourses which promote flexible working as a mechanism for the better reconciliation of work and family life, there is now considerable research evidence to show that employers' flexibilization strategies are intensifying work effort, extending the definition of working time and increasing work related stress rather than diminishing it. (Coyle, 2005: 87)

The decline in employment protection in several European countries, which is strongly associated with temporary employment (Glyn, 2006), is also problematic for care as it leaves people more economically insecure in their out-of-paid-work lives. While there is a debate in human resources thinking about the need to put the 'human' back into human resources (Bolton and Houlihan, 2007), there is an overwhelming problem within capitalist economic systems that are driven by the profit imperative, not least of which is its assumption that all human activities can be constructed in instrumental monetary terms (Sayer, 2007).

## Time conflicts: paid work vs. care work

Our Care Conversations showed that the ability to manage care work with paid work varied considerably, not only with income and family status, but also with one's terms of employment, the attitudes of individual employers, and the status of one's job. We found considerable variation in the levels of accommodation for carers in different organisations. People who were in employment situations where they were well-qualified for their jobs and where their skills were in demand had considerable flexibility in managing their care worlds, especially if they had supportive managers. Where people were not in a position to negotiate with their employers, either because of company policy or the inflexibility of their local managers, managing care and paid work was a considerable challenge. Poor people could not afford good child care and had to rely on their families for a guarantee of quality; when this was not available they were often forced to stay out of paid employment.

Debra was a married woman with two young children, one of whom had an intellectual impairment. She worked in a management position in a financial services company where there was considerable support for balancing care and paid work. She was able to negotiate a good part-time arrangement to accommodate the care needs of her children. Her ability to find an accommodating arrangement was a function of both her value to the company and the flexibility of the employer at central and local level. When asked if she was under pressure from her employer due to meeting the demands of child care she said:

> *I mean what has happened with me now I have been luckier than other people right, but mm, you know, the nature of my job is that I can say, I have said, on a number of occasions I have said 'well now this year it suits me to work half day Monday and then Wednesday and Friday, because Noel's appointments are you know whatever and whatever and is that okay?' ... And then next year, 'now this year I am going to work Tuesday and Thursday and half day Friday'. ... I mean generally the atmosphere in is very supportive, yeah, people are very supportive of each other whether they are peers or bosses. ... I do feel that I have had the freedom and not everybody even in today's society does but I have had the freedom to get the flexible job options that I wanted, work options. Mm ... I have enough money that I am comfortable and I get all the things I need. Mm you know I can choose to not work full time or you know and all of that, so that is very good.* (Debra, married to Alex, primary carer of one pre-school child and one primary school child)

The accommodations that were made for Debra were not available in all financial institutions however, and Clodagh, who was also married with young children, had been refused her request for part-time or job share arrangements:

> But I must say now really up to a point (pause) you're flexible ... but I wouldn't say as a company they are very family friendly. ... I know I am going to find it difficult getting reduced hours and I know people have found it very difficult to get hours to work their family life around it. (Clodagh, married to Séan, co-carer of three primary school children)

The attitude of local managers to care was a key issue determining levels of flexibility. People who had some accommodation from their employers for care needs were very aware from friends that this was not the norm. Susan, a lone mother, remarked:

> I would have went in and said 'I'm after getting a call from the school and I have to go', there was never a problem with that, I suppose because I didn't take the piss, you know what I mean, people can ... Like if I worked in [names of two big supermarket chains] there'd be no flexibility; there's none, I'm quite lucky in the organisation I work in. (Susan, single lone parent with one young son, aged 30 to 40, primary carer, employed full-time)

Clodagh's husband Séan worked for a distribution company where flexibility for carers was not on the agenda for employees at his level. He had to do his deliveries and if the person who replaced him in the job while he was on holidays was not available, the company expected him to do the work. His wages were directly tied to his delivery rates:

> For instance, last Christmas I had booked to take off after Christmas because I was minding them [the three children] and we had let the babysitter off that time – so the plan was 'I would take off the week after Christmas and into the new year and I would mind the kids' because Clodagh would be on and off working over the Christmas and New Year. But the relief man, being Christmas and all that, got sick himself and he didn't turn up so [name of company] rang me and said 'What is going to happen, there is nobody there?' So if I didn't do something about my runs and with the truck being parked it would have hit my wages and I would be down so I ended up going out in the evening when Clodagh came home and going in on New Year's Day making up loads in the warehouse to get someone to deliver. So that will give you the best example of what happens if I get sick like – even though that time it wasn't a case of me being sick, you know. (Séan, married to Clodagh with whom he has three young children, aged 40 to 50, co-carer, employed full-time)

Professional workers who were in business partnerships and who were successful in these, like Jane, were able to manage their child care on their own terms. Their financial independence enabled them and their partners to operate very care friendly practices in their private lives:

*Well they strive to have a work/life balance in the sense that they would respond if I was looking for... like the six weeks off that I took last year in parental leave. They facilitated that for me, they respected my needs around being off when my children were off. I know that is a statutory right to have it anyway but they did facilitate me to take that chunk of time. Yes in general I would say they have a good understanding of the need for balance.* (Jane, partner of Jill, primary carer of two primary school children)

While there were pressures with running one's own business in care terms, when the business was established and running well, much flexibility was possible. This was evident in Elizabeth's case:

*I leave about 9:30 in the morning, after we dress the kids and get the kids organised I leave after them, go for my coffee, ease into the day. Some days I could finish at 2pm and some days I mightn't be finished till 12 at night. Because I am self employed I work when the work is there, I don't go out looking for work, I don't want to get bigger because I have different priorities. I have enough money to support my life style with the clients I have.* (Elizabeth, partner of Nuala, secondary carer of two primary school children)

Sasha was at the other end of the social class spectrum in terms of her options. She was a lone parent with three children living on a carer's allowance since her last child was born. She did not have family support nearby so she had no options about returning to paid work although this was her wish. She did not have the practical support of a partner (from whom she was separated) to share her care responsibilities, and child care costs were too high relative to the types of jobs for which she was qualified. Even working part-time was not an option. She was only permitted to work for ten hours per week while on the carer's allowance but she could not get work for this period of time at the hours when she was free. Moreover, the work would have had to be within easy access of her home and the children's schools as she has no one else to pick them up:

*Like I haven't worked since he [the youngest child] was born and I got him into this playschool then. And he is in this playschool since he was ten months old. Then I was saying that I would go back to work when I got him into playschool. But there is no job that will take you for ten hours a week ... Like I am only allowed to work ten hours a week while I am on the carer's allowance.* (Sasha, single, caring for one pre-school and two primary school children)

Employment and care work are accommodated in some cases. The Conversations would suggest that there is greater flexibility for professional workers who are self employed and well established in their careers, and/or who have skills and experience that are valued by employers. A few people also noted that if their individual manager or supervisor had an understanding of care and its demands, this also helped in balancing paid and care work.

As noted in Chapter 4 however, most people did not think that care was valued by society or by employers and most did not think employers were willing to accommodate care time unless it was in their own interests to do so. Sara is an example of someone who had to work flexible hours, so she could care for her husband and adult daughter. While she did not claim her employers were especially unsympathetic, there was no particular account taken of her care responsibilities. It was assumed she would manage her caring around work times:

> ML: So would I be right then in thinking that the job is not just 9 to 5, are there other commitments?
> *Sara: No, no I would be going out three nights a week. One on Monday to X* [name of place], *Tuesday to one course and Thursday to another.*
> ML: But I suppose because of your arrangements with Phoebe at the moment ...
> *Sara: I can do it.*
> ML: You can do it because she is not home until Friday evening?
> *Sara: That's right, it all hinges on that. That is why I cannot go away to say Y when the group go on the Local Respite Break but I do go to the dinner on the Saturday night bringing Phoebe with me.* (Sara, married to John, caring part-time for daughter and husband)

Sara also had to manage the care of her husband each day and she organised her time around this:

> *I am able to come to work because my husband sleeps until about 12:00, I leave his breakfast all ready on the table and then I am home at 1:00 and get the lunch and then I am home again at 5:00 or 6:00.* (Sara, married to John, caring part-time for daughter and husband)

A number of people had suggested to Sara that she work part-time to manage care and paid work more easily. Sara noted however, that while part-time work seemed like an option, she would not choose this as 'all that would be part-time would be the money':

> *I did think of maybe only working mornings but if I only work mornings, the only thing that would be part time would be the money because I know I would be kept there until 3 or 4 o clock anyway. So I kind of have sold myself short enough before.* (Sara, married to John, caring part-time for daughter and husband)

## The gendered nature of care time

In Ireland as in many other countries there is a strong moral imperative commanding women to be the primary carers (O'Brien, 2007). Patriarchal practices of caring do not have to be newly established in every individual case or in every household; they are already encoded in the norms of femininity, masculinity and domesticity. For middle class women in particular, there is strong command to be 'Moral Mothers', to care competently and professionally (Hays, 1996; Williams, 2001). In all social classes, however, the morally encoded mother has attracted little analysis; women's domesticity persists as 'embodied history, internalised as second nature, and so forgotten as history' (Williams, 2001: 38, quoting Bourdieu). Equally for men, hegemonic masculinity is assessed in terms of male pay cheques and power (Connell, 1995). Being a primary carer, particularly in combination with paid work, means living a life of chronic time stress (Phipps *et al.*, 2001); this type of stress is not a typical part of the male trajectory.

Although men tend to spend more time on household work now than in the past, women still tend to do at least twice as much work in the household as men (Coltrane and Galt, 2000). Men also tend to spend less time caring for their children than women, and the time that they do spend tends to focus less on undertaking domestic tasks for children (cooking, cleaning, washing clothes, etc.) and more on play (Lewis, 2000). Fathers also view the time they give to care rather differently to women. They see time as abstract commitment, 'caring about' in a general sense rather than doing the more hands on, time consuming 'caring for' (McDermott, 2005). It is not surprising therefore, that employed wives experience less leisure and more stress than employed husbands (Coltrane and Galt, 2000).

Men become care commanders by cultural fiat; their roles as care assistants rather than primary carers comes not from their person nor even their wages, but rather from the gendered division of labour norms that are encoded in heterosexual relationships and in caring relationships generally. It is assumed that women will be the primary carers; where there are male and female partners in the household; both women and men assume this, so the matter is not for questioning. While there are negotiations around the amount of care that men and women do relative to each other, it is assumed that the management and organisation and responsibility for care will be taken by women if they are available to do it.

In the Care Conversations study we deliberately sought out men for interview who were primary carers. We enlisted the support of both the Carers Association and the Caring for Carers Ireland in this work. In each case, the associations pointed out that there were few men in their associations who were primary carers. Those men tended to be in households where there was no woman available to do the caring; this was not true of the women who were primary carers. The findings from the Care Conversations study confirmed those of Gerstel and Gallagher (2001) who found that men generally become primary carers only when there are no women available to do the work. In households where women were living with men, women tended to be the primary carers, especially in the case of children but also in relation to parents, including parents who were not co-resident.

### Gendered care time: heterosexual couples

Evidence of how gendered care norms trump economic rationalities was clear from the care arrangements in a number of the couple households where we interviewed; in two cases the wives had had higher salaries and more high status jobs than their husbands or partners prior to having children, yet in each case it was the woman who downsized her job and income to accommodate the care of her children. Debra had held a senior management post in a financial institution up to the time her second child was born. After the birth of her son who had an intellectual impairment, she left her full-time senior management post and went into a job-share arrangement. Cathy was in both more secure and pensionable employment than her husband. After the birth of her second child, she moved to a more local and less well-paid job. In neither case did their husband consider part-time or lower paid work.

In Cathy's case, she had moved job so she would not have to commute to work, which gave her more time with her children. The change of job also allowed her to care for her mother who was recently widowed. Cathy negotiated the care of the children with her husband in this new arrangement; he had to take responsibility for caring and collecting the children one day per week:

> *I think particularly now with this change of job, we would have negotiated stuff, you know because I had time to think about the fact that I was giving up a career in Dublin, taking a lower salary, the career structure was changing and then if that was going to happen, I didn't want to be actually going in for more [paid] child care, … I didn't want to go back to five days' child care, so that was when he … and we sort of negotiated that he would do the fifth day, you know, the Monday.* (Cathy, married to Michael, co-carer of two pre-school children)

What was clear from the conversation however is that Cathy regarded her husband's engagement in care one day each week as a concession, an optional act, not something that was inevitable in a shared care relationship:

> *I have to say now it was quite surprising to me that my husband **volunteered** that, because you know, he's self employed and potentially on the go all the time and that's actually been really good for him as a parent.* (Cathy, married to Michael, co-carer of two pre-school children) [Bolded text emphasis added]

The men we interviewed were not authoritarian characters; there was no evidence that they exercised a command and control style of authority.

Neither was there evidence that they generated the kinds of income that gave them significant power over their wives. Cathy admitted that her husband had moved his business to a new town and he was earning very little at the time of interview. The power they exercised over women in connection with care was an invisible form of control. Leaving primary care responsibilities to women was simply assumed to be in the natural order of things.

It was not surprising therefore than when we asked men in heterosexual households to talk about time pressures arising from their caring roles most of them said they had never really experienced it. Where there was joint caring, care roles and responsibilities were not subjects that exercised men in the same way as women as they did not see them as something for which they had primary responsibility. This was true even for those men who did a lot of care work and were joint carers of children like Séan. When asked if he had time for himself he noted that:

> *I wouldn't have much time alright, like you know. It is not something I have ever given a lot of thought to, you know. ... Time for myself! [laughing] Well you don't tend to think about that.* (Séan, married to Clodagh, co-carer of three primary school children)

For Séan, life was a continuous round of travel for his job, joint caring for his children with his wife Clodagh and visiting his parents at the weekend. His work hours were generally 6am to 4pm. He did not see himself needing time for himself, although he was aware that there would be no time for any other activities:

> *I don't really need time out. You are so tired when it is all done – it is nearly time to go to bed like – other than that I wouldn't need anything really. Definitely during the week, ... time for anything else is definitely out like, there is no question of it.* (Séan, married to Clodagh, co-carer of three primary school children)

Both Clodagh and Séan admitted however, that Clodagh took the primary responsibility for managing and organising their children's care, including leaving the two older children to school and the younger child to the play school each day. Clodagh also picked up her children from both primary school and play school at lunch time. Her view of time was very different to Séan; she was stressed by the lack of time and the need to manage paid work time and care time carefully. She described the constant rushing as 'a terrible way to live':

> *I am always hurrying them. I just would love just not to be constantly rushing. I mean the only time I don't rush is when I am collecting them in the evenings. ... [I would like] just time that I am not all the time telling them 'we are late get in, we are late come on, we are late come on, hurry up get out we are late, I am going to be late for work'! When I collect them at half two it's 'get in I am going to be late*

*to get back', I am constantly at that! You know, to ease the burden ... It is time ... I mean we are time poor! That is where we are most poor, we are time poor!* (Clodagh, married to Séan, co-carer of three primary school children)

Alex and Debra had two young children, one of whom had an intellectual impairment. When asked if he ever considered working part-time, given that Debra had a senior management post that she was giving up to job-share, Alex was clear that this was something neither he nor most men would consider:

*It may have been possible, it would have been highly unusual, I think it would still be unusual, although there are, I have heard of men who have done that kind of thing. I still think it would be highly unusual though, probably possible within the [name of insurance company] environment; it's a very open and friendly environment for that kind of thing. In the bank I am in now, probably not, and certainly in the first company I joined ..., it certainly wasn't the done thing ... Whether or not I would have wanted to do it, at the time, probably not, in fact at the time I didn't want to do it! It wasn't the sort of choice I would have made, you know.* (Alex, married to Debra, secondary carer of one pre-school child and one primary school child)

When asked as to why he felt this way, Alex attributed it to natural differences between women and men:

*I don't know! All I can think is that **it is just instinct for men not to want to give up work or to work part-time!** I don't know, there is a kind of genetic thing or, eh, I think it is just a difference between the way men and women are. I think there is just this desire for women to be much closer to the family and the kids. And for the man, that desire is not there so much, not saying that we don't love our kids but I think the desire is just different, you know.* (Alex, married to Debra, secondary carer of one pre-school child and one primary school child) [Bolded text emphasis added]

Although Alex left home between 7.30 and 8.00am each morning and did not return until almost 12 hours later, he did not think he needed more time to himself as he claimed spaces for himself in between. He went to the gym every morning for a half an hour before work, played football on Saturday afternoon and every Monday night. Debra had two hours without the children to herself on a Thursday. While Alex did try to spend time with the children before they went to bed, his view of having time with them was very different to Debra:

*I suppose every evening I do try and spend, you know even 10 or 15 minutes with each of them and typically Noel would be stuck into something on the telly. When he is in front of the telly he doesn't talk to anybody and Cathy is usually practising her dancing and eating her dinner and doing her homework. So it's difficult to get ten minutes with them but, you know* (Alex, married to Debra, secondary carer of one pre-school child and one primary school child)

Alex had prioritised his job in practice if not in theory. He was conscious of his standing in the company and wanted to improve on it:

*Alex: I need to be more visible in work and, you know, produce a number of things that in my three years in the other company I was, mm, I was able to, how will I put this, I was in the company at a very early stage, I was number 4 in the company so everyone that came in after me knew who I was but at this stage I am number 279, or people are wondering who I am and what am I doing. So there is a lot of pressure to say, to mm [pause].*
ML: To make your mark?
*Alex: Yeah exactly.* (Alex, married to Debra, secondary carer of one pre-school child and one primary school child)

Debra's view of time was very different to her husband. She experienced time pressures in a wide range of situations, both at home and at work. While she felt that some of the time pressures arose from her personal concern about keeping her home well:

*… when I am at home I find the housework pulls me or the list of jobs to do pulls me.*

Her main concerns were that:

*I don't have enough time for myself and I don't have enough time to play with the children.* (Debra, married to Alex, primary carer of one pre-school and one primary school child)

Debra was the primary organiser and manager of their children's care and the work of the household:

*I get up at 6 o'clock and go to bed at 10 o'clock and don't take much of a break in between.* (Debra, married to Alex, primary carer of one pre-school and one primary school child)

Sometimes she felt under pressure to spend more time at the office but could not do this as she was the person who collected the children at specific times. She also wanted to have time with her children:

*… the biggest pressure I find is that other people have capacity, you know, to work 40 hours a week, they can work 45 if they have a bad week. Whereas*

*I can't, I have to be out that door at half-four in the evening and I have very, very little capacity to do overtime. Partly because there aren't enough hours in the week and partly because mm I deliberately wanted to have as much time with my children outside the hours that I work. So the 20 hours a week that I am in work and travelling are the 20 hours that I don't have my children and ..., I don't have a hobby or anything like that, almost exclusively the rest of the time is spent with the kids.* (Debra, married to Alex, primary carer of one pre-school child and one primary school child)

Debra was not only caring for the children, she also organised the food for the house and attended appointments with her young son Noel (who has an intellectual impairment) at various clinics, and facilitated her young daughter's play time with her friends. She orchestrated the children's days. She described her two-and-a-half *days off* paid work, as follows:

*On the days I am not working then mm eh generally I would, well obviously I get up at half-six those days and have my shower and then get the children up. Mm the reason I have to get up so early again is because Noel is still at the baby stage so he takes probably a full hour just to get ready on his own. I leave about half eight, drop Cathy to school. Then I tend to run into the shops and get bread or just literally the couple of things I need that day. I bring Noel to playschool for a quarter-past-nine ... Tuesday afternoon is the only time I can bring Noel to appointments without having to drag Cathy, you know. ... Monday afternoon ... is for Cathy and her friends, you know, that is Cathy's day, but I obviously have Noel as well, ... Thursday because she has dancing and because she finishes school at half-two and dancing is at four you know we have to be fed in between because if we are not fed by then and cleared up then you are still clearing up at eleven that night. ... on Thursdays I have two hours to myself.* (Debra, married to Alex, primary carer of one pre-school and one primary school child)

### Gendered care time: wider relationships

The cultural command on women to be the primary carers was not simply operational in heterosexual marriage; it also operated between brothers and sisters. While men like Tony and Pearse were carers, each had become carers because there were no women in the family available to care for their respective parents, and in each case they were able to combine some employment in farming with caring. Moreover, their sisters were also a source of support.

Tony's sister Marian was married with children and had a good job; she looked after all the household washing for her mother and brother. Even though she was not the primary carer, Tony felt that Marian played a key support role in the care of her mother. She did not go abroad for her daughter's wedding, not only because it was far away but also because her mother would be without her support for the week:

> *Well we didn't go you see to (name of Cenral American country); it was too far away I felt and we'd be gone for a week. Again mother came into it.* (Marian, married sister of Tony, who is primary carer of mother)

Tom was the only person who named a brother as being a support in caring for a parent and he equated his support with that of his sister; he could call on him if he needed help in a crisis although he lived further away from him than a second brother who did not help:

> *My other brother Jim that … he wouldn't have a clue, whereas my younger brother John in Carlow … if I were to show him, if he was here he would help me. John would be the one that I would depend upon because John is eager, he is strong …*

However, the person who gave him practical help was his sister:

> *Mary is very good, she does my shopping. **And two things men can't, genetically can't do, are shop and iron** … So Mary is here for that and she is company and the kids are dotes. I am a surrogate father … if I had dad sitting out and I had to go out to something, maybe a funeral or whatever, Mary will put him to bed, she can manage the hoist.* (Tom, single, caring full-time for father) [Bolded text emphasis added]

Both Valerie and Maeve were carers of their parents. Both had brothers who took no responsibility for the basic caring work that is required on a daily basis with people who are physically very dependent. Valerie became a carer for her parents more by accident than by design. She had lived abroad most of her adult life and held a very well paid senior position in financial services prior to being a carer; she had, in her own words, 'a high powered position'. She was single and did not have children. She came home seven years previously to visit her parents. Both of them got sick at the time, so she stayed as neither her brother nor her sister lived in Ireland. Valerie found her sister to be a major support to her: she phoned her most days from the US and took time out to come home for extended periods to help her with caring for her parents:

> *She was here for a month and then they both got sick in October time … so she came again for six weeks, and then, she calls all the time, she's very good. She*

*phoned last night, and she talked about coming in May, she'll come for four to five weeks, and it is something to look forward to, and that's always good, its nice to have somebody closer to hand, you know.* (Valerie, single, caring full-time for both parents)

Valerie did not find her brother to be of much help as when he came to visit he expected her to care for him and his children:

*Oh he does come fairly often, but unfortunately he would descend with two children with him, and that's just an extra burden on me, to have to cook and clean for them as well.* (Valerie, single, caring full-time for both parents)

While Valerie recognised that her sister had more flexibility than her brother in making herself available to help with her parents (her children were in their late teens and early 20s), she still felt that her sister had to make a considerable effort to organise herself to come on her own to help care for their parents.

Maeve was the primary carer for her mother who was in her 90s; she was married and living with her husband and adult children. She also had two sisters and two brothers, all of whom lived nearby. Maeve did not regard either her brothers or sisters as sufficiently supportive; she was especially critical of her brothers, neither of whom ever took care of her mother. One brother, who had become a successful businessman, paid for the renovation of her mother's home at one time but never cared for her in person. Although Maeve was critical of her sisters (she felt that her sisters' husbands did not want her mother in particular), her sisters did take care of her mother each weekend, alternating the care between them:

*It is generally the three girls who do it. And the men, ... when there has been a family meeting, because it has just been relying on the three people, the two brothers will say 'yes we will take part BUT ...'* (Maeve, married to Frank, part-time carer of her mother)

Maeve did try to excuse her brothers however, noting the other demands on their time. She did not make any such excuses for her sisters although both of them were employed and one had a senior post.

*And my brother then again is a high flyer and he is married to a French girl and they have a house over in France as well. They travel over there quite a bit and he would be travelling anyway with business. My other brother has clotting problems and he is on warfarin and he has his mother-*

*in-law who would be a frequent visitor to his home.* (Maeve, married to Frank, part-time carer of her mother)

Sisters were also more important than brothers when it came to having support in caring for young children although the fact that these women were mostly in paid employment limited their ability to offer assistance. Clodagh explained how her sisters had been supportive at different times but could not be now as they were in full-time employment like herself:

> *I have a sibling nearby, I have a sister who lives out in Tuam, and she would take me out of a hole once or twice when I wouldn't have had anybody else to mind the children…But she has gone back to work fulltime.* (Clodagh, married to Séan, co-carer of three primary school children)

Susan was a lone parent and had great support from both her parents: she also had some occasional support from two bachelor uncles who lived near her parents who would collect her son if her parents were not available. She had two brothers, one of whom lived abroad and the other of whom was in college; they were younger than her and she did not see them as supports. Her sisters were her main social supports:

> *I still get to go out yeah, not every weekend, not now but before, I'm not a mad party animal anyway that I need to get out every weekend, I might have a bottle of wine in the house with the girls, the girls sometimes come around to me (and the girls meaning my two sisters as well), they'd come to me or I'd go to them.* (Susan, single, primary carer of second-level child)

These Care Conversations do not just confirm the point made in Chapter 5 that the care order is deeply gendered, but illustrate what that gendering means for the way men and women spend their time, day-to-day and year-to-year. Both in heterosexual couples and in wider family relationships, the assumption was that care was a woman's role, and therefore that it fell to women to allocate their time to care. Men found it easier to prioritise the time they gave to paid work, and sometimes even to leisure activities, over time spent on caring.

## Care's footsoldiers, tied by time: chasing, running, rushing

> *There aren't enough hours in the week.* (Debra, married to Alex, primary carer, of one pre-school child and one primary school child)

Primary care work involves an intense level of commitment and engage- ment that takes place within definite 'timescapes' (McKie *et al.*, 2002). The immediacy of care needs dictates time schedules; there is an urgency and powerlessness about caring that does not typically apply in other work situations. As Donal, a father of a young baby, observed:

> *In my paid job obviously I'm in control of what's going on, whereas, the child, when the child wants something the child has to have something, when the child is hungry, the child needs to be fed, whereas if I, if I want to schedule appointments I'd do it at a time that suits me.* (Donal, married to Geraldine, co-carer of one pre-school child)

It was not only the very young who needed care on call, it also applied to older people like Tom's father who had to be turned in bed to avoid bed sores. Being physically present at all times is also required where there are high care needs as Tom explained in relation to his father:

> *I don't leave him by himself, he can't be left by himself. I would be afraid, God forbid, if anything happened when I was out and he was here by himself.* (Tom, single, caring full-time for father)

There are multiple time markers in a given care labourer's day and these time markers are constant and repetitive even though they change with age and levels of vulnerability. Carers identified a very wide range of timed care tasks including times for cooking and feeding; times for delivering and collecting; times for lifting; times for changing nappies; times for washing and cleaning; times for homework; times for stories; times for medicines; times for listening; times for holding and caressing; times for challenging and negotiating; times for managing conflict and times for being.

The metaphors of 'running', 'chasing' and 'rushing' were very prevalent in the narratives, especially in women's narratives. Primary carers were constantly trying to catch time that was running away from them. Time was not something they could control and they spoke at length about the lack of time in their days. Paula, who was caring for her four sons alone, spoke about how the lack of time caused her to be stressed and become ill:

> *I'm always **chasing** my tail around the place and it's very stressful and I got sick from the stress ... I suppose the responsibility of working full time as a mother is hard because you are chasing your tail the whole time, you are trying to get time, I was only thinking about that last night, the way things are changing there is less and less time for conversations. My Paul would come in and sit down and talk to me about anything 'such and such is going to Turkey for his holidays etc' now he's just coming*

*to tell me that he is on report at school ... There is less time. I can't be there anymore than I am there.* (Paula, divorced mother, primary carer of one second-level school child and three adult children) [Bolded text emphasis added]

Clodagh, who was the joint carer of her three young girls, expressed similar sentiments:

*I am always **hurrying** them. I just would love just not to be constantly **rushing**.* (Clodagh, married to Séan, co-carer of three primary school children) [Bolded text emphasis added]

The hassle caused by constant deadlines was very stressful even for those caring full-time like Melanie, as caring for her adult children involved many meetings and travel to places of care:

*When you are all the time **rushing** and have all this on your plate it is not easy to be that patient or caring, do you know what I mean? ... Because I am all the time **running** with them, **running** them here and **running** them there. I know there's a bus and I know there is that service but with the trouble I have getting them up and out in time, it doesn't always work out!* (Melanie, married to Peter, full-time carer of husband and three adult children) [Bolded text emphasis added]

Unexpected events, such as accidents, exacerbated the time stresses of people who were already tied to tight schedules of work and care. This was true of Regina, the sole carer of her son, and a person who had no family support in Ireland:

*Last year he broke his foot, he had chicken pox, all sorts of things, high temperature, all sorts of things, great pain, **rushing** into the hospital, staying in the emergency, go with him, go to the doctor, do your volunteer work..., come in on time with the **deadlines** and all these things.* (Regina, divorced, primary carer of second-level child) [Bolded text emphasis added]

Having to balance several roles at the one time was also a source of stress; shopping, cooking and caring might all have to take place at the one time:

*You know if you're **running** late, like you're not getting going to be getting in and getting her settled till kind of half 5, so it does minimise your time. And if you weren't organised and you had to go to the shop that would add to it* *again.* (Geraldine, married to Donal, co-carer of one pre-school child) [Bolded text emphasis added]

Interestingly, the men we interviewed who were full-time carers did not express the same sense of time running away. While Tony admitted that he did not have much time to sit down during the day, he noted that:

*Well I have, I must say I am not totally rushed off my feet. I try to make time for myself.* (Tony, single, caring full-time for his mother and uncle)

Although Alex was caring for his two young children with his wife Debra, he did not feel overburdened by lack of time. He had scheduled two breaks for himself each week, on Saturday afternoons and Monday nights. He noted that:

*I usually have an hour or two to myself [each night] So I am never kind of, very rarely would I say 'oh god I need an hour off'. Debra would be much more prone to saying that than I would because she would obviously have them a lot more than I would.* (Alex, married to Debra, secondary carer of one primary and one pre-school child)

**Travel and time**

Human beings are not divisible; they cannot be in more than one place at a time. To be in another place to complete a new task means moving between spaces and this moving takes time. The separation of care spaces from work and education spaces in most societies means that travel time is a key element of care time, especially where distances are long or traffic exacerbates the travel time (McKie *et al.*, 2002).

Cathy explained that she had travelled 38 miles to and from her job each day, and that she had recently moved to a local job due to the hassle and time spent driving. While the distance was manageable at the outset it had become unsustainable after ten years:

*Well ... when I started first it was an hour, and it's an hour door to door comfortable, and then, it just got worse. It crept up to an hour and fifteen minutes, an hour and twenty minutes, and towards the end it was actually an hour and forty minutes ... and that was leaving at half past four, if I had to leave at half past five, I wouldn't have even dreamed of what time I would have got home, to be honest.* (Cathy, married to Michael, co-carer of two pre-school children)

People also travel within work and this also complicates care arrangements especially where it involves overnight stays. Both Alex and Séan had to travel in their jobs and both had overnight stays away from home; one night each week in Séan's case and two nights per month in Alex's situation. As both had young children, this meant that their partners had extra care work on these occasions and this was especially difficult for Clodagh (Séan's husband) who was tied to branch banking hours. On days when her husband was away working she had three different times of delivery and pick up for her three children. Not only had she to leave her children to school and the crèche, she also had to collect them at different times in the middle of the day. At the end of the day she had to collect them again from the childminder, feed them and help them with homework in the evening. She described the whole process of delivering and collecting the children as a 'nightmare' especially on Wednesdays when Séan was away:

> *I would drop them (the 2 oldest children) in the morning to school and drop ... (the youngest child) out to the baby minder and the traffic is so bad and I am trying to get into work on time. And then I am coming out of work [at lunch time] to drop her to pre-school on the first half hour of my lunch ... and then I have to collect the others at half 2. And on the Wednesday then with Séan away I have to do the collection as well from the childminder's [after work], so you know, the traffic is just so bad and it's just a nightmare!* (Clodagh, married to Séan, co-carer of three primary school children)

Clodagh explained that she had to work until 6pm in the evening to compensate for the extra time spent collecting and delivering the children during the day.

In Alex's case, the times at which he travelled could not be planned as flexibility was spatially, functionally and temporally determined by the needs of his employers (Coyle, 2005):

> *That is why the only thing... I didn't like in the last couple of years was the travel because it wasn't scheduled, you couldn't really schedule it properly. You couldn't say you were going to Manchester on Tuesday and Frankfurt on Saturday, it wasn't like that, it was much more when they (i.e., employers) needed it.* (Alex, married to Debra, secondary carer of one primary and one pre-school child)

## Time for yourself: class issues

Most of the carers claimed that they lacked sufficient time for themselves. Apart from one of the fathers (Alex) who continued to play soccer twice a week after his children were born, all other carers, both secondary and primary, had compromised on hobbies or interests. None of the women nor the men who were primary carers had hobbies that they pursued on a regular basis:

> *I have to be back, dinner has to be made, you know, you're always on the go, it is like, you feel yourself getting hyper but there's no time for you! I mean if you do get five minutes, somebody's shouting your name for one thing or the other.* (Valerie, single, caring full-time for both parents)

They were aware of the need for personal time; they missed having time for friends and experienced this as a loss:

> *And that's the thing about the whole thing is that you don't get enough time to meet with your friends or to have a yap, betimes I would snatch an hour with her [a friend] at lunchtime.* (Paula, divorced, primary carer of one second-level child and three adult children)

> *I have lost a lot of friends I would say. I have lost contact with a lot of friends. It is not just that it is also moving down here, moving from Dublin where a lot of our friends were based ... I mean I don't have the same time, I don't have the same freedom, I don't have the same energy to maintain relationships with other people.* (Jane, partner of Jill, primary carer of two primary children)

Other carers, especially mothers, missed simple things like having the house to oneself or going to the toilet in peace:

> *I think the thing you miss most is being even able to go to the loo and just shut yourself off, but that is the situation with small children, nothing to do with Noel's disability. That is just when you have small children.* (Debra, married to Alex, primary carer of one pre-school child and one primary school child)

Even when carers did take time to relax such as watching a favourite television programme, this did not mean they could do that on their own terms. In Sasha's case, two of her children were deaf so she would have to translate for the children while she was watching the programme:

> *When I do stop at half seven and I want to watch Eastenders or something because they cannot hear they are saying 'What are they saying, what are they saying?' and I have to be explaining because there is no subtitles and that I find that very tiring just to have to be explaining things all the time, you know.* (Sasha, single, caring for one pre-school and two primary school children)

Time to relax was not necessarily care-free time either especially for someone like Sasha who could not afford to pay for good child care. Her class status and her marital status impacted directly on her experience of time as there was no time that was free from worry about money and she had no financial support for her children from their fathers:

*Then it is nearly time to go to bed. Then I am thinking 'what am I going to do tomorrow, I have no money, where am I going to be able to get this from?' You know. If there is something coming up, you know like Easter or that, it is just mental torture on your brain, just wearing your head down!* (Sasha, single, caring for one pre-school and two primary school children)

While women who were employed full-time, like Clodagh and Jill, were also limited in what time they had for themselves, they were able to get this time by making arrangements with their partners, or by buying time for themselves through employing someone to do household chores. In Clodagh's case, both her husband Séan and herself recognised that each other needed time out and this made the demands of caring more manageable:

*... you might need chill-out times and I might say to him 'I have to go for a walk just to get my head clear for an hour' and I would and I would be fine. He will head back down to Monaghan or something and that is his chill-out or get away time. I would get into the car and go, you know, sometimes just go for a drive, just sometimes you do need time to yourself.* (Clodagh, married to Séan, co-carer of three primary school children)

The benefits of being upper middle class with a secure income was very visible in Jill's case. Her partner and herself had arranged for someone to come in twice a week to cook a meal and clean the house. This allowed Jill and Jane to have pleasurable love labouring time with their children:

*We were lucky, we get a bit of domestic help as well 2 mornings a week and we did that deliberately to free up ...We wanted quality time at dinner time every day of the week. So that we had at least from 5 o'clock in the evening until 8 o'clock at night ... the fact that we can get help for 2 mornings and dinners get made and the place gets cleaned up and ... allows us to totally enjoy being with them and being at home. We are very lucky, we are quite privileged and that is good for us.* (Jill, partner of Jane, primary carer of two primary school children)

Their situation was in sharp contrast to Sasha who was caring for her three children alone and living on social welfare payment:

*But I never get one [a break] like. I never like, ... like me sister is always saying to me 'you are always letting them go on everything, all the trips in the scouts and yet you don't go anywhere yourself'... I want the best for them and I want them to go away and see things and I don't want them to be saying in the scouts 'I cannot go away because me ma doesn't work and I have no da'.* (Sasha, single, caring for one pre-school and two primary school children)

Being poor not only meant that you had little resources for leisure, it also meant that you had to spend a lot of time waiting to access basic services. This further reduced the time you had for rest. Health appointments in public hospitals or visits to doctors were time consuming affairs as one had to wait in line as Melanie explained:

*Like you get a letter and you have to be there for 11 o'clock or something and then you are waiting there for hours and you are worrying about all the other things you have to do and places you have to be or who else you have to pick up.* (Melanie, married to Peter, full-time carer of husband and three adult children)

### Time for minding your health

There is considerable evidence that having too many care responsibilities can adversely affect your health (Cannuscio *et al.*, 2004; Hirst, 2003). We spoke with a number of the carers who were clearly endangering their own health due to the undue responsibilities they had for caring. This was especially evident among those who were caring alone with little family or respite support. Paula, who was caring for her four sons alone was suffering a number of health difficulties that she attributed directly to the difficulties of combining a full-time job with caring:

*No and I am finding that even more and more now that there is a cost factor involved and the cost to me for the caring that I do is to my health, it's to the detriment of [my health] ... if I don't take care of myself then I'm the one who falls down. So I am starting to realise that and I am very stressed this particular time of the year... I get alopecia in my head and I have problems with my stomach which isn't retaining food and they know it's all because of the stress. It's getting now that I am going to have to do something about it.* (Paula, divorced, primary carer of one second-level child and three adult children)

While carers like Valerie admitted she was not clinically depressed, she defined herself as feeling depressed at times and longing for respite to allow her to have time for herself:

*I would suffer from depression, obviously, naturally enough, I say, I just keep telling myself, whatever date it is, the respite is coming, and I'm going to get a break, as I say, without that, I don't know what I would do, because it does get me down, I say you know it does, it must, I must have something to look forward to, no matter how small.* (Valerie, single, caring full-time for both parents)

Nora was also a lone carer, in her case of adult children. She found it very stressful: when the stress and demands became too great she tended to go to the doctor. However, she did not find him particularly helpful, as he did not appear to fully understand her needs:

*Sometimes I get upset and then he offers to give me tranquillisers and I am not a person for tranquillisers, I saw my daughter taking too many of those things. I am the type that likes to fight the thing of my own, from my own strength! I don't like to have to take sleeping tablets or things like that. I can't afford to take sleeping tablets for someone might ring and I don't have any belief in taking them anyway.* (Nora, separated mother of three adult children, aged 70 to 80, caring full-time for adult son who has degenerative metabolic disease)

Melanie was also very distressed due to the intense demands on her from caring. While she was not ill at present, she feared that she would be in the future:

*Well even that stress now that I am under, I would be worried that I would eventually be so worn out that I wouldn't be able to take it, that my own health would end up breaking down.* (Melanie, married to Peter, full-time carer of husband and three adult children)

Being a primary carer is a demanding activity in terms of both physical and emotional health. Those who are without care supports and respite are especially vulnerable in health terms.

## Conclusion

Caring for others is a major task that is both labour intensive and time consuming. As time is a scare resource, caring for others is bounded by time limits, the most pressing of which is the time demanded by earning a livelihood.

Care's footsoldiers, those who did the daily, necessary work of care were those who experienced greatest time pressures; they were predominantly women. While women who were in full-time employment and also the primary carers were under the most pressure for time, often arising from commuting to work and/or delivering children to and from carers, they were not the only people who were short on time. Carers who were full-time primary carers adults with high care needs had little time for themselves to rest and relax. They described their care work as 'relentless' and 'unforgiving' in its time demands, especially in the absence of respite care services. All primary carers who lacked time for relaxation and leisure, for whatever reason, spoke of the negative impact of caring on their health, a finding which is well substantiated in other studies (Cannuscio *et al.*, 2004; Goldstein *et al.*, 2004; Hirst, 2003).

Neither those who were full-time carers nor those who combined paid work with caring exercised full control over their time. On the one hand, the care recipients dictated the terms and timing of caring arising from the immediacy of their care needs, be it the need to be fed, to be cleaned and bathed, or the desire for companionship. Full-time carers described themselves being tied to time; an intense desire to escape from this incessant time bind was evident, as Valerie explained in relation to her parents:

> *You feel like escaping, like you would just love to go now and spend the night out, or not to have to think oh God I have to be back, the bus is coming.* (Valerie, single, caring full-time for both parents)

On the other hand, those who were in paid employment, especially women carers in full-time employment, worked under two sets of competing time constraints, those of their employers and of their primary care recipients. While some professional workers exercised considerable control over their work and care times, due to their skills and incomes respectively, this was not true for other workers most of whom had to 'juggle' care and paid workers on an hourly basis. Even when carers were in paid work, they were often on *care-call* in case they were needed to collect a sick child from school or from a crèche. If they were not on call personally, they had to arrange for a child minder, sister, mother, father or friend to be on care-call.

While women were care's footsoldiers, men were more likely to be care's commanders. Their ability to command others to care was not a personal capability on the part of men; men's ability to command women to care arose from the cultural imperative imposed on women that assumed they were 'naturally caring', an assumption which, as we saw in Chapter 5, was contested by many women and by some men. There was also, however, a relation between time and social class. Carers in privileged classes were able to manage and attenuate the time demands of caring, while these demands were more inexorable for both men and women on low incomes, mostly people who were working class.

Looking beyond the gendered and classed nature of care time, the data also reinforced the point not all rationalities are economic, that there are care rationalities as well as economic rationalities. The time primary carers allocate to love labour is not simply a matter of their preferences between consumption and leisure, as typically modelled by economic theory. It is also a function of the moral imperative to care and the relational nature of care itself. Carers' understanding of their primary care relationships constrains their choices: it does not give them the option of having more free time, although they would clearly like to have some. While women are disproportionately socialised into care rationalities and men into economic rationalities, this is not inevitable. When men are primary carers, as were Tom, Pearse and Tony, they were as attentive and as burdened by guilt and commitment as women, although the stresses they experienced around time did not seem to be quite so acute. The cultural idol of a wholly rational, economic actor is a sociological myth. It works as a rhetorical device however to deny or dismiss the fundamental, interdependence of the human condition: As Sevenhuijsen has observed: 'Constructions of self-made autonomous man are based on the denial of care and dependency' (Sevenhuijsen, 2000: 24).

# 8
# The Impact of Economic, Social, Cultural and Emotional Capital on Mothers' Love and Care Work in Education

*Maeve O'Brien*

This chapter discusses the performance of love and care work in the paradigmatic context of mothering. It explores the care work mothers do in the field of education in particular. It suggests that the emotional care work performed by mothers in the educational field is an expression of what mothers understand as their love for their children (O'Brien, 2007). This forms part of the general mothering and domestic work that mothers do as part of their daily routines of care (O'Brien, 2005). The work of care, however, does not happen 'naturally' and effortlessly, and the capacities of mothers to activate economic, cultural, social and emotional capitals shape their care, and the exchange of that caring in the educational field.

While considerable attention has been given to the possession of economic, cultural and social capitals in reproducing educational advantage (Bourdieu, 1996), it is only more recently that the reality of activating emotional resources in supporting children's schooling has been explored and analysed (Allatt, 1993; O'Brien, 2007; Reay, 1998, 2002). This chapter explores how these capitals enable or constrain mothers' educational care work, and highlights relationships between economic, social and cultural capitals and the activation of emotional resources that facilitate mothers' care. The first section of the chapter draws on interdisciplinary discussions of care, mothering and schooling work from feminist sociology, moral philosophy and sociology of education to highlight the problematics of gender and care, and specifically the role of emotional capital in the way mothers support their children's education. This provides a backdrop for the rest of the chapter which draws on a qualitative research study with 25 mothers, and investigates how mothers activate resources in the performance of emotional care work at children's transfer to second-level education. The time of transfer from first to second-level schooling was selected as an exemplar of the doing of extensive educational care work by mothers, as it is a time of risk and uncertainty (Lynch and Moran, 2006; Reay and Ball, 1998; Reay and Lucey, 2000). Using Bourdieu's taxonomy of economic, social and cultural capital, and the related idea of emotional capital, this chapter shows that inequalities in all of these capitals had important consequences for mothers' abilities to provide educational care.

## Mothers' work and the role of care and capitals

### Emotional work, love labour and emotional resources

The unpaid care work that mothers perform in the home involves variable dimensions of caring, domestic work, physical child care work, emotional work, cultural work (childrearing including educational support) and sexual labour (Delphy and Leonard, 1992). While domestic and child care tasks are visible and commodifiable forms of work, the emotional work involved in caring is less tangible and often invisible and unrecognised. The 'love labour' (Lynch, 1989, 2007) that mothers perform for their children, including looking out for, thinking about and fostering relationships with them has an inalienable emotional dimension. However, the taken-for-grantedness and intangibility of love labour and the emotional work it includes have meant that the resources and energies required for its production have also been overlooked. Lynch (1989) has made an important distinction between love labour and emotional work. Love labour is heteronomous (see also Jaggar, 1995); it is an effort primarily concerned with the well-being of others, while emotional work may be used for emotional management in one's own interests or for example for profit (Hochschild, 1983). Nonetheless, emotions and emotional work are integral to loving and love labour. Feminist scholars have argued that it is the capacity of human beings to connect emotionally that facilitates attachment and care (Gilligan, 1982, 1995; Kittay, 1999; Nussbaum, 1995). Nussbaum (2001), Goleman (1995) and Damasio (1994, 2004) argue that emotions are essential to moral action and thinking, contribute to our emotional intelligence, and enable us to understand the position of others, and to care about and support them.

From perspectives spanning both sociology and psychoanalytic theory, Chodorow (1999) maintains that our feelings are essential to the making of personal meaning and identity. While Chodorow recognises that affect and feelings are shaped by cultural norms and the dominant gender order, they are also deeply personal and idiosyncratic. She argues that personal meaning is constructed in accordance with individual unconscious desires and affect. It is this socially gendered yet personal affect that enables and motivates mothers to care for and love their children, in ways that men and fathers traditionally do not (Duncombe and Marsden, 1996, 1998; Seery and Crowley, 2000). These culturally shaped emotions are fundamental to the efforts required in love and emotional labour, including listening, planning, organising, empathising, comforting and managing oneself in maintaining these emotional attachments (Hochschild, 1983, 1989).

Through the internalisation of caring ideologies, and a moral imperative to care, mothers' identities, regardless of positioning and resources, become inescapably bound to emotional caring (Bubeck, 2001; Hays, 1996; O'Brien, 2007). Notwithstanding the significance of emotions for caring, loving and the labour that involves, it is important to avoid generating essentialist and romanticised versions of mothers' love and emotional caring. Mothering work has real consequences for the carer (Nussbaum, 1995; Sevenhuijsen, 1998) and doing caring and love labour creates tensions in terms of mothers' time, and their energies and desires to pursue other goals and activities outside of caring.

## Mothers' care, love and education

Care and love have not been central concepts in educational debates, and traditionally, the emotional caring efforts carried out by mothers in education have been reduced to gender-neutral discourses of 'parental involvement'. Care and love have not been named as such in the growing body of literature on school choice and educational decision-making at the transfer to second-level education. Reay and Ball (1998) and Lynch and Moran (2006) have noted that discourses of school choice have constructed 'parents' as rational consumers in educational markets. This construction conceals the emotional efforts that are required, and generally performed by mothers, in managing schooling transitions and choices. Moreover, such constructions do not take into account the different capacities of parents to make educational choices and to care relative to their positionings and capitals (Gewirtz *et al.*, 1994; Reay, 1998).

The work of Lareau (1989), Walkerdine and Lucey (1989), Allatt (1993), Reay (1998, 2000) and Griffith and Smith (2005) has demonstrated the significant and often intensive educational care work produced by mothers relative to social class and the resources they can access. These authors also describe mothers' daily routines of performing educational work as having strong emotional components that require emotional energies or resources. Although Lynch (1989) has pointed out that not all emotional work qualifies as care, the educational work described by these authors certainly comes under the net of 'caring about' and 'caring for' one's children (Ungerson, 1990). The educational care work observed in their research suggests a wide range of ways of being caring, and doing care, including listening to children, guiding and making choices about schools and subjects, supporting children through assessments, homework support, meeting teachers, planning and organising meetings and transporting children to educational activities outside of school time.

## Mothers' access to capitals to care for and about children's schooling

Lynch (1989) has argued that even love labour, the work involved in fostering intimate relationships, requires resources. Bourdieu's metaphor of capitals can be used to analyse how resources reproduce social advantage and affect the doing of care. It appears that mothers' caring and loving take a particular trajectory in the educational field and become deeply imbricated with the capacity to access and activate dominant forms of cultural capital (Bourdieu, 1986). Those without access to cultural capital and other resources may find it difficult to achieve the kind of educational support required by the school system and have often been pathologised as mothers for lacking the forms of capital schooling requires. Walkerdine and Lucey's classic work (1989) suggests that middle class mothers have greater time and energy to do educational work because they do not have to engage in paid work outside the home. In addition, they argue that the possession of cultural capital and a middle class habitus[26] enables mothers to see the home as an extended site for educational work, where baking can be a maths lesson and gardening a science lesson. By contrast, working class mothers see formal educational support work as a separate activity from the daily care involved in domestic activities. Their restricted access to economic capital shapes the habitus and the possibilities for creating cultural capital in their children. The educational work middle class mothers do in the sense of transferring knowledge and skills is related to the task of providing care and emotional support for their children as they learn, and suggests that class differences in economic and cultural capital may also give middle class mothers an advantage in the degree of educational care they give their children.

In Allatt's (1993) exploration of routines of educational practices in middle class families, she describes how the cultural capital possessed by mothers is accessed via other forms of capital. She describes how mothers draw on cultural resources in tandem with social and economic capitals to pursue educational success and create pathways for the future 'happiness' of children. Allatt's work suggests that the possession of the classic forms of social, cultural and economic capital creates educational advantage and reproduces privilege through the activities of the mother and to a lesser degree the father. Drawing on Nowotny (1981), Allatt identifies a non-traditional form of capital, 'emotional capital' as being a carrier for other capitals/resources. Emotional capital is understood as a gendered and solidary capital, the skills, love, affection and willingness of mothers to spend time in caring for children, including their education. More recently, Lynch (2007) has distinguished emotional from nurturing capital, suggesting that nurturing capital is more specific to love labour while emotional capital can also be for profit or activated in pursuit of one's own interests.

## Activating emotional capital for care

Reay (1998, 2000) focuses on the problems facing mothers without cultural and economic capitals in trying to care in the educational field. She contests Lareau's (1989) claims that middle class mothers are more intensely emotionally involved in their children's schooling. Reay sees emotional involvement in education as a reality of all mothers' lives, regardless of social positionings and resources. She suggests that working class mothers, and those more marginally positioned, have to do greater levels of emotional work and invest greater emotional capital in their children's education than middle class mothers, although their investment often produces fewer results. Reay argues that the emotional efforts of marginalised mothers are less effective from a schooling perspective, as they cannot access other capitals that can be used in doing educational care. They often have a poor knowledge of the school system and little money to buy time, activities and artefacts that create advantage in schooling. Moreover, emotional capital, the emotional energies that mothers invest in caring for children's education, becomes depleted through poverty, loneliness, depression and hopelessness.

Reay (2000), echoing Lynch's distinction between emotional and nurturing capital, draws our attention to how emotional investment in education can be contrary to real care and love. She argues that increasingly, middle class mothers invest emotional and other capitals so intensely that it may be at the expense of children's well-being. These mothers, aware of current rhetorics of success and performativity in education, become implicated in cycles of control over children's time and choices which are contrary to real care.

## Mapping capitals in educational care

A recent qualitative study carried out with 25 mothers explored their emotional care work in the Irish educational context. The aim of the study was to contribute to our understandings of how caring is done by mothers in the educational field, to bring out the meaning care holds for them, and to investigate the inequalities associated with care production and provision relative to various resources. A theoretically diverse sample of mothers was selected to reflect varying social positionings and the resources associated with these for the doing of care.[27]

A discussion of the impact of capitals on mothers' love and care requires at least a brief description of the methods used to measure mothers' access to various capitals in their daily lives. This research drew upon Bourdieu's metaphor of capitals, as conceptual tools to capture mothers' idiosyncratic access to, and use of resources in the field of educational care work (see Reay, 2004). The research tried to represent this idiosyncrasy by mapping mothers along individual continua of capitals, namely economic, social, cultural and emotional capital.

Economic capital was categorised using the Irish average industrial wage in 2001 (I = 29,000 euro, see Layte *et al.*, 2001) as a ceiling for very low; those above this were categorised as low (I + 25%). The category adequately covered the next band (up to I × 2), with high capital at the upper end (> I × 2). Cultural capital was measured using educational credentials to locate mothers along the very low to high continuum from no educational qualifications to higher degrees (see Reay, 1998). While Bourdieu does not limit his metaphor of cultural capital to credentialised cultural capital, that is what was used here to describe mothers' levels of familiarity and 'success' within the school system. Social capital was a more difficult concept to capture but the continuum approach was used to position mothers relative to their access to social networks of support, networks that gave mothers credit and information in caring in the educational field (OECD, 2001).

With respect to emotional capital, egalitarian work on solidarity and emotional interdependency suggest that the emotional supports that one can draw upon at a particular point in time are significant for one's overall

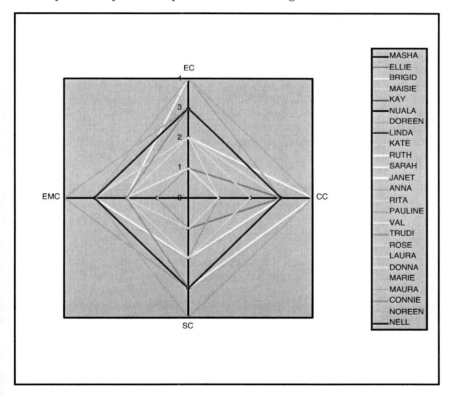

EC=economic capital, CC=cultural capital, SC=social capital, EMC=emotional capital

*Figure 8.1*   Mapping Economic, Cultural, Social and Emotional Capitals

EC = economic capital, CC = cultural capital, SC = social capital, EMC = emotional capital

*Note*: Diagram available at http://www.spd.dcu.ie/main/academic/education/staff _details/documents/OBrien_M_Phd_diagrams.pdf

capacity to activate emotional and nurturing capital (Lynch, 2007). Thus for analytic purposes it seemed reasonable here to base the mapping of a mother's accessible emotional capital on the level of personal emotional support she could access in her present 'carescape' (McKie *et al.*, 2002). Thus the mapping is limited to more tangible conscious and solidary aspects of emotional capital. Figure 8.1 illustrates the amounts of capitals accessible to the sample mothers in this study by attempting to map these resources in social space, where very low, low, adequate and high levels of each form of capital are assigned values of 1, 2, 3 and 4 respectively.

## Love and care at school transfer

While there are real differences in the ways that mothers can perform care for their children and support their education, particularly relative to their access to resources, it is important to comment on the shared experiences of mothers from different social positions in the doing of care.

All of the mothers described the time of their children's transfer from first to second-level education as one of uncertainty and change. It was a time in their children's lives that required mothers to perform intensive educational caring and general emotional support work. All mothers, regardless of social positioning, cared deeply about how this transition was negotiated because they believed that education was a key to the success and happiness of their children in the present, as well as in the future. Although understandings of 'happiness' are culturally and socially relative, all mothers performed educational care work towards that end (O'Brien, 2007).

Without exception, the mothers in this study felt that the transition from primary to second-level education was a significant educational and developmental move for their children. Most mothers had an awareness of an inevitable journeying, of a distancing and separation from their children as they entered a world where they would be required to be more autonomous and to meet social, personal and academic challenges in an increasingly performance driven and individualised school system and society (Beck and Beck-Gernsheim, 2001; Lynch and Moran, 2006). Nell summed up this complex transition:

> *I know our mothers worried but they didn't worry like this. It's all those other things out there as well, like a lot of their life is just spent trying to be cool, listen to the right music and say the right thing. It's not even the drugs thing at this stage … It's just he's only twelve and they have to know the words of the latest song and education has to squeeze in there, and they're squeezing the education in and that's very hard for them.* (Nell, middle class, married)

Mothers were aware that part of the transfer process involved a fine balance of letting go, and yet remaining emotionally available and acting in the interests of their children as they moved towards greater independence (cf. Kittay, 1999). This research found that mothers' education work in general, and the specific work at transfer, is performed against a backdrop of extensive general care work for their children. From the moment they woke up in the morning mothers set and maintained the emotional tone of the day in their families. First to rise, they were immediately engaged in emotional efforts to prepare children and themselves for the day ahead with a minimum of fuss and conflict. Mothers, irrespective of positionings and resources, maintained these efforts of 'caring for' and supporting children's schooling day-in and day-out.

Mothers' care work to support school transfer was extensive and also intensive at particular times or around specific situations that had to be negotiated as part of the transfer process. This work included: selecting a school, supporting children through assessment tests, securing a place in the chosen school, organisational work around uniforms, equipment and books, helping with new work regimes and timetables, and transporting children or arranging transport. Although none of these tasks are intrinsically forms of care work, what makes them care work in this context is the fact that they were things mothers needed to do in the course of meeting the needs of their children, a fact that made this work also highly emotional. Their care work also involved aspects of caring or loving that were about being rather than doing, especially being available to support and encourage children and listen to their concerns. Moreover, educational caring at transfer required that mothers have the confidence to communicate with teachers and principals where children were experiencing difficulties, or needed particular resources and supports. As discussed below, however, having the confidence to engage in this educational work was shaped by mothers' own experiences of education and their access to emotional and cultural capitals.

## Caring, loving and economic capital

Like most of Europe, primary and second-level education are provided free of charge in Ireland and economic capital should not have a major impact on students' participation in education. Research on participation rates at second- and third-level suggests however that socio-economic factors significantly affect the opportunities of young people to participate fully in the education system (Clancy, 1988; Clancy and Wall, 2000; Halsey *et al.*, 1980; Lynch and O'Riordan, 1998; O'Brien, 1987; O'Neill, 1992; Rudd, 1972).

All mothers in this study claimed that economic capital is required to care for children and their schooling at the transfer to second-level. They needed money not just to provide for new school equipment, books and uniforms, but also for other less visible and on-going schooling costs.

However, mothers differed considerably in the economic resources available to them to support their children's schooling.

This was most evident in the school choice process where mothers' horizons were set in accordance with the availability of economic capital (O'Brien, 2004). Mothers with access to economic capital appeared to experience greater emotional 'burdens' of choice as having economic capital to send their children to a range of schools meant a great deal of research and legwork had to be done, something that was outside the range of the possible for those on low incomes.[28] Only four of the 25 children in this study had transferred to fee-paying schools (only 8% of all Irish second-level schools are fee-paying).[29] Among the 14 middle class mothers in this study, fee-paying schools were routinely considered as an option, even if children did not eventually go to one.

Ruth, a married middle class mother of four, living on one income, felt the issue of fee-paying schools had become highly significant and stressful. Although economic capital was limited, Ruth and her husband prioritised finding the 'best' school for their son. Ruth had undertaken considerable emotional work (thinking, investigating, discussing and deliberating) to see if a fee-paying choice could be avoided, as the family would shortly be entering an even more economically difficult phase. Despite her anxiety about the monetary consequences of paying for private schooling, the school Ruth and her husband agreed was the 'best choice' was fee-paying:

> *When it came to Ben I was hoping that one of the local schools would be good enough and the local one is close, and non-fee-paying. We paid the deposit for the other one and he knew he could go. The fees are a huge commitment and we'll have to make sacrifices around that, but my feeling is if he's happy and he's developing it's worth it.* (Ruth, middle class, married)

Other middle class mothers also found themselves in this position. Having access to adequate, but not high, levels of economic capital created a possibility of sending children to fee-paying schools in an increasingly privatised system in Dublin in particular. But this possibility meant further emotional work and tensions for mothers as they pondered how they would spend money fairly on their children and distribute resources across the family.

The tensions experienced by mothers with low and very low incomes and from marginal positionings were different to those from the economically comfortable middle classes. Fee-paying schools were not even mentioned by the seven mothers in the study who were living on social welfare payments or a very low wage. These mothers spoke about the money management that they had to do just to purchase the basics, new uniforms, books and equipment for their children in the public educational system.

For those on low incomes, these demands were experienced as additional financial burdens in the effort to care for children.

Pauline, a separated mother of four demonstrated the stresses of caring without economic capital. She explained how choosing a school was shaped by an inescapable economic reality. For Pauline one of the criteria in making the choice between two local community schools (both located in designated disadvantaged areas) was the cost of school-books. She stated:

*I wouldn't have had the money for the other school either, because their books are too expensive, and the rental is only 50 euros in this school. I haven't the money for that and so I said I'd send him here and see how he gets on* ... (Pauline, working class, separated)

Pauline's perspective is indicative of how serious economic divisions operate, and how they are expressed emotionally in caring for children's schooling needs. For mothers on low incomes, meeting school requirements necessitated saving money throughout the year, so that there would be enough to pay the balance for school-books after they had availed of the small book grant scheme. Brigid, one of the Traveller women, talked about the emotional efforts required to have the money for schooling and to make sure her children 'had the right stuff':

*Like next year [costs] will go up. You have to pay for the uniform and the books, and you have to put a little bit by to make sure she has it. The only thing is the oldest gives a little bit of help with that and that's great. I don't think that she would go to school if she didn't have the right stuff and the kids'd be making a laugh of her.* (Brigid, Traveller, separated)

Indeed, all mothers in caring about their children felt that 'having the right stuff' was an issue to be negotiated. This applied not only to what the school stipulated was required in terms of uniform, but also having the type of shoes, schoolbags and runners that were acceptable to the children's peer group (Daly and Leonard, 2002).

Working class mothers, in particular, mentioned the stress caused by the 'hidden costs' of schooling. Laura, a working class mother, commented that primary school was 'good' because you could pay money off by the week, but it had to be 'up front' at second-level and that had to be managed. She also observed how hidden ongoing costs, such as ingredients for cookery classes, created hassles because as a mother you were not anticipating them:

*You have to pay up front and there's two of them and the older one came home the first day and asked for a hundred euro for papers (in transition year) and she's not even usin' them ... That cookery drives me mad, I wish they'd say ten euro each at the start, and she came home the other day and had to get two mangoes, where am I goin' to get two mangoes around here ... Cookery'd cost you a fortune ...* (Laura, working class, cohabiting)

In Standing's (1999) research on lone mothers and their schooling work for their children, she states that 'the school run' is one of the key organising factors for the mothers' daily routines. Although economic resources may not be an issue with respect to school journeys, even bus fare costs[30] were seen as a significant burden by low-income families and were a deciding factor with respect to choosing a local school. Masha, who recently came to Ireland from the Middle East, explained that transport was another burden in her situation and one that shaped her care and choices around education work:

*He [her son] will go just across the wall [to secondary]. If there are problems it's easy to sort them out. It's to save him from a far school, then there would be distance and we would have to have the transport, and that's another burden.* (Masha, immigrant on husband's student visa, married)

## Cultural capital, love and emotional care work

The amount and forms of cultural capital available to mothers were significant in the process of selecting particular second-level schools with and for their children. The emotional work involved in planning, information gathering, deliberating, discussing, weighing options, contacting and dealing with schools, was conducted most effectively by those with the cultural resources to do so, largely the middle class mothers. None of the working class, Traveller and non-national mothers in this study engaged in the selection process with the same intensity as the middle class group. Care work and how one is seen to care in the educational field is clearly shaped by one's access to knowledge and experience of the school system. The discussion below indicates how cultural capital shapes various aspects of mothers' educational care work.

### Selecting a second-level school

For all mothers school selection was about finding what they perceived to be the 'best' school. It is evident that 'best school' implied different sets of cultural meanings and expectations for mothers in different class and cultural groups. For middle class mothers, one of these expectations was that the school would provide a good holistic and advantageously academic education so children would be successful later in a career (cf. Allatt, 1993).

Janet, a single mother and a successful businesswoman had left school early herself. Having returned to education and obtained both a Leaving Certificate and a Bachelor's degree, she wanted to protect her child and send her to a school where her daughter would have the 'best opportunities' to develop and not be held back by others:

> *In that [working class] school, they're from difficult circumstances. I felt that maybe she would have to carry herself because there would be too much concentration on children with learning difficulties and other issues and problems. It was more what was going to suit her and some secondary schools are so bad you know the minute you go in the door.* (Janet, middle class, single parent)

For those mothers without dominant forms of cultural capital, choosing among a wide pool of schools was not a practice or issue that arose (cf. Bourdieu, 1984). None of the working class, non-national or Traveller mothers 'chose' to send their children to other than the local and familiar schools which, in all cases, were designated as disadvantaged and serving mainly working class populations. Nonetheless, although none of the working class or Traveller mothers had completed their formal education, they felt education was most important and they wanted their children to complete their schooling.

### Living near a good school

Cultural capital shapes emotional work in relation to school selection over prolonged periods of time. It appears to be embedded in the habitus and translates into practices that will facilitate educational trajectories from the moment the child is born (Allatt, 1993; Walkerdine and Lucey, 1989). This was evident in the discussions with middle class mothers who took it for granted that they would purchase homes in localities that were served by the kinds of schools that they would wish their children to attend. Sarah typically explained how she and her husband purchased their house with a view to caring for their children's education and sending their children to particular schools:

> *Basically we moved here and we enrolled her in the junior school. We had sussed out schools from an early stage. We decided early on that we would like her to go and although we have a [mixed] junior school that's closer and she could have walked across ... , but we heard reports that this [chosen school] was a good school, ... We both thought that because we both went to single-sex schools that we didn't want them to go to mixed schools.* (Sarah, middle class, married)

Not only had Sarah and her husband the cultural resources to discern the kind of schooling and particular schools they want their children to attend, but they also had the economic resources to follow through on the school choice that reflected their care.

## Staying in school

Three of the mothers were engaged in intense emotional work managing other care demands to keep their older children in school. Laura had two daughters attending two different second-level schools and her eldest wanted to leave school, as she was almost 16 and would be legally entitled to leave. Laura would not allow this because she wanted both her daughters to have better jobs than were available to her. Yet, Laura was worried that the care demands of her older daughter and of a new baby were jeopardising the transition of her middle child Cara and the potential for accumulating cultural capital:

> *Like I left at fourteen and I failed my Junior Cert ... It was sewing factories and shops and things and I don't want that for her, not for them, that's why she's got to stick it out ... When Eilish was goin' to secondary school, I had Cara but I didn't have the responsibility of a little baby and I feel that Cara might have missed out a bit.* (Laura, working class, cohabiting)

## Communicating with schools

One aspect of care work that is required at transfer is the contact and communication work of attending meetings and visiting schools. Schools varied in the types and frequency of contact they required of parents, but it was striking that none of the middle class mothers mentioned missing any meetings while four of the seven working class mothers mentioned that they had missed some meetings or opportunities to meet people at the schools.

In relation to attendance at initial school meetings, two of the four working class mothers who had missed meetings had partners that attended in their stead. The reason mothers gave for missing these meetings was that they had been away out of the city. It would appear that their habitus, shaped by their cultural capital, is more 'out of sync' with the habitus of the second-level school system than that of their more culturally advantaged middle class counterparts. These differences in how working class mothers care about their children's education and manage school meetings and contact does not imply a lack of interest or a lack of care. It appears that at an unconscious level they do not feel that they must or can always comply with school routines and demands.

Laura, a working class mother, explained that she could not get time off work during the working day when the parent/teacher meetings were held. The timing of school meetings may exclude parents from attending as the working class jobs they occupy may not allow time off for meetings. Although they would like to attend, they cannot. Laura commented:

> *Like there was a parent meeting yesterday but I couldn't go, but the teachers understood because I couldn't get time off work, and I told them I'd go up*

*and see the year-head in January. I rang the school.* (Laura, working class, cohabiting)

## Aspirations for children's schooling

The Traveller and working class mothers that participated in this study lacked educational qualifications and had little formal education. Thus, they cared for their children without understanding the nuances of the educational system and how it worked (cf. Lyons *et al.*, 2003). Indeed, for three of the mothers, even basic literacy was an issue. Consequently, almost all working class mothers and Traveller mothers had deep regrets and concerns about their own schooling and the impact this might have on their own children. For these mothers, their awareness of their lack of credentialised cultural capital made them determined that their children should complete their second-level schooling in order to have access to 'good' jobs or in a few cases to proceed to a third-level education.

There was a tension in how working class mothers experienced these aspirations for their children as they entered the second-level system. On the one hand, they wanted their children to be happy and supported their children's decisions to attend local schools with their friends. On the other hand, they knew that many students in the local schools still continued to leave before completion and this worried them.

In contrast, almost all the middle class and the two non-national mothers assumed that their children would complete their second-level education and transfer to college. The only middle class mothers who did not discuss college were two mothers of children with serious learning difficulties (Asperger's and Down's syndromes). Middle class mothers of children with dyslexia, for example, did not rule out the possibility of a college or university education. Their insider knowledge allowed them to seek appropriate supports for their children, and their care for these children was expressed in high educational aspirations.

## Social capital, spatial horizons and emotional work

It is possible here to distinguish between social and emotional capitals although they do overlap to a certain extent. Social capital is understood as relationships and networks that give one credit, information and support. Emotional capital is understood as the relations that give deep emotional support and enable mothers to invest emotional energy, love and affection in their children's care.

The sample of mothers in this study came from and lived in very different social circumstances and mixed with different sets of social groups. Within the school transfer process, one's social networks affect not only access to informal information about second-level schools, but also the capacity to act on that information (Reay and Ball, 1998).

Working class mothers generally associated with other mothers in similar social circumstances, and were informed through the local informal neighbourhood and kin networks. They had little opportunity to learn about other schools outside their immediate social and kin groups because they tended to move within 'closed' and 'local' networks. Their circumstances did not help them to exploit other possibilities in relation to choosing schools (cf. Connolly and Neill, 2001). Working class mothers worked hard at maintaining social bonds, and the social capital they built enabled them to survive within a 'closed' social world. This social capital however does not provide advantages in relation to schooling.

The emotional work that was required in relation to maintaining social networks among the working class mothers involved socialising and taking part in the life of the local community. It involved doing emotional work to get on with neighbours in the flat complexes and housing estates where they lived so as to provide a safe space for their children. Nuala, a working class mother of five, gave an insight into the energy involved and the importance of maintaining social bonds on her housing estate:

> *I'm the one who's here in the summer when they're [the children] off and if there's a gang in the garden and there's a problem I send them home, but sometimes the parents can be worse than kids … About secondary I'm not really worried like I was with Angela [her daughter] because they're [the boys] all going across together and they'll see each other.* (Nuala, working class, married)

Maisie and Brigid, two Traveller mothers, also relied on information from kin and neighbours in relation to education. The Travellers on their 'site' (housing estate) and their kin networks were valuable resources for keeping an eye on what was happening and checking out what young people were doing. The only social contacts that provided them with information or access about the school system were education programmes and the jobs they held in schools on community employment schemes.

The lives and social resources of working class and Traveller mothers contrasted starkly with that of Marie, a professional middle class mother. Marie observed that who you know can provide not only important information, but also can open doors that might otherwise be closed. Marie saw herself as an egalitarian and was loathe to exploit her own social capital, but when the happiness of her own child was at stake, this raised the question of using social advantages:

> *For my son, I've been unhappy with everything [at his school]. It was with pull, it's not the kind of thing that I would do but I mentioned it to somebody who then pushed all the right doors [to a private school]. So for me it was an eye-opener and I thought well obviously I should have been using those power*

*buttons all along and I wasn't really aware that it was such a big thing.*
(Marie, middle class, married)

Masha and Ellie were immigrants and outsiders in the school system despite their commitment to their children's education and their high academic ambitions. They were not part of any social groups that could offer support or access to information that would help them in caring for their children. They did not have access to the solidary support that working class and Traveller mothers did from kin and neighbourhood networks. They were very much isolated in trying to decode the workings of the school system and had to rely on comparisons with their experiences at home in their native Dubai and Nigeria. Moreover, Masha and Ellie's experiences of racist attitudes and treatment suggest that gaining access to social capital is very problematic. They were both at home full-time and were not allowed legally to work due to their visa status.[31] This cut off possible avenues of social contact and means of learning about the Irish school system.

## Emotional capital and educational care work

Allatt's (1993) understanding of emotional capital as the emotional skills, energies and resources that motivate one to act on behalf of one's child, suggest that emotional capital is an essential ingredient in care. In this chapter, it is assumed that the access mothers have had to intimate supports in the past as well as in the present is a major contributor to their emotional capital. However, the analysis here is confined to the emotional supports available to mothers in the present (as can be seen in the figure mapping mothers' access to the four capitals). The previous or early emotional nurturing that mothers may have had in their youth was beyond the scope of the study under discussion, although as many would suggest this is a significant aspect of our emotional well-being and capital over time.

### Caring and emotional capital within lesbian relationships

The two mothers in the sample who were in lesbian relationships were conscious of being involved in egalitarian emotional relationships. They felt that their partners were emotionally supportive around the 'hands on' educational work they performed. Rita, who had one child from a previous heterosexual relationship, described the experience of sharing the care with her partner as 'finding the crock of gold'. She appreciated how her partner sometimes got up first in the morning and drove her daughter to school so she could have 'a lie-in', a reality sharply in contrast with most heterosexual partnerships in this research. Rita described the building of her emotional capital through emotional support:

> *I was no less of a parent [before], but now I'm getting that nurturing myself, and in a way it comes in at all levels. Emotionally there's more of me to go round with her, whereas before I was spreading myself a bit thin all the time, a lot of the time really.* (Rita, middle class, cohabiting)

Anna, another lesbian mother, is not a biological mother but is a 'social' mother (De Kanter, 1993). Anna and Jean jointly decided to home educate their daughter Niamh during her primary school years. This involved negotiation in relation to the sharing of time and tasks. Both mothers cut their hours in paid work in order to be at home to teach and care for Niamh. Thus, Anna was not emotionally stressed about the new 'caring for' arrangements that schooling at second-level would involve. In contrast to the norm in most heterosexual partnerships in this study, both partners felt supported as they had negotiated and adjusted their hours spent in paid work:

> *Well, I have to be in for work at half eight and Jean is in the same place as me, but I'm tied for time as I have to be at a session and she has more flexibility. But I'll be waiting outside the gates ready to grab her and we'll have a bit of company and my day [in paid work] will be finished then.* (Anna, middle class, cohabiting)

### Heterosexual relations and emotional capital

Mothers in heterosexual partnerships whether cohabiting or married experienced varying but fairly low levels of emotional support in relation to the organisation of daily school support work. Even mothers who were involved in paid work, and who thereby experienced the dual demand of getting their children ready for school, and themselves organised for their jobs, did not always get emotional support for 'hands on' caring for children. In line with traditional gender ideology, middle class mothers, in particular, explained that this kind of support was not possible anyhow because of their husbands' commitments to long hours in paid work (see also Hays, 1996).

Notwithstanding mothers' responsibilities for primary care work, in the ten middle class families where the father and mother were living together, fathers were quite involved in the school choice process at an emotional level, even if they were unavailable for the donkeywork (David *et al.*, 1994). Mothers did the legwork and the background research but support was forthcoming from fathers particularly for meetings with school principals and in making the final decisions about which school children should attend.

Some mothers differentiated between practical and strategic support fathers offered about decisions, in contrast to emotionally engaging and time-consuming deliberations that mothers were engaged in. Noreen, a middle class mother, expressed this difference through understandings shaped by traditional gender ideology:

*Let me put it this way, men are more pragmatic. He'll just come in and look at a situation and say right ... For a woman the old heart strings enter in, possibly heart rules head.* (Noreen, middle class, married)

Mothers were not as resentful of the absence of hands on emotional support as might be expected. Traditional ideologies of gender and family enabled mothers to negotiate their primary care role (Hochschild, 1989). They perceived that there was emotional support in the background, or potential support, even if it was not available in a 'hands on' manner. Trudi exemplified this:

*It's important to know there's another parent there whose primary aim is probably the same as mine, to know that if I fall down or if I'm away he's there to take my place, and that he'll do it. He's very good and supportive, there's a family structure there.* (Trudi, middle class, married)

In Nell's view however, men did not understand the intensity of emotional work or recognise the need for investment of emotional capital in order to care properly:

*Men don't see it, though I know some men are different ... They want the child to progress, to be happy and not to get into trouble, but I think they expect that to happen without having to put in too much input. I think they lead by example and expect their children to follow them, to take their example and not necessarily discuss it with them, but just to follow their fathers.* (Nell, middle class, married)

In one case, Ruth, a middle class mother, indicated that her husband was more involved in giving emotional and practical support to the school selection process than to daily caring. Ruth described the benefits of sharing this task as significant for their relationship and her emotional energy:

*Well, he was involved from the start. He took a day off yesterday. We kind of mingled it [the work]. He approached the school as well, from our point of view [the relationship], it was very good, it was shared.* (Ruth, middle class, married)

For mothers who were living with partners or husbands and whose children had specific learning needs, the need for practical care support was fundamental to functioning. These mothers stated that they needed and did get varying degrees of practical support from partners for the children who needed most help in the family. Donna who had eight children and a child with Down's Syndrome making the transfer commented:

> *I've been doing everything and sometimes that gets really exhausting and I say to my husband 'will you do this run to school?' and it's that he wouldn't even think [of it] but he would do anything for you, but he doesn't think of it.* (Donna, middle class, married)

Practical support when provided was interpreted by mothers as emotional support, as it freed them to do other work, or to be less frustrated and torn in their attempts to care for children. Practical support in caring for children rebuilt mothers' emotional energies.

### Lone parents and emotional capital at transfer

Six of the seven lone parents in this study were living away from their own parents' homes. They were in a different situation from couples with respect to getting children organised for the school day. They did not have another adult living in the home who shared their concern for the children or who could potentially take over if required.

Linda, a middle class lone separated mother, had a demanding routine of rising at six and getting to bed by ten at night to cope with the demands of caring work and paid work. In the absence of a supportive partner, she described how she consciously drew upon her own internal resources, her emotional capital. Linda drew a distinction between the emotional support that one could derive from a sibling, a colleague or a boyfriend and what one might expect from a permanent and supportive partner:

> *I suppose my sister Sheila, she's a role model. She's a really good mother and she's there for me to talk a bit, but not like a partner on a daily basis. I don't discuss this with my partner [long-term boyfriend but not cohabiting]. That's a different relationship and I can't rely on it. I suppose in my work too, my principal, she's also alone and has difficulty with her son, so maybe I'm there more for her.* (Linda, middle class, separated)

Connie and Janet were both lone mothers who relied on both the emotional and practical support of their own parents to enable them to continue to work full-time and to care for their children. Connie and Janet acknowledged that they would have grave difficulties in managing their children and paid work without this support.

### Emotional capital and its relation to other capitals

Having no emotional support from others can lead to emotional isolation and exhaustion, particularly where other resources are limited. Pauline, a working class separated mother of five, tried to care for her children in economic poverty, and in a state of emotional trauma after the death of one of her children. Pauline's frankness in the interview provides a picture of the very real tensions experienced by mothers without capitals and in a situation of depleting emotional resources:

> *If I've problems at home, there's no point in hittin' them 'cos they only laugh at you. Mikie is getting' a bit of an attitude but I've discovered they do when they make their confirmation, and I get angry and say 'I'm going up to bed for bit of a lie down' and like the other day I said to them I'm sick of yez.*
> (Pauline, working class, separated)

This image of a mother caring without capital highlights the fragility of a mother's energy to care, but also the willingness of mothers to dig deep into their own emotional resources. Pauline was asked by service providers if she would take a short break but she could not. She described her 'love' for her children as all she had, so she continued to draw on her emotional energy although she was putting herself at risk of collapse.

It has been considered a truism that money cannot buy love, but in the daily routines of care that mothers performed to support their children's schooling, economic, social and cultural capital, in the right currency, enabled them to care and articulate their love. Moreover, these resources enabled mothers to restore their emotional energies for both care and their own well-being. Yet, these capitals could not replace the significance of emotional support as we have seen above; being emotionally cared for oneself builds one's emotional capital.

The problem of activating emotional capital without access to other capitals was obvious in the case of the most marginalised mothers, the Travellers and immigrant women. While three of these mothers had ongoing emotional support from intimate relationships, their economic impoverishment and lack of knowledge of the school system meant they still had to make far greater efforts to achieve a level of care in education that middle class mothers routinely achieved. Furthermore, ongoing daily struggles to survive, even when others may wish to emotionally support us, do not leave sufficient space for fostering one's own emotional well-being which is key to doing care. Traveller and immigrant mothers, and the very impoverished working class mothers, who expended so much energy just coping with basic day-to-day care work and schooling work, suffered physical and mental health related issues and regular tiredness and feelings of isolation. Going out to socialise or take time out for oneself was often out of the question, and lack of access to the social and economic benefits of well-paid work eroded the possibilities of receiving solidary support and recharging one's emotional batteries.

## Socially privileged mothers and anxiety

Anxiety and the erosion of emotional capital, in the broad sense of one's emotional energies, was not just confined to the poor and socially marginalised. Even those mothers with reasonable to high levels of economic, cultural and social capital worried and intensely cared about how their children were coping with the new school system. Having high levels of economic and cultural capital could intensify emotional concerns around care in the educational field. Indeed, the data show, as Reay (2000) has argued, that middle class mothers with access to the traditional capitals sometimes worried too intensely about their children's schooling. In this sample, none of the mothers displayed the movement from care to control, but nevertheless, the level of emotional energy that was expended on managing schooling showed that there is a normative requirement for mothers to do intensive caring in all social classes (Hays, 1996).

## Conclusion

While the intangibility of emotional care has often rendered it invisible in increasingly rationalised and bureaucratised public spaces, its presence in narratives of mothers' love and its expression in their daily caring suggest that mothers' emotional care work and love are deeply intertwined. This chapter has explored how mothers' expression of love for their children and the performance of care are mediated and shaped by access to resources.

Feminist scholarship, and the findings of the research presented here, suggest that mothers deeply internalise traditional gender ideologies around care, including a moral imperative that requires them to perform care regardless of the resources available to them. Thus, mothers are subject to a range of inequalities associated with the affective domain of life. At school transfer, they are expected to reproduce their children as students that can fit seamlessly with the norms and expectations of an increasingly performance-driven school system, regardless of whether they have the requisite capitals to facilitate this transformation. The taken-for-grantedness of care work and of the extensive educational work carried out by mothers is itself deeply problematic. This is further compounded by a lack of recognition of the resources required to maintain care and emotional work. While all mothers experience gender inequality in their assignment to care work as women, women differ in their experiences of caring and loving relative to the combinations of capitals they can access. Their educational care can be undermined by a lack of economic, social, cultural or emotional capital.

Cultural capital has been regarded as a highly significant resource in the educational field and the research presented here bears this out. Nonetheless, the data also indicate that material resources, in the form of income, impact on mothers' capacities to support their children's transition to second-level schooling. Moreover, having cultural capital without the material resources to realise 'the best educational choices' for children creates even further emotional work and anxiety for mothers. Social capital has the potential to privilege insiders in the system. Yet the kinds of social supports and capitals found between working class and Traveller women do ease the burdens of caring, despite the absence of privileged information and connections.

As a metaphor, emotional capital has not been theorised to the same extent as economic, social or cultural capitals, nor does it lend itself to direct or exact forms of measurement. Nonetheless, drawing on the literature and the narratives of care in this research, it is evident that emotional resources in both the broad sense of emotional energies we have acquired and the intimate emotional supports we can access in the present are fundamental to love and the work of caring. The ongoing care work mothers do in supporting children's education acts as a constant drain on their emotional energies and resources. Moreover, the experience of doing day-to-day caring and the schooling work necessary for the provision of good care forms a gendered knowledge that ties one to caring and to emotional investment. Where there is little access to economic, social and cultural capitals necessary to participation in education, emotional resources become highly significant for economically excluded and marginalised mothers (cf. Skeggs, 1997).

One can argue that money cannot buy love or the kinds of care that mothers perform to support their children and their schooling, but what is evident from this discussion is that economic resources do matter. From an equality perspective the recognition of care and emotional labour are a matter of urgency so that the extent of mothers' efforts are not rendered invisible. Moreover, it is only through that recognition of affective work that the issue of resources for the doing of care and how that plays out in the educational field can be addressed. The gender equality challenge around care is real, but this chapter confirms how other social differences relating to social class, emotional support and inequalities of resources affect mothers' care and education work.

# 9
# Caregiving Masculinities:
# An Exploratory Analysis

*Niall Hanlon*

This chapter presents findings from exploratory research about caregiving masculinities in Irish society. The chapter opens by addressing the gendered division of informal caregiving in families followed by a description of the research methodology. The remainder of the chapter discusses three themes identified in the analysis. The first theme focuses on the meaning of masculinity in the context of hierarchical and competitive relations among men. The second theme focuses on the way that breadwinning provides the dominant model for men's caregiving, prescribing and proscribing particular caring practices. The third theme focuses on tensions that arise for some men as they struggle with the role of 'feminised' caregiving in their lives.

Drawing on the theories of Connell (1987, 1995) and Bourdieu (2001) this small exploratory study tentatively draws three conclusions. Firstly, that the dynamics of masculinity preoccupy men with practices which are at least in tension with caregiving. Secondly, that breadwinner discourses and practices, whilst potentially drawing men into limited amounts of caregiving, are more likely to restrict the amount and types of care that men undertake. Thirdly, that there is considerable uncertainly among men about their role in 'feminised' caregiving and the value of 'feminised' attributes in their lives.

## Masculinities and caregiving

Caregiving is feminised in two senses. Firstly, women comprise the vast majority of both paid and unpaid caregivers in society (Gerstel and Gallagher, 2001: 214). Secondly, men's avoidance or evasion of caregiving facilitates gender inequalities experienced by women in social, political, economic and affective life (Baker *et al.*, 2004; Bubeck, 1995; Coltrane and Galt, 2000: 16; Hochschild, 1989; McMahon, 1999). While there are undoubtedly particular emotional payoffs from caregiving, it can also be psychologically burdensome and economically and socially exploited (Bubeck, 1995; Cullen *et al.*, 2004; Evandrou and Glaser, 2003).

Despite increasing resistance to male dominance (Giddens, 1992: 132) and important advances for gender equality in recent decades (Baker *et al.*, 2004: 207–211) the low level of men's caregiving, 'both within and beyond households, has appeared to be remarkably resistant to a wide range of demographic, social, and economic changes' (Gerstel and Gallagher, 2001: 199). This is despite men's work shifting from heavy manufacturing to traditionally feminised service sectors (Hayward and Mac án Ghaill, 2003: 26). Even societies with progressive policies on gender equality such as Iceland and Sweden struggle to realise gender equality in care work (Bjornberg, 2002; Seward *et al.*, 2006).

International research supports this assessment. McMahon's (1999) detailed review of men's caregiving emphasises a mismatch between quantitative and qualitative research, with quantitative research showing greater levels of caring equality. Qualitative research shows that women continue to do about double the care and domestic work of men and that women's increased participation in the formal labour market has not been matched by men's contribution to unpaid caring (Bubeck, 1995; Coltrane and Galt, 2000; Drew *et al.*, 1998; McMinn, 2007; O'Sullivan, 2007).

McMahon (1999) argues forcefully that the symmetrical family has not become the norm; he questions the extent of even modest advances towards caring equality. Men continue to take on the role of head of household in most cultures and tend to have more choice over their degree of involvement with children than women (Coltrane and Galt, 2000: 30; McMahon, 1999). Men generally prioritise careers over caregiving even when it defies economic rationality (Bubeck, 1995; Ranson, 2001: 146). McMahon (1999: 23) suggests that 'the typical husband enjoys a privileged position, with a greater right to leisure and to having his personal needs met by another'. Men's caregiving often involves higher status and enjoyable activities with greater emotional rewards (Brandth and Kvande, 1998; Gerstel and Gallagher, 2001; McMahon, 1999; Woodward, 1997: 267–269). Coltrane and Galt (2000: 30) note that 'Several decades of research...has shown that most women still perform the bulk of domestic work, remain the child-care experts, and continue to serve as the emotional managers for their families'.

Pessimistic interpretations of this situation argue that the evidence is symptomatic of men's continuing power and privilege. Male dominance is said to be shrouded by the myth of the 'new man' (Segal, 1997: 35). Minor increases in men's emotional support for their wives or partners, for example, is said to be a tactic to appease women for an unequal work-load (Delphy and Leonard, 1992). These findings lead some to conclude that men generally only undertake caregiving when there are no women available to do it for them (Gerstel and Gallagher, 2001; Noonan *et al.*, 2007).

Optimistic interpretations are more likely to emphasise that generational shifts in men's caring are occurring, albeit slowly. Men are seen as very capable of caring despite the fact that they rarely undertake primary caregiving

(Pringle, 1995). This includes, for example, men adapting traditional masculine work skills to the task of being full-time caregivers (Clarke, 2005; Russell, 2007). Specific groups of men including elderly men and gay men are more likely to undertake caregiving (Arber and Gilbert, 1989; Kramer and Thompson, 2005). Not discounting Delphy and Leonard's observation, men often take on a crucial role in supporting their partners' caregiving (Choi and Marks, 2006).

Research demonstrates that men's caregiving is structured by multiple economic, symbolic and emotional factors (Chesler and Parry, 2001; Coltrane and Galt, 2000; Reay *et al.*, 1998). This includes men's greater access to income, wealth and employment security as well as ideological factors including identity, subjectivity and differential status. Debates about men's lack of involvement in caregiving tend to focus on which of these factors is most significant or on their interrelationship. Against this background, this research set out to explore the hypothesis that dominant definitions of masculinities write out caregiving from men's lives.

## Research methodology

To explore the hypothesis ten key members from eight different types of men's group were interviewed. Men's groups were chosen because they typically reflect key male interests and identities, hold insights into men's resistances to gender equality (Connell, 2002: 150), and are often associated with the reproduction of male dominance (Brid, 1996; Hantover, 1998; Remy, 1990). Brid highlights the processes of emotional detachment, competition and sexual objectification of women that often occur in men's groups:

> *Homosocial interaction, among heterosexual men, contributes to the maintenance of hegemonic masculinity norms by supporting meanings associated with identities that fit hegemonic ideals while suppressing meanings associated with non-hegemonic masculinity.* (Brid, 1996: 121)

This is not true of all men's groups or essential to men's group processes. Some groups, such as gay, profeminist and many community development men's groups challenge hegemonic masculinities by facilitating alternatives to dominant masculinities (Kimmel and Mosmiller, 1992; Pease, 2000, 2002). The rationale of these groups is often to support men in resisting oppressive norms; for example, addressing men's violence and developing health initiatives. It is also erroneous to define groups simplistically in terms of pro- and anti-feminist/equality dualities, not least because of the multiplicity of feminisms and egalitarian perspectives. Even reactionary patriarchal men's groups can contain considerable differences in approach with some emphasising aspects of 'men's emotionality and shared (non-sexual) bonds between men' (Beasley, 2005: 181). Nonetheless, the nature of men's groups will typically activate and politicise masculine identities and prioritise masculine interests (Bradley, 1996). Gender identities are further activated by interview dynamics (Arendell, 1997; Campbell, 2003; Morgan, 1981).

Although it is difficult to estimate the number and diversity of men's groups in Ireland there appears to be a growing network of groups focused on supporting and advocating for men in various ways (Institute of Public Health, 2006; The Men's Project Directory, 2007). Added to this are men's clubs and societies, including sports, religious and business groups. The study was based on a purposeful sample of men's groups chosen to reflect inequalities including those based on social class, religion, age, geographical location, ethnicity, sexuality, and family and marital status (Government of Ireland, 1998, 2000) (Table 9.1).

*Table 9.1*   Research sample

| Interviewees* | Group Description |
| --- | --- |
| Dave and Tom | Community Development Men's Group |
| Declan | Construction Workers' Trade Union |
| Denis | Men's Club |
| Fran | Catholic Religious Group |
| Geoff and Alex | Gay Men's Support Group |
| Paddy | Older Men's Group |
| Paul | Fathers' Rights Group |
| Peter | Traveller Advocacy Group |

*Pseudonyms

Using standard thematic procedures (Braun and Clarke, 2006) the qualitative interviews with group members explored men's care relations generally, the specific caring concerns of each group and, occasionally, respondents' personal experiences.

## Relational masculinities

Connell (1995) proposes that men actively construct their masculinity in the context of the gender order that privileges men and disadvantages women. Men take a position in the gender order, or respond to the position they are placed within it, by actively constructing gender in daily life. Connell argues that men have collective interests in preserving a superordinate relation to women because the gender order provides men with symbolic, politic, economic and emotional/sexual privileges. Appreciating that men collectively extract a 'patriarchal dividend' from the gender order is key to understanding the social positioning of men as a group.

Connell points out that the gender order does not privilege all men equally, resulting in hierarchical and competitive relations among men. Femininities and subordinated masculinities are the most devalued within this order resulting in a tendency for men to distance and disassociate from these identities. On the other hand, hegemonic masculinities, gender practices that embody patriarchal legitimation and female subordination, are highly valued (Connell, 1995; Connell and Messerschmidt, 2005). Beasley (2005: 229) notes that hegemonic masculinities are ideals of male dominance that solidify masculine authority. Although culturally and historically variable, a feature of hegemonic masculinities is that they tend to write out and vilify 'feminine' attributes in men because they can undermine male dominance.[32]

Contradictions that arise between the imperatives to realise hegemonic masculinity and the negotiation of affective relational identities can result in 'crisis tendencies' in gender relations with negative effects on women's and men's well-being (Connell, 2002). For example, the incessant proving and machismo of competitive masculinities are associated with high rates of violence, injury, illness, mortality and imprisonment among men (Connell, 1995; Kimmel, 2000).

## The meaning of masculinity

The first theme to emerge from the interviews was that hierarchical and competitive masculinities were key features of men's relations. Heterosexuality, power, status and economic success were identified as important signifiers of socially valued masculinity, with each response reflecting the particular perspective of the group's relation to the gender order. Although the interviewees largely agreed about what the dominant signifiers were, many of them recognised the problems these created for members of their groups.

Denis associated masculine identity with public recognition and material possessions and exposed an acute sense that superiority and inferiority was a key dynamic of masculinity. For example:

> *[I]t is an old adage that if you come from a stately home, then you really don't care too much about how you look or what you drive around in. But if you come from a slightly more humble background, then ... you feel you've got to prove [yourself] to your neighbour that .... you need to be smart and you've got to be well-dressed, and you've got to be driving a nice shiny new Merc or a BMW or something.* (Denis, Men's Club)

Groups associated with less privileged men tended to emphasise how some men were socially excluded from advantages that other men receive:

> *Sometimes you hear about men being like a powerful group, a dominant group, an oppressive group. It isn't completely fair because these people don't feel it,*

*or see it, and their lives are not really like that ... society has been very uncaring for them ... [they're] shat on by the capitalist-patriarchal system* (Dave, Community Development Group)

Segal (1997) claims that men who are demoralised in public life often display power and status within the family. Tom and Dave emphasised the way many marginalised men resisted their social devaluation by achieving status, power and income within the community by other means, including illicit activities. Additionally they noted that some men oppressed others less powerful, including their wives, because they felt inadequate as men:

*[G]uys who realise they are in poor form because of something else and go home and have a row with the wife ... guys who would be on the housing waiting list and would have a meeting with the County Council people. [Then] go home in bad form and the wife would be saying 'you promised me we'd be in a house this time last year'. And everything blows up ... it's internalised and it's blamed on themselves not being articulate enough and not being able to state their case the same as a country fella, you know in the housing office.* (Tom, Community Development Group)

Subordinated men face particular difficulties developing a positive self-concept (Edley and Wetherell, 1997). Alex described how the subordination of homosexuality oppresses all men by defining masculinity and controlling men:

*Homophobia is used almost on a daily basis to police the boundaries of gender, to police masculinity and to set areas in behaviours and thoughts and attitudes of what is ok and what is not ok. That is still a very big stick for people to either beat themselves with or for people to get beaten with ... quite raw experience of homophobia and marginalisation ... stigmatisation or isolation which may have come from those experiences ... Or else internal wounds in terms of harm to their own self esteem, harm to their own self image ... People can be made feel that they are being left behind* (Alex, Gay Men's Group)

Paul argued that biological fathering was crucial for male identity and that family breakdown challenged the central role of fathers in families because it placed men in competition for authority as patriarchal authority figures. Discussing stepfathers in reconstituted families, he said:

*[D]oes that mean he is half a father and I'm the other half? Do they have two full fathers? Is he a step-up or step-down on me? Is he stepping on me, or over me, or under me? How do I feel about that or how does he feel about that? How do I feel about the fact that I might be doing it to some other man? Now that's a struggle for men!* (Paul, Separated Fathers Group)

Fran thought that men's sense of superiority over women was based on society treating men as more important:

> *[I]f the male gets preferential treatment in a family, what is that saying to him and how is that building his identity for the future? How is it feeding into his male dominant ego?* (Fran, Catholic Religious Group)

He thought that masculinity based on dominant attributes such as strength, aggression, resilience led to affective problems for men:

> *[P]eople come up against difficulties in their lives in terms of relationships, in terms of success and failure, in terms of jobs, in terms of qualifications, in terms of acceptance in peer groups. All of this is I'm sure connected, one way or another, with an inherent self-understanding that we have formed or is formed within us as we grow up.* (Fran, Catholic Religious Group)

Fran's discussion supported the view that men are under pressure to perform masculinity with bodies and emotions sometimes becoming sites of crisis (Connell, 1995). This view highlights the tension within masculinity studies between masculinities understood as constructions of power, prefacing men's tendencies to oppress women (Connell, 1995), and masculinities understood as embodied historical-emotional relations, prefacing how masculinities oppress as well as privilege men (Seidler, 2006, 2007). The former perspective places more emphasis on the power that men exercise over women: collectively through systems designed to favour men, and individually by recreating relations of superordination and subordination in daily life (Connell, 1995). The latter view challenges the central position of power in the construction of masculinities, emphasising that while power is important in understanding men's relationships, it is also a cover for men's vulnerability (Seidler, 2007).

Dave reflected the latter viewpoint when he described the mismatch between the social expectations of masculinity and the emotional ability of men from his group to meet these expectations:

> *[Y]ou're supposed to be strong with a woman at home, and so the lads are fed all that stuff. But the lads' capability of retaining those goals are completely different. So you're constantly being fed this thing that your success and self-esteem are based on A but if you get as far up as F you'll be doing well* (Dave, Community Development Group)

Contemporary masculinities theory appears to be giving greater recognition to the dynamic and relational, rather than fixed and static, processes and structures of power in personal life. Some men command and exercise less power than many other men and they may feel powerless because of 'racial' or class distinctions. This dynamic nature of power helps to account for men's contradictory power locations and experiences of powerlessness (Kaufman, 1994). At the same time, male power and privilege is obscured by a masculine sense of entitlement which positions white, middle-class and heterosexual masculinities as the gender norm against which other identities are measured (Kimmel, 2000).

## Breadwinner masculinities

Ireland's traditional strong male breadwinner model (Kennedy, 2001) is now declining in favour of a dual-breadwinner model (Creighton, 1999; Hilliard and Nic Ghiolla Phádraig, 2007; Meyer, 1998). Some dual-breadwinner models can advance gender equality when supported by progressive welfare systems (Rush and Richardson, 2007) but many continue to write out care from economic and social life relying on women as the default caregivers (Lewis, 2001). The result is a dominant family system where women are primary caregivers and only secondary earners and men are primary earners and only secondary caregivers.

Ferguson (2002) argues that hegemonic masculinity in Ireland was institutionalised as the good provider within heterosexual families. Breadwinning, rather than a broader definition of caring in terms of nurturing, was the traditional means that heterosexual Irish men used for constructing family caregiving masculinities (*ibid.*). However, breadwinning *per se* is not caregiving. Breadwinning practices may have caring elements and intentions and may be supportive of another's caregiving, but they do not generally involve caring activities. Breadwinning therefore provides a restricted conceptualisation of caregiving because the physical, cognitive and emotional work of caring are not its central activities (see Lynch, 2007). A breadwinner model defines men's caregiving in economic terms first and other aspects of caring as secondary. In this way, men define their caring based on full-time work in the public sphere and therefore escape the subordination and marginalisation involved in full-time caregiving.

The second theme that arose from the interviews was the way that breadwinner practices and ideology, which form the dominant model for men's caregiving, gave rise to particular tensions when they were threatened by dual-earner households, unemployment, retirement, and families departing from the heterosexual nuclear family norm. All of the groups, from different perspectives, were aware of the significance of breadwinning for men. This did not mean that they necessarily wanted men to adopt traditional breadwinner models. However, they saw breadwinning as the most socially valued way for men to access caregiver status. The interviews reflected a sense that if men were able to meet the valued expectations of breadwinning, they achieved a sense of masculine caring respectability, tied to the status of fathering and the emotional satisfactions of a secure family life. On the other hand, men who for various reasons could not meet these expectations were seen as excluded from its economic, status and affective rewards. *Family* and *Work Relations* were defined as two minor themes reflecting the way that different groups of men felt included and excluded from breadwinner caregiving.

## Family relations

Family relations that conform to the traditional norm of a married, hetero-sexual couple provide the context in which the breadwinner carer role is con-structed. Men whose families were modelled on this norm were happy to endorse it. For instance, Denis presented a romanticised and conventional view of breadwinner relationships as the natural order by defining masculine caring as oppositional and complementary to feminine caregiving:

> *It's nice that the woman is at home having the dinner on the table and looking after the kids and having them all washed, it's a different aspect [of caring], it's a different sort of pressure.* (Denis, Men's Club)

Complementary or difference perspectives that celebrate gender difference in caregiving deproblematise and rationalise caring inequalities between men and women. Often reflecting functional role and socialisation accounts they have been criticised for ignoring power and inequality (Brittan, 1989; Carrigan *et al.*, 1987; Kimmel, 2000). Their underlying functionality is often based on a biological essentialist ideology that endorses patriarchal relation-ships within families and wider society.

Traditional family relations were much more problematic for men who fell outside them, including separated fathers. Paul, a separated father, was parti-cularly hostile to feminism, suggesting that women supported by a feminised state had robbed men of breadwinning masculinity. He lamented the decline in 'patriarchy' which he felt had 'destroyed the self-esteem of men':

> *[It is] ... much more sustainable for [women] to go to the more reliable father which is the state, which is the substitute father who can pay you housing allowance, children's allowance, child care, crèche care, training if you want it, medical, than some guy who may or may not and you have to negotiate with him.* (Paul, Separated Fathers Group)

> *[G]ive him [separated father] a nice house and a car, the sort of resources you are prepared to give single mothers, and then sell that. Sure everybody would want to do it! There wouldn't be a woman left in the country with a child. You'd have every fella saying, 'I want one of them.'* (Paul, Separated Fathers Group)

Blaming women for the decline of traditional family relations is reflected in International Social Survey Programme research, which highlights a growing disapproval of single mothers among men in Ireland. Rush and

Richardson (2007: 96) identify the 'contemporaneous residual conservativism' of Irish men's attitudes towards lone mothers, compared to women's attitudes which tend to be more favourable. Although influenced by particular historical circumstances in Irish society, these conservative attitudes now occur in the context neoliberal market ideologies hostile to welfare dependency (ibid: 99). Discourses of lone mothers in liberal welfare states tend to define lone mothers both as a needy group and as a social problem rather than as a choice or as victims (Cheal, 2002).

Without excusing patriarchal relationships, it is important to appreciate their emotional content as this helps explain reactionary stances and the rhetoric of blame often levied towards single female parents (Leane and Kiely, 1997), or as excuses for male violence. For example:

*... domestic violence is a toxically incentivised industry with safety orders, protection orders ... vehicles for getting control of the family problem. I mean whoever gets the house, gets the car, gets the kids, gets the pension. That's what is up for grabs!* (Paul, Separated Fathers Group)

Paul presented the problems that separated fathers faced in accessing care relations (e.g. Corcoran, 2005; Ferguson and Hogan, 2004) as an assault by women on a traditional and proper gender order. Ironically, lamenting the decline of the traditional family based on stable marriages ignores the fact that this narrow conceptualisation of family life gives no role to single and separated fathers. Solidarity with lone mothers was absent despite the care gaps that confine the economic and social opportunities of all single parents.

The traditional breadwinner model's assumption of a heterosexual partnership also affects gay men's access to caring. Gay partnerships have no legal status in Irish society, with no rights to adoption, guardianship or marriage (Kee and Ronayne, 2002). Pointing out the diversity of situations in which gay men become fathers, including from previous heterosexual relationships and from having children with lesbian women, Geoff and Alex (Gay Men's Group) emphasised institutional discrimination and social stigma as particular problems. Geoff explained that unlike heterosexual men, gay men had to defend their rights to be fathers:

*Society's homophobia again can have a big impact [with] gay and bisexual men feeling afraid, in terms of bringing up kids, from society's homophobia because they shouldn't or they are bad parents or they can't be parents. But also then in terms of society's homophobic impact on the children themselves, in terms of the bullying that happens in school.* (Alex, Gay Men's Group)

Additional homophobic obstacles which gay fathers faced included society's association of homosexuality with paedophilia, which could make parenting a 'no go area' and a spoiled identity for many gay men (Goffman, 1981).

Gay separated fathers might also fear that prejudice against them would be exploited in court disputes:

> *There can be fears that [being gay] can be used as an issue in court around custody ... Or there may be still a lot of anger from their partner directed towards them ... [if they think] that the relationship broke down because they came out, so their sexuality can be identified in that broken relationship as a reason why the relationship failed.* (Geoff, Gay Man's Group)

As well as the fear of heterosexual prejudice, the 'social stigma' about being a gay father also came from other gay people, creating a silence about fathering:

> *It tends to be a bit of an unspoken on the gay scene, I know a number of men who have had children in previous relationships, some of them still have contact and play an active role and some of them don't. But I know a number of those men who are fairly open about it on the social scene but it is not something that is really talked about.* (Alex, Gay Men's Group)

Breadwinner caregiving in families, then, was primarily premised on heteronormative nuclear families. The numerous ways that men can fall outside, or become excluded from, these relations was a problem for men in constructing themselves as caregivers in families.

**Work relations**

A second element of the breadwinner caregiver model is an image of the man as a self-reliant, hard worker who faces a daily struggle to earn money in the hostile environment of the economy. Declan, reflecting on working class men, again gave voice to this picture of working relations:

> *[The] ... daily drudge having to slog in to the office or the factory ... [Many men] just do the 9 to 5 and get the hell out of it again and try and get home or get to the pub ... the man is out doing his best to make enough money as he can to raise the family, pay the mortgage.* (Declan, Construction Workers Trade Union)

Patriarchal family relations traditionally promised men an authoritative role within families in the context of a subordinated role in work (Hayward and Mac án Ghaill, 2003: 43). Paul emphasised the safety valve idea by the way the status and emotional fulfilment of being a father compensates men for unfulfilling working life:

> *[W]here guys are at work and they are not getting a lot of fulfilment from their jobs and they are not rated at work and you go home and your kids think you*

*are great. Like you can't fix anything at work but when you go home you can't
get anything wrong.* (Paul, Separated Fathers Group)

European research has emphasised that men are developing more relational
gender identities and are more responsive to caregiving but that they con-
front a 'deeply ingrained organisational masculinity in their job' (Holter,
2007: 425). Findings suggest that men face several difficulties in bringing
more caring ideals into practice including penalties such as decreased pay
and promotional opportunities for taking entitled leave or part-time work
(*ibid.*).

The expectation that men should be able to support themselves and their
families financially also creates problems for men in marginal economic
circumstances. Paddy thought that breadwinner identity, based on pride
and self-reliance, was crucial in understanding the reluctance of older men
to accept help from others:

> *Country people are very proud. Pride is an awful problem especially with
> single men or bachelor men like you know they would be too proud. I know
> people who would be living in very poor circumstances in very poor
> housing accommodation. Housing accommodation is available to them
> but they won't accept it because they wouldn't accept a hand out as they call
> it so it really is a problem with some people ... I feel it is something that
> happens in the generation of men and it probably goes back to the fact
> that a lot older men were children back when Ireland was a very, very poor
> place and life was very hard at the time during the Second World War
> and like a penny was a lot of money to a lot of people.* (Paddy, Older Men's
> Group)

Irish farming masculinities are traditionally based on 'breadwinning',
'independence', 'hard work' and 'pride' (Ní Laoire, 2002, 2005). Ni Laoire's
research shows that declining economic prospects for farmers are leading to
crisis as they struggle to stay on the land and live up to hegemonic farming
masculinities. Their chances of reproducing traditional patriarchal structures are also limited because of diverging gender roles and expectations
(*ibid.*).

Unemployed men face similar difficulties. Goodwin's (2002: 164) research
on men in north Dublin found that being unemployed made the men
'feel down, worthless, lazy, emotional, incapable, inactive, negative, lacking self-respect, weak and "not a real man"', because the men could not
define themselves as breadwinners. This was a major issue for marginalised
men:

> *The Traveller man perceives himself as the breadwinner full stop ... [I]f
> he feels that he is not contributing in a tangible way to the support and*

*the maintenance of his family, he feels a failure in some way. You know he feels he has let his family down.* (Peter, Traveller Advocacy Group)

Goodwin's research found that unemployment is more significant when men cannot find substitute means to construct themselves as bread-winners. As mentioned earlier, some of the men from Tom and Dave's group used the income and status of illicit activities to construct a sense of themselves as providers.

The image of the hard-working man supports the view that men's working life involves costs that can drain men's energies for love and emotional labour (Chapman, 2003; hooks, 2004: 94). Although men are net benefactors from gender relations (Connell, 1995), it needs to be borne in mind that privilege is unequally distributed, with white, middle-class, heterosexual, able-bodied men most protected against affective deprivations (Baker *et al.*, 2004: 8–9). Hegemonic masculinities set the agenda for men's relations and these are currently configuring around neoliberal philosophy privileging self-reliance and intense competitiveness, with the ideal worker defined as an independent rational actor who is perceived as mobile, flexible, and unattached (Hearn and Pringle, 2006). Men who fail to live up to this ideal cannot fully succeed in the role of breadwinner care-giver.

## Subordinated caregiving

The third theme emerging from the interviews centred on the tensions some men experience as they struggle with the role and meaning of 'feminised' caregiving in their lives. Doing 'feminised' care work challenged the men's sense of themselves as men. Bourdieu (2001: 30) emphasises the way masculinity distinguishes itself from the feminine by oppositional and complementary identities and social practices. He makes the observation that '[m]anliness … is an eminently relational notion, constructed in front of other men and against femininity, in a kind of fear of the female, firstly in oneself' (Bourdieu, 2001: 53). Viewing masculinity as the embodiment of social status distinctions through a long and continuous 'labour of socialisation', he emphasises the intensive socialisation process that strips masculinity of the feminine and embodies social practices of domination (*op cit:* 23, 49).

A sense of distinction was evident in the meanings the men gave to feminine caring showing how men experience a conflict between the need to achieve a sense of esteem and validation as men by embracing masculine-defined characteristics, and their desire to develop and sustain emotional intimacies and social relationships with others; relations typically defined as feminine.

Many of the men equated 'feminised' caregiving solely with 'soft' emotions, emotional intimacy, sensitivity, and 'tactile' physical caregiving. Reducing 'feminised' caregiving to emotional intimacy and physical nurturing hides the complex and multifaceted activities and relationships that comprise caregiving, including its mental (organisational/managerial) and physical aspects (Lynch, 2007; see Chapter 2). This 'feminised' understanding of caring made it seem more inaccessible than it might be since managerial and organisational attributes are traditionally thought of as 'masculine' virtues. Nevertheless, since care does involve emotions, intimacy, sensitivity and touch, the fact that these are traditionally seen as feminine presented a major obstacle to men's seeing themselves as carers. Respondents' views on the role of 'feminised' caregiving in men's lives varied from rejecting them to embracing them.

**Rejection**

Some of the men interpreted the expectation for men to do 'feminine' caring as a devaluation of men's caring roles. Paul felt that men were losing a sense of masculinity and becoming 'more like women' by developing 'feminine' care characteristics. Angry at what he saw as the 'feminisation of the word care' and with men presented as 'feelingless' and 'inarticulate' he wanted to see a revaluation of 'providing' as caring:

> *Society needs men to go to war; they need men to drive trains and fix the roads. The role of care [as] intimacy ... [is a] simplistic view of care is presented in the soft imagery of media and it denies other caring roles that men are playing.* (Paul, Separated Fathers' Group)

He gave nurturing caregiving a subordinated status to the romanticised roles of breadwinning:

> *You know I could be in here caring for my kids all night but if I don't get money to put the heating on then we'll all be cold and we'll die, we'll die, my children will die in my arms but they will die nonetheless.* (Paul, Separated Fathers' Group)

Believing that men's breadwinning carer role with their children was undermined and devalued, Paul was angry that men were finding it difficult to feel proud of their traditional roles as fathers, a situation exacerbated by what he saw as the lack of father's rights:

> *If the guy gets separated and the mother gets the house and he gets thrown out, where does he live? How does he have an environment whereby he can provide for his children the sense of, the ambiance of a home that can give him legitimacy and self-esteem within his relationship with his children? ... I'm looking*

*after my children on an equally shared basis and I want the respect for doing that. I am denied that! ... It's cost me money it's cost me a career.* (Paul, Separated Fathers Group)

Some of the men explicitly claimed that men hide their caring because it makes them feel inferior. This seemed especially important for older men, Traveller men and unemployed men. Paddy suggested that for poor elderly rural Irish farmers the association of caring work with femininity distanced these men from caregiving. Being a caregiver exacerbated their feelings of worthlessness because of expectations to be independent and self-sufficient. This mirrors other analyses that have found that illness, retirement and aging often signify emasculation for older men because they are the anti-thesis of hegemonic masculinity (Arber and Ginn, 1990). Similarly, Peter discussed how the 'external pressures and feeling that you are being laughed at and you're being called a woman' created the taboo on Traveller men's caregiving in public:

> *[This is] ... macho bullshit and peer pressure coming to bear on you so you find other ways of contributing, other ways of supporting ... [You] don't do it in public but you do it in the home, ... you wouldn't take a child out to the shop ... but you just might mind the child for an hour at home so it's not done in public view.* (Peter, Traveller Advocacy Group)

### Ambiguity

Some of the reflections were more uncertain about men's role in 'feminine' caregiving. This was most evident in discussions about gender differences in coping, where there was uncertainty among the different men about the value of stereotypically 'feminised' and 'masculinised' coping strategies:

> *I don't necessarily think that it's a case men need to be more like women in terms of mental health because I think women are very heavily socialised to be emotional and 'weak' ... [M]aybe [masculine] coping skills, you know, deserve more recognition as positive things.* (Dave, Community Development Group)

Uncertainty was also evident in discussions about changing masculinity:

> *[T]he lads should be able to access services, education, proper housing and health without first having to go through a process of de-masculinisation ... [N]o-one asks businessmen to sort out their feelings towards homophobia before they can access loans or business meetings ... [I]n community work set-tings the first thing on the agenda seems to be getting around talking about your feelings and sitting around counselling [rather than] why there is no accommodation or why there are twenty courses for women and none for men*

*... I think there's a real danger in focusing on men and emotional stuff in iso-
lation from the context of where men's lives are at ... [I]t's like focusing on one
aspect of an oppressed group's behaviour without seeing it all, you'd actually
be playing a part in the oppression.* (Dave, Community Development
Group)

Giddens (1992) argues that change in gender relations in families is driven
by women who are demanding relationships that are more egalitarian and
emotionally intimate as against men who tend to defend the status quo.
As traditional patriarchal structures supported by church and state are
declining, women have greater freedom to reject men who cannot meet
these emotional demands (Kennedy, 2001; Leane and Kiely, 1997). Even
Paul, who expressed traditional patriarchal views, was unsure about how
gender relations should be in contemporary society, as he shows referring
to the caring responsibilities of stepparents:

*There's the role play of what will happen in that new model. In other words,
will that new partner of mine become a replacement mother of my children? ...
Will I be the man of that relationship and do the non-caring things like provision of resources and will she now do the tactile things? How do we unravel
those struggles?* (Paul, Separated Fathers Group)

Yet if men are to meet the challenges of contemporary relationships, they
will be expected to develop traditionally feminised emotional skills and
relinquish a sense of masculinity based on notions of patriarchal authority.

## Embrace

Some of the men were less dismissive of 'feminised' caregiving and viewed
contemporary changes, as per Giddens, very favourably. Paddy reflected on
the historical status of women's work in rural Ireland and recognised the
multifaceted nature of caring. As well as being an injustice to women, he
noted that men's dependency on women's caring becomes an obvious
difficulty for men when women are not available to do it for them:

*[Men believed] that's women's work and that's men's work, ... especially as
far as the children was concerned. Rearing the children was left to women only
and the men went out to work in the morning especially in the rural areas
where there was farmers. They went out to work in the fields in the morning
and they came in when it was dark, and they were working so hard and tired.
And women to a certain extent let that happen because women felt 'ah well he
is working all day with a spade and that he's tired'. They didn't realise they
were probably working twice as hard inside looking after the children, cooking
meals, preparing meals, looking after livestock around the house. And they did
maybe give that status to men that maybe they didn't really deserve. It should*

*have been more as it is now with everybody shares and shares alike you know male or female.* (Paddy, Older Men's Group)

*A lot of men when they lose their partner, like they have never made a cup of tea in their lifetime, and when they lose their partner they have to be cooking for themselves. They don't cook what they should be cooking or eat what they should be eating and definitely it causes a problem ... [T]hey live on tea or bread as much as they can or boiled eggs and things. They don't get cooked vegetables or potatoes or cereal or anything like that.* (Paddy, Older Men's Group)

Declan supported a belief that men were increasingly sharing caregiving but associated men's slowness to change with masculinity:

*The people I look after would never have been categorised in the category of changing kids' nappies or minding children. That's changed a lot now and there's a lot of hurt and pride and all the rest, but they are coming round beginning to learn that's the way of the world now, and that's what it takes for families to survive and some are liking it ... Circumstances change people tremendously ... They are forced to dig down deeply into their emotions and find that they have what it takes to share with people and to bond with people and to help people around them.* (Declan, Construction Workers Trade Union)

Emotional constructions of particular masculinities as incommunicative and stoical have been identified as a source of psychological disturbance in men's lives, in extreme cases leading to depression and suicide (Clare, 2000; Cleary, 2005). This absence of emotional intimacy was seen as a big problem for some of the men:

*[There is] ... a lot of pent up sexual, emotional frustration in a lot of the lads ... [I]t would be 10 or 20 years since they have had a relationship with a man or a woman so there's a lot of pain there that's probably feeding the alcoholism and a lot of other stuff.* (Dave, Community Development Group)

Some of the men recognised men's problems with emotional communication especially in their friendships with other men and argued that becoming 'more like women' would improve men's lives. They embraced 'feminine' characteristics as beneficial for men and gender relations:

*Traveller men are still not at the stage where Traveller women are at in terms of talking about very personal issues ... Friendship among Traveller men is very limited in that it's either a football buddy, or a drinking buddy, or somebody you might go hunting with or horseracing ... [It is important to] arrive at a situation where Traveller men would be engaging with other Traveller men the same way women are engaging with each other ... that it doesn't diminish who you are and it doesn't make you less of a man if you talk about children to another man, or talk about sexual relations to another man.* (Peter, Traveller Advocacy Group)

'Feminised' caregiving has a subordinated status in men's lives because it contradicts dominant masculine norms. However, the intersection of different identities such as family status, class and age influences what men have to lose or gain from caregiving. It may be that men who feel assured of their status have less to lose by undertaking caregiving, whereas precariously held masculinity faces greater threats. Overall, the interviews mirrored other research where men guarded their masculinity from 'feminised' public displays including emotional intimacy (e.g. Cleary, 2005), but showed that some men were more open to change.

## Conclusion

Masculinities involve claims to power, status, and resources but additionally to love and care. A focus on masculinities and caregiving usefully illustrates the tensions and contradictions at the heart of men's lives. One of the main contradictions is between men seeking to maintain superordinate identities, embodied as a gendered habitus (Bourdieu, 2001), while at the same time reflexively renegotiating expectations of emotional intimacy and shared caring within contemporary relationships (Giddens, 1992). Ferguson (2002) argues that the gender order in Ireland is reconfiguring new masculinities based on reformed hegemonic practices but that there is also a counter trend of increasing individualisation, fluidity and reflexivity among men.

This chapter's analysis of interviews reflecting the lives of different groups of men has highlighted the widely acknowledged insight from masculinity studies that masculinity has a structure based on power and domination, although at the same time revealing the difficulties different men encounter in conforming to its norms. It additionally has shown that breadwinning continues to be the dominant referent for men's caregiving, defined in contrast to the kinds of care provided by women. Here again there were many men whose circumstances made it difficult for them to conform to this conception of masculinity, because their family relationships departed from the traditional model or they could not sustain the economic role of independent provider. Breadwinning seems to be a discursive resource that allows men to continue to perform and evaluate their masculinity based on economic achievement, power and public status, whilst at the same time to construct a sense of caring masculinity and access care relations. In this way, breadwinning supports hegemonic masculinities and is complicit with caregiving inequalities.

The meaning of caregiving creates different challenges when men step outside of this paradigm because its alternate commonly symbolises femininity and subordination. When thinking about men's resistance to caregiving, Delphy and Leonard (1992: 136) point out that caring activities *per se* are less significant than the relations of care production. The key issue, they find, is that caregiving is subordinated work most often done by women who have a subordinated status in society compared with men. The resistance and ambivalence expressed by men towards 'feminised' caregiving supports this view, although there were also men who welcomed change.

In general, the hypothesis that dominant definitions of masculinity exclude many aspects of caregiving from men's lives seems sound. That said, these definitions are not without major tensions and ongoing challenges. Consistent with Ferguson's claim there was a sense that some men were slowly adjusting to changing caregiving expectations, whilst others were resisting change and struggling with conflicting demands. Research demonstrates that breadwinner ideals but not practices are declining in Europe (Hearn and Pringle, 2006). It may be easier for men to talk the talk of caregiving than to walk the walk.

# 10
# Living in Care and Without Love – The Impact of Affective Inequalities on Learning Literacy

*Maggie Feeley*

In the general field of education, the role of the emotions has only begun to be explored in depth in the recent past. The work has focused on a range of issues such as: care and the school curriculum (Cohen, 2006; McClave, 2005); teachers' emotional labour (Hargreaves, 2000, 2001); the role of the affective domain in educational ideology (Lynch *et al.*, 2007); a school ethic of care (Noddings, 1992, 2006, 2007) and mothers' care labour in children's education (O'Brien, 2005, 2007; Reay, 2000). This chapter takes a new turn, towards the role of care in the learning of literacy. It describes the process and findings of a three-year ethnographic study carried out with survivors of institutional abuse in Irish industrial schools. In particular, the perspective moves from the teacher or parent as caregiver to the learner as a care recipient in a learning relationship.

The chapter begins by describing the research design and methodology and outlining the current context in which survivors of institutional abuse participate in adult learning. The prevalent theoretical conceptions of literacy are then summarised as a basis for examining literacy from an affective perspective. Finally, based on the findings, four types of *learning care*[33] relationships are described, based on the three-level conceptualisation of care relations set out in Chapter 2. They are primary, secondary and two types of tertiary learning care relations, where solidary learning relationships with peers in a civil society setting are distinguished from the enabling duty of care provided by the state. The chapter concludes that this understanding of the pivotal role of care in learning literacy may contribute to our understanding of persistent high levels of unmet literacy needs and of low participation in adult literacy provision.

## A relational method of inquiry

The research set out to explore the role played by affective aspects of equality in the learning of literacy. Both design and methodology required careful consideration and lengthy preparation because both literacy and care are sensitive areas not readily opened up to outsiders. After an exploratory period of working as a literacy tutor with a number of adult groups who had unmet literacy needs, the Lighthouse Centre[34] for adult survivors of institutional abuse in industrial schools became the ethnographic research site.

The ex-residents of care institutions were deemed the most appropriate partners for a number of reasons. Although these survivors had actually been resident in state educational establishments, they emerged with a higher proportion of unmet literacy needs than did their contemporaries in wider society (Government of Ireland, 1970; Raftery and O'Sullivan, 1999). In this, and in their experience of care, they were extreme or critical cases that Patton (1980) cites as useful in that they point up issues of wider concern.

The study sample, aged between 40 and 65, reflected the mainstream grouping involved in adult literacy (Department of Education and Science (DES), 2006). At the same time, the diverse nature of the community made it possible to explore the experience of both those with met and unmet literacy needs coming from a comparable learning and care environment.

The cohesive nature of the community meant that the process of gathering data was not only less intrusive than with other groups but actually contributed to a wider, emancipatory process of reflection and dialogue within the Centre. The solidary nature of the group also provided a supportive base for participants who might potentially have been upset by revisiting the details of a painful past. Most significantly, the primary care role of the state in the research participants' childhood removed the usual distraction of family deficit discourse and allowed the pivotal state duties to care and to educate, to emerge untrammelled (Hillyard *et al.*, 2004).

In total, 28 survivors took part in semi-structured interviews and a series of follow-up, feedback focus groups. The research sample was purposefully selected to be representative of age, gender, ethnicity, sexuality and learning disability within the core community. The entire process was collaborative including identification of potential participants. It was decided also to sample in terms of literacy status on leaving school so that comparison could be made between those who had learned literacy while in care in industrial schools and those who had not. Of necessity this required detailed insider knowledge and cooperation.

The data was further validated through methodological triangulation (Denzin, 1997) involving ten in-depth interviews with tutors, counsellors, legal representatives and others working closely with survivors. Cohen *et al.* (2000: 112) cite triangulation as a powerful means of 'demonstrating concurrent validity' in qualitative studies. Originally a navigational technique that used a number of markers to more accurately pinpoint a destination, triangulation analogously describes the use of a variety of methods and sources of data collection to confirm the validity and reliability of research data. This is particularly pertinent in ethnography where a single community is being studied and the possibility of collective memory exists (Olick and Robbins, 1998).

The affective focus of the empirical study, and the sensitive nature of the research topic, led organically to a relational research method. An ethnographic approach allowed time to build respectful relationships of trust with the research partners and to review and consult throughout the process with community members (Barton *et al.*, 2000; Carspecken and Apple, 1992; Edmondson, 2000; Pardoe, 2000). When adults become motivated to learn literacy, time becomes a significant imperative and adopting a practitioner research paradigm (Fowler and Mace, 2005) allowed this vital literacy work to proceed, and to ground the study throughout. It meant that the research agenda recognised and did not supersede the priorities of the research partners and the role of the researcher within the community became one of reciprocal learner.

## Irish industrial schools

Industrial schools were first established in Scotland, operated throughout Britain under the 1857 Industrial Schools Act and were extended to Ireland in 1868. They were intended as a complement to the Reformatory School system with the remit of providing state care and education for children whose family life was no longer viable. Although known to be exceptionally punitive, the schools were allowed to operate virtually without either challenge or sanction for almost 100 years. In 1970, the Kennedy Report (Government of Ireland, 1970) was highly critical of the system and the decades that followed saw survivors speaking out about their experiences and the extent of their multiple abuses becoming public (Doyle, 1988; Fahy, 1999; Flynn, 2003a, 2003b; Tyrell, 2006). In 1999, the Taoiseach, Bertie Ahern, admitted the awful reality of the repressive state care system and apologised to the survivors:

> On behalf of the State and all its citizens, the government wishes to make a sincere and long overdue apology to the victims of childhood abuse for our collective failure to intervene, to detect their pain, to come to their rescue … all children need love and security. Too many of our children were denied this love, care and security. Abuse ruined their childhoods and has been an ever present part of their adult lives reminding them of a time when they were helpless. I want to say to them that we believe that they were gravely wronged, and that we must do all we can now to overcome the lasting effects of their ordeals (An Taoiseach Bertie Ahern, 11 May 1999 as cited in Health Board Executive, 2002).

The Taoiseach acknowledged the importance of affective factors in the lives of children and the detrimental impact of a loveless and careless childhood on later adult lives. An inquiry was instigated to hear evidence of abuses and make compensatory payments to victims and this process is ongoing.

In June 2002, the State signed an Indemnity Agreement with 18 of the religious congregations who, for their part, contributed €12.5 million to enable the establishment of an Education Fund for survivors and their families (Education Finance Board, 2008). This was (implicit) recognition of the long-term, generational, harmful impact of affective and educational inequalities. In particular, unusually high levels of illiteracy were observed amongst those who attended industrial schools (Raftery and O'Sullivan, 1999). The Lighthouse Centre was established in 1999 by a group of survivors to provide healing through adult learning opportunities. Initially established without funding, the Lighthouse Centre now receives core funding through the Departments of Health and Education. Adult literacy is a core part of the work of the Centre.

'Survivors of institutional abuse' is the chosen term used by ex-residents of industrial schools who attend the Lighthouse Centre. A range of abuses has been reported by them including emotional, physical and sexual abuse. Neglect, including educational disadvantage, is also recognised by the Office of the Attorney General (2002) as a form of abuse eligible for compensation under 'loss of opportunity'. All those who attend the Lighthouse Centre have experienced one or more forms of abuse and many are working to improve their level of literacy.

## Changing perceptions of literacy

In the past the rich, the religious, the gendered cultural and political elite and the merchant classes have all used literacy to assert and sustain their dominant position and to maintain the subjugated position of others (Clanchy, 1979; Crowther *et al.*, 2001; Graff, 1981; Mace, 2001). Over time, as literacy has gradually become a more widespread resource in the West, so the relationship with inequality has persisted and the stigma attached to having unmet literacy needs has also grown. Literacy has historically reflected wider inequalities in society and yet this correlation is rarely articulated.

Treatments of literacy have taken three main forms: neoliberal discourses emphasising human capital, critical theory approaches focussing on agency and cultural activism, and New Literacy Studies (NLS), which sees literacy as a situated social practice. The dominant, neoliberal literacy discourse for the past decade has undoubtedly been one of 'falling standards' and the ensuing challenges for competitiveness across nations in the global capitalist market (Heckman and Masterov, 2004; Jones, 1997; Moser, 1999; Parsons and Bynner, 1997, 1998; Wagner and Venezky, 1999). The policy focus that results from such large-scale quantitative studies is on managing failed individuals and the perceived inability of the education system to furnish the market with sufficiently flexible and productive workers (Commission of the European Communities (CEC), 2001; Department of Education and Science (DES), 2000; Organisation for Economic Cooperation and Development (OECD), 1992, 1995, 1997). The constraint and inequality imposed on those who have been short-changed by the education system is discounted.

By contrast, critical literacy theorists have focused on agency and cultural activism as a means of transforming unjust social systems and their influence has transcended the field of education to wider movements of struggle (Aronowitz and Giroux, 1993; Freire 1972, 1985; Giroux, 1983; Gramsci, 1971, 1995; McLaren and Leonard, 1993). The work of Paulo Freire and of feminist scholars and educationalists radically influenced the development of the adult literacy movement in the 1970s and 1980s. Through defining and practising consciousness-raising, politicising the personal and acting collectively, they defined the parameters of an empowering and egalitarian approach to adult learning that continues to be present in some literacy work today (Barr, 1999; Freire and Macedo, 1987; hooks, 1994; McMinn, 2000; Thompson, 1997; Weiler, 1988, 1991). However, despite much optimism around critical approaches to literacy, the translation into transformative pedagogy has proved problematic. Freire (1972: 62) stressed that his dialogical, pedagogical practice was only authentic if 'infused with love' and a desire to end all oppression. It could not be automatically transposed onto other circumstances but needed to be part of a wider transformational context where conscious and collaborative struggle for change is a present and embracing reality. Such a context, that welcomes and nurtures critical egalitarian change, has proved elusive. For the most part now, adult literacy work in Europe takes place under the shadow of the Lisbon Strategy[35] and critical and affective aspirations are consequently restrained by funding imperatives, accreditation targets and the demands of a core curriculum.

Despite some intensification in the attention (and funding) given to adult literacy work as a result of the OECD adult studies of the 90s (OECD, 1992, 1995, 1997) literacy as a concept continues to relatively unproblematised. One exception to this theoretical void is the work of New Literacy Studies (NLS), which brings together a range of theoretical and empirical writing that challenges hegemonic, mainstream views of literacy. With evident Freirean and Gramscian influences, NLS has become an alternative voice. From an NLS standpoint it is proposed that literacy is not fixed but rather an evolving, socially situated phenomenon that is deeply interwoven with historical and power-related societal patterns (Barton and Hamilton, 1998; Crowther *et al.*, 2001; Gee, 1990, 1999; Ivanič, 1996; Street, 1984, 1995, 1999; Tett *et al.*, 2006). In particular, NLS emphasises the manner in which literacy is being reshaped by rapid developments in technological means of communication (Kress, 2003; Lankshear and Knobel, 2003).

Through contextualising and deconstructing literacy practices, NLS has sensitised us to the solidary contexts in which literacy and the uses of literacy are often defined. In their study of *Situated Literacies: Reading and Writing in Context,* Barton *et al.* (2000) bring together a range of recent research of the Lancaster School that exemplifies the NLS approach. The collection spotlights the diverse contexts in which real texts and lived literacy practices play a part, for example, in the specificity of a prison community (Anita Wilson); a Welsh farming community struggling with rising levels of agricultural bureaucracy (Kathryn Jones); a computer conferencing group for Canadian students wishing to improve their capacities in academic English (Renata de Pourbaix); and a Catholic community preparing for their children's First Holy Communion (Karen Tusting). These and a host of other studies place real and often undervalued literacies under the microscope as part of a contribution to reconceptualising literacy and recognising the real, complex role that literacy practices occupy.

NLS concentration on what people do and are required to do during literacy events is useful and counterbalances the growing mainstream *literacy deficit* narrative. On the other hand, the fact remains that, through no fault of their own, many people who wish to use literacy are unable to do so and this is also an important part of the story. NLS has not yet moved beyond the business of deconstruction to theorise literacy from a perspective that tackles the unequal nature of the social contexts in which literacy as a social practice happens. Similarly, affective aspects of literacy have yet to be considered.

## Four types of learning care relationships

The term *learning care* was developed in the course of the research to denote the complex affective attitude and effort involved in enabling the acquisition of literacy. Activity in the affective domain has a dynamic influence throughout every aspect of our interdependent lives (Engster, 2005). In particular, learning care refers to the impact of care on our capacity to absorb and retain new knowledge and skills. The process and outcome of literacy acts and events, and learning how to perform them, is almost always social and relational. Nevertheless, until recently, learning to read and write has been viewed as a purely cognitive matter (Lankshear and Knobel, 2003). Conceptualisation of the affective domain, in general, has also moved beyond the field of psychology. Where psychologists were primarily concerned with individual behaviours, work in sociology and philosophy brings the added insight of the influence of culture, ethics and social structures (Nussbaum, 2001; Turner and Stets, 2005). The importance of recognising affective matters as an important part of how and what we learn is increasingly being recognised in other areas of education (Cohen, 2006; Lynch *et al.*, 2007; Noddings, 1992, 2006, 2007). Here, the four types of learning care that this study has identified are proposed as a set of signposts for further reflection on how care, as praxis, might become transformative in literacy work.

The findings of this empirical study have indicated a model of *literacy learning care* that builds on the work of Lynch (2007; see also Chapter 2). She proposed a model of three concentric circles of care relations – primary, secondary and tertiary contexts where care is given and received. The history of survivors of institutional abuse is a stark reminder that not everyone in society benefits equally from caregiving. This in turn has a knock-on effect on all aspects of human development that care promotes and sustains, including literacy. The data suggest four discreet but interconnected sources of learning care, each of which has a contribution to make to literacy attainment.

1. The primary learning care relationships experienced within the family or alternative primary care centre.
2. Secondary learning care relationships in schools.
3. Solidary learning care experienced in civil society, with peer learners and communities of interest.
4. State learning care, defined as the attentiveness given by the state to ensuring structural equality (equality of condition) across all the contexts that influence family, school and community capacity to support literacy learning.

In the model of care outlined in Chapter 2 tertiary care has two discrete but interrelated dimensions – voluntary solidary care in civil society and statutory solidary care that is the responsibility of the state. The state is identified as an actor in the third sphere because it is the collective voice of the community, either showing solidarity for others in need of care or not. In the context of this study, it was important to distinguish between the solidarity the participants experienced within the civil society context of the Lighthouse Centre and the lack of solidarity they experienced from the state in its role of underwriting learning care at all three levels. Hence the two are separately described in the sections that follow. How the data helped clarify each level of learning care is discussed below.

## 1. Primary learning care relationships

For most people, the 'natural' locus of learning care is undoubtedly the family or primary care centre, where nurturing relationships promote and model all aspects of human development, including literacy. For the 28 participants in this research the main source of primary care was the industrial school although some had also had early or intermittent opportunities for care with their family of origin or in foster care. Fifteen respondents left school with their literacy needs met or partially met. The remaining 13 had attained little or no literacy.

In the majority (87%) of cases of those who had either met or partially met literacy needs when leaving school, there was a discernible link with levels of consistency in primary care relationships. Only two of these 15 had no recollection of either a home life or ongoing family contact during their time in residential care. Having some positive primary care was cited repeatedly as positively influencing literacy outcomes.

Similarly, of the 13 who finished school with unmet literacy needs, 11 (85%) had no family life or consistent family relationship while in care. Of the remaining two, one had an intellectual impairment and the other went into care at the age of eight with virtually no prior school attendance. The conclusive trend in the data therefore was of a strong link between some continuity of primary care and positive literacy outcomes.

The capacity of the respondents' families to offer care in the home was negatively influenced by extremes of poverty, the disrespect that comes from perceived moral inferiority and the powerlessness of those without privilege to challenge a rigidly authoritarian system. Where some degree of stability was possible in the home, and education valued and promoted, a positive experience of literacy could be traced back to an early age:

> *My life has been a pattern of in and out of care but I have very vivid memories of my life before I went, say when I was three or four ... learning words at home with my mother ... storytelling. And then when I did go to school we weren't allowed to eat until our homework was done. There is a bit of a perfectionist in me as well and maybe it's because I remember my mother always checking over our homework. You need that kind of approval. It is a kind of a nurturing thing you know?* (Carol, woman aged 50 years who left school with met literacy needs)

The quality of primary care was significant. Liam was a 42-year-old man who had moved in and out of care as a child. He lived at home consistently until he was three and although he had a number of siblings he always felt alone. His father was violent and his parents eventually split up after a stormy relationship to which he attributes his unmet literacy needs:

> *It would be very hard to learn if you feel that nobody cares about you. You are bound to build that wall and make sure that nobody gets in because that was my little nest where nobody could touch me. To me it is like I was deaf. I couldn't hear anybody. I blocked people out and didn't want to have anyone coming near me because I had never had someone caring about me. I can't remember hearing me Ma or Da saying loving things to me or showing me*

*love.* (Liam, man aged 42 years who left school with unmet literacy needs)

Where children had different affective experiences even within the same family they observed a corresponding difference in literacy outcomes within the institutional system. Brenda's literacy needs were met during her schooling whereas those of her younger sister remain unmet today. She attributes this directly to their divergent levels of primary care:

> *I lived at home with them until I was five and that is hugely influential because my sister was two [going into care] and you can see the three years that I got that she didn't get. The extra three years of nurturing from your own parent made a difference. She hadn't got the same foundation as I had as I would have had five solid years and she would have had only two. Even a little bit of encouragement that I got stood to me.* (Brenda, woman aged 55 years who left school with met literacy needs)

Once inside the institution there was no provision for nurturing relationships that might compensate for family absence. Girls as young as 12, who were resident in the institution and struggling to balance care and domestic duties with their own school work, looked after babies and small children. This was drudgery rather than care labour and they had neither the time nor the skill to encourage language or literacy development. Many had no literacy themselves.

Respondents' narratives describe the antithesis of affection. Authoritarianism and regimentation was the pervasive order of the day in a culture where children were identified with the perceived failings of their family. The goal of industrial schools was control and the production of docile, obedient manual and domestic labourers for deployment in religious enterprises or in wealthy families who required servants.

Those who were sustained in any affective family framework could be encouraged and motivated by that relationship or even the memory of it. Kevin had been at home until he was seven and could clearly name the role of primary care relationships in learning:

> *The way I look at it is that some people did well because they were connected with their families outside. They had their families to support them. They were able to concentrate better. Their thinking was different. People that did well at the school had their families looking after them.* (Kevin, man aged 56 years who left school with partially met literacy needs)

The motivation and impetus to learn literacy emerged, for most of those who were successful learners in the study (80%), from supportive and loving relationships and the desire to satisfy family expectations, even in circumstances of extreme hardship. Conversely, the absence of a primary care figure was seen to be a decisive negative factor. Those whose families were unable to keep them were passed on to those for whom care and learning care was work rather than love labour. In the industrial school system, abandonment and excessive discipline eclipsed care in children's lives. Even in later, more lenient regimes, discontinuity of staff meant that no single care figure existed with whom children could identify:

> *If a child comes from a family where there is lots of love and encouragement the child will reach their potential. But for someone like me who was brought up in a children's home, it is kind of even dodgier – because they have a family still (pause) their own biological family but then they have so many other people all over the years that have input in their lives, but who have walked away.* (Bob, man aged 41 years who left school with unmet literacy needs)

As adults, and often as parents and grandparents, survivors come to realise the centrality of care labour and to resent the irreplaceable lack of it in their early lives. For Jane, even the success of her own children and grand-children is tinged with regret for her own lack of primary learning care and lost opportunity:

> *Well I think it is very different for my granddaughter. When she picked up a book and was able to read it, I was so happy. You know? And it also made me feel (breaks down crying) what I would have been … with a normal (pause) let us put it this way. That is the kind of family I would have liked to come from.* (Jane, woman aged 57 years who left school with unmet literacy needs)

Any form of affectivity was discouraged in industrial schools and in the sphere of love labour it seemed as if an anti-relational ethos was pursued. In their critique of the industrial school system both the Kennedy Committee and the Compensatory Advisory Committee to the DES (2002) noted the dearth of personal relationships available to children. They observed the negative impact this had on all aspects of development, including learning opportunities:

> Research has shown that a most important factor in childhood and later development is the quality and quantity of personal relationships available to the child … The child who has not experienced good personal relationships will, in time, be lacking in emotional, social and intellectual stability and development. (Government of Ireland, 1970: 12)

Without such a recognition of the pivotal role of affection, the anti-relational ethos pervaded the industrial school in every aspect. A

Centre worker summarised her impressions of the narratives she has heard:

*The whole thing was separation though. You were separated from your family. The beds were separated. There was no touching and that was the whole ethos there.* (Lighthouse Centre worker)

Whether children knew their parents or not, it is clear that the absence of a primary carer from their lives did have a major impact on every aspect of their well-being and created a desolate backdrop to their early learning. As well as parents, other family connections were also significant. Often separation was extended to siblings who, because of age or gender or some other unexplained logistical factor, were placed in separate institutions and allowed no further contact with their brothers or sisters.

Derek, an Irish Traveller, described the sudden disappearance of his brother as a turning point in his literacy learning. Up until that point he was actually enjoying school and although 'the learning was a bit rough' he was happy and socially integrated and 'enjoying the interactive stuff'. Later in his narrative he explained his adult mistrust of groups and his inability to stay with any group learning process for any length of time. He was a loner who traced this trait to the betrayal and anger associated with his loss of his brother:

*Michael he is dead now. He used to be in the orphanage with me up until the age of ten. I think that was one of the main reasons (pause) why I do think that I couldn't read and write properly. When he was ten years old, I was seven, and when you reached ten years old you were taken away and put in another institution. And he was taken away at ten and I was left there. That was one of the main reasons why (pause) the turning points of my life. And so that (pause) was a blow and I couldn't concentrate, I couldn't learn.* (Derek, man aged 52 years, who left school with unmet literacy needs)

In the total institutional environment, even basic physiological care needs went unmet; children were hungry, cold and exhausted from exacting contract work. All were isolated from comfort and fearful of punishment, abuse and humiliation. Bedwetting was not uncommon in this stressful environment and resulted in public degradation on a daily basis. A common survival technique was withdrawal and self-protection that has extended into adult learning relationships:

*I would keep nice and quiet and still and I wouldn't be picked on or bullied or any of the other things. And it is the same with the literacy and all of that you know? I'll write it and nobody is going to see it. Does that make sense?* (Carol, woman aged 50 years who left school with met literacy needs)

The deep interface between learning literacy and being cared for emerged throughout the research process. Language and literacy development normally take place during a period of intense human dependency and so the interlinking of the processes is not surprising.

## 2. Secondary learning care relationships: the experience of schooling

Lynch and Lodge (2002: 11) have argued for schools and other places of learning also to be recognised as 'affective enterprises' where both teaching and learning are deeply and variously concerned with relationships of care and interdependence. The case is borne out, by default, in the findings of this study where fear and damaged self-esteem dominated accounts of literacy learning and the pervasive atmosphere in the classroom was one of tension. Kevin was seven when he went into care and became fearful of learning:

> *I didn't like the school there. I hated it. There was a terrible tense atmosphere. And like you would be looking at them to see if they were in a bad mood. There was always somebody getting a right beating. And you were tense all through the class and afraid. If you got something to do you would be scared. I didn't like it – it was too tense.* (Kevin, man aged 56 years who left school with partially met literacy needs)

Corporal punishment was widespread in the education system at this period but those with experience of both 'inside' and 'outside' schools observed difference in the degree of severity:

> *I went to regular schools so I can say they weren't party places either but they were light years away from this place. Nobody will ever know or be able to recreate the terror in those rooms – reigns of terror every day. It was horrendous.* (Bridget, woman aged 51 years who left school with met literacy needs)

In the teacher-learner relationship even the willing learner was anxious and fearful. Large classes were managed in a robotic, adversarial and often violent manner. Individual learning styles were not facilitated. Those who were left-handed were demonised and those unable to learn reading and spelling through primarily auditory methods were additionally disadvantaged.

In larger institutions, children attended 'inside school' where they had no contact with the outside world; in smaller institutions they were sent to the local national school where they joined children from the locality. In the 'outside school' children were constantly made aware of their inferior status and many spoke of being carelessly excluded at the back of the classroom. Inside the industrial school, within an already impoverished learning context, still further hierarchies existed. Irish Travellers, orphans, those perceived as morally defective because their parents were unmarried, those of mixed race and those with learning difficulties all attracted additional disparagement.

In retrospect, respondents wanted to be seen as individuals with learning needs that they could expect to have met. They wanted to be treated with patience and care and to have a teacher who would 'draw you out' and find a way of compassionately enabling learning.

Martin was in care from birth but in regular and constant contact with his mother. She was the cook in a wealthy Dublin family and he benefited from the discarded reading material and copybooks of the privileged sons in her place of work. He used these to supplement the poorly resourced learning he got in the industrial school. For this reason he was always ahead of his peers in literacy and to some extent able to observe classroom relations from this small comfort zone. The absence of kindness was apparent to him:

> ... it was harsh the way they taught you how to read and write. They didn't know any other way. You have to understand they didn't have any concept themselves of anything done at a level of decency or kindness. I mean kindness was alien to them, utterly alien. (Martin, man aged 64 years who left school with met literacy needs)

Until the age of ten when he moved to a more authoritarian regime, Matt lived in a convent where orphans were housed and educated. Uniquely, he described a positive, creative learning environment with art, music, storybooks, comics and seaside holidays. He did not remember boys and girls who were unable to read and write. When he moved to the industrial school he noted a visible difference:

> It was very intimidating. These men in black whereas the nuns were soft like with their blue habits. And when you went in there was all these big people and there was no colour anywhere. Like even in the convent there was colour everywhere. (Matt, man aged 64 years who left school with met literacy needs)

Matt maintained that those who were in that colourless, careless environment all their lives had little hope of learning. Bob, disappointed that his dyslexia went unattended, believed that the literacy learning relationship has to be infused with care:

> The teacher's heart and soul has to be in it to teach someone with special needs. It will come across. The child will see the love that the teacher has for

*what they do and the care will come across. 'I care and I want to teach you and I want to see you going forward.' Then that is like ... That is where the care starts.* (Bob, man aged 41 years who left school with unmet literacy needs)

Without primary or secondary advocates to champion the cause of their learning, the majority of those in industrial schools were at the mercy of people who had little belief in either the ability of children to learn literacy or the necessity for them to do so. Despite the nature of their professional role, teachers seemed to subscribe to the wider cultural perception that these children could best aspire to a life of subservience and did not really need to be literate. Tania articulates the implicit ethos enacted in industrial schools:

*You will never amount to anything. All you will be good for when you go out of here will be domestic work, laundries and that kind of thing. But sure how could you be any other way? Nobody wanted you. How could you have any brains because nobody wants you? So how can you be clever?* (Tania, woman aged 52 years who left school with met literacy needs)

An absence of primary care is used maliciously here to explain and legitimate the withholding of secondary learning care. The background presence of a primary carer was shown consistently in the data to make a significant difference to the secondary learning care received in the industrial school. The lack of a positive school learning experience in turn made learning in adulthood more daunting, suggesting that the types of learning care outlined have a dynamic and interconnected relationship.

## 3. Solidary learning care relationships: learning with peers

More than half of the participants in the research had begun to learn literacy in adulthood. Primary and secondary learning care relationships provided a bridge back into learning and there is much evidence in narratives of the premature death of those who did not make that transition. Successful adult relationships, the desire to make a positive contribution to children's lives, and the empowerment of the personal counselling process, were the most common motivational factors for participation in adult literacy.

Awareness of care matters in the process of facilitating literacy was a consideration for both learners and tutors. One man remarked that 'sometimes as an adult you can feel that you are being left at the back of the class too'. It is hard for adults to unlearn their fear of formal education. People display their long memories in almost imperceptible but ever-present responses. They wince at sudden movements, closed doors, loud noises or someone approaching from behind. They hit themselves for making mistakes in reading and spelling. As well as learning literacy they are also learning about making new relationships with others and with their past and tutors discovered the need to make room for this. Tutors are constantly patrolling the borders between past and present, deflecting and disarming negative echoes and substituting positive learning experiences:

> *I suppose that [building relationships] is part of the learning thing too because they have to talk and we wouldn't get beyond that sometimes. I always notice how people say particularly in the early stages, how different it is from learning they have done before and they can't get over that they are being treated as equals, and as adults, I suppose.* (Literacy Tutor)

A common legacy of industrial schools is that survivors feel uncomfortable with the complex dynamic of group learning and prefer a one-to-one learning arrangement where they can build up the confidence needed to move on. In this they demonstrate the need to retrace primary learning patterns. One-to-one literacy tutoring is provided by volunteers and reflects the realities of other types of unpaid care labour in that it is mostly carried out by women, who make immensely valuable contributions for little or no recognition.

Institutional life left little time or space for friendship or solidarity and group learning was not on the pedagogical menu. It was only in later life that survivors of abuse in industrial schools began to savour the benefits of community solidarity and the second chance it provided for learning literacy. As well as those whose return to learning was enabled by new relationships of primary care in adulthood, the bond that formed around a common experience of abuse and neglect has also been transformational in attracting people back to literacy:

> *I think that there is actually a lot of solace for people who maybe have felt quite alone that they come into a place and realise that people do have some form of shared history, some sort of shared continuing difficulties and that actually binds them together as a group. One of the features of the groups is that they do very much look out for each other, especially new members of the group. They try to welcome them in and a lot of support is actually peer-to-peer support.* (Lighthouse Centre Worker)

Gill left the industrial school with partially met literacy needs. She returned to learn as an adult and now teaches IT to adult groups. The consideration and care of her fellow adult learners was instrumental in sustaining her drive to progress:

> *The praise, the encouragement that you get from an adult group is sustaining. You know you would hand in a piece of work and a big fuss would be made*

*over you. Definitely it was positivity over negativity. It definitely made a differ-
ence. I stayed in adult education the whole way up after that.* (Gill, woman
aged 46 years, left school with partially met literacy needs)

## 4. The state's role in ensuring learning care

The majority of the research participants (68%) suggested that the state
neglected its direct responsibility to monitor the quality of care and education offered to them as children. Respondents described feelings of abandonment that transcended their immediate family and extended to the
wider population. They saw an irony in the fact that they were taken away
from families perceived to be unfit to offer care and supervision only to be
neglected in the alternative state provision:

> Despite the fact that orphanages were designed to educate us and
> protect us from the ills of society, we received only minimal education
> and most of us were illiterate. Lack of education deeply affected every
> aspect of our lives, leaving us unprepared for and fearful of the world
> outside the institution. (Fahy, 1999: 54)

Respondents attributed the loss of their primary care centre to wider structural inequalities. Unemployment, poverty, ill health, emigration, family
breakdown, moral opprobrium and cultural powerlessness resulted in children being taken into state care and subsequently experiencing abuses that
impacted negatively on their ability to learn literacy. State care-lessness was
therefore causal both in their original disadvantage and in their subsequent
neglect in the industrial school.

While home is undoubtedly the primary place of care, the capacity of the
family is determined by the state's achievements with regard to creating
equality in society. The state both enables and restricts the measures and
systems that shape how egalitarian a society is and whether its goods are
shared in a fair manner (Baker, 1987; Baker *et al.*, 2004). The legislative and
policy decisions made by the state, in practice, constitute choices about
learning care equality.

Bridget argued for an ideal, inclusive, participative view of the state
where interdependency is recognised and acted upon by all. Placing
borders around who we should have concern for meant she and others
were pushed to the margins of care. She proposed that our interdependence
brings with it responsibilities that make us accountable for what happens
to each other:

> *Do you know it might sound simplistic but it is every adult's responsibility to
> ensure that every child is educated? If we all just look after our own – that is
> why we were the way we were. Those adults who couldn't look after us were*

*equally abandoned by all the adults who could have helped out but instead abused them every way they could.* (Bridget, woman aged 51 who left school with met literacy needs)

## Conclusion

This chapter began by presenting the rationale, research design and theoretical context for this empirical study of literacy and affective aspects of equality. The findings from a three-year ethnographic, practitioner research process in the Lighthouse Centre for adult survivors of abuse in Irish industrial schools were then discussed. These findings strongly suggest that caring relationships have a pivotal role in successful literacy learning. For most of the last century, those consigned to state care experienced affective learning inequalities in each of three contexts. In their primary learning relationships in the institution, they were neglected, abused and humiliated. In their secondary learning relationships at school, they were treated carelessly and were harshly deprived of the chance to develop their capabilities, even in the most basic area of literacy. Thirdly, the state also, as surrogate guardian of institutionalised children, failed to ensure the provision of satisfactory care and education within the industrial schools. At the same time, through its role in accepting an inegalitarian education system and wider social structure, the state also ensured that some citizens received less learning care at every level than did others. These experiences of neglect and abuse sharply contrasted with the respondents' later experience of solidarity in the fourth context of the Lighthouse Centre.

The data also indicate the way that care in all four contexts facilitated literacy learning. In the austere environment of the industrial school, even small affective differences became discernible and survivors identified these as creating more conducive conditions for literacy to take some hold. In adulthood, it was learning care that emerged as transformational in the lives of those affectively and educationally disadvantaged in early life.

As a critical case sample, the literacy and care biographies of survivors of abuse in industrial schools reveal the reality of learning literacy while in the care of the state, but without love. They suggest that learning care, as a concept, has relevance for the contemporary field of literacy, and for learning in general.

# 11
## Conclusion

*Kathleen Lynch and John Baker*

Drawing on research in a wide range of fields in the social sciences and from feminist scholarship more generally, we distinguished in *Equality: From Theory to Action* between four main *contexts* where equality and/or inequality may be generated, the economic, political, cultural and affective systems. *Equality* contains a number of general hypotheses about inequality within each of these social systems and about the relationships between them, as well as the outline of a radical normative conception of equality, 'equality of condition', which can be applied either generally or to the specifics of each system. One of the core themes in *Equality* is the interaction of inequalities. Each of the main systems interact to promote or mitigate inequality along five key dimensions, namely (1) respect and recognition, (2) resources, (3) love, care and solidarity, (4) power, and (5) working and learning. The material in this book demonstrates quite clearly the multidimensional character of inequality within the affective system, and the ways in which inequalities in the economic, political and cultural systems impact on the affective sphere.

*Affective Equality: Who Cares?* has been primarily concerned with the empirical analysis of equality within one aspect of the affective system; it has focused on other-centred (primary care) relations, that sphere of social life that is primarily oriented to the care of intimate others (see Chapters 2 and 3). By means of a series of studies of primary care relations involving 30 Care Conversations and two focus groups (Chapters 3–7) and three further studies of mothers' emotional work in education, men's perception of masculinity and caring, and the relationship between care and literacy learning among people who had spent their childhoods in institutional care (Chapters 8–10), it has examined inequalities in the distribution of love and care labouring and, to a lesser degree, in the receipt of love and care. It has also examined the interrelationships between inequality in the affective system and the economic, political and cultural systems with respect to love labouring, and how this generates and reinforces inequalities in the affective system itself.

In this final chapter, we utilise the *Equality* framework to summarise the main findings of this book. We also set out the implications of the findings for the social scientific understanding of caring in egalitarian terms, and for the development of normative egalitarian theory. As the studies have been premised on the primacy of emotional work in the doing and receiving of love labouring, we begin by underlining the significance of emotions for caring.

## Emotions, care and equality

Our feelings are essential to the making of personal meaning and identity (Chodorow, 1999). We are emotional as well as intellectual beings, social as well as individual. At the individual level, all people have the capacity for intimacy, attachment and caring relationships. We can all recognise and feel some sense of affiliation and concern for others and we all need, at least sometimes, to be cared for. We value the various forms of social engagement that emanate from such relations and we define ourselves in terms of them. Bonds of friendship or kinship are frequently what bring meaning, warmth and joy to life. Being deprived of the capacity to develop such supportive affective relations, or of the experience of engaging in them when one has the capacity, is therefore a serious human deprivation. The emotional experience of being cared about is also a fundamental prerequisite for human development and for flourishing. Research in psychology and psychoanalysis demonstrates how the ability to care about others is firmly located in the development of attachment and feelings from infancy. While feelings are shaped by cultural and gender norms, they are also deeply personal and idiosyncratic (Chodorow, 1978). If the infant's needs for comfort and emotional warmth are not met with consistency at that stage in their lives, then the individual's capacity to develop into a mature human being, capable of feeling the distress and needs of others and indeed their own needs, is severely compromised. Being cared for is vitally important therefore, not just for physical survival, but because it enables us to feel and care for others throughout life.

The emotionally charged relations of solidarity, care and love help to establish a basic sense of importance, value and belonging, a sense of being appreciated, wanted and cared about. They play a vital part in enabling people to lead successful lives, and are an expression of our fundamental interdependence (Held, 1995b; Nussbaum, 1995).

Given their primacy in our lives, it is an important issue of equality, and therefore of justice, to ask who has access to, and who is denied, relations of love, care and solidarity. It is also vital to ask whether these relations are reciprocal or asymmetrical, whether they are structured by gender, class, race and/or disability, whether they are power balanced or power imbalanced, and whether societies operate in ways that help to satisfy or frustrate this human need. These are difficult questions to answer but this is the challenge we have begun to address in this book.

## Egalitarianism and affective inequality

As noted in Chapter 1, academic disciplines paid little attention to the affective system and its constituent inequalities before feminist scholarship started to investigate them, mostly since the 1980s. Even now, at least two decades later, issues to do with love, care and solidary relations and the work that goes into sustaining these, tend to be confined to branches of academic disciplines that are labelled as 'feminist' or 'radical' rather than being recognised as core academic concerns. The theme of affective equality has still to become truly integrated into mainstream sociology, education, economics, law and political theory.

To highlight the importance of relational and dependency-related inequalities, and to differentiate between these and economic, political and socio-cultural inequalities, in *Equality* we developed the concept of affective equality. We identified two primary forms of affective inequality: a) inequalities in the doing of love, care and solidary work, and b) inequalities in the receipt of love, care and solidarity. We acknowledged that these two forms of affective inequality are exacerbated by other dimensions of inequality. Lack of respect and recognition for care-related work exacerbates the inequalities involved in having to take a disproportionate responsibility for the burdensome aspects of love, care and solidarity. A culture in which care work is not recognised and rewarded also disempowers and impoverishes carers of all kinds. Having a low income and limited resources, either independently of being a carer or because of it, also makes care work more burdensome. It limits options for assigning some of the care tasks to others, and may leave carers with little time for rest or even energy to enjoy the pleasurable aspects of love, care and solidary work. Those who are assigned responsibility for love and care work are often powerless to determine the conditions under which they do this work, especially in the family sphere. Their powerlessness exacerbates the inequalities between themselves and those who are not carers by binding them to the necessity of caring and denying them the opportunity to exercise autonomy in other spheres of life.

Inequality in the doing of love, care and solidary work is but one side of affective inequality. Because humans are relational beings, entirely dependent on others at certain times in life, and interdependent throughout their existence, being denied access to love, care and solidarity is a serious human deprivation and an inequality in itself. While it can be argued that no one can ever experience too much love, care and solidarity, it is true nonetheless that people need certain basic forms of love, care and solidarity to survive and to flourish. Those who are denied love and attention in their intimate lives, or who do not have access to secondary forms of caring, be it from friends, neighbours, kin, colleagues or important service providers (such as teachers and health workers), or who live in societies that have little solidarity in terms of the distribution of wealth and other privileges, are denied access to crucial social goods. Inequalities between individuals, groups and societies can be mapped in terms of the degrees to which love, care and solidarity are available respectively to each.

In the next five sections we trace the various dimensions of affective inequality as they have arisen in Chapters 3–10 of this book. In so doing we demonstrate the depth, complexity and multidimensionality of affective inequality, as well as its gendered character and the ways it is reinforced by inequalities in other social systems. The affective system does not operate in structural isolation. It influences the operation of the political, economic and cultural systems, insofar as it enables or disables people to engage in those fields, be it by supporting them in love, care and solidarity terms or by failing to give support. The political, economic and cultural systems in turn, act back on the affective system, by either enabling people to do loving and caring and to show solidarity, or by disabling them owing to lack of resources, power or respect and recognition.

## Inequality in the work of love and caring: the gendered order of caring

Perhaps the most widely recognised fact about the doing of love and caring, referred to repeatedly in this book, is the gendered division of labour and the consequent inequality between women and men in the dimension of working and learning. Not only do women do most of the paid care work, they also do most unpaid care and love work. The patterns are the same in Ireland (Lynch and Lyons, 2008) as they are in other OECD countries (Bittman, 2004). The cultural system plays an important role in maintaining this inequality, most obviously in the way that it sets out and enforces gender roles, imposing on women the primary responsibility for caring and enforcing this role with a sense of moral obligation. Our findings confirm those of other feminist scholars, namely that unpaid family caring exists as a social space where women are the default lovers and carers unless there is no suitable woman available (Gerstel and Gallagher, 2001; Noonan *et al.*, 2007). Even where couples actively attempted to parent on an equal basis (Geraldine and Donal, and Clodagh and Séan, see Chapter 5), the persistence of the gendered attitudes of others (including family, friends and childminders from the crèche) made it virtually impossible to put this into practice. Because primary care work is indispensable, it has to be done for survival and development, and because women are not only socialised to do it, believing it to be in their nature, but morally sanctioned for failing to deliver on family love and care (O'Brien, 2007 and Chapter 8), the affective system plays a major role in generating gender inequality in society. This finding confirms our hypothesis in *Equality* that the affective system is a site of social relations that needs to be problematised if equality of condition is to be achieved, especially between women and men.

To understand why women are the default carers, lovers and solidary workers in society, one must understand their relational other, men, and especially men's relationship to caregiving. What the Care Conversations study shows, and what is confirmed in Hanlon's research (Chapter 9), is that caregiving is culturally encoded as feminine and as such it is an identity that most men actively avoid (Russell, 2007). None of the heterosexual men who were fathers and living with partners saw themselves (nor were seen by their partners) as the primary carers of their children. The men who were primary carers (of parents) had only taken on this responsibility because of their marital status and family status (all were single sons living with a parent) and unique economic circumstances: two were small farmers who had inherited their farms and were thereby able to combine care with some paid work, while the third held another legitimating public status (disability arising from previous employment). While Hanlon found that some understandings of caregiving are sanctioned as masculine activities (notably caring as providing for others through breadwinning), this conception of caring only reinforced hegemonic masculine identities, as it was premised on the assumption that women (and children) are dependent on men. One of major reasons that women continue to do the care, love and solidary work in society is because men fear that doing it will define them as feminine, and therefore inferior to other men. The fear of caregiving arises from a fear of association with femininity (Bourdieu, 2001).

Being a man is about being in command and control, it is not about being a carer. The primary carer status is a vulnerable one, and it is proscribed in the hegemonic masculinities code (Connell, 1995). Where men do identify with care roles organisationally, it is as managers of caring, roles in which they can avoid the more mundane and burdensome activities of caring (Russell, 2007). Even when working in female-dominated occupations, including caregiving, they symbolically distance themselves from feminised and subordinated activities (Simpson, 2004).

The irony of men being care commanders is that they are less likely to have opportunities to engage in the more emotionally involved aspects and forms of caring relationships. So although they are advantaged in status, power and income terms by defining themselves as breadwinning carers (Chapter 9), they can receive less care as they define themselves as not needing it.

Although the studies confirm the gendered order of caring, they also provide some resources for resistance to that order. On the one hand, although both women and men sometimes subscribed to the naturalness of gender roles, there was also a dissatisfaction and resistance on the part of women to their unequal care work burden (Chapter 5): the gendered order was not accepted without question. On the other hand, there was evidence of a genuine commitment among some men to take caring seriously (Chapters 5 and 9). Those men whose circumstances had placed them in caring positions exhibited a capacity to care and an orientation towards care that was similar to that of women in their sense of emotional attachment and moral obligation (Chapters 3, 5, 6), and they experienced the same obstacles of lack of recognition, lack of material support and lack of time (Chapters 4 and 7). These studies support the claim that the gendered order of care is not inevitable.

## Inequalities in receiving care: the role of the political system

The political system plays a pivotal role in determining the conditions for loving and caring in society as the affective system is highly regulated legally by the state. Laws proscribe certain forms of sexual contact and prescribe ideal family forms (Freeman, 1994; Nussbaum, 2000; O'Donovan, 1989). Legal discourse also helps to construct gender identity by applying notions of the 'good mother' (Biggs, 1997) or 'good father' in custody disputes, the 'deserving housewife' or homemaker in family property disputes (Smart, 1989). Law both reflects and constitutes social relations, it promotes certain ideals at the expense of others (by for example, telling us what types of 'families' deserve recognition) and plays a powerful role in shaping and regulating the form of care that a person receives.

In our Care Conversations, we found that in the primary family care sphere, love is an assumed food on the table of emotional life. The young teenagers with whom we held focus groups took the care and attention of their parents as a given (Chapter 6). It was something that was assumed and was not the subject of discussion or debate; it was deemed to be natural and inevitable. Notwithstanding this, Feeley's interviews with adults who had been in institutional care, and who had been neglected and/or abused in care, showed that neither love, care nor solidarity can be assumed in life (Chapter 10). Her research with survivors of institutional abuse showed how adults had experienced inequalities of care, not only in primary care, but also at the secondary and tertiary levels, due to neglect by guardians, teachers and the state respectively. The state had defined them in their childhood as only needing the most basic forms of protection (and even failed in that); they inherited the morally suspect identities attributed to their parents and with them a profound lack of love, care and solidarity. Their neglect in love and care terms had a huge impact not only on their emotional lives and relationships but also on their learning; most had left institutional care with a profound sense of emotional neglect, a neglect which seriously impeded their literacy learning.

## Inequalities of resources and the impact of the economic system

Inequalities of resources, originating for the most part in the economic system, have a profound effect on what they enable carers to do and care recipients to receive. These are compounded by cultural norms about family status that assume households with children are couple households, and increasingly, that they are couples with two incomes.

Social class is especially important in structuring affective inequalities. From the Care Conversations it was evident that those who were well-educated and had relatively high and secure incomes, such as Debra and Alex and Nuala and Elizabeth, had choices about how they organised their care world (Folbre, 2006). They could not only pay for supplementary care for their children, they also had the resources to call on supportive family care as needed. Low income carers and lone carers, be they caring for children or adult dependants, were heavily burdened in care terms, especially in the absence of affordable and accessible care-support services. While couple households could and did share care responsibilities, no matter how unequal that division of care may be, no such option existed for sole carers. Those who were sole carers of children and few economic resources, such as Sasha and Regina, had little independence of life; they experienced social isolation, stress, lack of leisure and general exhaustion. Those who were unpaid family carers of adults, including Melanie and Anita, were especially burdened by caring if they had low incomes and little support (Chapters 5 and 7). The demands of caring were exacerbated by a lack of hope of an independent future, and the challenge of living within an uncertain time frame.

O'Brien's study (Chapter 8) shows how the lack of resources, including economic, cultural and social capitals, all impacted negatively on one's ability to care for children and adults in the way that one would choose to do. Pauline's lack of economic capital precluded her from making any choices about the schools her four children attended, while in Laura's case it led to constant anxieties about unforeseen costs for schooling that she could not afford. In the Care Conversations (Chapter 5), Tom also found the hidden costs of caring for his father very burdensome, while Melanie was physically and mentally exhausted from undertaking her multiple care responsibilities on a very limited budget. The lack of economic capital did not just have direct costs, it had indirect costs in terms of the emotional resources required to do love labouring. O'Brien found that mothers' emotional capital was depleted through having to manage a deficit of economic capital. In this context, even those with cultural capital, such as Masha, were unable to activate this capital in the interests of their children, because they lacked social or economic capital.

Both the Care Conversations and O'Brien's study show that the experience of one parent carers is especially challenging (Oliker, 2000). Not only was the cost of child care premised on the assumption that it is funded from a double-income household budget, but lone parents also had to manage the emotional and social isolation that was part of being a lone parent family and is an important aspect of emotional capital. Emotional energy was also expended in managing the stigma that was often part of the single parent experience. Being poor and a lone parent confounded one's difficulties, as a lack of economic resources meant one was tied to caring mentally and emotionally, if not physically, all of the time. The one parent families with young children with whom we spoke had not availed of paid child care as they could not afford it.

While lone parents with young children struggled to manage care and paid work, or care and welfare, or paid work, care and education, they saw this as a clearly defined phase of life no matter how arduous. Carers of dependant adults, including Mary, Nora and Melanie, did not hold this view. They could see no definite end to their caring lives, lives that were often seriously constrained by lack of supports and services for those on low income. Caring for adult dependants, without adequate respite and care-support services, was seen as arduous and stressful. Carers outlined the constraints it imposed on them in terms of their health, income, pension, sleep, leisure and quality of life generally, findings which concur with those from similar studies (Bittman, 2004).

Another resource inequality that the Care Conversations brought out very clearly was inequality of time (Chapter 7). Time stress was an issue that affected all carers. They were pressed for time, always rushing, running and chasing time, and this severely limited the time they had for themselves and in several cases compromised their health and emotional well-being. However, the gender, class and family status differences that structure inequalities of care work, and the levels of economic resources and emotional capital available, also structure inequalities of time. Women were likely to be time-poor, whether they were engaged in full-time care or combining paid work with caring. This contrasted with evidence, in both two-parent households and wider family networks, that men had more free time. In families that were better off financially, time was more easily managed, by buying in domestic services. For obvious reasons, time pressure was also worse for lone carers than for households with two carers.

The moral obligations to care built into our culture's construction of kinship ties sometimes impose severe costs on family members particularly on women and/or those who are single and without child dependants. We are not suggesting that this sense of family obligation should be done away with, but we do want to point out the way in which its destructive inter-action with inequalities of resources could be significantly mitigated by a cultural shift that recognised a much stronger obligation on the part of society generally to support the care of all vulnerable members. As noted in Chapter 1 care needs to be reconstituted as a public good. Responsibility for ensuring that care work does not lead to poverty and social exclusion should be taken out of the private sphere and reframed as a collective responsibility. Under this renegotiated 'social contract' each individual engaging in caring labour would have a range of socio-economic rights met by the state, rather than by family member (see Fineman, 2004 for further discussion).

## Interdependency and inequalities of power

Because men are culturally defined as care commanders and women as care's footsoldiers, men exercise a silent power over women in relation to the day-to-day work involved in primary caring (Chapter 7). To expect a man to be a primary carer is to ask him to operate outside the accepted masculine gender code prescribed for men (Connell, 1995); it is, in many respects, to ask him to stop being a man. Some of the men we spoke with (like Séan) had never thought about the subject of care or discussed it, although they did do care work. Alex typified men who were clear that they did not want to be primary carers and who regarded being a primary carer as 'not the done thing' for men like himself (Chapter 5). Primary caring was defined by most men and women as essentially women's work, and only a small number contested this binary code (Chapter 5). Men exercised an implicit power over women's caring and loving capabilities and over the time they devoted to loving and caring, not through personal command, but through the power of the moral imperative on women to be primary carers, and the complementary masculine imperative that men only do primary caring when women are not available.

The Care Conversations revealed less predictable patterns when it came to power relations between carers and care recipients. Although care is often viewed as an asymmetrical relationship between a caregiver and a care recipient, it is almost always also a relationship of interdependency, mutuality and trust (Hansen, 2004; Strazdins and Broom, 2004). We cannot draw a neat dichotomy between carer and care recipient as if each were at polarised ends of giving and receiving love and attention. No matter how limited the reciprocity may be care relations have a reciprocal dimension, even if it is giving or withholding a nod or a hand to show appreciation on the part of a vulnerable care recipient. Where care is given within families or defined communities, care relations exist over protracted periods of time, and reciprocity may also occur intergenerationally rather than between particular pairs of caregivers and recipients. Relations of mutuality and reciprocity within care relations are not always visible to the outside observer, however. In the Care Conversations, Mary, who was widowed, spoke affectionately about the value of the company of her intellectually disabled son, for whom she was the primary carer, while Regina spoke about how she enjoyed the company of her 13 year old son for whom she was the sole carer. Anita (who was autistic) spoke about her love for her mother and Beth reciprocated, talking about how much she enjoyed her daughter, even though she also found care for her very demanding. Tom also conversed at length about the fun he had at times with his father and the satisfaction he got from caring for him so well (Chapter 6).

The interdependency of intimate relations impacts on how power works within the primary care sphere. While the carer does exercise power over the care recipient, and this is one of the reasons that disability researchers emphasise the importance of reducing unnecessary care dependencies for disabled people, it is a power that is tempered by cultural mores and conventions, by the survival needs of dependants, and by an assumption of trustworthiness that is often central to individual identities. Care is not always given on the carer's terms, not least because of the power of the care recipient to refuse certain forms of care and because of the cultural norms that operate in relation to care. People who are very vulnerable due to illness or infirmity can and do show appreciation for care or fail to show it; they can call on culturally available moral imperatives to enforce their care expectations, especially in relation to women (Bubeck, 1995; O'Brien, 2007). This was very evident in Valerie's and Maeve's cases where both of their mothers made it clear to them that they did not want to go into a nursing home. Monica, who was in her 70s and needed some care support, also spoke about how she pressed her daughter (especially) into caring for her when she was ill. Although she felt guilty about that, she could not help making demands at the time as her fear of leaving her own home and entering nursing home care was so great.

The imperative to care is not just culturally defined, it also arises from the deep dependency that characterises relationships between the carer and the very vulnerable; the command to care arises from having to provide for basic needs. The profoundness of the vulnerability of an intimate other calls forth a level of attention that may not be desired by the carer. Moreover, the failure to meet the survival and elementary care needs of vulnerable dependants is highly visible and this visibility also exercises its own control on carers. So while vulnerability can and does allow for the carer to exercise power over the care recipient, it also enables the care recipient to exercise some unspoken power over their carers as the neglect or abuse of care recipients can and does become visible often within a short time.

Love labourers are expected to be trustworthy and committed over extended periods of time. They do not do care work on a hire and fire basis like paid care labourers and as such are bound by sets of long-term expectations. Care recipients, on the other hand, exercise control over carers through the 'trust fund' that underpins primary care relations; it is this trust fund that generates guilt, guilt on the part of carers that they are not doing enough and on the part of the care recipients that they are expecting too much.

## Respect, recognition and love labouring

The impact of cultural values on caring is not confined to gender. We found two very different evaluations of caring, one in the public sphere and the other in the personal domain. In policy-making, employment and formal politics, carers and care recipients are not highly valued except at a rhetorical level. Most of those with whom we held conversations spoke about how politicians and employers did not respect their care responsibilities (Chapter 4). They felt that their caring lives were secondary in the eyes of the state and of most employers. They believed that the paid work world is *care-less*, in the sense that it does not have to accommodate caring unless legally required to do so.

All types of carers felt invisible and undervalued in their various forms of care work; they felt that care came last in the public order of priorities. Those who had been denied not only love, but also the secondary forms of care that were supposed to be provided for them by educators and by the state, were also aware of the lowly value placed on their care needs by most other adults (Chapter 10). They felt robbed of part of their life and incapacitated by their love and care losses.

Within the interpersonal world, however, love, care and solidarity work was highly valued and protected, often at a high personal cost to the carer. The life world of caring is a space where carers and care recipients verbalise the value of love and care for themselves. Moreover, carers are not passive recipients of negative labelling. They articulate a strong resistance to the lowly public evaluation of caring; they contest the values of the public spheres that assume the presence of love and care work while ignoring its existence and importance (Chapter 4). People are willing and able to contest economic rationalities and to articulate the primacy of nurturing rationalities.

The data show how human beings live in affective relational realities, especially in their primary care relations; they have emotional ties and bonds that compel them to act as moral agents, to act 'other wise' rather than 'self wise' (Tronto, 1991, 1993). Their lives are governed not only by the demands of economically and politically determined survival, but also by the rules of lay normativity (Sayer, 2005: 35–50).

## The social scientific implications of the findings

The findings from this work strongly endorse the message from 'care feminists', across the fields of economics, politics, law, sociology and social policy, that there is a need to redefine the understanding of the social scientific person from one that centres on the public persona, the economic, political and cultural actor in the public sphere, to one that recognises that people are endemically dependent and interdependent.

It highlights the fact that if we are concerned about the well-being of individuals in general, and gender equality in particular, we can no longer afford to ignore the significance of the affective dimensions of human experience. Human beings are at times autonomous, rational self-interested actors, but they are more than that. They are deeply social creatures who are part of a complex matrix of social and emotional relations that often give meaning and purpose to life, even though they can also constrain life's options.

### (a) Relational identities

The data show that primary carers, be they of dependant adults or children, defined their caring responsibilities as a core feature of their personal identities. This was especially true for mothers, whose lives revolved around their care responsibilities in a way that did not apply to fathers. However, whoever became primary carers, and sometimes they were men, also found their lives centred to a considerable degree on their love and care-related tasks. To say this is not to deny the importance of paid employment in defining personal identities (and the need to do paid work to earn a livelihood) but merely to note the importance of other-centred identities paralleling paid work identities. As noted in Chapter 4 priority was frequently given to love labouring work when major conflicts arose between it and career and income gains, especially by women.

The narratives of primary carers were characterised by a discourse of nurturing that was distinctly oppositional to the narratives of competition that pervade the public sphere both locally and globally (Boltanski and Chiapello, 2007; Coulter and Coleman, 2003). Narratives with respect to caring for children were focused on their happiness in the present and their security in the future; among those caring for adults and older people, the focus was on respecting their wishes and desires for comfort or for presence. Care recipients also defined themselves in terms of the quality of the care they received (and some of these also did care work for others). While care was assumed as a given among teenagers, older people were aware that care was a desirable good that they could not presume upon, as were those who were denied care in their childhood. The trust and attentiveness that was essential to good care was not assumed to be available in institutional care, either among carers or care recipients.

### (b) Nurturing rationalities vs economic rationalities

What is clear from all the studies reported in the book is that nurturing rationalities are different to economic rationalities. Almost all of the people with whom we spoke made some, and in some cases significant, economic and personal sacrifices in order to prioritise the care of those they loved. As most of those who were primary carers were women, most of the sacrifices were made by women (Chapter 5). Debra took a job share arrangement to spend more time with her two children and in particular to care for her son with intellectual disabilities. Geraldine worked an early shift (being at work at 7am) in order to have more time with her baby daughter in the evening; Maeve gave up taking in a student to supplement her income in order to care for her mother; Cathy moved to a lower paid job so that her husband and herself could have more time with their children; Jane took 6 weeks of unpaid leave in the summer in order to have time with her partner Jill and their two children; Tom and Tony devoted huge amounts of time to the care of their respective parents, and a sick uncle (in Tony's case), at a cost to their livelihoods and their social life; and Valerie gave up her prestigious career to be a full-time carer. All of the carers sacrificed free time for the sake of their care responsibilities, often at the cost of their own health and welfare.

People struggled to find words to name their care labours, variously describing it as demanding, joyful, stressful, time consuming, fun, natural, exhausting and fulfilling; the lack of a language to name the different forms of care could be a study in itself (see Uttal, 2002). The named reasons for caring varied, although for any one person there were multiple motives; at times it was a sense of duty and obligation that was the primary care narrative; other times the language of desire, longing and aspiration was more pronounced; the languages of guilt, hope, affection, responsibility and lack of choice were also dispersed throughout the conversations. Care was embedded in a set of relationships which had a history and an assumed future and so was integral to the sense of purposes, values and identities people held in life. To renege on *responsibility* for caring (even if some of the tasks had to be assigned to others) was to assign the person for whom one was caring an 'unwanted' caring status and to identity oneself as a person 'who was not caring'. These reasons for caring were deeply embedded in people's understandings of who they were, both as carers and as care recipients. Maeve, who was caring for her mother, exemplified this. She spoke about finding it difficult to care for her mother, who could be quite demanding, but whom she felt obligated to care for because of her sense of herself as a caring person, and because her mother would be deeply hurt if she was placed in residential care (see Chapter 5 for further discussion of this).

Caring was not seen therefore as a discrete set of tasks that could be separated completely from the relationship in which it was embedded, and the identities of those involved. Because of this, only certain aspects of care could be handed over to others or paid for at times without undermining the relational identity of both carer and care recipient. Care is not just a practical dilemma about a set of tasks to be undertaken, it is also an emotional and moral dilemma about who one is relationally and what is best care. While there are cultural and classed responses to the dilemma of organising care as Duncan (2005) has suggested, our data suggest that people know that there is an aspect to care, namely the love labouring dimension, which is inalienable. You cannot pay someone else to build or maintain your own relationship with intimate others regardless of you social class, gender or other statuses.

## (c) Care as work: a focus on love labouring

Most of the literature about care work treats it as a singular entity, classifying it largely in relation to the context or persons with whom it is associated, be it family care, institutional care, nursing care, home care, child care, elder care, etc. There is little understanding of which aspects of caring can be provided on contract and which cannot (Lewis and Giullari, 2005); the differences between secondary care labouring, which can be commodified, and love labouring, which cannot, are only minimally understood.

In Chapter 2 we provided a taxonomy for discriminating different forms of care, one that differentiates not only between interpersonal forms of care that are alienable and inalienable, namely between secondary care labouring and love labouring respectively, but also between interpersonal forms of caring and inter-institutional and group-related forms of caring, that is between love and secondary care labour on the one hand and social solidarity on the other. While we provide the intellectual rationale for the distinction between these three forms of care in Chapter 2, most of the book has been devoted to analysing the nature of one form of caring, love labouring, and exploring the equality issues that arise from the fact that this work cannot be commodified without being fundamentally altered and rendered as something else.

A major finding of the empirical studies on primary caring is that both carers and care recipients recognise the ways in which love labouring in particular cannot be assigned to others without altering the very nature of the intimate relationships involved. The importance of the analytical distinction between what is and is not alienable in care terms, what we can pay others to do on our behalf and what we cannot, must not be underestimated. It means that there is a form of caring which assumes a long-term, personal commitment from the primary carer(s) to nurture others. The Care Conversations show that while paid carers are vital for assisting the love labouring, they cannot substitute for it. Feelings and commitments that are an integral part of an ongoing relationship are not available for hire. While paid care services were regarded as indispensable for supporting love labouring (and grossly under-funded and under-resourced), they were seen as supplementary to love labouring rather than a substitute for it. Parents could and did pay people to care for their children. However, they recognised that although paid carers built their own relationship with their children they could not replace the parents' relationship (Himmelweit, 2005). Given the inalienability of love labouring, it was inevitable that primary care relations were deeply emotionally engaged, not only for carers but also, as shown in Chapter 10, for those who did not have love invested in them through nurturing.

Yet love labouring is defined as work by all of those who do it. It does not happen 'naturally' and effortlessly; it requires a huge investment of time, energy and effort. It is other-centred rather than materially productive work (although the latter depended on it to enable it to happen), but work nonetheless.

## Implications for normative egalitarian theory

In *Equality*, we distinguished between basic equality, liberal egalitarianism and equality of condition, each of which was defined in terms of the five dimensions already discussed. More specifically, we defined basic equality as being concerned with basic protections against inhuman and degrading treatment, including the most blatant forms of violence. We depicted liberal egalitarianism as concerned with the fair regulation of inequality by means of two pervasive ideas. First, there are stronger standards for the protection of the worst off, and, secondly, a commitment to some form of equal opportunity to succeed. We defined equality of condition as a radically egalitarian objective that aims at overall equality in the conditions of people's lives. In contrast to liberal egalitarianism, that could be called a principle of 'equal outcome', but it is perhaps more accurate to call it the principle that, overall, people should be roughly equally enabled and empowered to live their lives.

The research discussed in this book helps to clarify and expand the understanding of these conceptions of equality in a number of significant ways. First of all, it supports the idea of a multidimensional understanding of equality, because it shows that inequality in the affective realm is itself multidimensional. If, therefore, we want to promote equality in the affective sphere we need to attend to all five of its dimensions.

Secondly, it demonstrates some of the interrelations between equality in one dimension and equality in others. For example, a very strong theme in Chapter 4 was that the lack of material support for caregivers was seen by them as expressing a lack of recognition for caregiving. This is clearly one way in which we cannot expect to promote equality of recognition without simultaneously promoting equality of resources. Similarly, it is clear from the material discussed throughout this book that a shift in the gendered division of care labour, which belongs to the dimension of working and learning, is intimately connected with shifts in inequalities of recognition and resources. Greater equality of recognition and resources for caregivers would be, in the first instance, more beneficial to women than to men precisely because of the gendered division of care work, but this equality could itself have the effect of making care work more attractive to men. Conversely, one might reasonably hope that encouraging men to take on their fair share of care work would itself help to bring about greater equality of recognition and resources for caregivers.

Thirdly, the research discussed here, particularly in Chapter 10, invites a reconceptualisation of the dimension of love, care and solidarity. In *Equality*, this dimension was largely construed as concerned with providing and supporting positive relations of love, care and solidarity, and inequality was construed in terms of the differences between those who had access to these positive relations and those who did not. Little explicit attention was given to what may be called the negative counterpart of these relations – relations of hatred, abuse and social antagonism. Yet if there is an inequality of care between those who receive it and those who do not, there is clearly an even greater inequality in the same dimension between those who are cared for and those who are abused. We should therefore think of the range of the dimension of love, care and solidarity as extending in two directions and not just in one.

Fourthly, the research in this book raises some serious questions for liberal egalitarianism. A general feature of liberal egalitarianism is a commitment to some form of equal opportunity. One aspect of this position is the idea that social justice should be concerned with providing people with an opportunity to gain valued goods rather than to the goods themselves, because individuals should be free to accept or refuse the benefits they have access to. In the case of care, this distinction seems in many cases to lack any point. Children, the ill and the infirm need care itself; the idea of equal opportunity is in these cases a redundant concept. The carers featured throughout this book were not concerned with providing care recipients with an opportunity for getting love and care but with giving love and care themselves.

Another aspect of the liberal-egalitarian emphasis on equal opportunity is the idea of personal responsibility: that people should be held responsible for the choices they freely make. The affective sphere raises serious issues for this stance. Does the 'choice' to provide care count as a free choice for which caregivers should be held responsible? This choice occurs within the context of a social system that, as we have seen, places family members, and particularly women, under a moral imperative to provide care. That they thereby feel 'responsible' for others is not just a play on words but shows that the concept of responsibility itself is more complicated than liberal egalitarianism tends to portray it. Moreover, the moral imperative to care and therefore our responsibility for the care of others is partly constituted by people's need for care. Is a socially mediated response to a need a free choice for which the responder should bear the costs? These are rhetorical questions because it seems clear enough that these needs must be met by someone if societies are to function at all and therefore are the responsibility of society as a whole and not simply of family members. But acknowledging this social responsibility makes the distinction liberal egalitarians emphasise between personal choice and brute luck extremely problematic.

A fifth problem that the research in this book poses for normative egalitarian theory is the issue of how to develop social norms and institutions in ways that are actually capable of satisfying the needs for love and care that the material here so amply documents. Egalitarian theorists have paid some degree of attention to how we might design egalitarian economies, political systems, schools and even families, but these exercises have almost always been concerned with the other dimensions of equality. The key questions have concerned how these social institutions affect the distribution of income, wealth and cultural capital, how they generate or mitigate inequalities of opportunity, how well they can accommodate cultural and other group differences and the degree to which they can reduce inequalities of power. If love, care and solidarity matter then all of these institutional questions have to be revisited with a view towards assessing how well different institutions promote equality in this key dimension.

A central point of the research presented here is that certain kinds of care, what we call love labour, are inalienable and uncommodifiable. It may not always be possible to provide the love people need, but that does not make it any less of a loss. So in developing norms and institutions to deal with the issues of love, care and solidarity, it is going down an entirely wrong path to assume that all of this work can be allocated to public services or commodified for the sake of market-based providers. We are not denying that people contracted to care for others can also establish long-term loving relationships, but one cannot commit oneself by contract to love another, much less to do so on a life-long basis. In thinking about social norms and institutions, then, egalitarians must take seriously the objective of freeing both women and men from a level of commitment to paid work that is incompatible with meeting the love and care needs of others. This objective has wide-ranging implications for the economic system.

These points are related to a sixth question for egalitarian theorists, the question of rectification. As Anca Gheaus has argued (forthcoming), failures of love and care are all too frequent in contemporary societies, and even the best institutional designs are imperfect. These failures do not just harm people emotionally, but as Chapter 10 in particular has documented, have huge effects on other aspects of their lives. Should we aim to compensate those whose needs for love and care have been frustrated? How? Egalitarian theory has paid some attention to compensation for lack of material resources, lack of opportunities and physical impairments, but apart from Gheaus's work, little attention has been paid to compensation for lack of love and care.

Finally, the research in this book helps us to understand how equality of condition should be defined in the affective sphere. In the dimension of respect and recognition, perhaps its most important lesson is that recognition can be very tightly connected with other dimensions of equality. In Chapter 4, what came up time and again from caregivers was the view that the true measure of the lack of regard others had for their role was the lack of material support they were given, irrespective of public expressions by politicians of what a fine job they were doing. Perhaps a further investigation would reveal other, more symbolic forms of expressing recognition for care but its material expression was central to the perspective of these caregivers. This does not at all show that the dimension of respect and recognition is indistinguishable from that of resources, because it was clear from the Conversations that caregivers felt deeply about the lack of recognition for their work and not just about its under-resourcing.

In the dimension of resources itself, the research discussed here deepens our understanding of the range of resources we need to take account of in promoting equality of condition in the affective sphere. There is plenty of evidence here that inequality in material resources has a very strong impact of people's ability to provide care, but the research reveals other resources that are also crucial. Chapter 8 in particular showed that mothers' capacities to provide the care their children needed during the transition to secondary school were strongly influenced by their social capital, their cultural capital and their emotional capital, each of which influenced the others.

In relation to the dimension of love, care and solidarity, the research here contains a number of important insights. First of all, it confirms that this is a very important dimension of equality for many people. In particular, it is clear from the Care Conversations that many people prioritise relations of love and care over other dimensions of equality, and that they are therefore willing to incur low social esteem, poverty, time stress, powerlessness and lack of career prospects for the sake of maintaining their caring relationships. As mentioned above, it also shows that in many cases it seems pointless to characterise equality objectives in this dimension in terms of the opportunity for, access to, or capability for relations of love and care because what people in those cases need is love and care themselves, not just access to them.

The material in this book seems on the whole to confirm the model set out in Chapter 2 that distinguishes between primary, secondary and tertiary relations, although that model is intentionally schematic and allows for borderline cases. Most of the empirical work in this book concerns primary relations of care; there is some discussion of secondary relations but very little of tertiary relations. The characterisation of primary and secondary relationships given in Table 2.1 of Chapter 2 is largely confirmed by the cases discussed in Chapters 3–10, and so the material provides support for the idea that promoting equality of condition entails the kinds of commitment the table lays out. Perhaps the greatest challenge to the model in Chapter 2 is the claim discussed in Chapter 9 that the 'masculine' mode of caring for others does not consist in the emotionally intense, temporally prolonged and highly attentive activities set out in the Table 2.1, but in being the household breadwinner. The problem with the breadwinner view of care is that it cannot substitute for the kinds of primary care that people need; it entails either that breadwinners will themselves have a 'second shift' as primary carers, or that they will rely on and perpetuate a division of labour within the household that defines the caregiver as a dependant and has played a central role in sustaining gender inequality. It is of course to be welcomed that people in paid work should apply some of their earnings to the care of their dependants, but that is not an adequate response to the need for care.

In Chapter 1, we raised the question of whether equality in people's relationships of love and care was desirable, as distinct from being concerned with ensuring that everyone has access to the love and care they need. In the Care Conversations, caregivers repeatedly spoke positively about the reciprocal nature of their relationships with those for whom they cared, whether these were young children or other family members, and even in situations where the care recipient was highly incapacitated. These remarks certainly show that people valued reciprocal love and care, although it does not constitute a full case for making reciprocity an important principle of equality.

The material in this book also illuminates the idea of equality of condition in the dimension of power. In large-scale contexts, radical equality of power is most straightforwardly conceptualised in terms of democratic political structures. In the affective contexts focused on by most of this book, namely families and other households, power relations are more subtle. In some cases, caregivers clearly had significant power over care recipients and many of those were situations – such as the care of young children or of incapacitated adults – where this aspect of the power relationship was inevitably unequal. Even in cases where equal power is possible in principle, which in the case of children could be at quite a young age, there may be obvious good reasons for unequal power. What is less obvious is the case for the power that care recipients exercise over primary caregivers, sustained by high levels of dependency, the moral obligations primary caregivers feel, and by broader social norms about the gendered division of labour. Here again it was not always clear that equal power was a feasible alternative: if, for example, the care recipients were not really capable of abating their demands. But in such cases it is easier to see unequal power as an unavoidable wrong rather than a justified inequality. The social and moral norms governing caring are also a good example of the way impersonal, decentred power operates in the affective sphere. In this respect, the egalitarian ideal of equal power requires a deconstruction of those norms and their replacement by norms that are as far as possible equally empowering. This is not to say that no one should feel a moral obligation to care for others – quite the contrary. But it is to say that those obligations would not be oppressive in a society where caring was taken seriously and the burdens of caring were equally shared.

Finally, the material in this book helps us to clarify the idea of equality in the dimension of working and learning. There is ample evidence here that love and care do involve work. Although some respondents resisted that label, they did not deny that love and care were burdensome or that how love and care were arranged had an important effect on the extent to which their caring activities were satisfying and fulfilling or stressful and tedious. The evidence here also shows the persistence of the gendered division of love and care labour, which most of the women were justifiably unhappy with. So the general idea that equality of condition requires access to satisfying and fulfilling work, whether it is paid or unpaid, together with a reasonably strong form of occupational equal opportunity, inconsistent with the gendered division of labour, is supported by the material in this book. What is more problematic is the sense so often expressed by caregivers not just that they had no choice but to care, but also that they had a moral obligation to do so. Should we say that true equality in the dimension of working and learning entails that any sense of obligation is an infringement on freedom of occupational choice, and that everyone should be free to undertake love and care work or not, as they feel inclined? This is not a reasonable position, given that such work is a crucial and unavoidable condition for human survival, and therefore that we have a collective obligation to ensure that it is accomplished. At the very least, then, everyone has an obligation to contribute to supporting love and care work. The stronger claim that everyone has at least a *prima facie* obligation to engage in such work is certainly suggested by the contribution such a universal obligation would make to eroding the gendered division of care labour, but the case for that claim needs to be further developed.

Overall, then, the empirical material in this book raises important issues for normative egalitarian theory. In some cases the implications seem fairly straightforward. In others, the material highlights questions that egalitarian theorists need to address.

## Concluding remarks

This book set out to explore the subject of affective equality, focusing on the dynamics of care from an egalitarian perspective. It examined one particular dimension of care, namely love labouring, in depth: using data from four interrelated studies, it analysed the equality issues identified by a wide range of carers and care recipients. Love labouring, and associated care labouring, within families was examined from multiple perspectives, including those of carers and care recipients, women and men, mothers and fathers, working class and middle class people, and younger and older persons. The findings highlight the depth, complexity and multidimensionality, as well as the gendered character, of affective inequality. They demonstrate too the centrality of love labouring to personal identities, as well as its susceptibility to diminution owing to the lack of material supports, time and respect granted to it in the public sphere.

The studies also show that the affective system does not operate in structural isolation. It influences the operation of the political, economic and cultural systems, insofar as it enables or disables people to engage in those fields, be it by supporting them in love, care and solidarity terms or by failing to give support. The political, economic and cultural systems, in turn, act back on the affective system, by either enabling people to do loving and caring and/or to show solidarity, or by disabling them owing to lack of resources, power or respect and recognition. If, therefore, we want to promote equality in the affective sphere we need to challenge inequalities in all other social systems as well, namely the economic, the political and the socio-cultural. Without such a challenge, the inequality of resources, respect and recognition, and power that were identified as burdening love labouring will remain in tact.

# Appendix
# Methodological Note on 'Care Conversations' Study

## Context of 'Care Conversations' research

The 'Care Conversations' research was funded by the EU Programme for Peace and Reconciliation and was part of a larger study on *Equality and Social Inclusion* involving University College Dublin and Queen's University Belfast. The research was conducted over a 20-month period from February 2005 to November 2006.

## Methodological approach

We chose the term 'Care Conversations' to define the research approach as we wanted the meeting with carers and care recipients to be as spontaneous and informal as possible. This methodological approach equates closely with what Patton (1990) refers to as the 'informal conversational interview'; in this context, however, all the participants knew that the tape-recorded conversation taking place was part of a research project. The major stance here is to 'go with the flow', avoiding pre-determined questions in order to remain as open and adaptable as possible to the participant's nature and priorities. This approach meant that the conversation was highly individualised and relevant to the individual, producing information that we could not have anticipated in advance. The major advantage of this approach was that it facilitated the establishment of rapport between the researcher and the participant, thereby enabling participants to talk about their experiences and beliefs in an atmosphere of honesty, empathy and respect (Holloway and Jefferson, 2000: 100–103)

In these conversations about care, particularly love labouring (see Chapter 2 above for an analysis of this term), we wanted to explore how affective inequality, that is inequality in the doing and receipt of love, care and solidarity, impacted on people in different social situations, and in particular how gender, social class, marital and family status, age and other statuses impacted on carers and care recipients.

We wanted to examine the meaning of love and care in people's lives, be they carers of care recipients or both: how they defined as love and care, how they viewed the love and care work they did and care they received, and the conflicts and demands loving and caring posed, especially in relation to paid employment.

With this particular focus, a case-study approach (Travers, 2001) involving conversations with as many members of each care context as possible seemed appropriate; in most cases this involved members of the immediate family context. There are two main reasons why a case study method involving multiple perspectives was considered to be an appropriate analytical approach in relation to this study (Ribbens McCarthy *et al.*, 2003). First, because love labouring takes place in the context of a web of personal relationships and because care relationships are constructed and reconstructed through negotiations between members it seemed important to involve as many of these actors as possible. Second, while care is most often presented as a dichotomy between carers and care recipients, we considered that it was only by examining the accounts of both that the true nature of dependency and mutuality in

237

caring relationships can be understood. Gaining detailed knowledge of how love labouring operates from the perspectives of different carers and care recipients meant that we had to listen to and document multiple data sources as to how love and care relations operated within families. This took time and required a trusting and lengthy conversation in a comfortable setting rather than formal interviews. Our intention was to involve as many of the participants involved in each household in primary care relations as possible.[36] The case-study approach was to allow for an in-depth exploration of love labour practices and the subjective meanings ascribed to these practices by those giving and receiving care.

## Gaining access and consent

Access to potential participants was facilitated in the first instance by two national organisations which work closely and directly with carers and one community development organisation that works with lone parents. The two national care organisations referred to are *Caring for* Carers Ireland (see: http://www.caringforcarers.org/) and *The Carers' Association (see http://www.carersireland.com/);* in total, ten case studies were identified through these two organisations. The third organisation provides supports and services to lone parents and their children in Dublin; two further case studies were identified through this agency. (As it is a small organisation we are not naming it here to protect the anonymity of those who participated).

In addition, we used a number of employment and social networks (including the National Women's Council of Ireland, see http://www.nwci.ie) to identify potential participants who were part of a private household intimate care context but who were not members of either one carers' organisations. This allowed us to include those who did not strongly identify themselves in terms of giving or receiving care but yet were actually in one or both of these roles in their own lives. The remaining nine case studies were identified in this way. The 21 case studies involved carer and care recipients from nine counties (in all four provinces) in Ireland and involved carers in cities, towns and rural areas.

Finally, potential participants for the first of the two focus groups were identified through two youth service agencies, one of which comprised predominantly of middle class teenagers and the other of which was in a working class area. Both of these focus groups were in Dublin.

Much of the research period was spent developing links and relationships with key contacts in the research partner organisations and networks as well as with the respondents themselves. A user-friendly and jargon-free leaflet explaining the project and the types of carers and care recipients we wished to identify was produced and adapted for different organisations and groups. This leaflet included the names and contact numbers of both the principal investigator (Professor Kathleen Lynch) and researcher/interviewer (Dr Maureen Lyons); both were listed as available to answer any questions about the research or to address any issues raised for the participant following the 'care conversation'. Staff from the research partner organisations distributed the leaflets amongst their members and also spoke about the research to members who expressed an interest in participating. For example, one of the care organisations chose a residential respite weekend away to explain about the research and give members an opportunity to register their initial interest in participating in the study. This meant that the initial information about the project was communicated both through the leaflet and also filtered through the managers in the different organisations.

Potential participants were identified initially by the managers in the care organisations after they distributed the literature about the study. They arranged for the researchers to liaise with those who had expressed an interest in the study by telephone. The same methodology was employed in relation to potential participants identified through other organisational and social networks. After the telephone conversation, all potential participants agreed to meet and take part in the 'care conversation'. Where appropriate, the researcher also discussed with each person the possibility of including all others involved in the care situation, including other carers and care recipients. In all cases, participants acknowledged that they would have to get the consent of the person involved and would let the interviewer know on the day the 'care conversation' took place.

The majority (14 of the 21 case studies) of the care conversations took place in the participants' homes. For a further six case studies, the care conversations were conducted either in the participant's own workplace (three), the interviewer's workplace (two) or in a neutral venue (one), including a hotel. The care conversation for the remaining case study took place in a support service agency for lone parents.

### Types of care situations represented

Our study includes two main types of care situations. The first involved care of children (whether dependant or adult) by a parent(s) while the second involved care of an adult (spouse or parent) by a family member.

## 1. Care of children

In total, 15 of the 21 case studies involve *care of a daughter/son by a parent(s)*. These can be further divided into the following three subcategories:

- Nine of the 15 case studies involved *care of dependant children only* (i.e., all children under the age of 18)
- Five of the 15 case studies involved *care of adult children only* (i.e., all children over the age of 18) in all cases where dependency was *due to a physical, sensory or intellectual impairment*
- One of the 15 case studies involved *care of dependant children but the parent also had adult children*

*Care of Dependant Children only:* In total, nine of the 21 case studies involved *care of* dependant children only and included both lone mothers (three out of nine ) (*Susan; Sasha; Regina*) and those in couple relationships (both heterosexual and lesbian) (six out of nine) (*Cathy; Geraldine/Donal; Debra/Alex; Clodagh/Séan; Elizabeth/Nuala* and *Jane/Jill*).

In the case studies involving partnered carers, every effort was made to engage both partners in care conversations; this was achieved in relation to five of the 6 couples (all except *Cathy*). Of these, 9 case studies involved care of children less than 18 years, two (*Debra/Alex* and *Sasha*) involved family situations where at least one child had a physical, sensory or intellectual impairment. For reasons of access, resources and time, it was decided at the outset of the research to involve only adults in care situations, and so the views of dependant children were not elicited. (The focus groups with two separate groups of teenage children were organised separately to complement the adult perspective).

*Care of Adult Children only:* A further five of the 21 case studies concerned care of adult children only. Of these five, three involved lone mothers caring for adult children with physical and/or intellectual impairments (*Mary(widow) & Declan; Anita (separated) & Beth* and *Nora (separated) & Rory*) while two involved carers who were in partnered relationships (*Sara* and *Melanie*). Although married, both Sara and Melanie were primary carers for their children as in each case their spouse had developed a physical impairment and was unable to assist in care (and needed support himself at times).

In just two of the five case studies in this category, (involving *Anita* and *Nora*) were the adult children they were in care of also involved in the research. *Anita's* daughter *Beth*, who had an intellectual impairment and *Nora's* son, *Rory*, who had a progressive physical immunity disease opted to participate in the 'care conversation'.

*Care of Dependant and Adult Children:* Finally, one case study (*Paula*) involved a mixture of care of dependant and adult children. Paula had four children, three of whom still reside in the family home but only one is under 18 years. *Paula* initially thought that one of her sons would be interested in participating in the research; despite repeated efforts none of her three adult children wanted to hold a conversation with us.

## 2.  Care of family dependants other than children

In this category, all case studies involved the care of frail and sometimes ill or disabled older parent(s). Three of the six case studies involved a single (with no partner/not married) male carer (*Tom*, *Pearse* and *Tony*), one involved a single female carer (*Valerie*) and one involved a partnered female carer (*Maeve*). The only household where all carers and care recipients in this group agreed to hold a conversation was Tony's. His sister Marian, who assisted him in caring, and his mother, Mary Kate, all agreed to talk with us. In two of the three other case studies (*Tom* and *Maeve*), the carer considered the parent she/he was caring for to be too infirm to participate in a conversation about care. In *Pearse's case*, we did have a partial conversation with his mother but as she had a severe hearing loss we could not hold a meaningful conversation. She was present during the interview with Pearse but was only able to hear when either Pearse or Maureen (who was hosting the conversation) shouted really loudly.

In the sixth case study, the principal participant is a care recipient, a mother (now a widow) (*Monica*) who was being cared for by her co-resident single daughter. *Monica* did not want us to talk with her daughter claiming she said was too busy with work and other activities to be involved in the research.

### No Access: gatekeeping or hard-to-reach?

It is clear from the above that certain forms of 'gate-keeping', both on the part of carers and care recipients, was an issue in this study. While it was evident that some people were too ill to participate, it was not clear in other cases if care recipients were either unable or unwilling, or if this was simply the carer's view. We had to take the carer's word that they were unable/unwilling to hold a conversation, and in the case of Monica, the care recipient's word.

### Transcription, coding and analysis

A relatively unstructured schedule was used as an *aide-memoire* to ensure that all conversations covered a core set of themes/issues. In addition, each schedule was tailored to suit the particular care context; this involved the addition of particular themes/issues to provide additional information on each unique care situation. Equally, specific schedules were prepared for each of the care recipient conversations and focus groups, involving a set of core and additional issues/themes.

All taped conversations were transcribed in full and then coded and analysed using a computer-assisted software data analysis package, MAXqda.

| CS No. | Carers (Pseudonyms) | Care Recipients (pseudonyms) | Age of Carer | Family Status | Living Arrangement | Marital status | Socio-Economic Status | Description | Care Conversations |
|---|---|---|---|---|---|---|---|---|---|
| | Alex: see Debra | | | | | | | | |
| 6 | Anita | Beth, adult daughter in her 20s who has an intellectual impairment | 50–60 | Separated parent | Co-resident with Beth | Separated | Carer Full-time, with the exception of the hours Beth attends a day centre | Anita returned from the UK to find a better care arrangement for Beth. She is currently trying to find a full-time residential place for Beth. She is also mother of 2 other sons, one of whom lives abroad and the other nearby with his wife and young children. Because of his own care responsibilities he is not able to provide practical assistance to Anita. | CC with both Anita and Beth |
| 18 | Cathy | Amelia and Tara, pre-school daughters | 40–50 | Married parent | Co-resident with spouse Michael and CRs | Married | Employed Full-time | Cathy is employed full-time as well as being the primary carer for her two primary school-going children. She articulates the difficulty of finding a good care arrangement and the importance of same in being able to manage and balance these responsibilities. | CC with Cathy; Cathy indicated interest of husband to participate but he later decided that he did not wish to be involved |

| CS No. | Carers (Pseudonyms) | Care Recipients (pseudonyms) | Age of Carer | Family Status | Living Arrangement | Marital status | Socio-Economic Status | Description | Care Conversations |
|---|---|---|---|---|---|---|---|---|---|
| | Clodagh: see Séan | | | | | | | | |
| 20 | Debra | Cathy, primary school daughter. Noel, pre-school son who has an intellectual impairment. | 40–50 | Married parent | Co-resident with spouse and CRs | Married | Employed Part-time | Alex and Debra are married parents of 2 children, one of whom has an intellectual impairment. Despite being the more successful career wise, Debra has opted to work part-time and Alex to remain the full-time breadwinner. They provide a good example of deeply engrained gendered attitudes and practices and also added difficulties around care involving a child with an intellectual impairment. | CC with Alex and Debra; children not eligible to participate due to age |
| | Alex | | 40–50 | | | | Employed Full-time | | |
| | Donal: see Geraldine | | | | | | | | |
| 13 | Elizabeth | Owen, pre-school son, and Kate, pre-school daughter | 30–40 | Lesbian couple parent | Co-resident with partner and CRs | Cohabiting | Self-employed | Elizabeth and Nuala are a lesbian cohabiting couple whose work lives are organised around care responsibilities and | CC with Elizabeth and Nuala; children not eligible due to age |

| CS No. | Carers (Pseudonyms) | Care Recipients (pseudonyms) | Age of Carer | Family Status | Living Arrangement | Marital status | Socio-Economic Status | Description | Care Conversations |
|---|---|---|---|---|---|---|---|---|---|
|  | Nuala |  | 30–40 |  |  |  | Carer Full-time | choice for one to be full-time carer while other has breadwinner role. |  |
| 19 | Geraldine | Trisha, pre-school daughter | 30–40 | Married parent | Co-resident with spouse and CR | Married | Employed Full-time | Geraldine and Donal are married parents of one baby. They attempt to co-share parenting as equally as possible while both also in full-time employment and articulate gendered nature of society with regard to parenting. | CC with Geraldine and Donal; child not eligible to participate due to age |
|  | Donal |  | 30–40 |  |  |  | Employed Full-time |  |  |
| 11 | Jane | Richard and Cathal, primary school sons | 40–50 | Lesbian couple parent | Co-resident with partner and CRs | Cohabiting | Employed Full-time | Jane and Jill, a cohabiting lesbian couple, have 2 children. They have organised their work and daily lives around their children and care responsibilities. | CC with Jill and Jane; sons not eligible to participate due to age |
|  | Jill |  | 40–50 |  |  |  | Self-employed |  |  |
| 5 | Maeve | Brigid, elderly and infirm mother | 50–60 | Married parent | Co-resident with husband and part-time with her mother, who also spends some of the week with another sibling | Married | Carer Part-time & homemaking | Maeve lives in good economic circumstances with her husband Frank who is retired and is also of great practical and emotional support to her. Maeve and Frank's adult children are no longer living at home. | CC with Maeve; Maeve unwilling to involve her mother in research |

| CS No. | Carers (Pseudonyms) | Care Recipients (pseudonyms) | Age of Carer | Family Status | Living Arrangement | Marital status | Socio-Economic Status | Description | Care Conversations |
|---|---|---|---|---|---|---|---|---|---|
| 16 | Mary | Declan, adult son who has a physical and intellectual impairment | 50–60 | Lone parent | Co-resident with CR | Widow | Carer Full-time | Mary is a widow, having cared for her husband for a number of years before he died last year. She has been a full-time carer of her son (now in his 30s) since birth – he has a physical and intellectual impairment. | CC with Mary; Declan not eligible to participate due to nature of physical and intellectual impairment |
| 2 | Melanie | Susan and Patricia, adult twin daughters, and Deirdre, adult daughter, all of whom have intellectual and some physical impairments. Peter, husband, who has developed a physical impairment | 40–50 | Married parent | Co-resident with 3 daughters for whom she is caring and husband Peter | Married | Carer Full-time | Melanie has no support from extended family and receives very little aid/assistance from the State. She has had very little experience of care in her own earlier life and currently also experiences a certain amount of ill health. Melanie is also mother to college-going daughter Mary who is living away from home. | CC with Melanie; Husband willing to participate but unable to do so due to speech difficulty which is part of his physical impairment; adult children unable to participate due to nature of intellectual impairment |

| CS No. | Carers (Pseudonyms) | Care Recipients (pseudonyms) | Age of Carer | Family Status | Living Arrangement | Marital status | Socio-Economic Status | Description | Care Conversations |
|---|---|---|---|---|---|---|---|---|---|
| 14 | Denise, adult daughter in her 30s | Monica, a widow in her late 70s | 30–40 | Single daughter | Co-resident with mother | Single | Denise working Full-time<br><br>Monica a recipient of state pension | Monica is a Care Recipient living with her adult single daughter, Denise. She also has good support from other children who visit regularly with her grandchildren. She had negative experience of caring for her own mother while her children were growing up. | CC with Monica; Monica unwilling to involve her daughter in research |
| 17 | Nora | Rory, adult son (30–40) who has a physical impairment. Marita and Caitriona, adult daughters who have a milder form of the same condition and also suffer from mental ill health. | 70–80 | Separated parent | Co-resident with Rory | Separated | Pensioner and Carer Full-time<br><br>Rory unable to work due to physical impairment | Nora is caring for her son but there is a great deal of mutuality in this care relationship. Both also care for Rory's two sisters who live nearby. Nora has always been a carer despite having very little care in her own life as a child and in her marriage with her now ex-husband. | CC with Nora & Rory |

| CS No. | Carers (Pseudonyms) | Care Recipients (pseudonyms) | Age of Carer | Family Status | Living Arrangement | Marital status | Socio-Economic Status | Description | Care Conversations |
|---|---|---|---|---|---|---|---|---|---|
| | Nuala: see Elizabeth | | | | | | | | |
| 12 | Paula | Thomas, Stephen, Paul are 3 adult sons and Andrew is her 4th second-level school son | 40–50 | Lone parent | Co-resident with 3 of her 4 CRs | Divorced | Employed Full-time | Paula has 3 sons living with her – youngest still in school. Other son living away who now has a baby of his own. Paula very much involved in care of all 4 sons and grandchild. She finds work and home balance difficult. | CC with Paula; Paula wished her son to participate but efforts to organise this failed despite numerous contacts |
| 8 | Pearse | Mother in her 80s | 50–60 | Single | Co-resident with his mother | Single | Farming Full-time on small farm | Pearse, a small farmer, lives in very poor economic circumstances and living conditions. He has 2 sisters living in the same county but they are not involved in caring for their mother. | CC with Pearse; mother willing to participate but not possible due to her hearing impairment |
| 4 | Regina | Emmett, in 1st year in second-level school | 30–40 | Lone parent | Co-resident with CR | Divorced | Student Full-time | Regina, originally from Eastern Europe, came to Ireland as an asylum seeker with her young son. She suffers from physical ill health and struggles financially due to being a full-time student. | CC with Regina; Emmett not eligible to participate due to age |

| CS No. | Carers (Pseudonyms) | Care Recipients (pseudonyms) | Age of Carer | Family Status | Living Arrangement | Marital status | Socio-Economic Status | Description | Care Conversations |
|---|---|---|---|---|---|---|---|---|---|
| 10 | Sara | Phoebe, daughter with an intellectual impairment. John, husband who has recently suffered a stroke | 50–60 | Married parent | Co-resident with husband and on the weekends with Phoebe | Married | Employed Full-time | Sara is employed full-time and cares for her husband who has suffered a stroke (he is on his own during the day) and her daughter (who lives in residential centre Monday to Friday). | CC with Sara; Sara unwilling to involve her husband and Phoebe unable to due to nature of intellectual impairment |
| 15 | Sasha | Niall, Donal are in primary school and suffer from a sensory impairment Séan, is her 3rd pre-school son | 30–40 | Lone parent | Co-resident with CRs | Single | Carer Full-time | Sasha is a lone parent of 3 young children. Her two eldest sons have a sensory impairment and attend a special primary school; her relationship with their father broke up and she has little contact with him. Her 3rd child is in pre-school and she is caring for him full-time; she has little contact with his father. She would like to find employment as she finds it very difficult to survive on social welfare. She has good family support. | CC with Sasha; children not eligible due to age |

| CS No. | Carers (Pseudonyms) | Care Recipients (pseudonyms) | Age of Carer | Family Status | Living Arrangement | Marital status | Socio-Economic Status | Description | Care Conversations |
|---|---|---|---|---|---|---|---|---|---|
| 21 | Séan | Alicia, Ciara and Aoife, three primary school daughters | 40–50 | Married parent | Co-resident with spouse and CRs | Married | Employed Full-time | Séan and Clodagh are married parents of 3 primary school-going daughters. Care practice is one of equal sharing of care work. Interview good example of negative experience of managing employment and care, particularly in the context of the banking sector. | CC with Clodagh and Séan; children not eligible to participate due to age |
| | Clodagh | | 40–50 | | | | Employed Full-time | | |
| 1 | Susan | Sam: son who is in his 2nd year in second-level school | 30–40 | Lone parent | Co-resident with Sam | Single | Employed Full-time | Susan became pregnant in her final Leaving Cert year of Secondary School. Her immediate family are her main support structure. Sam's father is not involved in his life and is now living abroad. Susan has recently bought her own home. | CC with Susan; Sam not eligible to participate due to age |
| 7 | Tom | Elderly and infirm father in his 80s | 50–60 | Single | Co-resident with his father | Single | Unable to work owing to long-term illness/ physical impairment | Following an accident Tom is no longer able to work and is a full-time carer for his father. His other siblings help out with the care of his father from time to time. | CC with Tom; Tom unwilling to involve father in research |

| CS No. | Carers (Pseudonyms) | Care Recipients (pseudonyms) | Age of Carer | Family Status | Living Arrangement | Marital status | Socio-Economic Status | Description | Care Conversations |
|---|---|---|---|---|---|---|---|---|---|
| 9 | Tony | Mary Kate, mother. Uncle living in adjacent farm. | 40–50 | Single | Co-resident with his mother and uncle lives nearby | Single | Farming Full-time | Tony, farmer of a medium-sized holding, is carer for his mother and also for his uncle who lives at the adjoining farm. The main cost of caring to Tony is social isolation and loneliness due to the fact that his mother cannot be left on her own except for very short periods. Marian, his sister, who lives about 10 miles away, is a full time mother and homemaker/ farmer. She visits on a weekly basis and helps out with some of the practical aspects of care. Mary Kate is now elderly with impaired mobility. She has a very good relationship with both her son and daughter. She has another son who visits rarely. | CC with Tony, Mary Kate his mother and his sister Marian |

| CS No. | Carers (Pseudonyms) | Care Recipients (pseudonyms) | Age of Carer | Family Status | Living Arrangement | Marital status | Socio-Economic Status | Description | Care Conversations |
|---|---|---|---|---|---|---|---|---|---|
| 3 | Valerie | Both elderly and infirm parents. | 40–50 | Single | Co-resident with parents | Single | Carer Full-time | Valerie worked abroad and gave up a good career to return home and care for her parents. Her brother and sister are living abroad and so of little practical assistance to her. | CC with Valerie; Valerie unwilling to involve her parents in research |
| FG1 | Focus Group 1: Participants member a Youth Project (Middle Class) | | Teens, aged 14–17 | | | | Attending second-level school | Middle class group mainly from Dublin city and county. | CC with 7 teens, 4 boys and 3 girls |
| FG2 | Focus Group 2: Participants from, a community development project (Working Class) | | Teens, aged 13–17 | | | | Attending second-level school | Working class group from Dublin North Inner City | CC with 7 teens, 5 boys and 2 girls |

# Notes

1 Although in normal use 'affective' refers to the emotions and emotional relationships generally rather than to love, care and solidarity in particular, we use it here with this narrower focus for lack of a better general label for this field. The emotionality of such relationships is, however, one of their central features and the term 'affective' helps to keep this in view. Occasionally, where the context makes it clear, we use 'affective' in its wider sense and we sometimes make points about love, care and solidarity by reference to the general characteristics of emotional relations.

2 As Weber (1946/1958: 194) observed 'Whereas the genuine place of "classes" is within the economic order, the place of "status groups" is within the social order, that is, within the sphere of the distribution of "honour". From within these spheres, classes and status groups influence one another... But "parties" live in a house of "power". Their action is oriented toward the acquisition of social "power" that is to say, toward influencing a communal action no matter what its content may be.'

3 The lower status accorded to this work was not just a function of its subject matter, the personal, the private, the familial; it was also a function of the gendered character of those writing and teaching in these fields, most of whom were women.

4 This term 'cultural arbitrary' was used first by Bourdieu and Passeron (1977) to explain the ways in which powerful middle class groups imposed their values, language and modes of expression on working class students in formal education. This imposition was seen as natural, inevitable and desirable although it was entirely arbitrary and resulted in working class students failing in schooling contexts that were alien and hostile.

5 To recognise the patriarchal control of sociological research is not to deny that some leading scholars did recognise the role of patriarchy. In educational thought, for example, some male scholars made a space for feminist scholars to write and publish when it was far from politically fashionable (Walker and Barton, 1983). More recently, pro-feminist masculinity scholars, including Connell (1995, 2002), Lingard and Douglas (1999) and Mac an Ghaill (1994) have been especially important in reconstituting the relevant gender questions for education. By examining the discourses and practices that constitute the masculine, Connell, in particular, has problematised the conception of 'hegemonic masculinity', and in so doing has created a space for feminist educators to move beyond examining their otherness, their problematic status in a male-female binary. Bourdieu, while ignoring gender in most of his work, also came to recognise the key role of patriarchy in subordinating women (e.g. Bourdieu, 2001).

6 I think therefore I am.

7 Yet an analysis of the etymological roots of the word 'education' shows that it originated from the Latin verb *educare* (which means to nurture and to develop through care), rather than from the verb *educere* (which means to lead out).

8 We recognise that important distinctions can be drawn between the work of 'homo faber' (humans as makers of things), the labour of 'animal laborans' (the

251

work humans must do of necessity to maintain life itself) and the work of humans as 'animal rationale' (intellectual labourers) (see Arendt, 1958). These distinctions made by Arendt in *The Human Condition* do not focus however on care labouring in and of itself, although she does recognise that the work that women did in the private sphere was hidden away because of the type of work involved: 'Women and slaves belonged to the same category and were hidden away, not only because they were somebody else's property but because their life was "laborious", devoted to bodily functions' (*ibid.*: 72).

9  Gouldner defined domain assumptions as the personal values and assumptions that underpin research thinking, arising from personal experiences and statuses people may or may not reflect upon. They arise from our personal identities as women or men, ethnic majority or minority members, lesbian, gay or heterosexual, etc.

10  For critical insights into this debate, see Benhabib, 1992, ch 6; Held, 1995b; Kymlicka, 2002, ch 9.

11  See Shakespeare (2006) for an extensive review of different disability perspectives on this subject.

12  This reaction has invariably arisen whenever we have presented our equality framework to groups of political theorists.

13  This Chapter is an edited and revised version of a paper published by K. Lynch (2007) 'Love labour as a distinct and non-commodifiable form of Care Labour' *Sociological Review*, Vol. 54, No. 3: 550–570.

14  The term 'care' is used in the Chapter as a collective noun to refer to the combined activities involved in providing love, care and solidarity. This is not entirely satisfactory, but given the limitations of language it is not possible to find a more suitable generic noun to connote the range of human activities that are strongly other-centred.

15  For examples see Folbre, 1994, 2006 and Folbre and Bittman, 2004 (economics); Noddings, 1984 (education); Fineman, 2004 (law); Harrington Meyer, 2000 and Hochschild, 1989, 2001 (sociology); Held, 1995, Kittay, 1999, Nussbaum, 1995, 2000, and Tronto, 1993 (philosophy); Leira, 1992, Ungerson, 1995, 1997 and Williams, 2004 (social policy); Fraser and Gordon, 1997; Sevenhuijsen, 1998 and Hobson, 2000 (politics).

16  It is important to distinguish between emotional capital and the related but separate phenomenon of *nurturing capital*. While emotional capital (and the associated emotional work involved in love labouring and caring that produces it) is integral to nurturing capital, not all nurturing involves emotional work (and neither does all emotional work involve nurturing as Hochschild showed in her work, *The Managed Heart*). Nurturing can involve the enactment of practical tasks with limited emotional engagement at a given moment. The doing of nurturing tasks is generally motivated by feelings of concern for others, but the undertaking of the task itself may well be routinised at a given time and require low emotional engagement.

17  This is not to deny that love labouring can become routinised and emotionally disengaged especially when people are tired, stressed or unwell. However, the commitment to engage in the care of another is strongly affectively driven and this prior emotional engagement sets the context and frames the care relations. Even if love labour is undertaken without expressed feeling, it remains implicitly part of the relationship.

18  An example of this is the meitheal system of mutual co-operation that operated traditionally in rural Ireland especially around harvesting time (see Arensberg and Kimball, 2001: 255–257).

19  Although some define care as work for others that they cannot do for themselves (Tronto, 2002), this is a problematic conceptualisation of care as the boundaries between what people can and cannot do for themselves are not always easily drawn. At times, showing affection or appreciation for others may well mean doing a task for them which they are capable of doing (in the physical or mental sense). Relieving them of the task can be an expression of thanks, concern or appreciation which is a form of care in itself.

20  We speak of people 'wasting away' when they are very ill.

21  I think therefore I am.

22  In an *Irish Times* National Survey of 1000 women in 2007, there was a strong indication that Irish women's attitudes to gender issues are changing and becoming more feminist: 78% claimed that equality between the sexes was important (with 44% claiming it was very important) while 54% claimed the feminism was important. Financial independence was also highly prized with 65% saying it was very important and a further 26% saying it was quite important. Only 7% regarded it as unimportant (*Irish Times*, in association with Behaviour and Attitudes Marketing Research, reported September 27th : 6–7; see also *Irish Times*, September 28th 2007, weekend supplement).

23  In Ireland, a medical card provides means-tested free access to primary medical services. Eligibility for a medical card is, therefore, an indicator of low income.

24  Those he lists are: babies, children and young people; people with temporary illnesses or impairments; people with terminal illnesses; people with mild to moderate learning difficulties; people with profound learning difficulties; people with mental health problems; people who are elderly and frail; and people who are elderly and demented (Shakespeare, 2006: 136).

25  The work of Fiona Williams (2004) is an example of feminist work that takes account of the care recipients as indeed do others such as Sevenhuijsen (1998) and Kittay (1999).

26  Bourdieu defines the habitus as the sets of acquired and lasting schemes of thought, perception and action internalised by individuals in relation to the structural contexts in which they live.

27  A sample of 25 mothers from different social class groupings and across different social positionings were selected for this study in order to explore how mothers with access to different resources and occupying dominant and more marginal positionings carried out their educational care work. Mothers rather than parents were the focus of the study as a substantial body of scholarship has indicated that mothers rather than fathers are primary care workers and also do the bulk of educational support work. The study focused on the care children needed during their transition from primary school to secondary school in Ireland, a transition that normally takes place at the age of about 11–12. Interview quotations indicate the pseudonym of the speaker, her economic status and her marital status.

28  Parents in Ireland have quite a lot of choice if they have the relevant cultural and economic capitals and they can theoretically select among many schools as they are not compelled to send their children to schools within their own catchments. Lynch and Moran (2006) refer to the burdens of choice and the absence of choices respectively for those with and without economic and cultural capitals in a marketised second-level education system.

29  In Ireland, fee-paying schools are concentrated largely in the Dublin region and in a few large cities and towns. Most middle class parents outside these areas do not select and use fee-paying schools as they do not exist unless they choose boarding schools which are also very few in number.

30 Children with disabilities or who hold medical cards are entitled to free travel allowances to school.

31 The institutionalised racism involved in granting visas under very restricted conditions meant that the partners of those who got student visas or were waiting for working visas could not enter employment and missed out on the social and cultural capital gained through work which would have been of value for their children's education.

32 This does not always hold true. Attributes associated with women such as emotional intimacy may also be used to construct oppressive relations. Connell suggests that masculinities modernize to preserve dominance.

33 The concepts of *learning care* and *learning care labour* are based on the ideas of Kathleen Lynch and Eithne McLaughlin (1995) in 'Caring Labour and Love Labour' where they distinguish between types of emotional work and the extent to which both may be motivated by solidary intent.

34 The Lighthouse Centre is a pseudonym for an adult education and advice Centre established in Dublin by and for survivors of abuse in Irish industrial schools. The Centre provides a range of adult learning opportunities including literacy, anger management, art therapy and personal development. Advice is also available about family tracing, counselling, and legal matters. The Centre functions as a community centre and is attended on an average day by 80 people.

35 The European Council adopted the Lisbon Strategy in 2001 with the expressed aim of making the EU 'the most dynamic and competitive knowledge-based economy in the world capable of sustainable economic growth with more and better jobs and greater social cohesion and respect for the environment, by 2010' (CEC, 2001).

36 When we were planning the care conversations originally our aim was to undertake conversations with care recipients including children in families. However, the resources and timeframe available for the study were not sufficient for this purpose particularly with children. Moreover, there were considerable ethical, legal and access issues that would have had to be addressed if we were to talk with minors (under 16 years). To compensate for this conversational deficit, we did organise two focus groups with post-16-year-olds (mostly aged 16–18) who were living at home with parents and attending school. We chose two contrasting youth groups for these focus groups, one predominantly middle class and the other working class.

# Bibliography

Abel, Emily K. (1991) *Who Cares for the Elderly? Public Policy and the Experience of Adult Daughters* (Philadelphia: Temple University Press).

Adam, Barbara (1995) *Timewatch: The Social Analysis of Time* (Cambridge: Polity Press).

Adam, Barbara (2000) 'The Temporal Gaze: The Challenge for Social Theory in the Context of GM Food', *British Journal of Sociology* 51(1), 125–142.

Allatt, Patricia (1993) 'Becoming Privileged: The Role of Family Processes' in Inga Bates and George Riseborough (eds) *Youth and Inequality* (Buckingham: Open University Press).

Allen, Kieran (2007) *The Corporate Takeover of Ireland* (Dublin: Irish Academic Press).

Apple, Michael (2001) *Educating the 'Right' Way: Markets, Standards, God, and Inequality* (New York: Routledge/Falmer Press).

Arber, Sara and N. Gilbert (1989) 'Men the Forgotten Carers', *Sociology* 23(1), 111–118.

Arber Sara and J. Ginn (1990) 'The Meaning of Informal Care: Gender and the Contribution of Older People', *Ageing and Society* 10, 429–454.

Archard, David (1993) *Children: Rights and Childhood* (London: Routledge).

Arendell, Terry (1997) 'Reflections on the Researcher – Researched Relationship: A Woman Interviewing Men', *Qualitative Sociology* 20(3), 341–368.

Arendt, Hannah (1958) *The Human Condition* (Chicago: University of Chicago Press).

Arensberg, Conrad M. and Solon T. Kimball (2001) *Family and Community in Ireland*, 3rd edition (Ennis Co. Clare: CLASP Press).

Aronowitz, Stanley and Henry Giroux (1993) *Education Still Under Siege* (US: Bergin and Garvey).

Badgett, M. V. Lee and Nancy Folbre (1999) 'Assigning Care: Gender Norms and Economic Outcomes', *International Labour Review* 138(3), 311–326.

Baker, John (1987) *Arguing for Equality* (London: Verso).

Baker, John, Kathleen Lynch, Sara Cantillon and Judy Walsh (2004) *Equality: From Theory to Action* (Basingstoke: Palgrave Macmillan).

Ball, Stephen (2003) 'The Teacher's Soul and the Terrors of Performativity', *Journal of Education Policy* 18(2), 215–228.

Ball, Stephen, Carol Vincent, Sophie Kemp and Soile Pietikaien (2004) 'Middle Class Fractions, Childcare and the "Relational" and "Normative" Aspects of Class Practices', *The Sociological Review* 52(4), 478–502.

Ball, Stephen and Carol Vincent (2005) 'The "Child Care Champion"? New Labour, Social Justice and the Childcare Market', *British Educational Research Journal* 31(5), 557–570.

Barbalet, Jack (ed.) (2002) *Emotions and Sociology* (Oxford: Blackwell).

Barker, Drucilla (1998) 'Dualisms, Discourse and Development', *Feminist Economics* 13(3), 83–94.

Barnes, Marian (2006) *Caring and Social Justice* (Basingstoke: Palgrave Macmillan).

Barr, Jean (1999) *Liberating Knowledge: Research, Feminism and Adult Education* (UK: NIACE).

Barry, Jackie (1995) 'Care-need and care-receivers: Views from the Margins', *Women's Studies International Forum* 18, 361–374.

Barton, David and Mary Hamilton (1998) *Local Literacies: Reading and Writing in One Community* (London: Routledge).

Barton, David, Mary Hamilton and Roz Ivanic (eds) (2000) *Situated Literacies* (London: Routledge).

Beasley, Chris (2005) *Gender and Sexuality; Critical Theories, Critical Thinkers* (London: Sage).

Beck, Ulrich (2000) *Brave New World of Work* (Cambridge: Polity Press).

Beck, Ulrich and Elizabeth Beck-Gernsheim (2001) *Individualisation* (London: Sage).

Becker, Gary S. (1981) *A Treatise on the Family* (Cambridge, MA: Harvard University Press).

Beechey, Veronica (1987) *Questions for Feminism Unequal Work* (London: Verso).

Benhabib, Seyla (1992) *Situating the Self: Gender, Community, and Postmodernism in Contemporary Ethics* (New York: Routledge).

Bergmann, Barbara R. (1995) 'Becker's Theory of the Family, Preposterous Conclusions', *Feminist Economics* 1(1), 141–150.

Bettio, Francesca and Janneke Platenga (2004) 'Comparing Gender Regimes in Europe', *Feminist Economics* 10(1), 85–113.

Bettio, Francesca, Annamaria Simonazzi and Paola Villa (2006) '"Change in Care Regimes and Female Migration"; the "Care Drain" in the Mediterranean', *Journal of European Social Policy* 16(3), 271–285.

Bianchi, Suzanne, Mellissa Milkie, Liana Sayer and John Robinson (2000) 'Is Anyone Doing the Household Work? Trends in the Gender Division of Household Labour', *Social Forces* 79(1), 191–228.

Biggs, Hazel (1997) 'Madonna Minus Child, or Wanted Dead or Alive! The Right to Have a Dead Partner's Child', *Feminist Legal Studies* 5(2), 225–234.

Bittman, Michael (2004) 'Parenting and Employment: What Time-Use Surveys Show' in N. Folbre and M. Bittman (eds) *Family Time: The Social Organisation of Care* (London: Routledge).

Bjornberg, Ulla (2002) 'Ideology and Choice between Work and Care: Swedish Family Policy for Working Parents', *Critical Social Policy* 22(1), 33–52.

Bloom, Benjamin S. (ed.) (1956) *Taxonomy of Educational Objectives, the Classification of Educational Goals – Handbook I: Cognitive Domain* (New York: McKay).

Boland, Eavan (1995) *Object Lessons: The Life of the Woman and the Poet in Our Time* (Manchester: Carcenet Press).

Bolton, Sharon and Maeve Houlihan (eds) (2007) *Searching for the Human in Human Resource Management: Theory, Practice and Workplace Contexts* (London: Palgrave Macmillan).

Boltanski, Luc and Eve Chiapello (2007) *The New Spirit of Capitalism* (New York: Verso).

Borg, Carmel and Peter Mayo (eds) (2007) *Public Intellectuals, Radical Democracy and Social Movements* (New York: Peter Lang).

Bourdieu, Pierre (1984) *Distinctions: A Social Critique of the Judgement of Taste*, tr. Richard Nice (London: Routledge and Kegan Paul).

Bourdieu, Pierre (1986) 'The Forms of Capital' in J. G. Richardson (ed.) *Handbook of Theory and Research for the Sociology of Education* (Westport, CT: Greenwood Press).

Bourdieu, Pierre (1993) *The Field Of Cultural Production* (New York: Columbia University Press).

Bourdieu, Pierre (1996) *The State Nobility: Elite Schools in the Field of Power*, tr. L. C. Clough (Cambridge: Polity Press).

Bourdieu, Pierre (2001) *Masculine Domination* (Cambridge: Polity Press).

Bourdieu, Pierre and Jean-Claude Passeron (1977) *Reproduction in Education, Society and Culture*, tr. Richard Nice (London: Sage Publications).

Boyd, Susan (1999) 'Family, Law and Sexuality: Feminist Engagements', *Social & Legal Studies* 8(3), 369–390.

Bradley, Harriett (1996) *Fractured Identities: Changing Patterns of Inequality* (Cambridge: Polity Press).

Brandth, Berit and Elin Kvande (1998) 'Masculinity and Child Care: The Reconstruction of Fathering', *Sociological Review* 46(2), 293–313.

Braun, Virginia and Victoria Clarke (2006) 'Using Thematic Analysis in Psychology', *Qualitative Research in Psychology* 3(1), 77–101.

Brid, Sharon S. (1996) 'Welcome To The Men's Club; Homosociality and the Maintenance of Hegemonic Masculinity', *Gender and Society* 10, 120–132.

Brittan, Arthur (1989) *Masculinity and Power* (Oxford: Basil Blackwell).

Brody, Elaine M. and Avalie R. Saperstein (2004) *Women in the Middle: Their Parent Care Years*, 2nd edition (New York: Springer).

Brophy, Julia and Carol Smart (eds) (1985) *Women-in-Law: Explorations of Law, Family and Sexuality* (London: Routledge).

Browning, Martin, Francois J. Bourguignon, Pierre Chiappori and Vérie Lechene (1994) 'Income and Outcomes: A Structural Model of Intra-Household Allocation', *Journal of Political Economy* 102(6), 1067–1096.

Bubeck, Diemut (1995) *Care, Justice and Gender* (Oxford: Oxford University Press).

Bubeck, Diemut (2001) 'Justice and the Labour of Care' in Kittay, E. and Feder, E. (eds) *The Subject of Care: Feminist Perspectives on Dependency* (New York: Rowman and Littlefield).

Butler, Judith (1993) *Bodies That Matter* (New York: Routledge).

Butler, Judith (1999) *Gender Trouble: Feminism and the Subversion of Identity* (New York: Routledge).

Callan, Eamonn (1997) *Creating Citizens: Political Education and Liberal Democracy* (Oxford: Oxford University Press).

Callan, Eamonn (2004) *Creating Citizens: Political Education and Liberal Democracy* (Oxford: Oxford University Press).

Campbell, Elaine (2003) 'Interviewing Men in Uniform: A Feminist Approach?', *International Journal of Social Research Methodology* 6(4), 285–304.

Cannuscio, Carolyn C., Graham A. Colditz, Eric B. Rimm, Lisa F. Berkman, Camara P. Jones and Kawachi I. (2004) 'Employment Status, Social Ties, and Caregivers' Mental Health', *Social Science and Medicine* 58(7), 1247–1256.

Cantillon, Sara and Brian Nolan (1998), 'Are Married Women More Deprived than their Husbands?', *Journal of Social Policy* 27(2), 151–171.

Cantillon, Sara, Brenda Gannon and Brian Nolan (2004) *Sharp Household Resources: Learning from Non-Monetary Indicators* (Dublin: Institute for Public Administration).

Carrigan, Tim, Bob Connell and John Lee (1987) 'The "Sex-Role" Framework and the Sociology of Masculinity' in Gaby Weiner and Madeleine Arnot (eds) *Gender Under Scrutiny: New Enquiries in Education* (London: Open University).

Carspecken, Phil Francis and Michael Apple (1992) 'Critical Qualitative Research: Theory, Methodology and Practice' in M. LeCompte, W. L. Millroy and J. Preissle (eds) *The Handbook of Qualitative Research in Education* (San Diego: Academic Press Ltd.), 507–553.

(CEC) (Commission of the European Communities) (2001) *Making a European Area of Lifelong Learning a Reality* (Brussels: European Commission).

Chapman, Tony (2003) *Gender and Domestic Life: Changing Practices in Families and Households* (Basingstoke: Palgrave Macmillan).

Cheal, David (2002) *Sociology of Family Life* (Basingstoke, Hampshire: Palgrave Macmillan).

Cherniss, Cary, Melissa Extein, Daniel Goleman and Roger P. Weissberg (2006) 'Emotional Intelligence: What Does the Research Really Indicate?', *Educational Psychologist* 41(4), 239–245.

Chesler, Mark A. and Carla Parry (2001) 'Gender Roles and/or Styles in Crisis: An Integrative Analysis of the Experiences of Fathers of Children with Cancer', *Qualitative Health Research* 11(3), 363–384.

Chodorow, Nancy (1978) *The Reproduction of Mothering. Psychoanalysis and the Sociology of Gender* (Berkeley: University of California Press).

Chodorow, Nancy (1999) *The Power of Feelings* (New Haven: Yale University Press).

Choi, Heejeong and Nadine F. Marks (2006) 'Transition to Caregiving, Marital Disagreement, and Psychological Well-Being', *Journal of Family Issues* 27(12), 1701–1722.

Clanchy, Michael T. (1979) *From Memory to Written Record: England 1066–1307* (London: Arnold).

Clancy, Patrick (1988) *Who Goes to College? A Second National Survey of Participation in Higher Education* (Dublin: Higher Education Authority).

Clancy, Patrick and Joy Wall (2000) *Social Background of Higher Education Entrants* (Dublin: Higher Education Authority).

Clare, Anthony (2000) *On Men: Masculinity in Crisis* (UK: Chatto and Windus).

Clarke, Juanne N. (2005) 'Fathers' Home Health Care Work When a Child Has Cancer; I'm Her Dad; I Have to Do It', *Men and Masculinities* 7(4), 385–404.

Cleary, Anne (2005) 'Death Rather Than Disclosure: Struggling to be a Real Man', *Irish Journal of Sociology* 14(2), 155–176.

Cohen, Jonathan (2006) 'Social, Emotional, Ethical and Academic Education: Creating a Climate for Learning, Participation in Democracy and Well-being', *Harvard Educational Review* 76(2), 201–237.

Cohen, Louis, Lawrence Manion and Keith Morrison (2000) *Research Methods in Education* (UK: Routledge).

Coltrane, Scott and Justin Galt (2000) 'The History of Men's Caring' in Madonna Harrington Meyer (ed.) *Care Work: Gender, Class and the Welfare State* (New York: Routledge).

Connell, Robert W. (1987) *Gender and Power: Society, the Person and Sexual Politics* (Sydney, Allen & Unwin: Cambridge, Polity Press; Stanford: Stanford University Press).

Connell, Robert W. (1995) *Masculinities* (Cambridge: Polity Press).

Connell, Robert (2002) *Gender* (Cambridge: Polity Press).

Connolly, Paul and Julie Neill (2001) 'Constructions of Locality and Gender and their Impact on the Educational Aspirations of Working-Class Children', Conference Paper presented at *Addressing Issues of Social Class and Education* June 2001 (London: Institute for Policy Studies in Education).

Cook, Deborah (2001) 'Critical Perspectives on Solidarity', *Rethinking Marxism* 13(2), 92–108.

Corcoran, Mary P. (2005) 'Portrait of the "Absent" Father: The Impact of Non-Residency on Developing and Maintaining a Fathering Role', *Irish Journal of Sociology* 14(2), 134–154.

Cossman, Brenda and Judy Fudge (eds) (2002) *Privatisation, Law, and the Challenge to Feminism* (Toronto: University of Toronto Press).

Coulter, Colin and Steve Coleman (eds) (2003) *The End of Irish History? Critical Reflections on the Celtic Tiger* (Manchester: Manchester University Press).

Coyle, Angela (2005) 'Changing Times: Flexibilisation and the Re-organization of Work in Feminised Labour Markets' in L. Pettinger *et al.* (eds) *A New Sociology of Work* (Oxford: Blackwell).

Creighton, Colin (1999) 'The Rise and Decline of the "Male Breadwinner Model" in Britain', *Cambridge Journal of Economics* 23, 519–541.

Crowther, Jim, Mary Hamilton and Lynn Tett (eds) (2001) *Powerful Literacies* (UK: NIACE).

CSO (Central Statistics Office) (2003) *Census 2002: Volume 6 Occupations* (Dublin: Government Publications Office).

CSO (2007a) *Measuring Ireland's Progress* (Dublin: Government Publications Office).

CSO (2007b) *Women and Men in Ireland* (Dublin: Government Publications Office).

Cullen, Kevin, Sarah Delaney and Petrina Duff (2004) 'Caring, Working and Public Life' in *Equality Research Series* (Dublin: The Equality Authority).

Daly, Mary and Jane Lewis (2000) 'The Concept of Social Care and the Analysis of Contemporary Welfare States', *The British Journal of Sociology* 51(2), 281–298.

Daly, Mary (2001) *Carework: The Quest for Security* (Geneva: International Labour Office).

Daly, Mary (2002) 'Care as a Good for Social Policy', *Journal of Social Policy* 31(2), 251–270.

Daly, Mary (2005) 'Changing Family Life in Europe: Significance for State and Society', *European Societies* 7(3), 379–398.

Daly, Mary and Madeleine Leonard (2002) *Against All Odds: Family Life on a Low Income in Ireland* (Dublin: Combat Poverty Agency).

Damasio, Antonio (1994) *Descartes Error: Emotion, Reason and the Human Brain* (New York: Putnam).

Damasio, Antonio (2004) *Looking for Spinoza* (London: Vintage).

David, Miriam, Anne West and Jane Ribbens (1994) *Mothers' Intuition? Choosing Secondary Schools* (London: The Falmer Press).

De Kanter, Ruth (1993) 'Becoming a Situated Daughter: Later when I am big I will be daddy, so then we will also have a father in our house – Hannah four years old' in J. Van Mens-Verhulst, K. Schreurs and L. Woertman (eds) *Daughtering and Mothering: Female Subjectivity Revisited* (London: Routledge).

Delphy, Christine and Diana Leonard (1992) Familiar Exploitation: A New Analysis of Marriage and Family Life (Cambridge, MA: Polity Press).

Denzin, Norman K. (1997) 'Triangulation in Educational Research' in J. P. Keeves (ed.) Educational Research, Methodology and Measurement: An International Handbook (Oxford: Elsevier Science), 318–322.

Department of Education and Science (DES) (2000) Learning for Life: White Paper on Adult Education (Dublin: Government Publications).

Department of Education and Science (DES) (2002) 'Towards Redress and Recovery, Report by the Compensatory Advisory Committee, January 2002' (Dublin: Government Publications).

Department of Education and Science (DES) (2006) Joint Committee on Education and Science: Adult Literacy in Ireland (Dublin: Government Publications).

Dewey, John (1916) *Democracy and Education* (New York: Macmillan).

Doyle, Paddy (1988) *The God Squad* (Dublin: Raven's Art Press).

Doyle, Oran (2004) *Constitutional Equality Law* (Dublin: Thomson Round Hall).

Drew, Eileen, Ruth Emerck and Evelyn Mahon (1998) *Women, Work and the Family in Europe* (London: Routledge).

Duncan, Simon and Rosalind Edwards (1997) 'Lone Mothers and Paid Work – Rational Economic Man or Gendered Moral Rationalities?', *Feminist Economics* 3(2), 29–61.

Duncan, Simon, Rosalind Edwards, Tracey Reynolds and Pam Alldred (2003) 'Motherhood, Paid Work and Partnering: Values and Theories', *Work, Employment and Society* 17(2), 309–330.

Duncan, Simon, Rosalind Edwards, Tracey Reynolds and Pam Alldred (2004) 'Mothers and Child Care: Policies, Values and Theories', *Children & Society* 18(4), 254–265.

Duncan, Simon (2005) 'Mothering, Class and Rationality', *Sociological Review* 53(2), 50–76.

Duncombe, Jean and Dennis Marsden (1996) 'Extending the Social', *Sociology* 30(1), 156–158.

Duncombe, Jean and Dennis Marsden (1998) '"Stepford Wives and Hollow Men?" Doing Emotion Work, Doing Gender and "Authenticity" in Intimate Heterosexual Relationships' in S. J. Williams and G. Bendelow (eds) *Emotions in the Social Life: Critical Themes and Contemporary Issues* (London: Routledge).

Dworkin, Ronald (1977) *Taking Rights Seriously* (Cambridge, MA: Harvard University Press).

Edley, Nigel and Margaret Wetherell (1997) 'Jockeying for Positions: The Construction of Masculine Identities', *Discourse and Society* 8(2), 203–217.

Edmondson, Ricca (2000) 'Writing between Worlds' in Anne Byrne and Ronit Lentin (eds) *(Re)searching Women: Feminist Research Methodologies in the Social Sciences in Ireland* (Dublin: IPA).

Education Finance Board (2008) 'Education Finance Board – Home'. Available at www.educationfinanceboard.com. Accessed 12 May 2008.

Ehrenreich, Barbara and Arlie Russell Hochschild (eds) (2003) *Global Women: Nannies, Maids and Sex Workers in the New Economy* (London: Granta).

Eisner, Robert (1989) *The Total Incomes System of Accounts* (Chicago: University of Chicago Press).

England, Paula and Nancy Folbre (1999) 'The Cost of Caring', *Annals American Academy of Political and Social Science* 561, 39–51.

Engster, Daniel (2005) 'Rethinking Care Theory: The Practice of Caring and the Obligation to Care', *Hypatia* 20(3), 50–74.

European Commission (2004) *Rationale of Motherhood Choices: Influence of Employment Conditions and Public Policies* (Brussels: European Commission).

Evandrou, Maria and Karen Glaser (2003) 'Combining Work and Family Life: The Pension Penalty of Caring', *Ageing and Society* 23(5), 583–601.

Ewick, Patricia and Susan S. Silbey (1998) *The Common Place of Law: Stories From Everyday Life* (Chicago: University of Chicago Press).

Fahy, Bernadette (1999) *Freedom of Angels: Surviving Goldenbridge Orphanage* (Dublin: O'Brien Press).

Fahey, Tony and Eithne McLaughlin (1999) 'Family and State' in Anthony F. Heath, Richard Breen and Christopher T. Whelan (eds) *Ireland North and South: Perspectives from Social Science* (Oxford: Oxford University Press).

Feeley, Maggie (2007) 'Adult Literacy and Affective Equality: Recognising the Pivotal Role of Care in the Learning Relationship', PhD thesis (Equality Studies) (Dublin: University College Dublin).

Feldberg, Roslyn L. and Glenn, Evelyn Nakano (1979) 'Male and Female: Job versus Gender Models in the Sociology of Work', *Social Problems* 26(5), 524–538.

Ferguson, Harry (2002) 'Men and Masculinities in Late-Modern Ireland' in Pease, B. and Pringle, B. (eds) *A Man's World; Changing Men's Practices in a Globalised World* (London: Zed Books).

Ferguson, Harry and Fergus Hogan (2004) *Strengthening Families through Fathers: Developing Policy and Practice in Relation to Vulnerable Fathers and their Families* (Waterford Institute of Technology, Ireland: Centre for Social and Family Research).

Finch, Janet (1989) *Family Obligations and Social Change* (London: Polity Press).

Finch, Janet and Dulcie Groves (1983) *A Labour of Love: Women, Work and Caring* (UK: Routledge & Kegan Paul).

Fineman, Martha (1995) *The Neutered Mother, The Sexual Family and Other Twentieth Century Tragedies* (New York: Routledge).

Fineman, Martha (2004) *The Autonomy Myth: A Theory of Dependency* (New York: New Press).

Finkelstein, Vic (1991) 'Disability: An Administrative Challenge? The Health and Welfare Heritage' in M. Oliver (ed.) *Social Work: Disabled People and Disabling Environments* (London: Jessica Kingsley Publishers).

Flynn, Leo (1995) 'Missing Mary McGee: The Narration of Women in Constitutional Adjudication' in Gerard Quinn *et al.* (eds) (1995) *Justice and Legal Theory in Ireland* (Dublin: Oak Tree Press), 91–106.

Flynn, Mannix (2003a) *James X* (Dublin: Lilliput Press).

Flynn, Mannix (2003b) *Nothing to Say* (Dublin: Lilliput Press).

Folbre, Nancy (1994) *Who Pays for the Kids? Gender and the Structures of Constraint* (London: Routledge).

Folbre, Nancy (1995) '"Holding Hands at Midnight" The Paradox of Caring Labour', *Feminist Economics* 1(1), 73–92.

Folbre, Nancy and Michael Bittman (2004) *Family Time: The Social Organization of Care* (London: Routledge).

Folbre, Nancy (2006), 'Measuring Care: Gender, Empowerment and the Care Economy', *Journal of Human Development* 7(2).

Folbre, Nancy and Heidi Hartmann (1988) 'The Rhetoric of Self Interest: Ideology and Gender in Economic Theory' in Klamer, A., Mc Closkey, D. and Solow, R. (eds) *The Consequences of Economic Rhetoric* (Cambridge: Cambridge University Press).

Folbre, Nancy and Thomas Weisskopf (1998) 'Did Father Know Best? Families, Markets and the Supply of Caring Labour' in Benner, A. and Putterman, L. (eds) *Economics Values and Organisation* (New York: Cambridge University Press).

Foucault, Michel (1973) *The Birth of the Clinic. An Archaeology of Medical Perception* (London: Routledge).

Foucault, Michel (1977) *Discipline and Punish. The Birth of the Prison* (London: Penguin Books).

Foucault, Michel (1978) *The History of Sexuality. Volume 1. An Introduction* (London: Penguin Books).

Fowler, Ellayne and Jane Mace (2005) *Outside the Classroom: Researching Literacy with Adult Learners* (Leicester: NIACE).

Fraser, Nancy and Linda Gordon (1997) 'A Genealogy of "Dependency"' in Nancy Fraser, *Justice Interrupts: Critical Reflections on the 'Postsocialist' Condition* (New York: Routledge).

Fraser, Nancy (1997) 'Social Justice in the Age of Identity Politics' in G. B. Peterson (ed.) *The Tanner Lectures on Human Values* 19 (Salt Lake City: University of Utah Press), 1–67.

Freeman, Michael (1994) 'The Austin Lecture: The Private and the Public' in Derek Morgan and Gillian Douglas (eds) *Constituting Families: A Study in Governance* (Stuttgart: Franz Steiner Verlag), 22–39.

Freire, Paulo (1972) *Pedagogy of the Oppressed* (London: Penguin).

Freire, Paulo (1985) *The Politics of Liberation: Culture, Power and Liberation* (USA: Bergin and Garvey).

Freire, Paulo and Donaldo Macedo (1987) *Reading the Word and the World* (London: Routledge).

Gamoran, Adam (2001) 'American Schooling and Educational Inequality: A Forecast for the 21st century', *Sociology of Education* 74 (Special Issue), 135–153.

Gardner, Howard (1983) *Frames of Mind: The Theory of Multiple Intelligences* (New York: Basic Books).

Gardner, Howard (1993) *Multiple Intelligences: The Theory in Practice* (New York: Basic Books).

Gardner, Howard (1999) *Intelligence Reframed: Multiple Intelligences for the 21st Century* (New York: Basic Books).

Gardiner, Jean (1997) *Gender, Care and Economics* (London: Macmillan).

Gee, James P. (1990) *Social Linguistics and Literacies: Ideology in Discourses* (London: Falmer Press).

Gee, James P. (1999) 'The New Literacy Studies: From "Socially Situated" to the Work of the Social' in Barton, D., Hamilton, M. and Ivanic, R., *Situated Literacies* (London: Routledge).

Gershuny, Jonathan (2000) *Changing Times: Work and Leisure in Postindustrial Society* (Oxford and New York: Oxford University Press).

Gerstel, Naomi and Sally Gallagher (2001) 'Men's Caring: Gender and the Contingent Character of Care', *Gender and Society* 15(2), 197–217.

Gewirtz, S., S. Ball and R. Bowe (1994) 'Parents, Privilege and the Education Market Place', *Research Papers in Education* 9(1), 3–29.

Gheaus, Anca (forthcoming) 'How Much of What Matters Can We Redistribute? Love, Justice and Luck', *Hypatia* 24(4).

Giddens, Anthony (1992) *The Transformation of Intimacy; Sexuality, Love and Eroticism in Modern Societies* (Cambridge: Polity Press).

Gilligan, Carol (1982) *In a Different Voice* (Cambridge: Harvard University Press).

Gilligan, Carol (1995) 'Hearing the Difference: Theorizing Connection', *Hypatia* 10(2), 120–127.

Giroux, Henry (1983) *Theory and Resistance: A Pedagogy for Opposition* (US: Bergin).

Glendinning, Caroline and Jane Millar (eds) (1992) *Women and Poverty in Britain in the 1990s* (UK: Harvester Wheatsheaf).

Glendon, Mary Ann (1991) *Rights Talk: The Impoverishment of Political Discourse* (New York: Free Press).

Glenn, Evelyn Nakano (2000) 'Creating a Caring Society', *Contemporary Sociology* 29(1), 84–94.

Glucksmann, Miriam (1995) 'Why "Work"? Gender and the "Total Social Organization of Labour"', *Gender, Work and Organization* 2(2), 63–75.

Glyn, Andrew (2006) *Capitalism Unleashed: Finance, Globalization and Welfare* (Oxford: Oxford University Press).

Goffman, Erving (1981) *Stigma; Notes on the Management of Spoiled Identity* (UK: Penguin).

Goldstein, Nathan E., John Concato, Terri R. Fried, Stanislav V. Kasl, Rosemary Johnson-Hurzeler and Elizabeth H. Bradley (2004) 'Factors Associated With Caregiver Burden Among Caregivers of Terminally Ill Patients with Cancer', *Journal of Palliative Care* 20(1), 38–43.

Goleman, Daniel (1995) *Emotional Intelligence* (London: Bloomsbury).

Goleman, Daniel (1998) *Working with Emotional Intelligence* (New York: Bantam Books).

Goode, Jackie, Claire Callender and Ruth Lister (1998) *Purse or Wallet: Gender Inequalities and Income Distribution within Families on Benefit,* Tyne and Wear: Policy Studies Institute/Athenaeum Press.

Goodwin, John (2002) 'Irish Men and Work in North-County Dublin', *Journal of Gender Studies* 11(2), 151–166.

Gordon, Robert W. (1984) 'Critical Legal Histories', *Stanford Law Review* 36, 57–125.

Gotell, Lise (2002) 'Queering Law: Not By Vriend', *Canadian Journal of Law & Society* 17(1), 89–113.

Gouldner, Alvin W. (1970) *The Coming Crisis of Western Sociology* (London H.E.B. Heinmann).

Government of Ireland (1970) *Reformatory and Industrial Schools in Ireland* (Prl.1342, Kennedy Report) (Dublin: Government Publication).

Government of Ireland (1998) 'Employment Equality Act' Irish Statute Book Database.

Government of Ireland (2000) 'Equal Status Act' Irish Statute Book Database.

Grabb, Edward (2004) 'Conceptual Issues in the Study of Social Inequality' in James E. Curtis *et al.* (eds) *Social Inequality in Canada: Patterns, Problems, Policies* 4ᵗʰ edn. (Scarborough: Pearson Education Canada), 1–16.

Graff, Harvey J. (1981) *Literacy and Social Development in the West* (USA: Cambridge University Press).

Graham, Hilary (1983) 'Caring: A Labour of Love' in Janet Finch and Dulcie Groves (eds) *A Labour of Love: Women, Work and Caring* (London: Routledge and Kegan Paul).

Gramsci, Antonio (1971) *Selections from the Prison Notebooks* (ed. and tr.) Quentin Hoare and Geoffry Nowell-Smith (London: Lawrence and Wishart).

Gramsci, Antonio (1995) *Further Selections from the Prison Notebooks* (ed. and tr.) Derek Boothman (London: Lawrence and Wishart).

Green, F. (2001) 'It's Been a Hard Day's Night: The Concentration and Intensification of Work in Late Twentieth Century Britain', *British Journal of Industrial Relations* 39(1), 53–80.

Green, Francis (2006) *Demanding Work: The Paradox of Job Quality in the Affluent Economy* (Princeton NJ: Princeton University Press).

Grewal, Daisy and Peter Salovey (2005) 'Feeling Smart: The Science of Emotional Intelligence', *American Scientist* 93(4), 330–339.

Griffith, Alison and Dorothy Smith (2005) *Mothering for Schooling* (New York: Routledge Falmer).

Grigolo, Michele (2003) 'Sexualities and the ECHR: Introducing the Universal Sexual Legal Subject', *European Journal of International Law* 14(5), 1023–1044.

Gürtler, Sabine (2005) 'The Ethical Dimension of Work: A Feminist Perspective', *Hypatia* 20(2), 119–136.

Halford, Susan and Pauline Leonard (2001) *Gender, Power and Organisations* (Basingstoke: Palgrave Macmillan).

Halsey, Albert, Anthony Heath and John Ridge (1980) *Origins and Destinations* (Oxford: Clarendon Press).

Hanlon, Niall (2009) *Masculinities and Affective Equality: The Role of Love and Caring in Men's Lives,* Unpublished PhD thesis submitted to University College Dublin.

Hannan, Damien F. and Louise F. Katsiaouni (1977) *Traditional Families?: From Culturally Prescribed to Negotiated Roles in Farm Families* (Dublin: ESRI).

Hansen, Karen (2004) 'The Asking Rules of Reciprocity in Networks of Care for Children', *Qualitative Sociology* 27(4), 419–435.

Hantover, P. Jeffrey (1998) 'The Boy Scouts and the Validation of Masculinity' in Kimmel, Michael S. and Messner, Michael A. (eds) *Men's Lives* (USA: Allyn and Bacon).

Hargreaves, Andy (2000) 'Mixed Emotions: Teachers' Perceptions of their Inter-actions with Students', *Teaching and Teacher Education* 16(8), 811–826.

Hargreaves, Andy (2001) 'Emotional Geographies of Teaching', *Teachers College Record* 103(6), 1056–1080.

Harrington Meyer, Madonna (2000) 'Introduction: The Right to- or Not to-Care' in Madonna Harrington Meyer (ed.) *Care Work: Gender, Class and the Welfare State* (New York, London: Routledge).

Harvey, David (2005) *A Brief History of Neoliberalism* (Oxford: Oxford University Press).

Hays, Sharon (1996) *The Cultural Contradictions of Motherhood* (New Haven: Yale University Press).

Hayward, Chris, and Máirtin Mac án Ghaill (2003) *Men and Masculinities* (Buckingham: Open University Press).

Health Board Executive (2002) 'The National Counselling Service First Report' (Ireland: HBE).

Hearn, Jeff and Keith Pringle (eds) (2006) *European Perspective on Men and Masculin-ities: National and Transnational Approaches* (Hampshire, UK: Palgrave Macmillan).

Heckman, James and D. Masterov (2004) 'The Productivity Argument for Investing in Young Children', *Working Paper No 5* (Washington DC: Committee on Economic Development).

Held, Virginia (1995a) 'The Meshing of Care and Justice', *Hypatia* 10(2) Spring, 128–132.

Held, Virginia (ed.) (1995b) *Justice and Care: Essential Readings in Feminist Ethics* (Boulder, CO: Westview Press).

Hilliard, Betty and Máire Nic Ghiolla Phádraig (eds) (2007) *Changing Ireland in International Comparison* (Dublin: The Liffey Press).

Hillyard, Paddy, Christina Pantazia, Steve Tombs and David Gordon (2004) *Beyond Criminology: Taking Harm Seriously* (London: Pluto Press).

Himmelweit, Susan (2002) 'Making Visible the Hidden Economy: The Case for Gender-Impact Analysis of Economic Policy', *Feminist Economics* 8(1), 49–70.

Himmelweit, Susan (2005) *Can We Afford (not) To Care: Prospects and Policy,* New Working Paper Series Issue 15, July 2005 (London School of Economics, Gender Institute).

Hirst, Michael (2003) 'Caring-Related Inequalities in Psychological Distress in Britain During the 1990s', *Journal of Public Health Medicine* 25(4), 336–343.

Hobson, Barbara (2000) 'Economic Citizenship: Reflections through the European Policy Mirror' in B. Hobson (ed.) *Gender and Citizenship in Transition* (London: Macmillan), 84–117.

Hobson, Barbara (ed.) (2000) *Gender and Citizenship in Transition* (London: Macmillan).

Hochschild, Arlie Russell (1983) *The Managed Heart: Commercialization of Human Feeling* (Berkeley: University of California Press).

Hochschild, Arlie Russell (1989) *The Second Shift: Working Parents and the Revolution at Home* (New York: Viking).

Hochschild, Arlie Russell (1997) *The Time Bind* (New York: Henry Holt).

Hochschild, Arlie Russell (2001) *The Time Bind: When Work becomes Home and Home becomes Work,* 2nd edition (New York: Owl Books).

Hogarth, Terence, Chris Hasluck and Gaëlle Pierre (2000) *Work-Life Balance 2000: Baseline Study of Work-Life Balance Practices in Great Britain'* (London: Department for Education and Employment).

Holloway, Wendy and Tony Jefferson (2000) *Doing Qualitative Research Differently: Free Association, Narrative and the Interview Method* (London: Sage).

Holter, Oystein Gullvag (2007) 'Men's Work and Family Reconciliation in Europe', *Men and Masculinities* 9(4), 425–456.

hooks, bell (1994) *Teaching to Transgress – Education as the Practice of Freedom* (New York: Routledge).

hooks, bell (2000) *All About Love* (New York: William Morrow & Co).

hooks, bell (2004) *The Will to Change: Men, Masculinity and Love* (New York: Washington Square Press).

Hughes, Bill, Linda McKie, Debra Hopkins and Nick Watson (2005) 'Love's Labour Lost? Feminism, the Disabled People's Movement and an Ethic of Care', *Sociology* 39(2), 259–275.

Hunt, Alan (1993) *Explorations in Law and Society: Toward a Constitutive Theory of Law* (New York: Routledge).

Institute of Public Health (2006) *All Ireland Men's Health Directory* (Belfast: Men's Health Forum in Ireland).

Irigaray, Luce (1977) 'Women's Exile', Trans. Couze Venn. *Ideology and Consciousness* 1, 62–76.

Irigaray, Luce (1991) 'The Sex Which is Not One' in Warhol, R. R. and Herndl, D. P. (eds) *Feminisms: An Anthology of Literary Theory and Criticism* (New Brunswick, NJ: Rutgers University Press), 350–356.

Ironmonger, Duncan (1996) 'Counting Outputs, Capital Inputs, and Caring Labour', *Feminist Economics* 2(3), 37–64.

Ivanič, Roz (1996) 'Linguistics and the Logic of Non-Standard Punctuation' in Nigel Hall and Anne Robinson (eds) *Learning about Punctuation* (Clevedon: Multilingual Matters).

Jackson, Stevi (1999) 'Feminist Sociology and Sociological Feminism: Recovering the Social in Feminist Thought', *Sociological Research Online* 12 (http://www.socresonline. org.uk/4/3/jackson.html).

Jackman, Martha and Bruce Porter (1999) 'Women's Substantive Equality and the Protection of Social and Economic Rights Under the Canadian Human Rights Act' in *Status of Women Canada, Women and the Canadian Human Rights Act: A Collection of Policy Research Reports* (Ottawa: Status of Women Canada), 43–112.

Jaggar, Alison (1995) 'Caring as a Feminist Practice of Moral Reason' in Virginia Held (ed.) *Justice and Care: Essential Reading in Feminist Ethics* (Boulder: Westview Press).

James, Veronica C. and Jonathan Gabe (eds) (1996) *Health and the Sociology of Emotions* (Oxford: Blackwell Publishing).

Jones, Philip W. (1997) 'The World Bank and the Literacy Question: Orthodoxy, Heresy and Ideology', *International Review of Education* 43(4), 367–375.

Kaufman, Michael (ed.) (1994) *Men, Feminism, and Men's Contradictory Experience of Power* (London: Sage Publications).

Kee, John, and Kaye Ronayne (2002) 'Partnership Rights of Same Sex Couples' (Dublin: The Equality Authority).

Kemper, T. D. (1990) 'Social Relations and Emotions: A Structural Approach' in T. D. Kemper (ed.) *Research Agendas in the Sociology of Emotions* (Albany, New York: State University of New York Press), 207–237.

Kennedy, Finola (2001) *Cottage to Créche: Family Change in Ireland* (Dublin: Institute of Public Administration).

Khadiagala, Lynn (2002) 'Negotiating Law and Custom: Judicial Doctrine and Women's Property Rights in Uganda', *Journal of African Law* 46(1), 1–13.

Kimmel, Michael S. (2000) *The Gendered Society* (New York: Oxford University Press).

Kimmel, Michael S. (2005) *The Gender of Desire: Essays on Male Sexuality* (Albany, New York: State University of New York Press).

Kimmel, Michael S. and Tom Mosmiller (eds) (1992) *Against the Tide: Pro-Feminist Men in America, 1776–1990* (Boston: Beacon Press).

Kimmel Michael S. and Michael A. Messner (eds) (1995) *Men's Lives* (Needham Heights, MA: Allyn and Bacon).

Kittay, Eva Feder (1999) *Love's Labour* (New York: Routledge).

Kirby, Peadar (2002) *The Celtic Tiger in Distress: Growth with Inequality in Ireland* (Basingstoke: Palgrave Macmillan).

Klare, Karl E. (1992) 'The Public/Private Distinction in Labour Law', *University of Pennsylvania Law Rev* 130, 1358–1361.

Kramer, Betty, J. and Edward H. Thompson, Jr. (eds) (2005) *Men as Caregivers* (New York: Prometheus Books).

Krathwohl, David R., Benjamin S. Bloom and Bertram B. Masia (1964) *Taxonomy of Educational Objectives: The Classification of Educational Goals: Handbook ii: Affective Domain* (New York: David McKay Company).

Kress, Gunter (2003) *Literacy in the New Media Age* (London: Routledge).

Kymlicka, Will (2002) *Contemporary Political Philosophy: An Introduction*, 2$^{nd}$ edition (Oxford: Oxford University Press).

Lacey, Nicola (2004) 'Feminist Legal Theories and the Rights of Women' in *Gender and Human Rights*, Knop Karen (ed.) (Oxford: Oxford University Press), 13–56.

La Valle, Ivana, Sue Arthur, Christine Millward and James Scott (2002) *Happy Families* (York: Policy Press, Joseph Rowntree Foundation).

Lankshear, Colin and Michele Knobel (2003) *New Literacies: Changing Knowledge and Classroom Learning* (Buckingham: Open University Press).

Lanoix, Monique (2007) 'The Citizen in Question', *Hypatia* 22(4), 113–129.

Lareau, Annette (1989) *Home Advantage* (Lewes, Sussex: The Falmer Press).

Layte, Richard, Bertrand Maitre, Brian Nolan, Dorothy Watson, Christopher T. Whelan, James Williams and Barra Casey (2001) *Monitoring Poverty Trends and Exploring Poverty Dynamics in Ireland* (Dublin: Economic and Social Research Unit).

Leane, Máire and Elizabeth Kiely (1997) 'Single Lone Motherhood – Reality Versus Rhetoric' in Anne Byrne and Madeleine Leonard (eds) *Women and Irish Society* (Belfast: Beyond the Pale Publications).

Leira, Arnlaug (1992) *Welfare States and Working Mothers: The Scandinavian Experience* (Cambridge: Cambridge University Press).

Leonard, Madeleine (2004) 'Bonding and Bridging Social Capital: Reflections from Belfast', *Sociology* 38(5), 927–944.

Lewis, Charles (2000) *A Man's Place in the Home: Fathers and Families in the UK* (York: Joseph Rowntree Foundation).

Lewis, Jane and Barbara Meredith (1988) *Daughters Who Care: Daughters Caring for Mothers at Home* (London: Routledge and Kegan Paul).

Lewis, Jane (1998) *Gender, Social Care and Welfare State Restructuring in Europe* (Aldershot: Ashgate).

Lewis, Jane (2001) 'The Decline of the Male Breadwinner Model: Implications for Work and Care', *Social Politics* 8(2), 152–169.

Lewis, Jane (2003) 'Economic Citizenship: A Comment', *Social Politics* 10(2), 176–195.

Lewis, Jane and Susanna Giullari (2005) 'The Adult Worker Model Family, Gender Equality and Care: The Search for New Policy Principles and the Possibilities and Problems of a Capabilities Approach', *Economy and Society* 34(1), 76–104.

Lingard, Bob and Peter Douglas (1999) *Men Engaging Feminisms: Profeminism, Backlashes and Schooling* (Buckingham: Open University Press).

Lister, Ruth (1997) *Citizenship: Feminist Perspectives* (Basingstoke: Macmillan).

Lister, Ruth (2001) 'Towards a Citizens' Welfare State: the 3 + 2 'R's of Welfare Reform', *Theory, Culture and Society* 18(2–3), 91–111.

Lopes, Paula N., Daisy Grewal, Jessica Kadis, Michelle Gall and Peter Salovey (2006) 'Evidence that Emotional Intelligence is Related to Job Performance and Affect and Attitudes at Work', *Psicothema* 18, 132–138.

Lundberg Shelly, Robert Pollak and Terry Wales (1997) 'Do Husbands and Wives Pool Their Resources? Evidence from the UK Child Benefit', *Journal of Human Resources* 32(3), 463–480.

Lynch, Kathleen (1989) 'Solidary Labour: Its Nature and Marginalisation', *Sociological Review* 37(1), 1–14.

Lynch, Kathleen (2006) 'Neo-Liberalism and Marketisation: The Implications for Higher Education', *European Educational Research Journal* 5(1), 1–17.

Lynch, Kathleen (2007) 'Love Labour as a Distinct and Non-Commodifiable Form of Care Labour', *Sociological Review* 54(3), 550–570.

Lynch, Kathleen and Anne Lodge (2002) *Equality and Power in Schools: Redistribution, Recognition and Representation* (London: Routledge/Falmer).

Lynch, Kathleen, Maureen Lyons and Sara Cantillon (2007) 'Breaking Silence: Educating Citizens for Love, Care and Solidarity', *International Studies in Sociology of Education* 55(3), 550–570.

Lynch, Kathleen and Eithne McLaughlin (1995) 'Caring Labour and Love Labour' in Clancy, Patrick, Sheila Drudy, Kathleen Lynch and Liam O'Dowd (eds) *Irish Society: Sociological Perspectives* (Dublin: IPA), 250–292.

Lynch, Kathleen and Marie Moran (2006) 'Markets, Schools and the Convertibility of Economic Capital: The Complex Dynamics of Class Choice', *British Journal of Sociology of Education* 27(2), 221–235.

Lynch, Kathleen and Claire O'Riordan (1998) 'Inequality in Higher Education: A Study of Class Barriers', *British Journal of Sociology of Education* 19(4), 445–478.

Lyons, Maureen, Kathleen Lynch, Sean Close, Emer Sheerin and Philip Boland (2003) *Inside Classrooms: The Teaching and Learning of Mathematics in Social Context* (Dublin: Institute of Public Administration).

Lyons, Maureen, Kathleen Lynch and Maggie Feeley (2006) 'Rationalities of Care', Paper presented at *Equality and Social Inclusion Conference* (Queen's University Belfast), 1–4th February.

Lynch, Kathleen and Maureen Lyons (2008) 'The Gendered Order of Caring' *163–184*, in *Where are We Now? New Feminist Perspectives on Women in Contemporary Ireland* (Dublin: New Ireland Press).

Mac An Ghaill, Máirtín (1994) *The Making of Men: Masculinities, Sexualities and Schooling* (Buckingham: Open University Press).

MacDonald, Martha, Shelley Phipps and Lynn Lethbridge (2005) 'Taking Its Toll: The Influence of Paid and Unpaid Work on Women's Well-Being', *Feminist Economics* 11(1), 63–94.

MacKinnon, Catherine A. (1987) *Feminism Unmodified: Discourses on Life and Law* (Cambridge MA: Harvard University Press).

McCann, Michael W. (1994) *Rights at Work: Pay Equity Reform and the Politics of Legal Mobilization* (Chicago: Chicago University).

McClave, Henry (2005) 'Education for Citizenship: A Capabilities Approach', PhD thesis (Equality Studies) (Dublin: University College Dublin).

McDermott, Esther (2005) 'Time and Labour: Fathers' Perceptions of Employment and Childcare' in Lynn Pettinger, Jane Parry, Rebecca Taylor and Miriam Glucksmann (eds) *A New Sociology of Work?* (Oxford: Blackwell).

McDonnell, Patrick (2007) *Disability and Society: Ideological and Historical Dimensions* (Dublin: Blackhall Publishing).

McGinnity, Frances, Helen Russell, James Williams and Sylvia Blackwell (2005) 'Time Use in Ireland: Survey Report' (Dublin Economic and Social Research Institute).

McKie, Linda, Susan Gregory and Sophia Bowlby (2002) 'Shadow Times: The Temporal and Spatial Frameworks and Experiences of Caring and Working', *Sociology* 36(4), 897–924.

McLaren, Peter and Peter Leonard (1993) *Paulo Freire: A Critical Encounter* (New York: Routledge).

McMahon, Anthony (1999) *Taking Care of Men; Sexual Politics in the Public Mind* (Cambridge, UK: Cambridge University Press).

McMinn, Joanna (2000) *The Changers and the Changed,* Unpublished PhD Thesis, Equality Studies Centre (Dublin: University College Dublin).

McMinn, Joanna (2007) 'Imbalance in the Sharing of Care and Household Responsibilities', *Equality News* 23 (Dublin: The Equality Authority).

Mace, Jane (2001) 'Signatures and the Lettered World' in Crowther, Hamilton and Tett (eds) *Powerful Literacies* (UK: National Institute of Adult and Continuing Education (NIACE)).

Manji, Ambreena (2003) 'Remortgaging Women's Lives. The World Bank's Land Agenda in Africa', *Feminist Legal Studies* 11, 139–162.

Manji, Ambreena (2005) '"The Beautiful Ones" of Law and Development' in Doris Buss and Ambreena Manji (eds) *International Law: Modern Feminist Approaches* (Oxford; Portland: Hart), 159–171.

Masschelein, Jan and Martin Simons (2002) 'An Adequate Education in a Globalised World?', *Journal of Philosophy of Education* 36(4), 589–608.

Meagher, Gabrielle (2002) 'Is it Wrong to Pay for Housework', *Hypatia* 17(2), 52–66.

Melucci, Alberto (1996) *The Playing Self: Person and Meaning in the Planetary Society* (Cambridge: Cambridge University Press).

Meyer, Traute (1998) 'Retrenchment, Reproduction, Modernisation: Pension Politics and the Decline of the Breadwinner Model', *Journal of European Social Policy* 8(3), 195–211.

Millett, Kate (1969) *Sexual Politics* (London: Granada Press).

Minow, Martha (1987) 'Interpreting Rights: An Essay for Robert Cover', *Yale Law Journal* 96, 1860–1915.

Minow, Martha (1990) *Making All the Difference: Inclusion, Exclusion, and American Law* (Ithaca, NY: Cornell University Press).

Minow, Martha and Mary Lyndon Shanley (1996) 'Relational Rights and Responsibilities: Revisioning the Family in Liberal Political Theory and Law', *Hypatia* 11(1), 4–29.

Moran, Marie (2006) 'Social Inclusion and the Limits of Pragmatic Liberalism: The Irish Case', *Irish Political Studies* 20(2), 181–201.

More, Gillian (1996) 'Equality of Treatment in the European Community Law: The Limits of Market Equality' in Anne Bottomley (ed.) *Feminist Perspective on the Foundational Subjects of Law* (London: Cavendish), 261–278.

Morgan, David (1981) 'Men, Masculinity and the Process of Sociological Enquiry' in Roberts, H. (ed.) *Doing Feminist Research* (London: RKP).

Morris, Jenny (1991) *Pride Against Prejudice* (London: Women's Press).

Morris, Jenny (1993) *Independent Lives?: Community Care and Disabled People* (Basingstoke: Macmillan).

Moser, Claus (1999) *A Fresh Start: Improving Literacy and Numeracy* (London: Department for Education and Employment).

Murphy-Lawless, Jo (2000) 'Reinstating Women's Time in Childbirth', *AIMS Journal*, Spring 2000, 12(1).

Naffine, Ngaire (1990) *Law and the Sexes: Explorations in Feminist Jurisprudence* (Sydney: Allen & Unwin).

Nedelsky, Jennifer (1993) 'Reconceiving Rights as Relationship', *Review of Constitutional Studies* 1(1), 1–26.

Nelson, Julie (1994) 'I, Thou and Them: Capabilities, Altruism, and Norms in the Economics of Marriage', *American Economic Review* 84(2), 126–131.

Nelson, Julie (1996) *Feminism, Objectivity, and Economics* (London: Routledge).

Nelson, Julia A. and Paula England (2002) 'Feminist Philosophies of Love and Work', *Hypatia* 17(2), 1–19.

Ní Laoire, Caitríona (2002) 'Young Farmers Masculinities and Change in Rural Ireland', *Irish Geography* 35(1), 16–27.

Ní Laoire, Caitríona (2005) '"You're Not a Man at All!" Masculinity, Responsibility and Staying on the Land in Contemporary Ireland', *Irish Journal of Sociology* 14(2), 94–114.

Noddings, Nel (1984) *Caring: A Feminine Approach to Ethics and Moral Education* (Berkeley, CA: University of California Press).

Noddings, Nel (1992) *The Challenge to Care in Schools: An Alternative Approach to Education* (New York: Teachers College Press).

Noddings, Nel (2006) 'Educating Whole People: A Response to Jonathan Cohen', *Harvard Educational Review* 76(2), 238–242.

Noddings, Nel (2007) *Philosophy of Education*, Second Edition (Boulder, Colorado: Westview Press).

Noonan, Mary, C., Sarah Beth Estes and Jennifer Glass, L. (2007) 'Do Workplace Flexibility Policies Influence Time Spend in Domestic Labour?', *Journal of Family Issues* 28(2), 263–288.

Nowotny, Helga (1981) 'Women in Public Life in Austria' in C. F. Epstein and R. L. Coser (eds) *Access to Power: Cross National Studies of Women and Elites* (London: George Allen and Unwin).

Nussbaum, Martha C. and Amartya Sen (eds) (1993) *The Quality of Life* (Oxford: Oxford University Press).

Nussbaum, Martha C. and Jonathan Glover (eds) (1995) *Women, Culture and Development: A Study of Human Capabilities* (Oxford: Oxford University Press).

Nussbaum, Martha C. (2000) *Women and Human Development: The Capabilities Approach* (Cambridge: Cambridge University Press).

Nussbaum, Martha (2001) *Upheavals of Thought: The Intelligence of Emotions* (Cambridge: Cambridge University Press).

O'Brien, Maeve (1987) *Home Study Relations in Inner-City Dublin: A Case Study*, Unpublished M. Ed. Thesis (Dublin: University College Dublin).

O'Brien, Maeve (2004) *Making the Move: Students', Teachers' and Parents' Perspectives of Transfer from First to Second-Level Schooling* (Dublin: Marino).

O'Brien, Maeve (2005) 'Mothers as Educational Workers: Mothers' Emotional Work at their Children's Transfer to Second-Level Education', *Irish Educational Studies* 24(2–3), 223–242.

O'Brien, Maeve (2007) 'Mothers' Emotional Care Work in Education and its Moral Imperative', *Gender and Education* 19(2), 159–177.

O'Brien, Maeve (2008) 'Gendered Capital: Emotional Capital and Mothers' Care Work in Education', *British Journal of Sociology of Education* 29(2), 137–148.

O'Connor, J. S., A. S. Orloff and S. Shaver (1999) *States, Markets, Families: Gender, Liberalism and Social Policy in Australia, Canada, Great Britain and the United States* (Cambridge: Cambridge University Press).

O'Connor, P. (1998) 'Women's Friendships in a Post-Modern World' in R. G. Adams and G. Allan (eds) *Placing Friendship in Context* (Cambridge: Cambridge University Press).

O'Donovan, Katherine (1989) 'Engendering Justice: Women's Perspectives and the Rule of Law', *University of Toronto Law Journal* 39, 127–148.

O'Mahony, Paul (1997) 'Mountjoy Prisoners: A Sociological and Criminological Profile' (Dublin: Stationery Office, Government Publications).

O'Neill, C. (1992) *Telling It Like It Is* (Dublin: Combat Poverty Agency).

O'Sullivan, Eoin (1998) 'Juvenile Justice and the Regulation of the Poor: 'Restored to Virtue, to Society and to God' in Ivana Bacik and Michael O'Connell (eds) *Crime and Poverty in Ireland* (Dublin: Round Hall Sweet & Maxwell), 68–91.

O'Sullivan, Sara (2007) 'Gender and the Workforce' in O'Sullivan, S. (ed.) *Contemporary Ireland A Sociological Map* (Dublin: University College Dublin Press).

Oakley, Ann (1976) *Housewife* (Harmondsworth: Penguin).

Oakley, Ann (1989) 'Women's Studies in British Sociology: To End at Our Beginning?', *The British Journal of Sociology* 40(3), 442–470.

Organisation for Economic Cooperation and Development (OECD) (1992) *Education at a Glance: OECD Indicators* (Paris: OECD).

Organisation for Economic Cooperation and Development (OECD) (1995) *Literacy, Economy and Society: Results of the First International Adult Literacy Survey* (Paris: OECD).

Organisation for Economic Cooperation and Development (OECD) (1997) *Literacy Skills for the Knowledge Society* (Paris: OECD).

Organisation for Economic Cooperation and Development (2001) *The Wellbeing of Nations: The Role of Human and Social Capital* (Paris: OECD).

Okin, Susan Moller (1989) *Justice, Gender, and the Family* (New York: Basic Books).

Olick, Jeffrey K. and Joyce Robbins (1998) 'Social Memory Studies: From "Collective Memory" to the Historical Sociology of Mnemonic Practices', *Annual Review of Sociology* 24, 105–140.

Oliker, Stacey J. (2000) 'Examining Care at Welfare's End' in Madonna Harrington Meyer (ed.) *Care Work: Gender, Class and the Welfare State* (New York, London: Routledge).

Oliver Michael (1990) *The Politics of Disablement* (Basingstoke: Macmillan).

Oliver, Michael (1993) 'Re-Defining Disability: A Challenge to Research' in Swain, J., Finkelstein, V., French, S. and Oliver, M. (eds) *Disabling Barriers – Enabling Environments* (London: Sage).

Oliver, Mike and Colin Barnes (1991) 'Discrimination, Disability and Welfare: From Needs to Rights' in Bynoe, I., Oliver, M. and Barnes, C. *Equal Rights For Disabled People* (London: Institute for Public Policy Research).

Olsen, Frances (1983) 'The Family and the Market: A Study of Ideology and Legal Reform', *Harvard Law Review* 96(7), 1497–1578.

Pahl, Raymond (ed.) (1988) *On Work: Historical, Comparative and Theoretical Approaches* (Oxford: Basil Blackwell).

Pardoe, Simon (2000) 'Respect and the Pursuit of "Symmetry" in Researching Literacy and Student Writing' in David Barton, Mary Hamilton and Roz Ivanic (eds) *Situated Literacies* (London: Routledge), 149–166.

Parkin, Frank (1971) *Class Inequality and Political Order* (London: McGibbon and Kee).

Parsons, Samantha and John Bynner (1997) 'Numeracy and Employment', *Education and Training* 39(2&3), 43–51.

Parsons, Samantha and John Bynner (1998) *Influences on Adult Basic Skills. Factors Affecting the Development of Literacy and Numeracy from Birth to 37* (London: Basic Skills Agency).

Parsons, Talcott and Robert F. Bales (1956) *Family: Socialization and Interaction Process* (London: Routledge & Kegan Paul).

Pateman, Carole and Charles Mills (2007) *Contract and Subordination* (Cambridge: Polity Press).

Patton, Michael Q. (1980) *Qualitative Evaluation Methods* (US: Sage).

Patton, Michael Q. (1990) *Qualitative Evaluation and Research Methods*, 2nd edition (Newbury Park, CA: Sage).

Pease, Bob (2000) 'Researching Pro-feminist Men's Narratives: Participatory Methodologies in a Postmodern Frame' in Barbara Fawcett, Brid Featherstone, Jan Fook and Amy Rossiter (eds) *Researching and Practicing in Social Work: Postmodern Feminist Perspectives* (London: Routledge).

Pease, Bob (2002) '(Re)Constructing Men's Interests', *Men and Masculinities* 5(2), 165–177.

Pettinger, Lynne, Jane Parry, Rebecca Taylor and Miriam Glucksmann (eds) (2005) *A New Sociology of Work?* (Oxford: Basil Blackwell).

Phipps, Shelley, Peter Burton and Lars Osberg (2001) 'Time as a Source of Inequality Within Marriage: Are Husbands More Satisfied with Time for Themselves than Wives?', *Feminist Economics* 7(2), 1–21.

Pickard, Susan and Glendinning, Caroline (2002) 'Comparing and Contrasting the Role of Family, Carers and Nurses in the Domestic Health Care of Frail Older People', *Health and Social Care in the Community* 10(3), 144–150.

Pieterse, Marius (2004) 'Coming to Terms with Judicial Enforcement of Socio-Economic Rights', *South African Journal on Human Rights* 20(3), 383–417.

Pigou, Arthur (1932) *The Economics of Welfare* (London: Macmillan).

Pildes, Richard (1998) 'Why Rights are not Trumps: Social Meanings, Expressive Harms and Constitutionalism', *Journal of Legal Studies* 27(2), 725–763.

Pillinger, Jane (2000) 'Redefining Work and Welfare in Europe: New Perspectives on Work, Welfare and Time' in Gail Lewis, Sharon Gewirtz and John Clarke (eds) *Rethinking Social Policy* (London: Sage).

Pringle, Keith (1995) *Men, Masculinities and Social Welfare* (London: UCL Press).

Putnam, Robert (1995) 'Bowling Alone: America's Declining Social Capital', *Journal of Democracy* 6(1), 65–78.

Qureshi, Hazel (1990) 'A Research Note on the Hierarchy of Obligations Among Informal Caregivers – A Response to Finch and Mason', *Ageing and Society* 10(2), 455–458.

Qureshi, Hazel and Elinor Nicholas (2001) 'A New Conception of Social Care Outcomes and its Practical Use in Assessment with Older People', *Research, Policy and Planning* 19(2), 11–26.

Raftery, Mary and Eoin O'Sullivan (1999) *Suffer Little Children: The Inside Story of Ireland's Industrial Schools* (Dublin: New Island).

Ranson, Gillian (2001) 'Men and Work; Change – or No Change? – in the Era of the "New Father"', *Men and Masculinities* 4(1), 3–26.

Rawls, John (1993) *Political Liberalism* (New York: Columbia University Press).

Rawls, John (1999) *A Theory of Justice*, Revised Edition (Oxford: Oxford University Press).

Rawls, John (2001) *Justice as Fairness: A Restatement* (Cambridge, MA: Harvard University Press).

Reay, Diane (2000) 'A Useful Extension of Bourdieu's Conceptual Framework?: Emotional Capital as a Way of Understanding Mothers' Involvement in their Children's Education', *Sociological Review* 48(4), 568–585.

Reay, Diane (2004) 'It's All Becoming a Habitus: Beyond the Habitual Use of Habitus in Educational Research', *British Journal of Sociology of Education* 25(4), 415–431.

Reay, Diane (2005) 'Doing the Dirty Work of Social Class? Mothers' Work in Support of their Children's Schooling', *The Sociological Review* 53(2), 104–115.

Reay, Diane and Ball, Stephen (1998) '"Making Their Minds Up": Family Dynamics and School Choice', *British Educational Research Journal* 24(4), 431–448.

Reay, Diane, Sarah Bignold, Stephen J. Ball, and Alan Cribb (1998) '"He Just Had a Different Way of Showing It" Gender Dynamics in Families Coping with Childhood Cancer', *Journal of Gender Studies* 7(1), 39–52.

Reay, Diane and Lucey, Helen (2000) 'Children, School Choice and Social Differences', *Educational Studies* 26(1), 83–100.

Remy, John (1990) 'Patriarchy and Fratriarchy as Forms of Androcracy' in Jeff Hearn and David Morgan (eds) *Men, Masculinities and Social Theory* (London: Unwin Hyman).

Ribbens McCarthy, Jane, Janet Holland and Val Gillies (2003) 'Multiple Perspectives on the "Family" Lives of Young People: Methodological and Theoretical Issues in Case Study Research', *International Journal of Social Research Methodology* 6(1), 1–23.

Roberts, Dorothy E. (1997) 'Spiritual and Menial Housework', *Yale Journal of Law & Feminism* 9(1), 51–80.

Romero, Mary and Eric Margolis (eds) (2005) *The Blackwell Companion to Social Inequalities* (Oxford: Blackwell).

Roseneil, Sasha (2004) Why Should We Care about Friends: An Argument for Queering the Care Imagery in Social Policy, *Social Policy and Society* 3, 409–419.

Rousseau, Jean-Jacques (1762) *Émile* (London: Dent (1911 edn.)).

Rudd, Joy (1972) *Report on National School Terminal Leavers* (Dublin: Germaine Publications).

Rush, Michael, and Valerie Richardson (2007) 'Welfare Regimes and Changing Family Attitudes' in Betty Hilliard and Máire Nic Ghiolla Phádraig (eds) *Changing Ireland in International Comparison* (Dublin: The Liffey Press).

Russell, Richard (2007) 'The Work of Elderly Men Caregivers: From Public Careers to an Unseen World', *Men and Masculinities* 9(3), 298–314.

Sahlins, Marshall D. (1972) *Stone Age Economics* (New York: Aldine de Gruyter).

Sayer, Andrew (2005) *The Moral Significance of Class* (Cambridge: Cambridge University Press).

Sayer, Andrew (2007) 'Moral Economy and Employment' in Sharon Bolton and Maeve Houlihan (eds) *Searching for the Human in Human Resource Management* (London: Palgrave).

Scales, Ann C. (1986) 'The Emergence of Feminist Jurisprudence: An Essay', *Yale Law Journal* 95(7), 1373–1402.

Scheingold, Stuart (1974) *The Politics of Rights* (New Haven: Yale University Press).

Seery, Brenda L. and M. Sue Crowley (2000) 'Women's Emotion Work in the Family: Relationship Management and the Process of Building Father Child Relationships', *Journal of Family Issues* 21(1), 100–127.

Segal, Lynne (1997) *Slow Motion: Changing Masculinities, Changing Men* (London: Virago).

Seglow, Jonathan (2005) 'The Ethics of Immigration', *Political Studies Review* 3(3), 317–334.

Seidler, Victor (2006) *Transforming Masculinities: Men, Cultures, Bodies, Power, Sex and Love* (London and New York: Routledge).

Seidler, Victor (2007) 'Masculinities, Bodies, and Emotional Life', *Men and Masculinities* 10(1), 9–21.

Sen, Amartya K. (1990) 'Gender and Co-operative Conflicts' in I. Tinker (ed.) *Persistent Inequalities: Women and World Development* (New York: Oxford University Press).

Sennett, Richard and Cobb, Jonathan (1977) *The Hidden Injuries of Class* (Cambridge: Cambridge University Press).

Sevenhuijsen, Selma (1998) *Citizenship and the Ethics of Care: Feminist Considerations on Justice, Morality and Justice* (London: Routledge).

Sevenhuijsen, Selma (2000) 'Caring in the Third Way: The Relation Between Obligation, Responsibility and Care in the Third Way Discourse', *Critical Social Policy* 20(1), 5–37.

Shachar, Ayelet (2003) 'Children of a Lesser State: Sustaining Global Inequality Through Citizenship Laws', *Jean Monnet Working Paper 2/03*.

Seward, Rudy R., Daele E. Yeatts, Iftekhar Amin and Amy Dewill (2006) 'Employment Leave and Fathers' Involvement with Children, According to Mothers and Fathers', *Men and Masculinities* 8(4), 405–427.

Shakespeare, Tom (2006) *Disability Rights and Wrongs* (London: Routledge).

Shildrick, Margret (1997) *Leaky Bodies and Boundaries: Feminism, Postmodernism, (Bio)ethics* (London: Routledge).

Siegel, Reva B. (1994) 'Home as Work: The First Woman's Rights Claims Concerning Wives' Household Labour, 1850–1880', *Yale Law Journal* 103(5), 1073–1217.

Silbaugh, Katharine (1996) 'Turning Labour into Love: Housework and the Law', *Northwestern University Law Review* 91, 1–86.

Skeggs, Beverly (1997) *Formations of Class and Gender* (London: Sage).

Skeggs, Beverly (2004) *Class, Self, Culture* (London: Routledge).

Smart, Carol (1989) *Feminism and the Power of the Law* (London: Routledge).

Smart, Carol (1989) 'Power and the Politics of Child Custody' in Carol Smart and S. Sevenhuijsen (eds) *Child Custody and the Politics of Gender* (London: Routledge).

Smith, Dorothy E. (1987) The *Everyday World as Problematic: A Feminist Sociology* (Boston: North-eastern University Press).

Standing, Guy (2001) 'Care Work: Overcoming Insecurity and Neglect' in Mary Daly (ed.) *Care Work: The Quest for Security* (Geneva: ILO).

Standing, K. (1999) 'Negotiating the Home and School: Low Income, Lone Mothering and Unpaid Schoolwork' in L. McKie, S. Bowlby and S. Gregory (eds) *Gender, Power and the Household* (Basingstoke: Macmillan Press).

Sternberg, Robert J. and Richard K. Wagner (eds) (1986) *Practical Intelligence: Nature and Origins of Competence in the Everyday World* (Cambridge: Cambridge University Press).

Sternberg, Robert J. (2002) *The Evolution of Intelligence* (London: L. Erlbaum Associates).

Strassman, Diana (1993) 'Not a Free Market: The Rhetoric of Disciplinary Authority in Economics', from *Beyond Economic Man, Feminist Theory and Economics* (eds) M. Ferber and J. Nelson (Chicago: The University of Chicago Press).

Strazdins, Lyndall and Dorothy H. Broom (2004) 'Acts of Love (and Work): Gender Imbalances in Emotional Work and Women's Psychological Distress', *Journal of Family Issues* 25(3), 356–378.

Street, Brian (1984) *Literacy in Theory and Practice* (Cambridge: CUP).

Street, Brian (1995) *Social Literacies: Critical Approaches to Literacy in Development, Ethnography and Education* (London: Longman).

Street, Brian (1999) 'New Literacies in Theory and Practice: What are the Implications for Language in Education?', *Linguistics in Education* 10(1), 1–24.

Stychin, Carl F. (1995) *Law's Desire: Sexuality and the Limits of Justice* (New York: Routledge).

Swain, Scott Orin (1985) 'Male Intimacy in Same-Sex Friendships' (United States California: University of California, Irvine).

Taub, Nadine and Elizabeth Schneider (1998) 'Perspectives on Women's Subordination and the Role of Law' in David Kairys (ed.) *The Politics of the Law: A Progressive Critique*, 3$^{rd}$ edition (New York: Basic Books), 328–355.

Taylor, Rebecca F. (2004) 'Extending Conceptual Boundaries: Work, Voluntary Work and employment', *Work, Employment and Society* 18(1), 29–49.

TenHouten, Warren D. (2006) *Time and Society* (New York: State University of New York Press).

Tett, Lynn, Mary Hamilton and Yvonne Hillier (2006) *Adult Literacy, Numeracy and Language: Policy, Practice and Research* (UK: OUP).

The Men's Project Directory (2007) http://www.mensproject.org/mendir/index.html.

Thompson, Jane (1997) *Words in Edgeways: Radical Learning for Social Change* (Leicester: NIACE).

Toynbee, Polly (2007) 'Re-thinking Humanity in Care Work' in S. Bolton and M. Houlihan (eds) *Searching for the Human in Human Resource Management* (Basingstoke: Palgrave Macmillan), 219–243.

Travers, Max (2001) *Qualitative Research Through Case Studies* (London: Sage Publications).

Tronto, Joan C. (1991) 'Reflections on Gender, Morality and Power: Caring and Moral Problems of Otherness' in S. Sevenhuijsen (ed.) *Gender, Care and Justice in Feminist Political Theory* (Utrecht: University of Utrecht).

Tronto, Joan C. (1993) *Moral Boundaries: A Political Argument for an Ethic of Care* (New York: Routledge).

Tronto, Joan C. (2001) 'Who Cares? Public and Private Caring and the Rethinking of Citizenship' in Nancy J. Hirschmann and Ulrike Liebert (eds) *Women and Welfare: Theory and Practice in the United States and Europe* (New Brunswick, NJ: Rutgers University Press).

Tronto, Joan C. (2002) 'The "Nanny" Question in Feminism', *Hypatia* 17(2), 34–51.

Tronto, Joan C. (2003) 'Time's Place', *Feminist Theory* 4(2), 119–138.

Turner, Jonathan and Jan Stets (2005) *The Sociology of the Emotions* (USA: Cambridge University Press).

Twigg, Julia and Karl Atkin (1994) *Carers Perceived: Policy and Practice in Informal Care* (Buckingham: Open University Press).

Tyrell, Peter (2006) *Founded on Fear* (Dublin: Irish Academic Press).

U.S. Department of Labour, Bureau of Labour Statistics (2007) 'Occupational Employment Statistics'. http://www.bls.gov/oes/current/oes_stru.htm#35-0000 Date accessed 13$^{th}$ June 2008.

Ungerson, C. (1990) 'Why do Women Care?' in J. Finch and Groves, D. (eds) *A Labour of Love: Women, Work and Caring* (London: Routledge and Kegan Paul).

Ungerson, Clare (1993) 'Commodified Care Work in European Labour Markets', *European Societies* 5(4), 377–396.

Ungerson, Clare (1995) 'Gender, Cash and Informal Care: European Perspectives and Dilemmas', *Journal of Social Policy* 24(1), 31–52.

Ungerson, Clare (1997) 'Social Politics and the Commodification of Care', *Social Politics* 4 Fall(3), 362–381.

Ungerson, Clare (2000) 'Thinking about the Production and Consumption of Long-Term Care in Britain: Does Gender Still Matter?', *Journal of Social Policy* 29(4), 623–643.

Uttal, Lynet (2002) *Marking Care Work; Employed Mothers in the New Childcare Market* (New Brunswick, NJ: Rutgers University Press).

Vandervoort, D. J. (2006) 'The Importance of Emotional Intelligence in Higher Education', *Current Psychology* 25(1), 4–7.

Vincent, Carol and Stephen Ball (2001) 'A Market in Love? Choosing Preschool Child Care', *British Educational Research Journal* 27(5), 633–651.

Vogel, Ursula (1988) 'Under Permanent Guardianship: Women's Condition under Modern Civil Law' in Kathleen B. Jones and Anna G. Jónasdóttir (eds) *The Political Interests of Gender: Developing Theory and Research with a Feminist Face* (London: Sage), 135–159.

Vogler, Carolyn (1994) 'Money in the Household' in M. Anderson, F. Bechhofer and J. Gershuny (eds), *The Social and Political Economy of the Household* (Oxford: Oxford University Press).

Waerness, Kari (1984) 'The Rationality of Caring', *Economic and Industrial Democracy* 5(2), 185–211.

Waerness, Kari (1987) 'The Rationality of Caring' in Anne Showstack Sassoon (ed.) *Women and the State: The Shifting Boundaries of Public and Private* (London: Hutchinson).

Waerness, Kari (1990) 'Informal and Formal Care in Old Age: What is Wrong with the New Ideology in Scandinavia Today?' in Clare Ungerson (ed.) *Gender and Caring: Work and Welfare in Britain and Scandinavia* (London: Harvester: Wheatsheaf).

Wagner, Daniel and Richard Venezky (1999) 'Adult Literacy: The Next Generation', *Educational Researcher* 28(1), 21–29.

Waldron, Jeremy (1993) 'When Justice Replaces Affection: The Need for Rights' in *Liberal Rights: Collected Papers 1981–1991* (Cambridge: Cambridge University Press), 374–391.

Waldron, Jeremy (2000) 'The Role of Rights in Practical Reasoning: "Rights" Versus "Needs"', *Journal of Ethics* 4(1–2), 115–135.

Walker, Steven and Len Barton (eds) (1983) *Gender, Class and Education* (Lewes, Sussex: Falmer Press).

Walkerdine, Valerie and Helen Lucey (1989) *Democracy in the Kitchen: Regulating Mothers and Socialising Daughters* (London: Virago).

Waring, Marilyn (1988) *As If Women Counted – A New Feminist Economics* (San Francisco: Harper & Row).

Weiler, Kathleen (1988) *Women Teaching for Change: Gender, Class and Power* (US: Bergin and Garvey).

Weiler, Kathleen (1991) 'Freire and a Feminist Pedagogy of Difference', *Harvard Educational Review* 61(4), 449–474.

West, Robin (2003) 'The Right to Care' in Eva Feder Kittay and Ellen K. Feder *The Subject of Care: Feminist Perspectives on Dependency* (Rowman and Littlefield), 88–114.

West, Robin L. (2004) *Re-imagining Justice: Progressive Interpretations of Formal Equality, Rights, and the Rule of Law* (Aldershot: Ashgate).

White, Julie A. and Joan C. Tronto (2004) 'Political Practices of Care: Needs and Rights', *Ratio Juris* 17(4), 425–453.

Wihstutz, Anne (2007) 'When Children Take on Responsibility – House and Care Work by Children in Family and Community', *SWS-Rundschau* 47(1), 100–123.

Wilkinson, Richard G. (2005) *The Impact of Inequality: How to Make Sick Societies Healthier* (Abingdon: Routledge).

Williams, Joan (2001) *Unbending Gender: Why Family and Work Conflict and What To Do About It* (New York: Oxford Press).

Williams, Joan (2001b) 'From Difference to Dominance to Domesticity: Care as Work, Gender as Tradition', *Chicago-Kent Law Review* 76, 1441–1493.

Williams, Fiona (2004) *Rethinking Families* (London: Central Books, Calouste Gulbenkian Foundation).

Witz, Anne (1992) *Professions and Patriarchy* (London: Routledge).

Wong, Simone (1999) 'When Trust(s) is Not Enough: An Argument for the Use of Unjust Enrichment for Home-Sharers', *Feminist Legal Studies* 7, 47–62.

Wood, Richard (1991) 'Care of Disabled People' in Gillian Dalley (ed.) *Disability and Social Policy* (London: Policy Studies Institute).

Woodward, Kath (1997) 'Motherhood, Identities, Meanings and Myths' in Kath Woodward (ed.) *Identity and Difference* (London: Sage Publications).

Woolley, Frances and Judith Marshall (1994) 'Measuring Inequality Within the Household', *Review of Income and Wealth* 40(4), 415–431.

Yeates, Nicola (1999) 'Gender, Familism and Housing: Matrimonial Property Rights in Ireland', *Women's Studies International Forum* 22(6), 607–618.

Young, Iris Marion (1990) *Justice and the Politics of Difference* (Princeton: Princeton University Press).

Yuval-Davis, Nira (1997) 'Women, Citizenship and Difference', *Feminist Review* 57 (Autumn), 4–27.

# Index

*Note*: Page numbers followed by 'f' and 't' refer to figures and tables, respectively.